Palgrave Adva

Palgrave Advances offers a series of innovative books which orientate graduate and upper-level students within the current state of a field of study. Bringing together leading international scholars, each text surveys, questions and pushes the boundaries of the discipline. Foregrounding new research, these books seek to map the future direction of the field and as such are invaluable for students, scholars and lecturers.

More information about this series at
http://www.palgrave.com/gp/series/14721

Simon Kövesi • Erin Lafford
Editors

Palgrave Advances in John Clare Studies

palgrave
macmillan

Editors
Simon Kövesi
Oxford Brookes University
Oxford, UK

Erin Lafford
Department of Humanities
University of Derby
Derby, UK

Palgrave Advances
ISBN 978-3-030-43373-4   ISBN 978-3-030-43374-1   (eBook)
https://doi.org/10.1007/978-3-030-43374-1

Cover illustration: © 'Crowland Abbey' by Peter De Wint, The Print Collector / Alamy Stock Photo, Image ID: R0R23W

This Palgrave Macmillan imprint is published by the registered company Springer Nature Switzerland AG.
The registered company address is: Gewerbestrasse 11, 6330 Cham, Switzerland

ACKNOWLEDGEMENTS

All images in Chap. 3 '"Sweet the Merry Bells Ring Round": John Clare's songs for the drawing room' by Kirsteen McCue are reproduced with the kind permission of The British Library Board, ©The British Library Board.

A Note on the Texts

All references to Clare's writings are to the following editions except where otherwise stated:

> *Early Poems, Middle Period, Later Poems*
> *Letters*
> *Natural History*
> *By Himself*

In each essay, references to Clare's poetry are by volume, page, and line number in the first instance, and then by line number within text for repeated references. References to Clare's letters are by date and page number. References to Clare's prose writings are by page number.

Contents

LIST OF ABBREVIATIONS

Barrell	Barrell, John. *The Idea of Landscape and the Sense of Place, 1730–1840: An Approach to the Poetry of John Clare*. Cambridge: Cambridge University Press, 1972
Bate, *Biography*	Bate, Jonathan. *John Clare: A Biography*. London: Picador, 2003
By Himself	Clare, John. *John Clare By Himself*. Edited by Eric Robinson and David Powell. Ashington and Manchester: MidNAG/Carcanet, 1996
Critical Heritage	*Clare: The Critical Heritage*. Edited by Mark Storey. London: Routledge & Kegan Paul, 1973
Deacon	Deacon, George. *John Clare and the Folk Tradition*. London: Sinclair Browne, 1983; repr., London: Francis Boutle, 2002
Early Poems	Clare, John. *The Early Poems of John Clare 1804–1822*. Edited by Eric Robinson and David Powell, assoc. ed. Margaret Grainger. 2 vols. Oxford: Clarendon Press, 1989
JCSJ	*The John Clare Society Journal*. (1982–). Continuing series
John Clare in Context	*John Clare in Context*. Edited by Hugh Haughton, Adam Phillips and Geoffrey Summerfield. Cambridge: Cambridge University Press, 1994
Letters	Clare, John. *The Letters of John Clare*. Edited by Mark Storey. Oxford: Clarendon Press, 1985
Later Poems	Clare, John. *The Later Poems of John Clare 1837–1864*. Edited by Eric Robinson and David Powell, assoc. ed. Margaret Grainger. 2 vols. Oxford: Clarendon Press, 1984

Middle Period	Clare, John. *John Clare, Poems of the Middle Period 1822– 1837.* Edited by Eric Robinson, David Powell and P.M.S. Dawson. Oxford: Clarendon Press. Vols 1–2: 1996 Vols 3–4: 1998. Vol. 5: 2003
Natural History	Clare, John. *The Natural History Prose Writings of John Clare.* Edited by Margaret Grainger. Oxford: Clarendon Press, 1983
Nor.	*Northampton Manuscript, John Clare Collection, Northamptonshire Libraries and Information Service.* As listed in [David Powell], Catalogue of the John Clare Collection in the Northampton Public Library. Northampton: County Borough of Northampton Public Libraries, Museums and Art Gallery Committee, 1964
PD	Clare, John. *Poems Descriptive of Rural Life and Scenery.* First edition. London: Taylor and Hessey, 1820
Pet.	*Peterborough Manuscript, Central Library, Peterborough. As listed in Margaret Grainger, A Descriptive Catalogue of the John Clare Collection in Peterborough Museum and Art Gallery.* [Peterborough]: [Peterborough Museum Society], 1973
VM	Clare, John. *The Village Minstrel and other Poems.* 2 vols. London: Taylor and Hessey, 1821

Notes on Contributors

Katey Castellano is Professor of English at James Madison University and author of *The Ecology of British Romantic Conservatism, 1790–1837* (Palgrave, 2013). Her research focuses on commons, landscape, and animals in Romantic-era literature. She has recently published essays in *European Romantic Review* (2015), *Studies in Romanticism* (2017), *Environmental Humanities* (2018), and *Commemorating Peterloo: Violence, Resilience, and Claim-making in the Romantic Era* (2019).

James Castell is Lecturer in English Literature at Cardiff University since 2014; he has completed a research fellowship at Hertford College, Oxford, and holds a PhD from St John's College, Cambridge. His research is concerned primarily with nature poetry from Romanticism to the present. He focuses, in particular, on encounters with animals, various approaches to the question of 'life', and the importance of sound in accounts of the environment. He has published on William Wordsworth, John Clare and Ted Hughes, as well as on the relationship between the sciences and the humanities. He is a director of the Cardiff ScienceHumanities Initiative.

Scott Hess is Professor of English and Environmental Sustainability at Earlham College in Richmond, Indiana. He is the author of *William Wordsworth and the Ecology of Authorship: The Roots of Environmentalism in Nineteenth-Century Culture* (2012) and *Authoring the Self: Self-Representation, Authorship, and the Print Market in British Poetry from Pope Through Wordsworth* (2005). His book project explores how authors' 'genius' became associated with specific natural landscapes during the nineteenth century in both Great Britain and the United States, shaping modern ideas of nature and the origins of the environmental movement.

Andrew Hodgson is Lecturer in Romanticism at the University of Birmingham since 2016; he holds a PhD from the University of Durham. He is author of *The Poetry of Clare, Hopkins, Thomas, and Gurney: Lyric Individualism* (Palgrave Macmillan, 2019) and of essays on Gray, Clare, Hopkins, Brooke, Larkin and rhyme in Romantic poetry. He is working on a book about love in Romantic writing.

Sarah Houghton-Walker is Fellow of Gonville & Caius College, Cambridge, and is Co-Director of the Centre for John Clare Studies. She has a particular interest in marginal figures and groups which is reflected in her work on Clare: her first book focused on his religion, and her second book explored the ways in which the figure of the gypsy was represented in the Romantic period. She has published various articles on Clare and on Romantic writing more generally, and is beginning a study of the poet James Withers. Her major project examines conjunction and repetition in Romantic-period poetry.

Simon Kövesi is Professor of English Literature at Oxford Brookes University. He researches working-class writing from the Romantic period through to contemporary literature. He is editor of the *John Clare Society Journal* and a fellow of the English Association. His books include *John Clare: New Approaches* (2000), *James Kelman* (2007), *New Essays on John Clare: Poetry, Culture and Community* (2015), and *John Clare: Nature, Criticism and History* (2017). He is currently working on a book entitled *Literature and Poverty: 1800–2000*, and a paperback edition of Pierce Egan's 1821 smash hit *Life in London*.

Erin Lafford is Postdoctoral Research Fellow in English at the University of Derby, and holds a PhD from the University of Oxford. Her research focuses mainly on Romantic and long eighteenth-century literature, particularly on its intersections with medical and environmental thought. She is currently completing her first monograph, *John Clare and the Poetry of Illness*, and has published or forthcoming essays on John Clare, Robert Bloomfield, William Gilpin, William Cowper, William Blake, Gerard Manley Hopkins, and Elizabeth Bishop. She is also the book reviews editor for the *John Clare Society Journal*.

Sara Lodge is Senior Lecturer in English at the University of St Andrews, specialising in nineteenth-century literature and culture. Her books include *Thomas Hood and Nineteenth-Century Poetry: Work, Play, and Politics* (2007), *Jane Eyre: An Essential Guide to Criticism* (Palgrave, 2008) and *Inventing Edward Lear* (2018). She has published many articles and chapters, including work on John Clare, John Keats, Charles Lamb, the literary annuals, the Brontës and on the comic body in the long nineteenth century. She is particularly interested in poetry, in periodical culture and in writers who are also artists.

Kirsteen McCue is Professor of Scottish Literature and Song Culture and Co-Director of the Centre for Robert Burns Studies at the University of Glasgow. She has published widely on Romantic song culture, most recently in *The Oxford Handbook to British Romanticism*. She is the editor of James Hogg's *Songs by the Ettrick Shepherd* and *Contributions to Musical Collections and Miscellaneous Songs* for the Stirling/South Carolina research edition of Hogg's works and editor of the forthcoming *Burns's Songs for George Thomson* for the new Oxford *Works of Robert Burns*.

Michael Nicholson is Assistant Professor of English at McGill University. His book, *After Time: Romanticism and Anachronism*, explores the new ecopoetic strategies of anachronism that English poets from a broad range of backgrounds developed to contest the increasing dominance of strictly standardized models of imperial time. He has published essays on Clare, Wordsworth, and Byron in *ELH*, *Genre*, and *ECTI*. An additional piece on the scientific aspects of Mary Shelley's creature recently appeared in *Science Fiction Studies*. At McGill, he co-directs the SSHRC-funded 'Poetry Matters' project.

David Stewart is Associate Professor of English Literature at Northumbria University. He has published widely on Romantic-period literary culture, including work on periodicals, print culture, and landscape, and writers such as Lord Byron, Thomas De Quincey, James Hogg, and Letitia Elizabeth Landon. He is the author of two books: *Romantic Magazines and Metropolitan Literary Culture* (Palgrave Macmillan, 2011) and *The Form of Poetry in the 1820s and 1830s: A Period of Doubt* (Palgrave Macmillan, 2018).

Stephanie Kuduk Weiner is Professor of English at Wesleyan University, Connecticut. She has published widely on nineteenth-century British poetry, including articles about political expression, print and oral cultures, representations of sensory experience, and literary explorations of the history and multiplicity of the English language. She is the author of *Clare's Lyric: John Clare and Three Modern Poets* (2014) and *Republican Politics and English Poetry, 1789–1874* (Palgrave, 2005).

James Whitehead is Lecturer in English at the Research Institute for Literature and Cultural History, Liverpool John Moores University. His 2017 monograph *Madness and the Romantic Poet* considers the idea of mad genius as it was connected to poets and poetry in the nineteenth century and beyond, and includes several sections on John Clare. Clare will also figure in his ongoing book project on the history of autobiographical narratives of madness and mental illness.

LIST OF FIGURES

**'Sweet the Merry Bells Ring Round': John Clare's Songs
for the Drawing Room**

Introduction

Simon Kövesi and Erin Lafford

The year 1820 was a remarkable year for John Clare. His life as a poet was launched in January via a puff piece by Octavius Gilchrist, the second essay proper in the first issue of the newly revived *London Magazine*, directed along liberal lines by the experienced editor John Scott. Gilchrist's 'Some Account of John Clare, an Agricultural Labourer and Poet' appears sandwiched between 'Reflections on Italy Seen in 1818 and 1819' and a critical take on Walter Scott's novels.[1] In this same month Clare's first collection—*Poems Descriptive of Rural Life and Scenery*—was published, to widespread acclaim. A month after the book appeared, a poem quoted and discussed in John Taylor's introduction—'The Meeting'—was set to an original composition by Haydn Corri, slotted into a decades-old pasticcio comic opera *The Siege of Belgrade* (originally by composer Stephen Sorace and librettist James Cobb) and sung on stage by Madame Vestris at

S. Kövesi (✉)
Oxford Brookes University, Oxford, UK
e-mail: skovesi@brookes.ac.uk

E. Lafford
University of Derby, Derby, UK
e-mail: e.lafford@derby.ac.uk

© The Author(s) 2020
S. Kövesi, E. Lafford (eds.), *Palgrave Advances in John Clare Studies*, Palgrave Advances,
https://doi.org/10.1007/978-3-030-43374-1_1

1

the Theatre Royal, Drury Lane, in what was Vestris's first ever performance on the London stage.[2] Vestris played the heroine: a witty Turkish
peasant called Lilla. Clare missed that run of the opera but recollected that
he 'felt uncommonly thrilled at the circumstance'.[3] He visited London for
the first time in March and, across an extended visit, socialised with his
publishers' and patrons' circles of writers, lords, and ladies, some of them
famous and influential. On the way to London, Clare had travelled by
coach, again for the first time.[4] Probably responding to one of Clare's later
visits to London, Thomas Hood observed Clare and Charles Lamb:

> in wending homewards on the same occasion through the Strand, the
> Peasant and Elia, *Sylvanus et Urban*, linked comfortably together; there
> arose the frequent cry of 'Look at Tom and Jerry—there goes Tom and
> Jerry!' for truly, Clare in his square-cut green coat, and Lamb in his black,
> were not a little suggestive of Hawthorn and Logic, in the plates to 'Life
> in London'.[5]

Like the Tom and Jerry of Pierce Egan's smash hit tour de force *Life in
London* (1821), Clare had fun in the capital. He enjoyed the city's unique
mix of theatres, bookshops, print-shop windows, boxing bouts, salons,
dinner clubs, pubs, the sheer crowds in the streets—and no doubt much
else besides. 'I had often read of the worlds seven wonders in my reading
Cary at school but I found in London alone thousands', he gasped.[6] He
even sat for William Hilton, who painted his portrait in his prime—a work
which remains to this day the best image of Clare. The first book of poetry
sold well: reviewed widely, and mostly positively, the volume went to four
editions that same year. His work, his life, and his circumstances were
scrutinised often. Clare and a lover had fallen pregnant before the close of
1819, and with a bit of arm-twisting from his new patrons (according to
Jonathan Bate's authoritative account[7]), the poet married Martha Turner,
who gave birth to their first child in June of 1820. Even including such
domestic pressures, Clare could be justified in positively anticipating a life
of writing success stretching out in front of him. He could look forward
to money coming in that would change his and his family's lives, and alter
all of his future prospects. He was, arguably, not wrong or naïve to do so:
the chances of his ongoing success looked good, considering the circumstances in which he was born and in which he and his family had laboured
for so long, and where he now found himself in early 1820. Granted,
things did not quite work out the way this early promise suggested; and

yes, Clare was always a poet of loss and regret for times past, though he was from the very start of his writing life. But the loss of hope, increasing alienation, and isolation that tend to predominate in accounts of Clare are not the only notes we can hear in either his work or his life.

Rather than rehearse the usual stories of decline, madness, and neglect, we ought to linger on just how well Clare did in that remarkable first year in the exciting, knockabout world of the mainstream literary scene, which reflected and informed a Britain of 1820 in all its political and social turmoil. It was not an auspicious time. In the same month Clare's book was published, George III died and the country looked to his widely despised successor, the profligate George IV (the notorious 'Queen Caroline affair'—over his treatment of his long-estranged wife—was to divide the country viciously that same year[8]); the government was preparing militarily for insurrection in many towns and cities (especially in Glasgow and London), partly in response to the Peterloo massacre in Manchester in September 1819; while at the same time rebellion was building in Ireland; in January the country was in the grip of a catastrophically cold winter (in some cases, it was a winter that was fatal for the poor and infirm).[9] For Clare, by happy contrast, as the reviews and readers' letters started coming in, things seemed to improve happily indeed.

A lot of wise and talented people had faith in Clare. They backed and supported him as much as they could, and he enjoyed it. A little later in the 1820s, Clare reflected that his poems 'have gained me many pleasures and friends that have smoothed the rugged road of my early life and made my present lot sit more easily on the lap of life and I am proud of the notice they have gained me'.[10] All writers write to be read, to be noticed, and to be responded to. Clare was keen for an audience, and keen for appreciation, here described as being paid welcome 'notice' that he did not shy away from, even as he went on to find some discomfort in the 'exposure' (as Adam Phillips has it) that comes with being a published poet.[11]

If the terrain of Clare's early personal life could be described as 'rugged', the road from that set of circumstances to publication was always likely to be a rocky one. Given where and how he lived, it is remarkable his work made it anywhere at all. That local booksellers, with aspirations to publishing prowess, took an early interest in his work, and were prepared to invest time and money in it—to take a real risk on Clare in business terms and in a public fashion too—all stands as a testament to the evident quality of his early writing. This level of attention also suggests the nascent poet had a keen ability to forge networks to his own advantage, and for what we might anachronistically call his 'career'. For all Clare's seeming modesty—fragility, even, as some have had it—the poet clearly had enough private confidence in the merit of his work to show it to influential people. 'Luck' has little to do with his trajectory, though to read his own accounts, and those of many of his biographers and myth-makers, his modesty was such that one might think his poetry was dragged out of him. He is frequently presented as the most private and cautious of 'humble' poets, as someone who was hesitant to the point of debilitation, meaning that any publication at all was miraculous. It can be tempting to read Clare's as a poetic career produced miraculously as if by a virgin birth, not made of the energy and wit of plans and designs. However, stories of miracle and luck deny the presence of ordinary human work and considerable personal effort. Clare's prose stories of his own isolated, solitary musings which mark him out for the villagers, from an early age, as a strange lad, have to be balanced with the enriching fact—evidenced throughout his correspondences most particularly—of his affable sociability (as well as what John Goodridge claims for Clare's deep sense of 'community'[12]), and of his ability to court and maintain relationships that would do him and his aspirations some good. For all his awkwardness, Clare's was a sociability that operated in a wide variety of circumstances and social settings, and this speaks to a remarkable set of adaptive social skills. With a class system as rigidly policed as that of Clare's time, one to which all genuflected, conversing with someone of a much higher social and economic standing was not at all easy.

What stories of Clare's shyness, modesty, and humility often elide is the evidence that he was always immensely clubbable and performative: just as labour in unenclosed fields was work carried out in tandem with village peers (sometimes, especially before enclosure, with the whole village, including people of all social classes in the same seasonal task), so too was playing fiddle and singing songs in pubs in Helpston, or in the wider country with the gipsies he purposefully sought out. Musical fun was not a solo affair for Clare, though of course song could provide a sense of reassuring company when work proved solitary, as it does for young Hodge of 'Rural Morning' in *The Village Minstrel*:

> Young Hodge the horse-boy, with a soodly gait,
> Slow climbs the stile, or opes the creaky gate,
> With willow switch and halter by his side

Prepar'd for Dobbin, whom he means to ride;
The only tune he knows still whistling o'er,
And humming scraps his father sung before,
As "Wantley Dragon," and the "Magic Rose,"
The whole of music that his village knows,
Which wild remembrance, in each little town,
From mouth to mouth through ages handles down.[13]

Song acts as a familial bond, as a kind of guarantor of community, as a comforting social glue, as a canon of memory, and as cultural history. Work, poetry, reading, and the study of nature sometimes took Clare off alone, but his learning and his culture were always sociably founded. By his own account Clare's father was a singer; Clare understood song, intimate listeners, and—we can assume—the rough justice of vocally critical audiences too.[14] He had a formative, early grasp of the potency of performance, and of the sociability of story and song. As Ronald Blythe insightfully suggests, a 'village was, still is in some ways, the least private place on earth'.[15] Community and human contact—when not wanted—can be oppressive, of course. Privacy costs money, and was a rare enough commodity in Clare's life, especially as his desires became more studious. But for critics to ignore the huge cultural resources that the young poet could draw on in the rush to describe what his education 'lacked' in comparison to other Romantic-period poets is to ignore the rich store of life experiences and oral culture he had to hand. When the young Clare turned all of his oral and musical energy and understanding towards textual life, he wrote with a determination to be read and sounded out, as much as a fiddle player plays to be heard. It is no surprise that sound is everything in Clare's work, to which some of our essays in this collection certainly attest. It was surely with a sense of purposeful confidence—layered over with the necessary presentational patina of an apologia of diplomatically cap-doffing class consciousness—that Clare was able to tap into the rich cultural and entrepreneurial life that was so active, and so vital, in small towns across Britain in the early nineteenth century. His confidence in these varied and widening social circumstances takes literary shape in the sheer range of topics, poetic forms and modes with which he happily experimented in the 1810s, and which were to shape the diverse range of work in *Poems Descriptive* of 1820.

Read the Clare of the 1810s and very early 1820s—and of 1820 in particular—and you encounter someone of buoyant confidence engaged in a wide variety of correspondences, with all manner of interested parties. There are occasional rages at being double-crossed and swindled too, along with collapses of confidence and activity. But Clare's sociable and business-like engagements with—what was across 1820 at least—an ever-increasing number of well-connected people (and excited corresponding readers), are never only humble or passive. The fair at Market Deeping was where he met J. B. Henson in 1814, the first bookseller to take Clare on; in 1818 Henson advertised a subscription towards a prospective publication, seemingly at Clare's own expense.[16] The bigger and more wealthy wool town of Stamford was another hub of bookish connections for Clare; not coincidentally, it was the town where he bought his first book of poems (James Thomson's *The Seasons*), with his own hard-won money. Stamford was the home of Edward Drury, who was to be the bridge to publication with his cousin John Taylor. Taylor's London-based firm, which he ran with James Hessey, was to go on to publish Clare's first three collections across the 1820s. That Clare swiftly got caught up with interested parties, and then used other (more useful, more powerful, better connected) types to unlock agreements with the earlier ones—all on this rocky road to print—is something that can be read in support of versions of Clare's naivety and social and commercial awkwardness. These moments can also be read as evidence of the way Clare was pushed and pulled around. Nevertheless, the early, blunt severances, first from Henson, then from Drury, can also reveal a pretty determined aspect to Clare's agency as he quickly pushes through from conversations in local bookshops to a life in print: from the provinces to the capital, from the margins to the centre. Clare can even seem ruthless in the pursuit of his ambitions to get published. His is an agency we can see working busily, even while people like Henson and Drury both assert their claims, through investment, to Clare's work. By way of example, here is a letter from Drury to Clare, quoted in full (and for which biographer Jonathan Bate offers a rich context[17]). Drury wants Clare to break ties with Henson, and come under his wing. His missive is a pitch for business:

Dec. 24, 1818

Dear Sir,
    Your epistle (and the favors enclosed) found me in full occupation with the bustle of market-day. And I have scarcely time to prepare an answer by the time your messenger said he would call. However, I cannot allow an opportunity to slip of encouraging you to place full and undivided confi-

dence in Mr. Richard Newcomb, junior, who has both the power and the will of doing every service that can be wished.

There can be no reason why you should not come over to Stamford on Sunday—every thing shall be so arranged to suit your wishes; and if you will signify to Mr. Henson that you have determined to relinquish the plan of publishing your poems in the form announced we can, if you could, decide on the most proper steps to be taken; I shall have no objection to purchase the MSS of your writing, on speculation. Or w^d· conclude such an agreement with you, (in which any money sh^d· not be requisite) or sh^d· leave you perfectly independent of my proceedings.

I have too much love for Poësy not to take Pleasure in helping the trembling and diffident efforts of a second Burns, or Bloomfield; and therefore,

remain,

Your Assured Friend,

E. B. Drury

***Come on Sunday at All Events.

A Note to Mr. Henson, as follows w^d· fully effect your purpose—

"Sir,

By the Bearer pray return the MSS of Poetry, &c., you have in possession, and I beg to signify that I do not intend to present my writings to the public, for the present."

I am etc"

(P.S. The above is only a suggestion E.D.)[18]

To an extent, Clare is being played here: having visited him once, Drury is now trying to prise the poet away from Henson—even going so far as to offer a way of doing so that Clare could copy out verbatim—while also proffering a link to the son of the owner of the *Stamford News*, who has 'the power and the will' Drury thinks Clare needs to get on. Drury seems to be saying 'Instead of Henson, come with me to the big time, and money and power will be yours'. The final sweetener in the double suggestiveness of alliterated labouring-class poets ('Burns, or Bloomfield') that Clare should be looking to follow is possibly there because Drury wants to end with the poet knowing this is all for a higher purpose—not for money and power—even though the letter has been precisely about that. Drury is selling, and selling hard: money, connection, power, print, and a place amongst a labouring-class tradition of recent stars are glittery carrots dangled in front of the next 'peasant poet'. The level of control Drury is grasping for, and which he would continue to claim even as Clare moved on to the relationship with Taylor and Hessey (a relationship Drury accidentally proffered for Clare of course), would see the poet's patience quickly wear thin. As Clare wrote as early as December 1819 to his local helpmeet the Reverend Isaiah Knowles Holland of Market Deeping, on the issue of having a copy of his first collection of poems presented to local landowner Lord Milton: 'I am affraid Drury will Interest himself in the matter [.] A Shabby Booksellers Word will be no advantage to me as self Interest is the Cause'.[19] The range of relationships far beyond his social class or his known locality that Clare is relying upon, leveraging, and sometimes rubbishing—even here in this momentary snippet of canny assessment and snippy disparagement—is astounding. In critiquing Drury's 'self-interest' Clare is asserting his own, exactly a year after his relationship with Drury began, and the month before his book was launched through Drury's cousin.

Clare was no holy fool, and while constantly patronised, he was not easily pushed around or duped. While critics have long condemned Drury for his slippery machinations,[20] still some degree of congratulation should surely be directed at Clare: for not doing exactly as prescribed in this letter (though Henson was dropped, he was still writing to Clare in March 1830 pleading poverty and suggesting they work together on his next book); for using Drury's familial connections to his advantage; for using Drury as a stepping stone to the truly influential, metropolitan platform that, firstly, Stamford writer Octavius Gilchrist offered, and, secondly, the London-based Taylor and Hessey allowed; and for then severing ties with Drury altogether—much to the businessman's chagrin. Messy though this relationship became, Clare reveals a remarkable resilience, adaptability, and insight: to read self-interest in people he encountered and to be wary of it, but also to use albeit exploitatively inclined people for his own, sometimes successful, ends. It is worth reaffirming that beyond the business end of poetic endeavour, intelligent, well-read, and highly capable people wanted Clare's company before he was a success. In January 1820, laid up in bed with a swollen foot, having read his own review of Clare's forthcoming collection, Gilchrist wrote to Clare in terms so warm it is hard to imagine a friendlier way to close a brief letter:

> Believe me, I shall always be glad to hear of any good fortune that betides you, and I shall be always more willing than able to promote it [...] As a

general remark for your use, our dinner hour is always (company excepted)
two o clock, and you will always find a knife and fork at your service. Ever
faithfully,

Yours   Oct. Gilchrist

Jan. 14, 1820[21]

Gilchrist's next extant letter, written a week a later, is full of praise for the
qualities of Clare's first volume, published just before on 16 January 1820.
The poems, Gilchrist protests jokily:

[...] have disappointed me,—they have disappointed me greatly, for they are
still better than I looked to find them. Tenderness and feeling and a mind
awake to the beauties of nature I expected to find,—but there is occasionally
a grasp of thought and strength of expression,—as in "What is Life?"—
which I was not quite prepared for [...].[22]

In the past 200 years since his first book of 1820, critical attention to
Clare's work has ebbed and flowed, and if his posthumous reputation has
occasionally hit rocky patches, it has never been blocked altogether. Clare
has never been entirely forgotten (though that's a myth still told, and
retold).[23] In the last 30 years, as a result in part of the incrementally
expanding availability of reliable scholarly texts, critical work on Clare has
grown exponentially. We reach the point now that the voices collected in
this volume make entries into a voluble, voluminous set of existing and
varied conversations. Clare's work and life continue to be a rare and robust
stimulus to an array of critical approaches and agendas. The wide variety
of topics in his work and contexts that spark interest means that trying to
cover the wealth of critical praxis Clare has inspired in one volume poses a
challenge. If not quite comprehensive, this collection offers a series of
distinct routes into Clare's life and writing that we the editors feel best
represent some of the most persistent and emergent critical avenues still to
be explored, that all in their own way speak to Clare as the canny, artful
poet of sociability and performance discussed in this introduction. We
hope these chapters will be informative for readers new to Clare, while also
being a collection of rigorous new areas of engagement for more experienced ones.

Setting the scene for this collection are three chapters on contexts of
poetic production and dissemination. David Stewart offers a corrective to
the deeply engrained story that Clare's time was up before he got going,

because poetry was on the wane. Stewart's research into the widely ignored years between the heights of canonical Romanticism and the powerhouse fiction of the Victorian period proper suggests a different story. Here, Clare is found to be an adaptable writer, one aware of shifts in tastes and trends, alert to the emerging power of annuals, and experimentally adept at responding to new styles of verse. As we have pointed out above, Clare grew into rhyme, story, and performance through song, the fiddle, and the sociability of the pub and the gipsy campfire; yet his engagement with song culture, and assessments of how song culture responded to and adapted his work, remains a quiet corner of Clare studies (with the only substantive exception being George Deacon's foundational study of 1983[24]). Musical scholar Kirsteen McCue has found a treasure trove of settings of Clare's work, heretofore unknown to scholarship, and her chapter reappraises Clare as collector and lyricist, affirming, as she puts it, 'his position amidst a sparkling firmament of famous songwriting contemporaries, including Robert Burns, James Hogg and Thomas Moore'. Following a parallel trajectory, Stephanie Kuduk Weiner looks in detail at Clare's song collecting and his song writing, and considers how his understanding of music informed his verse, exploring the ways in which he experimented playfully across text and sound in his own compositions: she examines him, then, as a 'multi-media' artist.

Offering a wide variety of close readings of poetry across his oeuvre, Sara Lodge, Andrew Hodgson, and Sarah Houghton-Walker examine the formal aspects and innovations of Clare's poetry. Lodge reads Clare's landscapes into his literary experimentations, and finds him as embedded in responses to literary traditions as he is engaged with digging into real topographies. Hodgson pursues the metrical patterns of Clare's pulsing line across various verse forms, and finds that a 'sensitive rhythmic artistry underpins Clare's affecting and sophisticated control of timing and tone', as he puts it. Focusing on the 1827 poem *The Shepherd's Calendar*, Houghton-Walker looks at Clare's use of repetition—locating 'irregularity as an aspect of natural regularity'—and reminds us that Clare's poetry presents listening as being core to communal connection and social meaning.

In the current critical climate, the predominant reason readers discover Clare, the agenda teachers pursue in presenting his work in classrooms, and the motive for journalists and scientists quoting from his work, is our wide gamut of environmental and ecological concerns. It is important to remember that our climate-conscious contexts are not identical to Clare's.

Damaged or not, the promise of nature's permanence and an evergreen return at spring was more of a certainty for the culture of Clare's time, in ways that cannot be offered to our own. Indeed, does the word 'nature' indicate the same kinds of processes, beings, and even feelings that it could in Clare's time? Yet, for all that distance, there remains a huge amount to be learned, explored, and enjoyed in pursuing Clare's sheer attentiveness, his innovative 'botanising' expertise, and his passion for and understanding of the natural world, his own environment, and his explorations of what human environmental damage can effect. He seems to model a commitment to being in a place that is as rare as it is inspiring. This collection therefore contains three chapters that offer fresh perspectives on Clare's proto-ecological concerns. Often Clare is regarded as the poet of the microcosm: one who focuses on the grain of sand rather than the heaven beyond; an eye to the moss on a branch, rather than the whole forest. Yet in directing attention to the movements of animals in Clare's verse, James Castell charts much wider skies than critics usually pursue, and finds that the poet is 'fascinated by the dynamics of both physical and poetic space' in ways that might usefully 'nuance existing coordinates of ecocriticsm'. Katey Castellano puts 'work' to work, in garnering a new understanding of how Clare presents the work of animals, particularly in the case of industrious birds, whose endeavours never cease to amaze the poet. Birds' work, in Castellano's close reading of the poetry, multiply extends the commons, meaning birds forge a kind of rebellion against private property with their own built determinations of territories. Scott Hess theorises multiple subjectivities in Clare's understanding of the natural symbolic order: the poet's rendering, Hess argues, of encounters with natural bodies is always tending to the multiple, the de-centred, and the collaborative, and his proto-ecological consciousness is always aware of and in touch with an array of species, not just the human.

Innovative representations of the material world of nature are not Clare's only concern. He is a poet who is acutely aware of his own mind and body, as much as he is attentive to the subjectivity of an animal, or the mood of a cloud. In Michael Nicholson's chapter, we find that in times of national difficulty (the contexts of his first two collections of 1820 and 1821), Clare represents a complex human and natural world of stress and 'strain', and builds a community of 'distress' by way of shelter from the storm. Offering a corrective to frequent characterisations of Clare as a 'hypochondriac', and assessing the class dynamics and prejudices in the widespread use of the term in Clare's day, Erin Lafford finds that the poet's heightened bodily awareness can serve as much more than a mere marker of affectation or private obsessiveness: hypochondria can offer a new lens through which to read Clare's poetic subjectivity and experiments in relation to physical and mental suffering, and can frame his participation in a wider Romantic culture of imaginary illness. James Whitehead closes our collection with a similarly corrective account of readings of Clare's later asylum verse that have tended to cloak his work in the misery of institutionalisation: Whitehead considers the sociable aspects of the early Victorian asylum, the regimes that encouraged poetic composition, and reads symptomatic examples of Clare's work in that refreshed context of production. Two hundred years after his first book was published, and in celebration of his significance today, this collection of critical, archival, and theoretical essays offers a fresh and stimulating set of inroads to help readers of all kinds and with all sorts of interests to pursue and examine Clare's unique work, his unique contexts, and his remarkable life. He is a poet who remains the most uncommon of commoners.

NOTES

1. *London Magazine* (January 1820), 1: 1–22. Gilchrist's essay on Clare, 7–11. Appears in *Critical Heritage*, 35–42.

2. For the libretto of this opera see James Cobb, *The Siege of Belgrade: A Comic Opera in Three Acts* (Dublin: printed and sold by the booksellers [1791?]), and for the original music, see *The Siege of Belgrade: an Opera in Three Acts, As Performed as the Theatre Royal Drury Lane, the Music Principally Composed by Stephen Sorace* (London: J. Dale, [1791?]). For a reproduction of the playbill for the 19 February 1820 performance featuring Clare's poem 'The Meeting' being sung by Madame Vestris during her first ever performance on the London stage, see Augustus Harris, *A Collection of Playbills from Drury Lane Theatre 1819–1820* (London: s. n., 1819–1820), available at British Library online: Digital Store Playbills 16, playbill 14 of 230, http://explore.bl.uk/.

3. *By Himself*, 136.

4. For a richly detailed account of Clare's first visit to London, see Bate, *Biography*, 165–72.

5. Thomas Hood, 'Literary Reminiscences, No. IV', in *Hood's Own: or, Laughter from Year to Year* (London: A. H. Baily and Co., 1839), 555–68 (555).

6. *By Himself*, 136.

7. Bate, *Biography*, 170–2.

8. For Clare's responses to this national controversy, see Sam Ward, '"This is radical slang": John Clare, Admiral Lord Radstock and the Queen Caroline Affair', in *New Essays on John Clare: Poetry, Culture and Community*, ed. Simon Kövesi and Scott McEathron (Cambridge: Cambridge University Press, 2015), 189–208.

9. These contexts are examined in detail in Malcom Chase, *1820: Disorder and stability in the United Kingdom* (Manchester: Manchester University Press, 2013). For a focused literary-critical account of the radical causes, conspiracies, and controversies of the time, see John Gardner, *Poetry and Popular Protest; Peterloo, Cato Street and the Queen Caroline Controversy* (Basingstoke: Palgrave Macmillan, 2011).

10. *By Himself*, 163.

11. Adam Phillips, 'The exposure of John Clare', in *John Clare in Context*, 178–88.

12. John Goodridge, *John Clare and Community* (Cambridge: Cambridge University Press, 2013).

13. 'Rural Morning', *VM*, 2: 67.

14. See *By Himself*, 2.

15. Ronald Blythe, 'Clare in Hiding', in *Talking About John Clare* (Nottingham: Trent Books, 1999), 39.

16. A list of notes penned by Taylor and Hessey in early 1820 shows them trying methodically to unpick the history of Clare's dealings and agreements with Henson and Drury; it also reveals how Taylor and Hessey dealt with the tangled legacy of these relationships in their own work towards getting Clare in print. This is offered as Appendix 1 of Mark Storey's *Letters*. Item 2 in the list reads: 'Clare paid Henson [£] 1/5/0 for the Prospectuses, & was even compelled to discharge the Reckoning at the Public House which Henson had incurred by coming over to Helpstone for the Money'. *Letters*, 685.

17. Bate, *Biography*, 117–18.

18. British Library, Egerton MSS 2245, fol. 10r.–11v.

19. Clare to Isaiah Knowles Holland, December 1819, *Letters*, 19–20 (20).

20. See, for example, the stimulating opening chapter of Roger Sales, *John Clare: A Literary Life* (Basingstoke: Palgrave Macmillan, 2002), 1–27.

21. Gilchrist to Clare, 14 January 1820. British Library, Egerton MSS 2245, fol. 19r.

22. Gilchrist to Clare, 21 January 1820. British Library, Egerton MSS 2245, fol. 27r–28v (27v).

23. Accounts of Clare's critical reception can be found in the editors' introductions to existing essay collections such as Hugh Haughton, Adam Phillips and Geoffrey Summerfield, eds., *John Clare in Context*, 1–27; John Goodridge, ed., *The Independent Spirit: John Clare and the Self-Taught*

Tradition (Helpston: The John Clare Society and The Margaret Grainger Memorial Trust, 1994), 13–24; Simon Kövesi and Scott McEathron, eds., *New Essays on John Clare: Poetry, Culture and Community* (Cambridge: Cambridge University Press, 2015), 1–13. See also the introduction to *Clare: The Critical Heritage*, ed. Mark Storey (London: Routledge & Kegan Paul, 1973), 1–26. This exemplary collection is essential to understanding the history of Clare's critical reception.

24. George Deacon, *John Clare and the Folk Tradition* (London: Sinclair Browne, 1983; repr., London: Francis Boutle, 2002).

Bibliography

Barrell, John. *The Idea of Landscape and the Sense of Place, 1730–1840: An Approach to the Poetry of John Clare*. Cambridge: Cambridge University Press, 1972.

Bate, Jonathan. *John Clare: A Biography*. London: Picador, 2003.

Blythe, Ronald. 'Clare in Hiding'. In *Talking About John Clare*, 39–47. Nottingham: Trent Books, 1999.

Chase, Malcolm. *1820: Disorder and Stability in the United Kingdom*. Manchester: Manchester University Press, 2013.

Chilcott, Tim. *'A real world & a doubting mind': A Critical Study of the Poetry of John Clare*. Hull: Hull University Press, 1985.

Clare, Johanne. *John Clare and the Bounds of Circumstance*. Kingston, ON: McGill-Queen's University Press, 1987.

Clare, John. *The Village Minstrel and Other Poems*. 2 vols. London: Taylor and Hessey, 1821.

———. *The Natural History Prose Writings of John Clare*. Edited by Margaret Grainger. Oxford: Clarendon Press, 1983.

———. *The Later Poems of John Clare 1837–1864*. 2 vols. Edited by Eric Robinson and David Powell, assocc. ed. Margaret Grainger. Oxford: Clarendon Press, 1984a.

———. *The Letters of John Clare*. Edited by Mark Storey. Oxford: Clarendon Press, 1985.

———. *The Early Poems of John Clare 1804–1822*. 2 vols. Edited by Eric Robinson and David Powell, assocc. ed. Margaret Grainger. Oxford: Clarendon Press, 1989.

———. *John Clare: Poems of the Middle Period 1822–1837*. 5 vols. Edited by Eric Robinson, David Powell and P. M. S Dawson. Oxford: Clarendon Press, 1996–2003.

———. *John Clare By Himself*. Edited by Eric Robinson and David Powell. Ashington and Manchester: MidNAG/Carcanet, 1996.

———. *John Clare The Major Works*. Edited by Eric Robinson and David Powell. Oxford: Oxford University Press, 1984b; repr. 2004.

Cobb, James. *The Siege of Belgrade: A Comic Opera in Three Acts*. Dublin: Printed and sold by the booksellers, 1791?.

Deacon, George. *John Clare and the Folk Tradition*. London: Sinclair Browne, 1983; repr., London: Francis Boutle, 2002.

Gardner, John. *Poetry and Popular Protest; Peterloo, Cato Street and the Queen Caroline Controversy*. Basingstoke: Palgrave Macmillan, 2011.

Gilchrist, Octavius. 'Some Account of John Clare, an Agricultural Labourer and Poet'. *London Magazine* (1820): 7–11.

Goodridge, John. *John Clare and Community*. Cambridge: Cambridge University Press, 2013.

Goodridge, John, and Simon Kövesi, eds. *John Clare: New Approaches*. Helpston, Peterborough: The John Clare Society, 2000.

Goodridge, John, ed. *The Independent Spirit: John Clare and the Self-Taught Tradition*. Helpston: The John Clare Society and The Margaret Grainger Memorial Trust, 1994.

Gorji, Mina. *John Clare and the Place of Poetry*. Liverpool: Liverpool University Press, 2008.

Harris, Augustus. *A Collection of Playbills from Drury Lane Theatre 1819–1820*. London: s.n., 1819–1820.

Haughton, Hugh, Adam Phillips and Geoffrey Summerfield, eds. *John Clare in Context*. Cambridge: Cambridge University Press, 1994.

Hood, Thomas. 'Literary Reminiscences, No. IV'. In *Hood's Own: or, Laughter from Year to Year*, 555–68. London: A. H. Baily and Co., 1839.

The John Clare Society Journal. Vols. 1–38. John Clare Society, 1982–2019.

Kövesi, Simon. *John Clare: Nature, Criticism and History*. London: Palgrave Macmillan, 2017.

Kövesi, Simon and Scott McEathron, eds. *New Essays on John Clare: Poetry, Culture and Community*. Cambridge: Cambridge University Press, 2015.

Letters to John Clare. Egerton Manuscript 2245–50. The British Library, London.

Martin, Frederick. *The Life of John Clare*. London and Cambridge: Macmillan, 1865.

Phillips, Adam. 'The Exposure of John Clare'. In *John Clare in Context*, edited by Hugh Haughton, Adam Phillips and Geoffrey Summerfield, 178–88. Cambridge: Cambridge University Press, 1994.

Sales, Roger. *John Clare: A Literary Life*. Basingstoke: Palgrave, 2002.

Sorace, Stephen. *The Siege of Belgrade: an Opera in Three Acts, As Performed as the Theatre Royal Drury Lane, the Music Principally Composed by Stephen Sorace*. London: J. Dale, 1791?.

Storey, Edward. *A Right to Song: The Life of John Clare*. London: Methuen, 1982.

Storey, Mark. *The Poetry of John Clare: A Critical Introduction*. London and Basingstoke: Macmillan, 1974.

———, ed. *John Clare: The Critical Heritage*. London: Routledge & Kegan Paul, 1973.

Tibble, J. W and Anne. *John Clare: A Life*. London: Michael Joseph, 1932; revised edition 1972.

Ward, Sam. "'This is radical slang'": John Clare, Admiral Lord Radstock and the Queen Caroline Affair'. In *New Essays on John Clare: Poetry, Culture and Community*, edited by Simon Kövesi and Scott McEathron, 189–208. Cambridge: Cambridge University Press, 2015.

Poetry's Variety: John Clare and the Poetic Scene in the 1820s and 1830s

David Stewart

The later 1820s and 1830s have often been presented as a dead-end not only for Clare but for poetry as a whole. Publishers, many claim, were afraid of publishing poetry, and that which was published was trite religious sentimentality aimed at middle-class female readers. Clare, following the success of his first two volumes in 1820 and 1821, began to find himself isolated. The *London Magazine* circle dispersed, his plans to publish *The Shepherd's Calendar* and *The Midsummer Cushion* hit block after block, and, finally, readers seemed to have lost interest in him, their attention fixed by new fashions. Scholars have recently challenged this view of the period's poetry, its readerships, and its market, to reveal a culture that had indeed changed since Clare first appeared in print in 1820, but that was far more vital and far more varied than such a view allows.[1] This was a time of significant flux in the financial markets and real acceleration in print technology, changes that had knock-on effects on poets and

D. Stewart (✉)
Northumbria University, Newcastle upon Tyne, UK
e-mail: david.stewart@northumbria.ac.uk

© The Author(s) 2020
S. Kövesi, E. Lafford (eds.), *Palgrave Advances in John Clare Studies*, Palgrave Advances,
https://doi.org/10.1007/978-3-030-43374-1_2

17

publishers. It was also a period in which Clare was highly active as he sought to adapt to the changes around him. Rather than seeing Clare as a victim of a period too busy with steam-driven commerce to hear his voice, this chapter shows that he was productively engaged with this period of flux. The period from the mid-1820s to the mid-1830s, a period often presented as one of retreat and isolation for Clare, a time when his plans to address the public seemed to be thwarted at every turn, was in fact one of remarkable experimentation, during which he opened himself up to a changing and highly diverse poetic scene.

POETRY AND ITS MARKETS

Clare's publishing career—beginning in success in 1820 before dropping off into ever greater struggles to find a market—seems to map neatly on to the history of sales of poetry in Britain. The year 1820 saw the highest number of individual volumes of new poetry yet published in a single year: 957.[2] The 1825–26 stock-market crash took down a number of publishers, most famously Archibald Constable, but it also had a severe impact on Clare's publisher, John Taylor. After that, as Roger Sales puts it, '[t]he bottom [...] dropped out of the market' for poetry.[3] The poet, periodical writer and editor Thomas Pringle said as much to Clare in 1831: 'Poetry they say is quite unsaleable—and even Wordsworth and other well known writers cannot find a purchaser for their MSS'.[4] The picture maps neatly onto conventional literary periodisation of Romantic and Victorian eras: 1820 also saw volumes published by Keats, Wordsworth, and Shelley, but by 1835, when Clare's *The Rural Muse* finally appeared, a young Charles Dickens was on his way to fame as a new kind of prose writer.

Studies of the period between, roughly, 1824 and 1840 are beginning to increase, and in doing so reveal a highly active literary marketplace. The idea that there was no market for poetry is simply untrue. When Clare published *The Rural Muse* in 1835 his book joined at least 569 new volumes of poetry published that year.[5] Whatever Pringle might have said, Wordsworth's *Yarrow Revisited* (1835) was a success, but this did not come as a particular surprise to a poet whose volumes had been selling increasingly well right across the 1820s. The year 1835 was no sudden return to form for the poetry market; the production of new volumes of poetry remained largely consistent across the mid-1810s into the 1830s at above 500 volumes per year. Individual volumes of verse were not the only means by which poets reached readers. The literary annuals—elegantly bound miscellanies published for the Christmas gift market, containing original verse and prose alongside steel-plate engravings of works of art— were one of the publishing phenomena of the era.[6] Clare published at least 39 poems in annuals in this period.[7] There were many other periodical publications—daily, weekly, and monthly—that provided a space for a wide variety of poets. Poetry anthologies found a market, many of them designed to sell in Europe and the British colonies.

There were a great variety of kinds of poetry that found substantial audiences in this period, all of which Clare was aware of. The fact most noted by Romantic and Victorian scholars is the success of female poets. Letitia Elizabeth Landon and Felicia Hemans, the two bestsellers, were joined by many others, including Mary Russell Mitford and Maria Jane Jewsbury. Other writers found success in different modes. Clare's friend George Darley produced ethereal, metrically innovative aestheticism. Such work proved common among relatively obscure poets such as Thomas Lovell Beddoes and Thomas Wade as well as subsequently canonical fig- ures like Tennyson and Browning. Clare corresponded frequently with Darley, and enjoyed playing up to the aggressive rejection of a supposedly 'feminised' poetic culture such poets adopted, mocking the 'trumpeting clamour about her L.E.Ls. Hemans's Dartford Moorians'.[8] Many critics have taken him at his word in his rejection of Hemans and Landon (L.E.L.) in this letter, but, as I will go on to argue, his poetry indicates a far greater openness to the 'feminine' poetry that dominated this era's poetry market, as well as a fascination with counter-positions like those Darley adopted.

Many other styles of writing were available to Clare. Thomas Hood may have rejected one of Clare's poems for an annual publication, but Hood's punning, comic verse—found also in the work of John Hamilton Reynolds (a friend of Clare's), or the work of Winthrop Mackworth Praed—was another success of the period.[9] John Keble's *The Christian Year*, first published in 1827, went through 13 editions by 1835; Clare's friend James Montgomery had success in this vein of consolatory Evangelical poetry, often written with the colonies and missionaries in mind, as did Robert Montgomery and Bernard Barton. Political poetry remained important, though the publication format shifted. The year 1820 was a peak for sales of individual new volumes because so many political poems were published in this year of crisis. Poets did respond to Catholic Emancipation and the Reform Bill in verse, but they tended to publish their poems in newspapers and magazines rather than individual volumes. Scholarship of these developments is growing, and the texts of this era are far easier to access as a consequence of scholarly editions and digital reproductions. Clare criticism is now well placed to rethink his relations with this complex, unstable, but productive era.

These literary developments from the mid-1820s were powered by technological, political, and social shifts. The steam-powered press had been in use since 1814, but it was not until the mid-1820s and 1830s that it became widely used, increasing print runs and reducing costs.[10] From the mid-1820s steel-plate engravings in annuals and periodicals diffused relatively cheap, high-quality reproductions of visual art to a much wider audience. Periodicals like the *New Monthly Magazine* and the literary annuals offered venues of self-fashioning for middle-class readers who assumed in this era a new cultural confidence. Ben Wilson describes, as an aspect of these changes, a new era of 'cant' dominated by a rising middle-class Evangelicalism that made the rambunctious early 1820s culture of Byron's *Don Juan* and Pierce Egan's *Life in London,* both of which Clare was aware of, seem increasingly inappropriate for mainstream consumption.[11] The radical political agitation of the Peterloo era had been largely defeated, but bubbled under and coloured the often anxious discussions about Catholic Emancipation (1829) and the Reform Bill (1832). The 1825–26 stock-market crash was a product of a new kind of speculative financial activity. Angela Esterhammer has explored how this period's technological and financial shifts affected its literary productions such as improvisational poetry, the periodical press, and the Silver Fork novel. The dominance of the periodical press, combined with a period of heightened (and often catastrophic) stock-market speculation, prompted in literary writers a fascination with 'hasty action that lacks a solid or profound basis, that responds to contingencies and constructs its own (pseudo-)reality'.[12]

The principal characteristic of the literary market of the later 1820s and 1830s, then, was not its deathly quietness, but rather a speedy changefulness that made it bewilderingly hard to map. Clare's work was not stymied by his context, but drew creatively upon it. Clare scholars have recently become attuned to the ways in which his creativity benefitted from his interactions with his contemporaries in the literary market.[13] This scholarship has developed two aspects of Clare that I wish to build on here: these interactions present him as connected rather than isolated, and they also indicate Clare's openness to new forms of creativity. As Simon Kövesi puts it, this is 'a Clare who changed his mind and his models of creative conception, who theorised the writing of poetry and the forging of writerly identities'.[14] Critics have not, so far, explored in detail the connections

Clare forged in the literary market of the later 1820s and early 1830s, in part because in this period, poets like Landon, and publishing venues like the annuals, have themselves been presented as being of marginal critical interest. It is important, I argue, that we explore Clare's engagements with that world, and that we value the new turns his creative self-fashioning took. By placing Clare in dialogue with his fellow products of this era of flux and doubt, a new sense of Clare's mobile interactions with his contemporary readers and writers emerges.

CLARE'S POETICS OF DOUBT

Jonathan Bate makes the intriguing suggestion that Clare in the later 1820s might have become a periodical essayist and revealed a manner with 'not only the personal touch, but also the sententiousness and insight, together with the humour and the gift of irony, that characterise the essays of Hazlitt and Lamb'.[15] Something like that, combined, I will suggest, with an unfixed quality that marks the era as a whole, emerges in a prose essay Clare prepared around 1829–30, which he referred to as the 'Letter to A C'.[16] The 'Letter to A C' is an unlikely addition to the Clare canon, little studied by scholars. I wish to present it as a model of the kinds of interactive creativity Clare developed in this era.

The 'Letter to A C' is a prose essay written as a letter to Allan Cunningham, a friend of Clare's who began life as a stonemason in Nithsdale in Southwest Scotland before establishing himself in the literary and cultural scene of London.[17] The essay is headed 'On the Wonders of inventions curiositys strange sights & other remarkables "of the last forty days" in the Metropolis in a Letter to A Friend'. The format of the letter to a friend, and indeed the format of the country cousin writing about the trip to the city, was an established feature of the magazine culture of the 1820s.[18] Clare enjoyed his fourth extended stay in London between February and March 1828, but the essay does not depend so much on Clare's actual visit as it does on his knowledge of the metropolitan print culture of his era. 'Of the last forty days' suggests a biblical timeframe—and indeed religion plays a central part in the letter—but it also hints at the central feature of the essay: its encounter with a culture moving so fast that any attempt to write about it produces at best baffled wonder.

Clare adopts the persona of the astonished rural friend hearing rumours and reading reports of the latest London phenomena. The essay becomes a headlong rush that leaves the reader grasping for a point of stability.

Clare draws out what Esterhammer calls the 'ephemerality, superficiality, and theatricality' of the oft-discussed 1820s idea of the 'march of intellect', the relentless onward progress of a steam-driven age.[19] Rather than the confident gaze of one who has mastered what he sees, Clare's bemused, excited, mobile manner reflects an era in which there is no clear link to past traditions and no possibility of confidently projecting towards a future. 'When will wonders have an end', he exclaims, mingling ecstasy with frantic despair:

> when shall we become standard in knowledge when shall it be said—"The force of genius can no farther go"—the last forty days has left me behind a modern "Reading made easy"—where am I … the units & common place materials of things hardly know me in my astonishments—can it be so far in the year of the world as 5590—am I so far among the improvments of time & so ignorant. (27)

The year 1825 saw the implementation of the 'Act for Ascertaining and Establishing Uniformity of Weights and Measures', and it would be the steam trains that Clare comments on in the essay that prompted the standardisation of time zones later in the century.[20] But these measurements seem not to provide a reliable method of accounting. 'Where am I' Clare asks: the question is about fixing a location in time as well as space, neither of which seems possible. Shadowing this doubt is another question: 'who am I'?

Clare shows us a world in which quack doctors promise miracle cures, preachers preach eternal salvation and the coming revelation, and politicians promise the earth. The spirit of the age is one of multiplicity, of relentless change, and of doubt. At the end of one great list of signs and wonders (ghosts, learned pigs, Methodists), Clare remarks 'not that their authenticitys are beyond my beleef—they are only left behind it … aye very far behind it' (24). The essay might be understood as an account of what went wrong with Clare's relation with the literary market in the 1820s. An age of stock-market speculations, ephemeral wonders, fashionable poetry, and even more fashionable 'Silver Fork' novels leaves Clare's quiet rural observations behind. Instead, Clare is reduced to trying to follow the trend in this rather desperate way, in prose that makes a Bartholomew Fair show of him as a country bumpkin bowled over by modernity.

Yet Clare, as Kövesi has argued, was just as capable of flight and play as he was of 'authenticity'; indeed, 'authenticitys' becomes in Clare's essay another element of the theatricality he adopts and reflects. Clare's performative 'anxietys' (25) are a teasing reflection on the speculative excitements and uncertainties of his period. In the 1830 annual *The Keepsake*, published towards the end of 1829, one can find an essay supposedly written in 2130 describing the extraordinary speed of modern life (it dismays Lord A that it took him a full seven and a half hours to travel from Edinburgh to London, beggars speak Latin, and Irish street sweepers speak French, while Lord and Lady D have hired a steam porter). Clare's essay works so well in this period because it suggests that things can only accelerate further. 'Booksellers perhaps thrive best on speculations' (29), Clare ponders, and the 'Letter to A C' was one of many literary speculations he essayed alongside his fellow writers for fellow readers who were often just as thrilled and overwhelmed as he is here. It offers us, in its ephemerality, its speculative quality, its theatricality, its embrace of a poetics of doubt, a model for reading Clare's interactions with a diverse, steam-powered poetic scene.

CLARE IN *THE ANNIVERSARY*

In this section I will consider one speculative product of this era, one in which Clare's poetry rubbed shoulders with a diverse variety of types of culture. *The Anniversary: Or, Poetry and Prose for MDCCCXXIX* was published by John Sharpe of Piccadilly on 1 November 1828, and was edited by Allan Cunningham. The book was one of the many annuals designed to be gifts for the Christmas and New Year markets. Annuals captured much of the mix of technological innovation and speculative finance that marked the era. The first British annual was published in November 1822 by Rudolf Ackermann. Annuals were beautifully bound and presented volumes that made use of the latest steel-plate engraving techniques to offer unusually high-quality reproductions of art. These were presented alongside original contributions commissioned by the leading writers of the age. The costs involved were enormous, and publishers had to sell many thousands of copies simply to break even. But they were a huge success, and had a significant impact on the literary market, especially the market for poetry. By 1832 there were 63 annuals in the shops in Britain.[21]

The Anniversary was offered for sale at 21 shillings, bound in silk, and according to Cunningham's biographer it stood up well in a crowded market with pre-sales of 6000 copies.[22] Annuals were designed to be given as Christmas or New Year gifts. My own copy is inscribed for Eliza M. Clark by 'her aff^{te} Aunt Eliza', the dedication written on a beautifully presented inscription page featuring a wood cut by W. Harvey and J. Thompson of a stockinged cavalier offering a book to an elegant maiden with a large crucifix round her neck and a guitar cradled in her right arm, all embowered in a sylvan scene. The page might account for the half-buried scorn many Clare scholars have for this period and products of it like *The Anniversary*: the presentation of poetry as a matter of upper-class elegance; the performance of the tropes of feudal chivalry in a mercantile middle-class setting; the very beauty of the page suggesting that style matters more than substance; stylised 'sylvan' nature rather than authentic rural reality; poetry very clearly a matter of commercial exchange; the dominance of middle-class ideas of decorous femininity; the pointed artifice of the whole that claims nature as yet one more product for sentimental consumption; the large crucifix pointing to a society of religious cant keen to condemn those who stray from society's diktats rather than any spiritual feeling.

Clare had good reason to be angry with much of this, but he was willing to try the annuals on for size. He wrote to John Taylor that

> these Annuals are rather teazing to write for as what one often thinks good the Editors returns back as good for nothing while another gives them the preference & what one thinks nothing of they often condescend to praise— Allan Cunninghams is the best Annual of the whole.[23]

Writing for the annuals was not always easy (Cunningham sent him three sovereigns for a poem, though others forgot to pay him at all), but Clare is intrigued rather than enraged.[24] A closer look at the contents of *The Anniversary* lets us see the creative potential Clare found in such print places.

Cunningham includes an additional inscription page with a poetic and pictorial representation of the year. His idea was to evoke the recurrence of sentiment across the year (each month a reminder of the bond between giver and receiver that the book represents) mirrored in the recurrence of seasonal patterns ('anniversary' spelled out as twelve pictorial letters: 'anniversarie'). Alongside it, though, Cunningham offers instructions on how one might inscribe it: 'To Lady Teazle, on the Anniversarie of her wedding day, from Sir Peter'. The reference to R. B. Sheridan's satire of sentimental hypocrisy, and the particular reference to the rather less than ideal marriage between the Teazles in *School for Scandal* (1777), jars somewhat if we assume (as Sheridan, and Cunningham, do not) that sincere sentiment cannot coexist with worldly wit. Such humour is in fact common in the annuals and the poetic culture of the period. Frederic Mansel Reynolds, editor of *The Keepsake*, included, for example, a cynical and witty epigram on love in high society immediately following P. B. Shelley's essay 'On Love', and one finds similar humour in annual work by the likes of Maria Jane Jewsbury and Barry Cornwall (and, indeed, by Clare, as I will discuss below).[25] Beginning with the pages that frame the volume, then, *The Anniversary* is, as Clare put it, a 'teaze', but it is a teasing game that readers and writers are invited to play together.

Cunningham drew on his connections in the London art world to secure outstanding engravings of paintings. These included T. Crostick's engraving of J. M. W. Turner's painting of Fonthill abbey and H. Robinson's engraving of Thomas Gainsborough's 'The Young Cottagers'. Caroline Bowles delivers one of her musings on country churchyards (a series that she started in *Blackwood's Magazine*), in which her gloom is suddenly dissipated by a skylark. James Montgomery (a correspondent of Clare) offers a poem of religious sentiment about the longing for home that celebrates imperial missionaries. Mary Russell Mitford's 'Going to the Races' is a casually xenophobic sketch of provincial life: one sister accompanies a proud farmer to Ascot where they see King George IV ('the greatest sovereign of the world' [46], it seems), while her silly, vain sister, dressed up like 'a parrot tulip, or a milliner's doll, or a picture of the fashions in the Lady's Magazine, or like any thing under the sun but an English country girl' (51), makes a fool of herself by preferring a French dandy who proves unreliable. Clare's friend George Darley provides two poems, both of which depend on beautifully observed metrical patterns, and both of which link love, death, and femininity in a slightly queasy mix. 'The Wedding Wake' describes a dead woman, the softly lulling rhythm evoking a scene in which time is slowed to a deathly crawl:

> Like a dark stream, her raven hair
> Wanders adown her brow;
> Look how the weetless, reckless air
> Moves its dead tresses now! (73)

John Wilson's 'Edderline's Dream' is similar: it draws on Coleridge's 'Christabel' in its unusual metre, and its depiction of a woman frozen in time evokes the work of the two most important poets of the period, Letitia Landon and Felicia Hemans (and went on to influence Edgar Allan Poe's 'The Sleeper'). Local traditions and dialects often feature in annuals, though there is a slightly stronger emphasis on this in *The Anniversary* than in others, notably by James Hogg and Cunningham himself. T. Crofton Croker's 'Paddy Kelleher and his Pig: A Tale' is an amusing shaggy hog story set in Buttevant, County Cork. It provides in a comic key the theme so often found in Landon's and Hemans's poetry of someone returning from the dead.

It would be a mistake to assume that the politics of the annuals were simply quietist. Clare's favourite piece in *The Anniversary* was 'The Glowworm' by A. Ferguson.[26] The poem is in the 'standard Habbie' stanza associated with Robert Burns and written in a mix of Scots and English. It begins as a pastoral tale of local tradition, before accelerating outwards into a strident condemnation of the class structure. The lower classes are in tatters, while others 'with lordships in their pocket, / Rise glorious as a Congreve rocket' (69):

> The earth is yours, and all that's on it:
> Deep have ye plowed, and thick ye've sown it
> With human bones. (70)

The burning rage about the injustice that creates 'honest poverty' stands in fascinating counterpoint to the poems and engravings elsewhere (Cunningham's gloss on Sir William Beechey's painting 'The Little Gleaner' for example) that find in poverty contentment and authenticity.[27] Robert Southey's digressive, comic, miscellaneous 'Epistle from Robert Southey, Esq. to Allan Cunningham' (fascinatingly similar to Clare's 'Letter to A C', written at the same time) offers a very different and defensively Tory political perspective. It too finds the annual a space of creative play. Annuals, more than many of their critics recognise, were diverse, and the form proved a place of experiment rather than a straitjacket. Clare's work begins from a spirit of openness to these 'teazing' publication venues.

Clare's contribution to *The Anniversary*, 'Ode to Autumn' (known as 'Autumn' in the MS version, opening 'Syren of sullen moods and fading hues'), sits on pages 75–79, following Ferguson's 'Glowworm' and George Darley's 'The Wedding Wake' and succeeded by Clare's friend

Eliza Emmerson's sentimental 'The Return'.[28] I will quote the poem as it appears in *The Anniversary*. It begins, 'SYREN! of sullen woods and fading hues, / Yet haply not incapable of joy,—/ Sweet Autumn, I thee hail!' (75). It feels like a triumph of culture over nature. The apostrophe to the personified spirit of the season, placed in small capitals and crowned with an exclamation mark, folds the natural passage of the seasons into a set of conventions that are functions of poetic cliché and the art of the printer. The poem that follows is rarely discussed by Clare scholars. That might be understandable: the voice that emerges seems so conventional (the laboured 'haply', the distanced 'poetic' inversion 'I thee hail', the feeling that he is producing an annual poem simply to make money), and it is Clare's wild individualism that we have tended to prize. It is, I think, a poem that draws on conventions and habits, but we need not simply dismiss it on that basis.

'Ode to Autumn' does indeed fit very neatly into the annual mode: readers now will—quite rightly—notice the allusions to Keats's 'To Autumn', but annual readers would also have enjoyed this as one of very many annual poems on the seasons, and a fitting complement to the seasonal 'Anniversarie' frontispiece to the volume.[29] The autumn scenes that he presents are precisely habitual and are offered to readers as a communal experience that they can share not just with the poet but with other communities. Eliza M. Clark and her affectionate Aunt Eliza are one such community, and they form a wider community of the thousands of readers of *The Anniversary* and similar annuals containing similar reflections.

Later in the poem we are invited to:

> [...] mark the hedger, front with stubborn face
> The dank rude wind, that whistles thinly by,
> His leathern garb, thorn proof,
> And cheeks red hot with toil! (77)[30]

The precision of the depiction (a wind at once 'dank' and 'thin') is typical of Clare, though not unlike the rest of the annual. Mary Russell Mitford's provincial sketches were one of the fashions of the age, and they depend on a similar interchange between precise detail (a depiction of a wagtail 'with an up and down motion, like a ball tossed from the hand' [53]) and an impulse to track common 'types' of human behaviour (such as the spoiled young girl who has her head turned). Clare's hedger is similar: he is 'the' hedger, yet threatens to become a vivid individual. The description of labour here (or the fact that the hedge itself is a product of farming 'improvement' and enclosure) lacks the political charge of Ferguson's 'The Glowworm', though following that poem by only a few pages readers might well see Clare's 'Plough'd lands, thin travell'd by half hungry sheep' (77) a little differently. Equally, though, the seeming contentment of the cow boy with his 'unpremeditated song' (77) might recall the complacent vision of rural labour Cunningham presents in response to the engraving of William Beechey's cloying painting 'The Little Gleaner' (58–59).

Clare's celebration of autumn is a season that is 'Disorderly divine' (78): this is the glory of 'dappled things' that have inspired poets before and after him. Clare's poem is many-hued too, a miscellany, and that miscellaneous quality emerges not from his resistance to the homogenising impulse of his period's print culture, but in collaboration with it. I have suggested some of the ways that the poem draws on modes of writing in the pages around him, in *The Anniversary*, and in the other annuals on sale in the bookshops at Christmas in 1828. Clare frequently wrote, as he did in 'Ode to Autumn', of venturing into 'solitudes, where no frequented path / But what thine own foot makes, betrays thine home' (75). Such accounts fit well the idea that labouring-class poets were, as Clare said to Cunningham, 'intruders and stray cattle in the fields of the Muses' who had to find their own unique track.[31] I do not wish to deny that, but Clare was in demand as an annual writer because he could create poems that sympathised with the desires of the thousands of *Anniversary* readers who took walks in the woods and liked to read poetry and prose that could guide them as they looked. As Richard Cronin has argued in his essay on Clare's interactions with Cunningham as part of the *London Magazine* circle, Clare enjoyed the opportunities for self-conscious play with identity, authenticity, and belonging that many in this period employed.[32] Clare's 'Ode to Autumn' is a highly conventional poem that describes habitual actions, but it is by means of these conventions and habits that he helped form a community with his annual readers. The poem's miscellaneous quality comes into being not because it has either resisted the annual mould or been forced into it, but because it is a collaboration with his editor Cunningham, with fellow writers like Mitford, Emmerson, Ferguson, Wilson, and Darley, and with readers like Eliza M. Clark and her affectionate aunt.

CLARE'S VARIETY

I will finish this chapter by pointing to some of the ways that Clare's work comes into focus, in ways that are rarely considered by Clare scholars, when those works are viewed through the kaleidoscopic culture of this period. Clare had sent two poems to Allan Cunningham, intended for publication in the next volume of *The Anniversary* (due to be published at the end of 1829), before the publisher surprisingly cancelled the arrangement and began a magazine instead. Both of these poems suggest Clare's capacity to adopt diverse styles. 'Helpstone Statute or the Recruiting Party' is a narrative poem of rural custom very much in tune with Cunningham's writing, and with contributions to the 1829 *Anniversary* by Crofton Croker and James Hogg.[33] 'May Morning: Addressed to E. L. E. by the Northamptonshire Peasant' was eventually published in *The Amulet* for 1834.[34] The poem is addressed to Clare's regular correspondent (and fellow *Anniversary* author) Eliza Emmerson. It comes with an epigraph from George Darley's *Sylvia; or, the May Queen* (1827), an appropriate choice for a poem about May, but an unusual one too. As I have already discussed, Clare knew Darley and his work well. *Sylvia* is a highly varied verse drama, taking in dreamy-eyed songs to the fairies, drunken comedy, and references to radical reform. Clare's epigraph acts as something of a tease to readers who cannot be sure what kind of poem is to follow.

His poem is, in fact, relatively straightforward: a celebration of a female poet who has also supported the muses, with some consideration of the way that 'fashion's praise' has given laurels that 'never grew on Parnass' hill' (300). When Cunningham received the poem to E. L. E., he thought Clare had written a poem in praise of L. E. L., Letitia Elizabeth Landon. The mistake is an interesting one. Had Clare been writing to L. E. L., he really ought to have included more elaborate praise of the leading poet of the era than the brief mention that 'thou canst touch the minstrel-wire' (298). One might expect Clare, given his opposition to 'trumpeting clamour about her L.E.Ls. Hemans's Dartford Moorians', would react with scorn to Cunningham's error: instead he says that Cunningham 'flatters me much by praising them & also by thinking them worthy of the Poetess', and that he would be 'proud' should Landon also commend them.[35] The mistake is revealing not so much because the poem sounds like praise of Landon, as because, in its rejection of fashion, its allusions to minstrelsy, its praise of Scott, Byron, and nature, and its hint of melancholy at the lot of this particular poet, it seems like an imitation of her. Landon's poetry frequently depended on the idea that the figures she represented are veils through which the reader views the real Landon. Although there is undoubtedly some truth in this, it was also true, as critics have recognised, that Landon enjoyed the theatrical possibilities of such a set-up.[36] Her references to minstrelsy and the medieval past are pointedly and self-consciously filtered through an awareness of the printed, mercantile products in which those allusions appeared. Clare, a poet so open to the possibilities of self-fashioning that print offered, learned much from this. His attitude to gender is a matter of ongoing debate, and his place in a market so dominated by female writers complicates that further. Clare enjoyed being rude about the dominant female poets of his era in letters to friends like Darley, but he was constantly fascinated by the poetic innovations around him. His work indicates his active sympathy with his fellow poets, male and female, and his fellow readers, many of whom were female.

Clare also wrote poems of religious sentiment in the later 1820s and 1830s, such as 'On a Child Killed by Lightning' that appeared in *Forget Me Not* for 1829.[37] The poem is typical of the poems often found in annuals and magazines in this period: a brief description of an event, followed by a consolatory moral:

> Thus Providence will oft appear
> From God's own mouth to preach;
> Ah! would we were as prone to hear
> As Mercy is to teach!

Felicia Hemans is perhaps the poet who did this best, but it is a highly common mode: one example in the same edition of *Forget Me Not* is James Montgomery's 'Epitaph on a Gnat, Found Crushed on the Leaf of a Lady's Album' that finds a deeper moral in this frail reminder of the 'labour of Omnipotence' (67). As Sarah Houghton-Walker has shown, Clare's engagement with religion was complex and sustained across his career; a poem like this should certainly not be dismissed as piecework.[38] The form of the poem—the structure that moves from striking event to moral conclusion—is one that Clare picked up in the culture around him, and in doing so he was both engaging with readers who clearly found much value in such sentiments, and with a broader culture of religious revival in the period that Clare drew on in the prose essay he wrote at the same time, the 'Letter to A C'.

The period offered Clare a highly miscellaneous culture of poetry writing, and his poetry responds to that. Clare's poetry of this period is notably varied in tone, so much so that making a coherent 'Clarean' voice of it is difficult. Perhaps we ought to, as Clare suggests in the 'Letter to A C', look for 'authenticitys' rather than a singular 'authenticity'. 'To Harry Stoe Van Dyk' is a witty, spry verse epistle, but when it appeared in *The Pledge of Friendship* for 1828 it would not have stood out particularly. Comic verse was very common: in *The Amulet* for the same year, Thomas Hood offers a very loose translation of Horace that laments that 'I hunt in vain for eglantine, / And find my blue-bell on a sign / That marks the Bell and Crown!'.[39] Clare's 'The Maid of the Hall' (*Friendship's Offering*, 1827) adopts bouncing anapaests to celebrate the social whirl of the dance; it kept good company with poets like Winthrop Mackworth Praed whose 'The Fancy Ball' (*New Monthly Magazine*, December 1828) and 'Goodnight to the Season' (*New Monthly Magazine*, August 1827) are notably similar if we permit the change of scene from rural dance to metropolitan ball. 'Adventures of a Grass hopper' (*Juvenile Forget Me Not*, 1829, an annual for children) again adopts sprightly anapaests in a poem that is disarmingly unusual in its depictions of rural poverty, and yet highly suited to its place of publication in turning to the young female reader to suggest she learn the lesson of the grasshopper and make sure not to be idle. It is no surprise to see the poem singled out for praise in a review of the 1829 annuals in the *Eclectic Review*.[40]

The 1820s and 1830s were a bookish time, with the literary annuals and their steel-plate engravings, watered silk bindings, and protective slipcases standing as one example of the innovations that made books prized possessions to be shown off in the home. Critics have emphasised how bookish Clare was too.[41] A poem written in 1828, 'Evening Pastime', hints at Clare's capacity to be at once a highly individual voice and also to fit his work neatly for the volumes in which he appeared. The sonnet describes the sociable pleasures of evening, the fire 'crackling', his wife brewing tea, the children 'who edge up their chairs' to tell stories and listen to their father reading from Thomson, Cowper, or Bloomfield. The choice of Bloomfield is distinctive, and the children 'edg[ing] up their chairs' gives a touch of living reality that marks Clare out. But more than anything, I would suggest, this is an act of sympathy with the reader who holds the quarto volume of *Friendship's Offering* for 1829 in their hands, reading, quite possibly, in a very similar social setting.[42] By tuning in, as Clare did so well, to the diversity of the period's poetic market, we can see more clearly both what marked Clare out from his peers, and what he shared.

In Clare's 'Ode to Autumn', he describes the season as 'disorderly divine'. The description might well be taken as an account of Clare's work in the mid-1820s and 1830s. The 'Letter to A C' is perhaps his most astonishing (and even bewildering) experiment, but the period as a whole was one of experiment in which Clare tested out the diverse set of forms thrown up by a print culture that seemed increasingly hard to map. I have presented a largely positive picture of Clare's creative encounters with poetry in this period, but I do not wish simply to overwrite the difficulties Clare found. But something is lost if we see Clare as being only either in opposition to his age, or forced to produce work against his better instincts merely to make money. The idea that Clare was ever a poet interested in creating works independently of his readers misses the vitality that his creative processes took from such interactions with readers, publishers, and other models of poetry. In recent years scholars have adopted a more open attitude to the poetry and print culture of this period. As that work continues, Clare critics have the opportunity to view his work's variety as a teasing, creative response to an age both 'teazing' and fascinating.

NOTES

1. See especially Richard Cronin, *Romantic Victorians: English Literature, 1824–1840* (Basingstoke: Palgrave, 2002), Gregory Dart, *Metropolitan Art and Literature 1810–1840: Cockney Adventures* (Cambridge: Cambridge University Press, 2012), Tim Fulford, *The Late Poetry of the Lake Poets: Romanticism Revised* (Cambridge: Cambridge University Press, 2013), Maureen McCue, Rebecca Butler and Anne-Marie Millim, eds., *Writing in the Age of William IV, Yearbook of English Studies* (2018), David Stewart, *The Form of Poetry in the 1820s and 1830s: A Period of Doubt* (Basingstoke: Palgrave Macmillan, 2018) and Beatrice Turner, *Romantic Childhood, Romantic Heirs: Reproduction and Retrospection, 1820–1850* (Basingstoke: Palgrave Macmillan, 2017).
2. I am drawing on J. R. de J. Jackson's digital *Jackson Bibliography of Romantic Poetry* http://jacksonbibliography.library.utoronto.ca [accessed 14/4/19] (based on his earlier print *Annals of Verse*), the fullest lists of book production in the Romantic period available. Work is ongoing on the lists, and these numbers do not include the literary annuals.

3. Roger Sales, *John Clare: A Literary Life* (Basingstoke: Palgrave, 2002), 7.
4. Quoted in Bate, *Biography*, 370.
5. For this figure, see Jackson.
6. For a thorough overview of the birth of the annual phenomenon, see Katherine D. Harris, *Forget Me Not: The Rise of the British Literary Annual, 1823–1835* (Athens: Ohio University Press 2015). On Clare and the annuals see Lindsey Eckert, "'I'll Be Bound": John Clare's "Don Juan", Literary Annuals, and the Commodification of Authorship', *Nineteenth-Century Literature* 69.4 (2015): 427–54 and Stephen Colclough, 'Designated in Print as "Mr John Clare": The Annuals and the Field of Reading, 1827–1835', *JCSJ* 24 (2005): 52–68.
7. I draw this figure from Harris, 289–90. Eckert's figure of 45 includes poems in *Spirit and Manners of the Age* which is not strictly an annual.
8. *Letters*, 397.
9. Hood rejected Clare's 'The Rural Muse', suggesting 'one of your Songs to Mary ... would be just the thing': *Letters*, 443.
10. See James Raven, *The Business of Books: Booksellers and the English Book Trade, 1450–1850* (New Haven: Yale University Press, 2007).
11. See Wilson, *Decency and Disorder: The Age of Cant 1789–1837* (London: Faber and Faber, 2007). On Clare's nostalgia for the earlier 1820s, see Sales, *John Clare*, 148.
12. Angela Esterhammer, '1824: Improvisation, Speculation, and Identity-Construction', *BRANCH: Britain, Representation and Nineteenth-Century History*. Ed. Dino Franco Felluga. Extension of *Romanticism and Victorianism on the Net*. Web. [accessed 14/4/2019], unpag.
13. John Goodridge has explored these interactions most fully in *John Clare and Community* (Cambridge: Cambridge University Press, 2013); see also Paul Chirico, *John Clare and the Imagination of the Reader* (Basingstoke: Palgrave Macmillan, 2007), on Clare, other writers, and communities of readers, and Adam White, *John Clare's Romanticism* (Basingstoke: Palgrave Macmillan, 2017), on Clare and the 'major' Romantics.
14. Simon Kövesi, *John Clare: Nature, Criticism and History* (Basingstoke: Palgrave Macmillan, 2017), 9.
15. Bate, *Biography*, 352.
16. P. M. S. Dawson edited this essay from the manuscript and published it in 2001: 'Clare's "Letter to Allan Cunningham": An Unpublished Prose Work', *JCSJ* 20 (2001): 21–37. Dawson's edition includes a very helpful introduction and much-needed explanatory footnotes. References are to this edition. An advertisement for its publication appeared in the Stamford *Champion* on 2 February 1830, though Dawson's is the first publication.
17. On Clare and Cunningham, see Richard Cronin, 'John Clare and the *London Magazine*', *New Essays on John Clare: Poetry, Culture and*

Community, eds. Simon Kövesi and Scott McEathron (Cambridge: Cambridge University Press, 2015), 209–27.

18. For example, Peter George Patmore's series of 'London Letters to Country Cousins' in the *New Monthly Magazine* (1824–5). Clare may also have in mind Pierce Egan's Corinthian Tom and his country friend Jerry Hawthorn in *Life in London* (1820).

19. Esterhammer, '1824', unpaginated.

20. The Act was passed on 17 June 1824 and implemented on 1 June 1825. The number 5590 may refer to the Hebrew year, equivalent to 1829/1830 CE.

21. See Harris, 283.

22. The editions I have seen are bound in boards and leather, though it was offered for sale at 21s bound in green silk. See David Hogg, *The Life of Allan Cunningham* (London: Hodder and Stoughton, 1875), 281. A facsimile edition is available currently via Google Books.

23. *Letters*, 451.

24. For Cunningham's payment see *Letters*, 457. See *Letters*, 458, on S. C. Hall failing to pay Clare, and 424 on receiving 20 guineas a sheet for contributions to *Forget Me Not*.

25. *Keepsake* (1829), 49.

26. *Letters*, 457. Possibly Adam Ferguson, Esq., of Woodhill (1783–1862).

27. A theme that Clare himself essayed in 'The Quiet Mind', a poem in the 1828 *Amulet* signed 'The Northamptonshire Peasant'; see *Middle Period*, 3: 300–2.

28. *Middle Period*, 3: 258–68.

29. John Goodridge has explored in depth Clare's relations with Keats, noting how deeply he was engaged with Keats's 'To Autumn': see *Clare and Community*, 74–5.

30. The comma before 'front' seems an editorial error.

31. *Letters*, 303.

32. See Cronin, 'John Clare and the *London Magazine*'.

33. *Middle Period*, 3: 163–74.

34. It was also published in the *Stamford Champion* in 1830. The title given in the Oxford edition is 'To—on May Morning'; *Middle Period*, 3: 279–85.

35. *Letters*, 397, 460, 461.

36. See, for example, Glennis Stephenson, *Letitia Landon: The Woman behind L.E.L.* (Manchester: Manchester University Press, 1995) and Jill Rappoport, 'Buyer Beware: The Gift Poetics of Letitia Elizabeth Landon', *Nineteenth-Century Literature* 58.4 (2004): 441–73.

37. Clare, *Middle Period*, 3: 285–6; it appears on page 272 of *Forget Me Not*. I quote from the *Forget Me Not* version.

38. See Sarah Houghton-Walker, *John Clare's Religion* (Farnham: Ashgate, 2009); on this poem see page 200.
39. *The Amulet* (1828), 87.
40. *The Eclectic Review*, 30 (November 1828): 477.
41. See, for example, Chirico and Goodridge.
42. The poem appears on page 60 of *Friendship's Offering*, from which I quote; see *Middle Period*, 4: 161–2.

BIBLIOGRAPHY

Bate, Jonathan. *John Clare: A Biography*. New York: Farrar, Straus and Giroux, 2003.

Chirico, Paul. *John Clare and the Imagination of the Reader*. Basingstoke: Palgrave Macmillan, 2007.

Clare, John. *The Letters of John Clare*. Edited by Mark Storey. Oxford: Clarendon Press, 1985.

———. *Poems of the Middle Period, 1822–1837*. 5 vols. Edited by Eric Robinson, David Powell and P. M. S. Dawson. Oxford: Clarendon Press, 1996–2003.

Colclough, Stephen. 'Designated in Print as "Mr John Clare": The Annuals and the Field of Reading, 1827–1835'. *JCSJ* 24 (2005): 52–68.

Cronin, Richard. 'John Clare and the *London Magazine*'. In *New Essays on John Clare: Poetry, Culture and Community*, edited by Simon Kövesi and Scott McEathron, 209–27. Cambridge: Cambridge University Press, 2015.

———. *Romantic Victorians: English Literature, 1824–1840*. Basingstoke: Palgrave Macmillan, 2002.

Cunningham, Allan, ed. *The Anniversary: Or, Poetry and Prose for MDCCCXXIX*. London: John Sharpe, 1828.

Dart, Gregory. *Metropolitan Art and Literature 1810–1840: Cockney Adventures*. Cambridge: Cambridge University Press, 2012.

Dawson, P. M. S. 'Clare's "Letter to Allan Cunningham": An Unpublished Prose Work'. *JCSJ* 20 (2001): 21–37.

Eckert, Lindsey. '"I'll Be Bound": John Clare's "Don Juan", Literary Annuals, and the Commodification of Authorship'. *Nineteenth-Century Literature* 69.4 (2015): 427–54.

Esterhammer, Angela. '1824: Improvisation, Speculation, and Identity-Construction'. *BRANCH: Britain, Representation and Nineteenth-Century History*. Edited by Dino Franco Felluga. Extension of *Romanticism and Victorianism on the Net*. https://www.branchcollective.org/?ps_articles=angela-esterhammer-1824-improvisation-speculation-and-identity-construction.

Fulford, Tim. *The Late Poetry of the Lake Poets: Romanticism Revised*. Cambridge: Cambridge University Press, 2013.

Goodridge, John. *John Clare and Community*. Cambridge: Cambridge University Press, 2013.

Harris, Katherine D. *Forget Me Not: The Rise of the British Literary Annual, 1823–1835*. Athens: Ohio University Press, 2015.

Hogg, David. *The Life of Allan Cunningham*. London: Hodder and Stoughton, 1875.

Houghton-Walker, Sarah. *John Clare's Religion*. Farnham: Ashgate, 2009.

Jackson, J. R. de J., ed. *Jackson Bibliography of Romantic Poetry*. http://jackson-bibliography.library.utoronto.ca [accessed 14/4/19]

Kövesi, Simon. *John Clare: Nature, Criticism and History*. London: Palgrave Macmillan, 2017.

McCue, Maureen, Rebecca Butler and Anne-Marie Millim, eds. *Writing in the Age of William IV, Yearbook of English Studies*. Cambridge: Modern Humanities Research Association, 2018.

Rappoport, Jill. 'Buyer Beware: The Gift Poetics of Letitia Elizabeth Landon'. *Nineteenth-Century Literature* 58.4(2004): 441–73.

Raven, James. *The Business of Books: Booksellers and the English Book Trade, 1450–1850*. New Haven: Yale University Press, 2007.

Sales, Roger. *John Clare: A Literary Life*. Basingstoke: Palgrave Macmillan, 2002.

Stephenson, Glennis. *Letitia Landon: The Woman behind L.E.L.* Manchester: Manchester University Press, 1995.

Stewart, David. *The Form of Poetry in the 1820s and 1830s: A Period of Doubt*. London: Palgrave Macmillan, 2018.

Turner, Beatrice. *Romantic Childhood, Romantic Heirs: Reproduction and Retrospection, 1820–1850*. London: Palgrave Macmillan, 2017.

White, Adam. *John Clare's Romanticism*. London: Palgrave Macmillan, 2017.

Wilson, Ben. *Decency and Disorder: The Age of Cant 1789–1837*. London: Faber and Faber, 2007.

'Sweet the Merry Bells Ring Round': John Clare's Songs for the Drawing Room

Kirsteen McCue

It is well known that John Clare's first poetic creations were 'imitations of my fathers Songs'.[1] He recounted destroying many of them, then trying some in performance, but the locals 'only laughd at and told me I need never hope to make songs like them'.[2] Regardless of this early criticism, by the time of the first published collections of his poetry in the early 1820s Clare was already being marked out as 'an individual, as meritorious as remarkable in the annals of song'.[3] Fast forward to the twentieth century, and he is held up as the ancestor of the great English twentieth-century song collectors Cecil Sharp and Ralph Vaughan Williams, who gathered material from local singers on wax cylinders (rather than amending what they heard as they notated it). Following Margaret Grainger's work on Clare as collector of ballads in the 1960s,[4] George Deacon's 1983 study, *John Clare and the Folk Tradition*, revealed that there are few comparable songwriters with such collections in the Romantic period.[5] Critics have,

K. McCue (✉)
Centre for Robert Burns Studies, University of Glasgow, Glasgow, UK
e-mail: Kirsteen.McCue@glasgow.ac.uk

© The Author(s) 2020   37
S. Kövesi, E. Lafford (eds.), *Palgrave Advances in John Clare Studies*, Palgrave Advances,
https://doi.org/10.1007/978-3-030-43374-1_3

rightly, noted the strong links between Clare's songs (collected and created) and those of Robert Burns (1759–1796), James Hogg (1770–1835), and, to a lesser degree, Thomas Moore (1779–1852).[6] While Burns and Hogg bear many similarities—both, like Clare, are rural, working-class writers heavily influenced by their own local and national demotic song traditions—neither of them leaves behind such a concentrated and 'gathered' manuscript record. However, Burns, Hogg and Moore arguably gain much more contemporary notoriety and success because their songs are picked up and published with musical notation both in large national song collections and in separate song-sheets for a growing domestic performance market.

Deacon's study concentrates principally on the local dimensions of Clare's manuscripts, and he explores the osmosis (backwards and forwards) between popular chapbooks and broadsides with the songs Clare notates and sometimes amends.[7] As he reveals, 'The Meeting', Clare's original song beginning 'Here we meet too soon to part',[8] gains a certain popularity beyond such text-only garland, broadside and songster versions because of an early musical setting by the composer Haydn Corri.[9] In his study Deacon mentions two further musical settings of Clare's songs published during the poet's lifetime: he had been unable to find a copy of the first, 'The Banks of Broomsgrove', and the second, 'Sweet the Merry Bells Ring Round' (Figs. 1, 2, 3, and 4), represented just one of several songs Clare had apparently written for the composer F. W. Crouch to set. Deacon cites these two examples as 'outstanding queries', but few scholars have since explored these, or any other Clare song settings in any depth. The recent exception is Simon Kövesi's detailed and expansive discussion of 'The Meeting', which he uses to illustrate just how far-reaching Clare's work could be when it was, as he states, 'let loose from the chains of nature and place'.[10]

Bryan N. Gooch's and David Thatcher's catalogue of *Musical Settings of Early and Mid-Victorian Literature*, published in 1979, includes a comprehensive list of musical settings of Clare's texts by composers from Clare's own day right up to settings by Benjamin Britten in the 1950s and Trevor Hold and others in the 1970s.[11] Using their work as a starting point and undertaking further investigation, the following settings of Clare's songs have (so far) been located. Excepting the American publication of 'The Meeting', these were all produced in London and are given below in suggested chorological order of publication.[12] The list includes

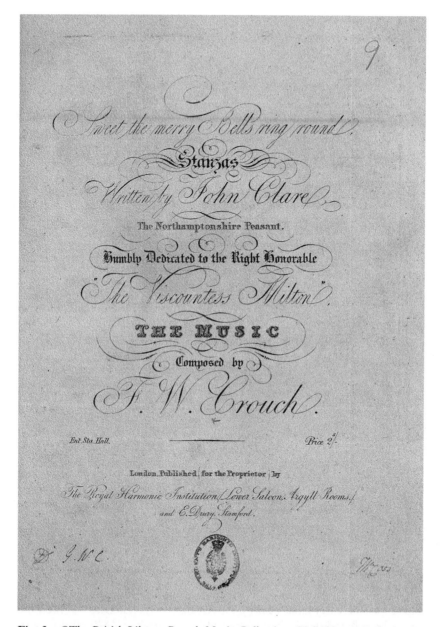

Fig. 1 ©The British Library Board, Music Collections H.3691.e.(9.) 'Sweet the Merry Bells Ring Round', John Clare and F.W. Crouch, c. 1820. Title page

Fig. 2   ©The British Library Board, Music Collections H.3691.e.(9.) 'Sweet the Merry Bells Ring Round', John Clare and F.W. Crouch, c. 1820. First page of musical setting

Fig. 3 ©The British Library Board, Music Collections H.3691.e.(9.) 'Sweet the Merry Bells Ring Round', John Clare and F.W. Crouch, c. 1820. Second page of musical setting

Fig. 4   ©The British Library Board, Music Collections H.3691.e.(9.) 'Sweet the Merry Bells Ring Round', John Clare and F.W. Crouch, c. 1820. Third and final page of musical setting

titles of songs (with first lines) and information about composers, associated performers (where applicable) and publishers:

- 'The Meeting' ('Here We Meet Too Soon to Part'). There are at least three different musical settings dating from ca. 1820 to ca. 1856, as follows.

  - Setting of Clare's 'The Meeting' associated with the singer Mr Broadhurst (no composer's name given): published by I. [J?] Waring of 55 Fleet Street.[13] This song-sheet possibly dates from ca. 1820.[14]
  - Setting by Haydn Corri, associated with singer Madame Vestris (1787–1856): published by F. T. Latour of 50 New Bond Street. The song was definitely performed at Drury Lane in 1820. This musical copy is likely to date from ca. 1826 to ca. 1830, as Latour established his own business around 1826 at this address, and it was then taken over by the better-known Samuel Chappell in 1830.[15]
  - Setting by unnamed composer of Clare's poem adapted to the air 'Ditanti Palpiti' [sic] by Gioachino Rossini (from his opera Tancredi of 1813). This version is associated with singer Catherine ('Kitty') Stephens (1794–1882): published by George Shade, East side of Soho Square. Shade was based at 21 Soho Square from ca. 1817 until 1840. This setting is thought to date from ca. 1825.[16]
  - Setting by T. B. Phipps (1796–1849) of Rossini's 'Di Tanti Palpiti', as sung by Mr Williamson: published by G. Graupner, No. 6 Franklin Street, Boston, U.S.A. Possibly published between ca. 1821 and ca. 1824.[17]

- 'Evening Bells' ('Sweet the Merry Bells Ring Round'). Setting by Frederick William Crouch (ca. 1783–1844). Dedicated to the Viscountess Milton: published 'for the Proprietor' by the Royal Harmonic Institution, published early 1821 (see Figs. 1, 2, 3, and 4).[18]
- 'To-day the Fox must die' ('The cock awakes the rosy dawn'). Sung and composed by William Kirby (n.d.).[19] Dedicated to Captain T. Brett & the 8th Hussars: published Preston of 71 Dean Street, Soho. Probably published ca. 1825 (certainly between 1822 and 1834).[20]
- 'Song' ('O the voice of woman's love'). Setting by Edwin J. Nielson (b. 1812): published by Joseph Alfred Novello at 67 Frith Street, Soho Square. Probably published ca. 1830 (certainly between 1829 and 1834) as the company moved to Dean Street in 1834.[21]

- 'Ballad' ('I dreamt not what it was to woo'). Setting by John William Hobbs (1799–1877). This setting is associated with singer Clara Novello (1818–1908): published by T. E. Purday of 50 St Paul's Church Yard linked to Collard & Collard (previously Clementi & Co). Thomas Edward Purday was at that address between ca. 1834 and 1862 as he took over the firm of Collard and Collard in 1834. Probably published ca. 1840.[22]
- 'The Banks of Broomsgrove' ('There's the daisy, the woodbine, the crowflower so golden'). Music by John Barnett (1802–90): no publisher's details given on copy, though this may be the setting connected to publisher James Power in ca. 1825. Most probably published ca. 1856.[23]
- 'Ballad' beginning 'Winter's gone, the summer breezes'. Setting by Sir William Sterndale Bennett (1816–75) and published by Novello, Ewer & Co. at 1 Berners Street. W. and 80 and 81 Queen Street E. C. and by Diston & Co in Boston, New York and Philadelphia. Novello, Ewer & Co. were at that address from December 1867 until the end of 1906. Performance noted as 1855; possibly not published until after 1867.[24]

This list includes songs other critics have already mentioned and one or two additional pieces besides. It does not mention the wider distribution of Clare's song texts in chapbooks, broadsides and elsewhere, nor is it inclusive of other American printings of the songs. Needless to say, there are potentially other song-sheets as yet unknown. As Kövesi has noted, 'Immediately Clare's work was made public […] professional musicians evidently saw in it the potential for musical setting and performance'.[25] This is evidenced by tracking the texts of the musical settings listed here. Four of them appeared in the first two collections of Clare's poetry, namely *Poems Descriptive of Rural Life and Scenery* of 1820 (appearing in four editions across 1820 and 1821) and *The Village Minstrel and Other Poems* of 1821.[26] The content of *Poems Descriptive* was arranged as 'Poems', 'Songs and Ballads' and 'Sonnets'; in *The Village Minstrel* songs and ballads were distinguished only by 'Song' or 'Ballad' prefixed to their titles. Unlike those of Burns, Hogg and Moore, these lyrical texts were rarely printed with an associated tune title, even though, as Deacon states, Clare's poetry often 'has a musicality redolent of the tunes he played and assiduously collected'.[27] The text of 'The Meeting' appeared in John Taylor's introduction to *Poems Descriptive*,[28] though Clare had also sent a copy of it to his Stamford friend Edward Drury in his letter of [20 December 1819], noting that 'the one in the Book varies a great deal from my improved one, which I here send you'.[29] 'To-day the Fox Must Die', subtitled 'A Hunting Song', also appeared in *Poems Descriptive*.[30] 'The Banks of Broomsgrove' and 'Winter's Gone' had both been included in the second volume of *The Village Minstrel* in 1821.[31] 'O the voice of woman's love' appeared later in *The Rural Muse* of 1835, though the musical setting most probably dates from the year before this.[32] The exceptional text here is 'Sweet the Merry Bells Ring Round', which was written in 1819–20, but does not appear in print in either of the first poetry collections (Figs. 1, 2, 3, and 4).[33]

Other texts were included in the periodical press, adding to their attractiveness for composers and music publishers. 'I dreamt not what it was to woo' seems to have first appeared, under its new editor John Scott, in the *London Magazine* in July 1821.[34] Bate notes that the magazine included a few samples of Clare's work from *Poems Descriptive* as 'tasters'.[35] 'Winter's Gone' also appeared there in November 1821, to promote the recent publication of *The Village Minstrel*.[36] As already discussed 'The Meeting' had unrivalled contemporary success amongst Clare's songs, and it was also lifted up quickly by newspaper editors. For example, it is mentioned in *The Morning Post* for 21 February 1820, which refers to Madame Vestris's performance and reprints the poem; in the *Lancaster Gazette and General Advertiser, for Lancashire, Westmorland, &c* for 1 April 1820, to promote *Poems Descriptive*; and, later, in *Freeman's Journal and Daily Commercial Advertiser* for 2 March 1821, which refers specifically to Haydn's Corri's setting of the song within Thomas Dibdin's comic opera *The Cabinet* at the New Theatre Royal, Dublin.[37] This information illustrates how far such popular songs could range; making mention of performances by celebrated singers was a marketing tactic to further sales of printed copies and, as Clare later noted, such song copies only helped sales of the poetry collections too.

Collations of these texts with those in the musical settings reveal that most often composers were using the first formal appearances of the songs as copy text. Most have the usual orthographic changes and nearly all settings repeat certain words or lines for musical emphasis. A number of songs also remove verses entirely. Thus the Broadhurst version of 'The Meeting' and the settings featuring Rossini's melody exclude the third verse of the Clare text in *Poems Descriptive*; Bennett's setting of 'Winter's Gone' omits verse 3; and 'The Banks of Broomsgrove' omits lines 4–8 and lines 1–4 of verses 2 and 3 respectively, and removes the final verse of the song altogether from *The Village Minstrel* version.

These first musical appearances of Clare's songs coincide with what Sam Ward has shown to be something of a white-hot period of songwriting for Clare around 1820.[38] Both Ward and Jonathan Bate recount that Clare's Stamford friends Ed Drury and Octavius Gilchrist were particularly keen to encourage Clare to write songs, and both had a clear eye on the musical market. While Taylor worked closely with the poetic manuscripts for *Poems Descriptive*, Drury had a hands-on approach in helping Clare select songs for potential publication.[39] Gilchrist introduced Clare to a different kind of musical soirée, not quite like those to which he was accustomed at his local hostelry 'The Bluebell' and in his own home.[40] Introductions and visits to Milton Hall, local winter seat of the Fitzwilliam family, and time spent in the company of Viscount Milton (to whom Clare dedicated his *Poems Descriptive*) and his wife (to whom Crouch dedicated his musical setting of 'Sweet the Merry Bells') may well have made Clare aware of a different performance context for songs. But undoubtedly his first London visit with Gilchrist in March 1820 opened Clare's eyes to the opportunities musical performances might afford him and his work.

On their arrival in London, the duo frustratingly missed a scheduled performance by Madame Vestris of 'The Meeting' at the Theatre Royal Drury Lane,[41] but this failure notwithstanding, Clare wrote afterwards that he 'felt uncommonly pleased at the circumstance' of his own song being heard in such a grand setting.[42] Gilchrist's brother-in-law, J. C. Burkhardt, took Clare to the 'fairey land' of Vauxhall Gardens where he must have heard popular songs.[43] It was during this first London visit that Clare met up with Taylor's publishing partner James Hessey, and where his patron Lord Radstock introduced him to Mrs Eliza Emmerson.[44] Again, it was through Taylor that Clare dined with contemporary writers and artists, meeting, amongst others, the Scots writer Allan Cunningham (1784–1842), one of whose many areas of interest was song collecting, editing and writing.[45] Cunningham had been aiding Robert Hartley Cromek with his *Remains of Nithsdale and Galloway Song* of 1810, instigating much discussion about the authenticity of some of the 'collected' songs and ballads, which were in fact penned by Cunningham himself.[46] Cromek had invited Cunningham to London before the publication of *Remains* and gave Cunningham useful connections to further his career in the city.[47] Cunningham was a close friend of James Hogg, who Clare also held in high regard. Alongside his existing admiration for the lyrics of Burns and

Moore one might reasonably conclude that Clare's first visit to the metropolis thus both stimulated his appetite for wider musical dissemination of his songs and, moreover, gave him a range of useful contacts for that purpose.

'The Meeting' could be seen as Clare's song 'calling card' at this moment, with its appearances across wide-ranging print media and performance in the theatre by such notable champions as Lucia Vestris and Kitty Stephens. As Taylor noted, this song was directly inspired by Burns's love song 'O were I on Parnassus hill', which had already appeared with a Burns's choice of tune ('My love is lost to me') in the *Scots Musical Museum* in 1792 (3: 255) and in Thomson's *Select Collection of Original Scottish Airs* in 1798 (no. 29).[48] Burns's correspondence with his song editors illustrates that he had strong opinions about the melodies for his songs, even if he had little control over their musical settings or arrangements.[49] However, because Clare rarely had direct contact with the production process, the settings of his songs never use melodies he may have had in mind; they are all newly composed, excepting the re-use of the Rossini aria listed above for some settings of 'The Meeting'. 'Sweet the Merry Bells Ring Round' is one song from the period where we know Clare was directly involved. Encouraged by Drury to select some of his songs for London composer F. W. Crouch, Clare recalls that he sent 'a great quantity of Songs written purposly for an intended publication with music by Crouch 5 or 6 of them was published but what profit they made I cannot tell I got nothing'.[50] Of this group, only 'Sweet the Merry Bells' has since been located and the British Library copy has the imprint of the Royal Harmonic Institution alongside one 'E. Drury, Stamford' on its elaborate title page (see Fig. 1). Leanne Langley has explained that the Institution was developing a commercial enterprise at precisely this moment, with its shop opening in 1819.[51] It is frustrating that we have no further details about Clare's involvement here, but we do know that Taylor was unhappy with this venture and displeased that Clare received no remuneration for his texts.[52]

Whatever the reason, Clare's enthusiasm for Drury's song projects dwindled when he returned home from that first London visit. In May 1820 Drury wrote to Clare of his disappointment, explaining that he had told 'Power & others' that Clare's songs were 'of the first order of excellence' even those 'not adapted for Music'.[53] That James Power was interested and saw potential in Clare's songs was notable, for his company was one of the most powerful music publishing houses in the city, with a growing list of domestic music. Ward reveals that correspondence in the summer of 1820 between Clare and Hessey, and Clare and Captain Markham E. Sherwill, continues to refer to the production of 100 songs for 'Powers'. But the project was never completed. As Ward suggests, Power was perhaps diverted at this time by a copyright battle in the courts with his brother William, in relation to their joint publication of Thomas Moore's multi-volume *Irish Melodies*.[54] But, along with Taylor's concerns, Hessey had reservations about Clare's plan. Further disquiet, expressed by Lord Radstock and Eliza Emmerson (who was in a state of 'some distress' at the thought of Clare publishing songs that were disreputable in comparison with his poetry), presented a serious impediment.[55] Had the connection with Power been more closely established, the story of the wider circulation of Clare's songs with music might have been very different. But only one song, as far as we are aware, was taken up by Power and that was several years later.

On 22 September 1825, Hessey wrote to Clare to warn the poet that Power would be in touch to ask permission to publish 'The Maid of Broomsgrove', recently set to music by composer John Barnett.[56] Clare's response to Power, dated 24 September, states that he had no objections to Barnett's setting, and he explained that he was 'convinced that the setting any Song to good music from a Volm. of Poems goes a great way to make the book popular'.[57] Inspired by Hessey, Clare requested a royalty payment or 'trifle' for use of his text,[58] and he received a sum of £2 on 29 September. He was then encouraged by Eliza Emmerson to consider writing more new songs for Power and to charge 2 guineas a piece: apparently she had changed her mind about the worthiness (and commercial viability) of Clare's songs.[59] As Alan Vardy has noted, another admirer of Clare's songs, Charles Hodgson, also asked permission to publish Clare's 'My love thou art a nosegay sweet' in November 1825, and the same royalty payment appears to have been part of the deal.[60] No one has found a copy of 'The Maid of Broomsgrove' dated 1825, but the British Library houses a copy which it believes appeared around 1856. It gives Clare's name in its heading and also states that 'The Words of this Ballad are Published by Permission of the Author'. However, it has no elaborate title page (as many contemporary song-sheets do) nor any additional publisher information barring the number '975' in the middle of the bottom of each page. While this is most probably the same setting as that published by Power in 1825, the BL catalogue entry identifies that this particular copy was one of several miscellaneous songs produced in the 1850s under the title 'Cyclopaedia of Music'. Clare's song appears as no. 103 of a large number of contemporary song settings including those by distinguished musical figures Ludwig van Beethoven, Joseph Haydn, G. F. Handel and Thomas Arne.

The connection with Power in 1825, not to mention Clare's growing awareness of such commercial opportunities, seems to have coincided with a second spell of focused songwriting activity for Clare. During his third visit to London in the summer of 1824 he became acquainted with Harry Stoe Van Dyk (1797–1828).[61] Van Dyk's obituary, published a year after his untimely death, states that, inspired by Byron and Moore, he 'was engaged during the two or three last years of his life in writing songs for publishers of music'.[62] Several of these songs were set by John Barnett, including a series of minstrel songs featuring (with an obvious nod to Moore) 'A Highland Minstrel Boy'.[63] As Deacon has shown, Van Dyk was corresponding with Clare in February 1825 about 'many beautiful tunes' and 'provincial ballads'.[64] He appears to have been interested in the relationship between Clare's poetic text and music as mentioned in his letters to Clare in 1827,[65] and he was especially keen on seeing and sourcing a music publisher for Clare's manuscript collection with the working title:

National and Provincial Melodies
Selected from the Singing
and Recitations
of
the Peasantry in and about
Helpstone and its neighbourhood
with some alterations and corrections
Necessarily required[66]

The existence of this collection (albeit in fair-copy manuscript) raises several important issues. Clare's reference to gathering songs and recitations of the local 'Peasantry' chimes with James Currie's first presentation of the work of Burns in 1800.[67] Clare's title underlines his role as 'collector', but it also alludes to the editing and amending (the altering and correcting) of songs. Deacon notes that this collection in fact included more newly composed songs than it did songs from 'the field'. This illustrates that Clare, once again, was functioning in a very similar way to Burns and to James Hogg. One of Hogg's early ventures had been a small selection of songs published by Edinburgh music publisher Nathaniel Gow and Sons in 1819 with the title *A Border Garland*. Although Hogg was already contributing songs to other larger Scottish national song publications in the 1810s, this little collection helped label Hogg as the song man of his local border region.[68] Clare's little collection, discussed in detail in this volume by Stephanie Kuduk Weiner, might have served a similar purpose for him. But, once more, it was not to be.

Perhaps Clare was diverted by the delays around the publication of *The Shepherd's Calendar* in 1827, or was dissuaded by Van Dyk's unexpected early death the following year. However, it is tantalizing to think that if Clare had succeeded in completing this English 'national and provincial' song project and seen it into print with musical notation, then this would have been one of the first published collections of English songs during the Romantic period. Clare understood that if his songs had been published by Power they would have appeared much like Moore's *Irish Melodies*. Ireland, Wales and notably Scotland, all witnessed a vogue for such published collections from at least the 1770s onwards, but there is still a mystery as to why equivalents were so much rarer in England. Aside from a small number of documented manuscript collections (Clare's ought to be included in this), critics have so far agreed that the English nation had to wait until considerably later—for William Chappell's revelatory *A Collection of National English Airs, Consisting of Ancient Song, Ballad and Dance Tunes of the Olden Time* of 1838–40 and John Broadwood's *Old English Songs* of 1843—to begin to redress this balance.[69]

There was one final missed opportunity for Clare's songs in the 1820s and early 1830s. Allan Cunningham, who Clare met on his first London trip, produced his text-only multi-volume set *The Songs of Scotland: Ancient and Modern* [...] in 1825. He was well connected with both the *London Magazine* and *The Athenaeum* between 1822 and 1834, yet his correspondence with Clare across this period seems to focus more on poetry and prose than on song.[70] Cunningham was a good friend of another Scotsman, Thomas Pringle (1789–1834), who contacted Clare in the summer of 1828 to request some pieces for the annual *Friendship's Offering*.[71] Clare saw this as a fine opportunity and duly sent two poems ('To the Wren' and 'A Spring Morning') which, as editor, Pringle included that winter. Clare's letter to Pringle of 29 August 1829, makes particular mention of Pringle's 'best song of Teviotdale', a lyric sometimes referred to as 'The Emigrant's Farewell'. It had first appeared in *The Athenaeum* in 1821 and was then included by Thomson (set by J. N. Hummel) in his *Select Collection of Original Scottish Airs* in 1826.[72] The song lyric had appeared within the longer narrative poem 'Glen-Lynden. A Tale of Teviotdale' in *Friendship's Offering* for 1829 (thus in the same issue as Clare's poems). Clare was enthusiastic about this and several other Pringle lyrics, but neither Pringle nor Cunningham appears to have taken up the cause of Clare's songs nor made other fruitful connections for him. In comparison, two of Hogg's songs appeared with musical notation in a rival annual, *The Musical Bijou*, in 1829.[73] Another of his songs (without music) appeared in *Friendship's Offering* of 1830, and four others (with music) were included in the musical magazine *The Harmonicon* in 1829 and 1832. This magazine was owned by renowned music publisher Goulding & D'Almaine, who had also printed *The Border Garland* (an expanded version of Hogg's earlier Edinburgh production) in 1829. One of Hogg's *Harmonicon* songs was set by one Edwin J. Nielson,[74] who also set Clare's 'O the voice of woman's love' at around the same time. Clare may not have been aware of Hogg's comparative success with London music publishers, but he was most certainly aware of his prowess as a song writer, referring to his admiration for Hogg's ballad 'on the Herding at eve from the pasture' in a letter to Pringle of 8 February 1832.[75] It transpires that Clare had most probably seen Hogg's love song 'When the kye comes hame', in the *Stamford Champion* on 1 February 1831, just after the publication of Hogg's text-only collection *Songs by The Ettrick Shepherd*.

We have little information about how the later settings of Clare's songs came about, but there is a neat connection between 'I dreamt not what it was to woo' and 'Winter's Gone'. The first of these ballads, set to music by singer and composer John Hobbs, was performed by Clara Novello, daughter of music publisher Vincent, who made her concert debut in 1832. She was a highly successful performer, befriending the young Felix Mendelssohn at whose Leipzig Gewandhaus concerts she sang in the 1830s, and she was much admired by Rossini and others. While the majority of Clare's song settings were by fairly mediocre, if popular, composers of the moment, William Sterndale Bennett, who set 'Winter's Gone', was regarded as a significant musician in his own right: his first piano concerto was reviewed favourably in *The Harmonicon* in 1833, while he was a student at the Royal Academy of Music in London. Later that year he was heard by visitor Felix Mendelssohn, who subsequently mentored him as his career developed. It was undoubtedly through Mendelssohn that this young English composer came to know Karl Klingemann, who accompanied Mendelssohn on his famous trip to Scotland in 1829. And, as noted on the copy of 'Winter's Gone', it was Klingemann who translated the texts for Bennett's 'Six Songs' Op. 35, which included the Clare setting: 'Winter's gone, the summer breezes / Breathe the shepherd's joys again: Winter's Macht is überwunden / Weithin schallt des Schäfer's Sang'. Of all the musical settings listed, this one, as Trevor Hold has stated, is 'a fine song and deserves to be better known'.[76] It was clearly created far in advance of its possible publication date of 1867. A London performance, given by 'Miss Novello' with Bennett accompanying, is mentioned in *The Morning Post* for 14 March 1855, and it describes this setting as 'a perfect gem, a piece of artistic truth which, like the diamond, shines on every side with equal lustre'.[77]

Eric Robinson's view that Clare 'wanted to write songs that people like himself would enjoy. He did not wish to separate himself from ordinary men and women'[78] might be reconsidered in light of these musical settings. Closer examination illustrates that these songs, created for parlour or drawing room performance, also roamed into the theatre and onto the concert platform. There is little evidence of Clare's knowledge of such performances (aside from the Madame Vestris event), so it is impossible to know what he would have thought about his songs appearing in such different environments. The final published songs with music are a strange selection of mostly predictable pastoral love songs—perhaps not presenting the best of Clare's lyrical voice. They were mostly created by now little-known composers, but several were performed by celebrated singers and produced by a number of key music publishing houses of their day. Examining these publications, while further exploring the two periods of Clare's song activity in 1820 and 1825–27, provides solid evidence to support Sam Ward's view that these songs, so often sidelined in criticism, because they are regarded as less 'authentic', still illustrate something of Clare's 'literary ambitions'.[79]

There are many reasons why Clare's songs did not receive the musical attention they deserved. Clare's own disposition—he presents a picture of vulnerability compared to the strident self-confidence of Hogg, for example—alongside his complex relationships with opinionated editors and literary mentors did not make things straightforward.[80] The failed attempts of both Drury and Van Dyk to see independent song projects to fruition, and the disappointment in Cunningham and Pringle to ignite further interest, were followed by years of mental illness for Clare from the mid-1830s until his death. Accounts of his final asylum years suggest, however, that he remained preoccupied with songs and song culture. Adam White tracks, in detail, the strong affiliation with Burns in many of the lyrics Clare produced in his final years alongside his fascination with Byron's *Hebrew Melodies*.[81] It may just be possible that Clare, within himself, continued to feel unfulfilled in the musical marketplace.

NOTES

1. *By Himself*, 98.
2. Ibid.
3. From an Unsigned Review, *Literary Gazette*, 246 (6 October 1821), 625–8, in *Critical Heritage*, 141.
4. Margaret Grainger, *John Clare: Collector of Ballads* (Peterborough: Peterborough Museum, 1964), 7. Grainger is keen to underline Clare's prominence as a collector of both text and music, which is unusual for this period: she likens him to James Johnson with whom Burns works closely on *The Scots Musical Museum* (1787–1803); however, Johnson does not work in the field in the same way as Clare. See *The Scots Musical Museum*, ed. Murray Pittock (Oxford: Oxford University Press, 2017).
5. See Deacon, *passim*. For the relationship between Clare's roles as collector, creator and imitator, see also Terence Hoagwood, *From Song to Poetry: Romantic Pseudo-songs* (Basingstoke: Palgrave Macmillan, 2010), 16–20. The Welsh writer Iolo Morganwg (1747–1826) also collected tunes: see Daniel Huws, 'Iolo Morganwg and Traditional Music' in *A Rattleskull Genius: The Many Faces of Iolo Morganwg*, ed. Geraint H. Jenkins (Cardiff: University of Wales Press, 2009).
6. See Valentina Bold, 'James Hogg and the Scottish Self-taught tradition' in John Goodridge ed. *The Independent Spirit: John Clare and the Self-Taught Tradition* (Helpston, 1994), 69–86; Ronald Blythe, 'John Clare in Scotland', *JCSJ* 19 (2000), 73–81; Adam White, 'The Love Songs and Love Lyrics of Robert Burns and John Clare', *Scottish Literary Review*, 5:2 (Autumn/Winter 2013), 61–80; Adam White, *John Clare's Romanticism* (London: Palgrave Macmillan, 2017), 297–301. For Moore see Bate, *Biography*, 161–2, 21 and 492.
7. Clare often refers to this material himself: see, for example, *By Himself*, 68.
8. Deacon, 64–5.
9. Garlands and songsters were most often text-only anthologies of popular lyrics. Broadsides frequently appeared with illustrative wood-cuts, but rarely with musical notation. For Haydn Corri see Deacon, 67; Bate, 157.
10. Simon Kövesi, *John Clare: Nature, Criticism and History* (London: Palgrave Macmillan, 2017), 61. Further brief discussion of some of the early settings is found in Trevor Hold, 'The Composer's Debt to John Clare', *JCSJ* 1 (1982), 25–9. But Hold's article is as interested in twentieth-century settings of Clare by Gurney, Britten and himself.
11. Bryan N. Gooch and David Thatcher, *Musical Settings of Early and Mid-Victorian Literature: A Catalogue* (Michigan: Garland, 1979). Entries for John Clare, 186–96.
12. Defining exact publication dates for most song-sheets with musical notation across this period is a complex and tricky business. Few are dated on

the copies. Here the dates given are those defined by the British Library catalogue entries, further nuanced by date ranges given for the relevant publisher in Charles Humphries and William Charles Smith, *Music Publishing in the British Isles from the Beginning to the Middle of the Nineteenth Century* [...] (London: Cassell and Company, 1954). Some, such as 'Winter's Gone', are newly suggested dates relating to reception of performances in the periodical press. See also Yu Lee An, 'Music Publishing in London from 1780–1837 as reflected in Music Publishers' Catalogues of Music for Sale: A Bibliography and Commentary' (Unpublished PhD: Canterbury, 2008).

13. Waring is not listed by either Humphries or Smith nor by Frank Kidson in *British Music Publishers, Printers and Engravers: London, Provincial, Scottish and Irish* (London: W. E. Hill, 1900). However, one J. Waring, a pianoforte-maker and dealer, is mentioned as being based at 51 Exmouth Street, Spa Fields, London around 1822: see http://www.lieveverbeeck. eu/Pianoforte-makers_England_w.htm.

14. Copy located in Music Collections at the Bodleian Library, Oxford. Also discussed in Kövesi, 55–6 and 75, who thinks 1820 might be too early a date for this song-sheet. Mr Broadhurst's name appears regularly on contemporary song-sheets published in London, though little detail is known of his biography. He is noted as teacher of several of the singers who performed at Vauxhall Gardens see: http://www.vauxhallgardens.com/vauxhall_gardens_singers_page.html.

15. British Library: H.1650.yy.(15).

16. British Library: H.3691.d.(21.). There are several copies of this setting, including later 1830s copies published by J. Duncombe (the same setting), and others dating from the 1850s. This melody, originally featured in Rossini's opera *Tancredi* of 1813, was hugely popular at the time: there are numerous sets of variations for piano and even a parody by Ignaz Moscheles in 1825. Catherine (Kitty) Stephens was one of the most popular singers of the period. A protégée of the London theatre composer Sir Henry Bishop, she performed across the London Theatre and at Vauxhall. She would become Countess of Essex in 1838.

17. Thanks to Derek B. Scott for drawing my attention to this setting. There are numerous American printings of Phipps's setting listed on Worldcat, including several that appeared between 1824 and 1826 in Philadelphia published by G. E. Blake of 13 South 5th Street. Thomas Bloomer Phipps is associated with several contemporary song-sheets. 'Mr Williamson' is the named singer (possibly one 'R. Williamson') on several American song-sheets including others published by Gottlieb Graupner, a German-born musician who established a music school and publishing business in Boston, Massachusetts, after emigrating there from London in the late 1790s. See

Douglas A. Lee, rev. Debra L. Hess, 'Gottlieb Graupner [Graubner]', *Grove Music Online* (2014). https://www.oxfordmusiconline.com/grovemusic/view/10.1093/gmo/9781561592630.001.0001/omo-9781561592630-e-1002256734.

18. British Library: G.806.a. (45.). Crouch was author of a *Complete Treatise on the Violoncello*, published in 1826, and his father was William Crouch, organist of Old Street Church, London.

19. A William Kirby and a Mrs William Kirby are listed as performers at the Adelphi Theatre, London between 1816 and 1827: https://www.umass.edu/AdelphiTheatreCalendar/actr.htm.

20. Thanks to Sam Ward for drawing my attention to this setting. British Library: G.805.a.(7.). The 8th Hussars had just returned to England in 1819 after a period of service in Nepal. Preston is another of the significant music houses of the moment, producing a large catalogue of domestic music and the key publisher of George Thomson's *Select Collections* of Scottish, Welsh and Irish airs from the early 1790s to the late 1840s. See Kirsteen McCue, '"An individual flowering on a common stem": melody, performance, and national song', in *Romanticism and Popular Culture in Britain and Ireland*, ed. Philip Connell and Nigel Leask (Cambridge: Cambridge University Press, 2009), 88–106.

21. British Library: H.2832.b. (22.). Nielson was a popular composer of song-sheets and other domestic pieces, notably for the harp. The Novello family business was probably the most famous of the music publishing houses of the moment (established in 1811), with an impressive catalogue including much domestic music. See Humphries and Smith, 246–7. See also Fiona M. Palmer, *Vincent Novello (1781–1861) Music for the Masses* (Aldershot: Ashgate, 2006).

22. British Library: H.1654.ee. (18.). J. W. Hobbs was another contemporary popular setter of songs. He was a noted singer: a tenor and member of the choirs of King's, Trinity and St John's, Cambridge then at St George's Windsor. He became a gentleman of the Chapel Royal.

23. British Library: H.2342./103. Barnett was one of the most popular composers of the moment, producing much of the incidental music for farces, melodramas and burlesques and a wide range of domestic music including songs. He was well connected with singers, composers and theatrical entrepreneurs including Henry Bishop, Lucia Vestris and S. J. Arnold. See Nicholas Temperley and Nigel Burton, 'John Barnett', *Grove Music Online* (2001). https://www.oxfordmusiconline.com/grovemusic/view/10.1093/gmo/9781561592630.001.0001/omo-9781561592630-e-0000002090. See also *Letters*, 348.

24. British Library: Hirsch M.769. (8.). Part of Sterndale Bennett's *Six Songs* Op. 35.

25. Kövesi, *John Clare*, 53–61. This quotation, 55.
26. Bate notes that these first two collections were far more popular and the two later collections *The Shepherd's Calendar* (1827) and *The Rural Muse* (1835) never gained comparable sales. Bate, *Biography*, 150.
27. Deacon, 13. Clare's tune collections are distinct from his manuscripts of song and ballad texts (Deacon, 14–15).
28. *Early Poems*, 1: 436. Taylor includes the text as part of his introduction to *Poems Descriptive of Rural Life and Scenery* (1820), xxiii.
29. Clare's letter to [?Edward Drury], of [ca. 20 December 1819], *Letters*, 20–1.
30. In *Poems Descriptive*, 170–2. See also *Early Poems*, 1: 400. The text of this song also appears in *The Sportsman's Vocal Cabinet, comprising an extensive Collection of Scarce, Curious and Original Songs and Ballads relative to Field Sports*, ed. Charles Armiger (London, 1833), 116–17, without attribution to Clare.
31. 'The Banks of Broomsgrove' appeared as 'Song' in *The Village Minstrel*, 2: 138–40; see also *Early Poems*, 2: 438–9. 'Winter's gone' appeared as 'Ballad' in *The Village Minstrel*, 2: 34–6; see also *Early Poems*, 2: 334–5.
32. *The Rural Muse*, 52. See also *Middle Period*, 4: 10–11.
33. This song is included in *Early Poems*, 2: 254–5. Manuscript versions are listed by the editors Robinson and Powell, and more details are given in John Goodridge, ed., *First-Line Index to the Published and Unpublished Poetry of John Clare* (undated). http://www.johnclare.info/flindex.html.
34. See *London Magazine* (July 1821), 76, signed 'John Clare'. See also *Middle Period*, 4: 23–4. Clare's anticipation about receiving a copy of the *London Magazine* appears in a letter to John Taylor of 11 August 1821, *Letters*, 206–8. See also Clare's correspondence with Taylor in July and August 1821, *Letters*, 206–8.
35. Bate, *Biography*, 222.
36. *London Magazine* (November 1821), 540–8. The 'Ballad', 543.
37. There are later mentions of 'The Meeting' in *Hampshire Telegraph and Sussex Chronicle* (11 January 1845), where the song is referred to as a perfect conclusion to an evening of entertainment (referring to a festive party hosted by Captain Wilcox onboard HMS Sultan, berthed in Portsmouth) and in the *Caledonian Mercury* (27 January 1851), the *Aberdeen Journal* (29 January 1851) and the *Dundee Courier* of the same date, referring to Clare while noting that he is still an inmate of a lunatic asylum (all three use the same text).
38. Sam Ward, 'Melodies in the Marketplace: John Clare's 100 Songs', *JCSJ* 25 (July 2006), 11–30. Bate, *Biography*, 214–15.
39. Ward, 13–14. Ward notes that there was, for example, a list of 20 songs sent by Drury on 17 May 1820.
40. Bate, *Biography*, 131.

41. Ibid., 166.
42. *By Himself*, 136.
43. Ibid., 132. Songs performed at Vauxhall were frequently then published as single song-sheets, advertising the particular performers associated with the renditions at the Gardens.
44. Ibid., 130.
45. Clare's vignette of Cunningham, *By Himself*, 145.
46. Denis M. Read, *R. H. Cromek, Engraver, Editor, and Entrepreneur* (Farnham: Routledge, 2011), 134–5.
47. See Leslie Stephen and Hamish Whyte, 'Allan Cunningham (1784–1842)', *ODNB* (2004). https://www.oxforddnb.com/view/10.1093/ref:odnb/9780198614128.001.0001/odnb-9780198614128-e-6918.*ODNB*.
48. John Taylor's introduction to *Poems Descriptive* makes this clear comparison as a way to suggest Clare's debt to Burns but also to show that his 'execution' was quite different, xxiv.
49. See *The Scots Musical Museum* (2017) and *Burns's Songs for George Thomson*, ed. Kirsteen McCue (Oxford: Oxford University Press, 2020 [forthcoming]).
50. Deacon, 67, quotes Clare from Peterborough MS. D14. *By Himself*, 168 and 313n4.
51. See Leanne Langley, 'Regent's Harmonic Institution', *Grove Music Online* (2001). https://www.oxfordmusiconline.com/grovemusic/view/10.1093/gmo/9781561592630.001.0001/omo-9781561592630-e-0000042367.
52. *Letters*, 154–7. See Clare's letters to John Taylor of February 1821. Storey notes that Taylor's letter to Clare of 14 July 1821 referred to Crouch's setting as 'very silly & common-place' (156).
53. Drury to Clare, 16 May 1820: British Library, Egerton MSS 2245, fol. 124v, as quoted at greater length in Ward, 14.
54. James Power secured an injunction against his brother William publishing the eighth number of *Irish Melodies* in Dublin in July 1821. See Una Hunt, *Sources and Style in Moore's Irish Melodies* (Abingdon: Routledge, 2017), 2.
55. Ward, 18.
56. *Letters*, 348. The letter quoted is Clare's response to Power dated 24 September 1825. The information about Hessey's letter of 22 September is given in Storey's notes.
57. Ibid. See also Hoagwood, 18–19. Hoagwood draws attention to Clare's awareness of the 'commercial advantages' of his songs, 19.
58. Ibid.
59. Ibid.
60. Alan Vardy, *John Clare, Politics and Poetry* (Basingstoke: Palgrave Macmillan, 2003), 113.
61. *By Himself*, 154; Bate, *Biography*, 296–8.

62. *The Annual Biography and Obituary for the year 1829*, 13 (London, 1829), 183.

63. The Van Dyk/Barnett songs are frequently issued by New York publishers including James L. Hewitt of 137 Broadway and Dubois and Stodart of 149 Broadway for several decades from around 1824 to the 1880s; and in Boston by Parker and Ditson of Washington Street. Also 'Knights may woo & ladies listen' appeared with a musical setting by J. B. Cramer and published by Cramer, Addison & Beale of 201 Regent Street, London, most likely between 1824 and 1828.

64. Deacon, 22 quotes from Clare's letter of 14 February 1825 in Nor. 15, 56.

65. Ibid. Van Dyk's letter of 14 August 1827, Pet. Fl. 92.

66. Ibid. Deacon quotes from Pet. A41.

67. See Currie's 'Some observations on the character and condition of The Scottish Peasantry' prefixed to his 'Life of Robert Burns with a criticism on his Writings' in *The Works of Robert Burns*, ed. James Currie (Liverpool, 1800), 1.

68. *James Hogg: Contributions to Musical Collections and Miscellaneous Songs*, ed. Kirsteen McCue (Edinburgh: Edinburgh University Press, 2014), 209–39.

69. See *ODNB*, Henry Davey, rev. Peter Ward Jones, 'William Chappell (1809–1888)' (2004). https://www-oxforddnb-com.oxfordbrookes.idm.oclc.org/view/10.1093/ref:odnb/9780198614128.001.0001/odnb-9780198614128-e-5130. Davey and Ward Jones suggest that Chappell, born into the famous music publishing family of Samuel Chappell (ca. 1782–1834), was inspired to undertake his English project by a boastful Scottish colleague, who noted how strong the tradition was North of the Border. It has been argued that England was too busy flying the flag for the newly emerging 'British' nation at this time, and thus its energies were diverted from a notably 'English' project. See *Romantic National Song Network* (University of Glasgow) https://rnsn.glasgow.ac.uk/.

70. *The Modern Scottish Minstrel*, ed. Charles Rogers (London, 1855), 3: 1–8. *Letters*, 456–7; 463; 489; 492—these are letters dating from 1828–29. Cunningham endeavours to help Clare and get something into *The Atheneum* across October and November 1832. *Letters*, 600; 604.

71. Pringle had returned to London from South Africa in 1827 to edit *Friendship's Offering*. See *ODNB*, David Finkelstein 'Thomas Pringle (1789–1834)' (2004). https://www.oxforddnb.com/view/10.1093/ref:odnb/9780198614128.001.0001/odnb-9780198614128-e-22807. Hogg's poems appeared in the annual of 1829, 334 and 416.

72. *A Select Collection of Original Scottish Airs*, ed. George Thomson (London, 1826), 5: 231.

73. *The Musical Bijou* (London, 1829) 2–7, 100–3; see also *James Hogg: Contributions to Annuals and Gift Books*, ed. Janette Currie and Gillian Hughes (Edinburgh: Edinburgh University Press, 2006), 143–53.

74. Nielson also set songs by James Hogg which appeared in the musical magazine *The Harmonicon*. See *James Hogg: Contributions to Musical Collections*, 461–76. For Nielson's setting see 472–3. Nielson set two further Hogg songs 'I hae naebody now' and 'Maggy o' Buccleuch' between ca. 1833–40, ibid., 599–614.
75. *Letters*, 572–3.
76. Hold (1982), 26.
77. *The Morning Post*, 14 March 1855: article titled 'Mr. Sterndale Bennett's Concerts' at Hanover-square rooms', reviewing the first concert in the series held on 13 March 1855.
78. *John Clare, Autobiographical Writings*, ed. Eric Robinson (Oxford: Oxford University Press, 1986), xv.
79. Ward, 11.
80. Paul Chirico, *John Clare and the Imagination of the Reader* (Basingstoke: Palgrave Macmillan, 2007).
81. White, 76–7.

BIBLIOGRAPHY

An, Yu Lee. 'Music Publishing in London from 1780–1837 as Reflected in Music Publishers' Catalogues of Music for Sale: A Bibliography and Commentary'. Unpublished PhD. Canterbury, 2008.
Armiger, Charles, ed. *The Sportsman's Vocal Cabinet, Comprising an Extensive Collection of Scarce, Curious and Original Songs and Ballads relative to Field Sports*. London, 1833.
Bate, Jonathan. *John Clare: A Biography*. London: Picador, 2003.
Bold, Valentina. 'James Hogg and the Scottish Self-taught Tradition'. In *The Independent Spirit: John Clare and the Self-Taught Tradition*, edited by John Goodridge, 69–86. Helpston: John Clare Society, 1994
Blythe, Ronald. 'John Clare in Scotland'. *JCSJ* 19 (2000): 73–81.
Burns, Robert. *The Scots Musical Museum*. Edited by Murray Pittock. Oxford: Oxford University Press, 2017.
———. *The Works of Robert Burns*. Edited by James Currie. Liverpool, 1800.
Chirico, Paul. *John Clare and the Imagination of the Reader*. Basingstoke: Palgrave Macmillan, 2007.
Clare, John. *John Clare By Himself.* Edited by Eric Robinson and David Powell. Ashington and Manchester: MidNAG/Carcanet, 1996.
———. *John Clare, Autobiographical Writings*. Edited by Eric Robinson. Oxford: Oxford University Press, 1986.
Deacon, George. *John Clare and the Folk Tradition*. London: Sinclair Browne, 1983; repr., London: Francis Boutle, 2002.
Gooch, Bryan N. and David Thatcher. *Musical Settings of Early and Mid-Victorian Literature: A Catalogue*. Michigan: Garland, 1979.

Goodridge, John, ed. *First-Line Index to the Published and Unpublished Poetry of John Clare* (undated). http://www.johnclare.info/flindex.html.

Grainger, Margaret. *John Clare: Collector of Ballads*. Peterborough: Peterborough Museum, 1964.

Hoagwood, Terence. *From Song to Poetry: Romantic Pseudo-songs*. Basingstoke: Palgrave Macmillan, 2010.

Hogg, James. *James Hogg: Contributions to Annuals and Gift Books*. Edited by Janette Currie and Gillian Hughes. Edinburgh: Edinburgh University Press, 2006.

———. *James Hogg: Contributions to Musical Collections and Miscellaneous Songs*. Edited by Kirsteen McCue. Edinburgh: Edinburgh University Press, 2014.

Hold, Trevor. 'The Composer's Debt to John Clare'. *JCSJ* 1 (1982): 25–9.

Humphries, Charles and William Charles Smith. *Music Publishing in the British Isles from the Beginning to the Middle of the Nineteenth Century* [...]. London: Cassell and Company, 1954.

Hunt, Una. *Sources and Style in Moore's Irish Melodies*. Abingdon: Routledge, 2017.

Kidson, Frank. *British Music Publishers, Printers and Engravers: London, Provincial, Scottish and Irish*. London: W. E. Hill, 1900.

Kövesi, Simon. *John Clare: Nature, Criticism and History*. London: Palgrave Macmillan, 2017.

McCue, Kirsteen. '"An Individual Flowering on a Common Stem": Melody, Performance, and National Song'. In *Romanticism and Popular Culture in Britain and Ireland*, edited by Philip Connell and Nigel Leask, 88–106. Cambridge: Cambridge University Press, 2009.

Palmer, Fiona M. *Vincent Novello (1781–1861) Music for the Masses*. Aldershot: Ashgate, 2006.

Read, Denis M. *R. H. Cromek, Engraver, Editor, and Entrepreneur*. Farnham: Routledge, 2011.

Rogers, Charles, ed. *The Modern Scottish Minstrel*. London, 1855.

Storey, Mark, ed. *Clare: The Critical Heritage*. London: Routledge & Kegan Paul, 1973.

———, ed. *The Letters of John Clare*. Oxford: Clarendon Press, 1985.

Thomson, George, ed. *A Select Collection of Original Scottish Airs* [later *Melodies of Scotland*], 6 vols (London: Preston [later Coventry & Hollier], 1793–1851).

Vardy, Alan. *John Clare, Politics and Poetry*. Basingstoke: Palgrave Macmillan, 2003.

Ward, Sam. 'Melodies in the Marketplace: John Clare's 100 Songs'. *JCSJ* 25 (July 2006): 11–30.

White, Adam. 'The Love Songs and Love Lyrics of Robert Burns and John Clare'. *Scottish Literary Review* 5.2 (Autumn/Winter 2013): 61–80.

———. *John Clare's Romanticism*. London: Palgrave Macmillan, 2017.

'Sea Songs Love Ballads &c &c': John Clare and Vernacular Song

Stephanie Kuduk Weiner

What is the relation between music and poetry for Clare? How do his poems draw on his life as a musician and on the tunes he played and knew, many by heart? How should we understand his many poems in song forms? This chapter approaches these questions by examining a group of transcripts and imitations of vernacular song on which he worked during the 1820s and early 1830s. These compositions are multi-media affairs, professing a direct connection to music and intended not only for reading but also, even primarily, for singing. All indications are that Clare hoped to publish them in a songbook modelled on collections of Scottish song and Thomas Moore's *Irish Melodies* (10 vols. 1808–34), and he came close to doing so.[1] Had Clare succeeded, songs that he collected, reworked, and composed with music in mind might have been printed with music on the page. He might have collaborated with composers to notate the tunes to which he had fitted words and to set original lyrics to new music. We

S. K. Weiner (✉)
Department of English, Wesleyan University, Middletown, CT, USA
e-mail: sweiner@wesleyan.edu

S. Kövesi, E. Lafford (eds.), *Palgrave Advances in John Clare Studies*, Palgrave Advances,
https://doi.org/10.1007/978-3-030-43374-1_4

would then have classed Clare with Moore, Robert Burns, and other Romantic poet-songwriters, and we would have listened to his words with an ear for the melodies that went with them. Clare's unpublished song collection is one of the great missed chances of the era.

But thankfully that is not the end of the story. A number of Clare's poems were set to music during and shortly after his lifetime, giving voice to his words in concert halls and drawing rooms throughout Britain and around the world, as Kirsteen McCue explains in this volume.[2] And, as I explore here, although he never published a songbook, the transcripts and imitations he worked on with that aim in view survive in both draft- and fair-copy manuscripts. Clare also kept working with these pieces—and with the musical resources they exemplify and, no doubt, helped him master—after the dream of producing a song collection had faded. In this chapter I examine this set of 'Sea Songs Love Ballads &c &c', as he referred to them in a letter to his publisher John Taylor.[3] Drawing on the pioneering work of George Deacon, I analyse how music and poetry enrich one another in these songs, which, unusually in Clare's corpus, can often be connected to particular tunes. I also search for the clues he left, as he shaped and reshaped these compositions, about which aspects of songs he thought were characteristic or wanted to harness for his own writing. Even when the words of a song or song-poem cannot be tied to a particular tune, Clare certainly composed them with reference to the musical and meaning-making structures of songs, to the musical cultures of the day, and surely, on occasion, to specific, yet unknown, melodies. Clare's songbook project directs our attention to features of vernacular song and music custom that were salient for him, and it helps us make educated guesses about how those unknown tunes may have complemented his lyrics. In all these ways, it offers a key to unlocking the musical vitality of the hundreds upon hundreds of songs—songs for both singing and reading—that Clare composed over the course of his life.

CLARE'S SINGING BOOK

Song collections are prime examples of print commodities that are significantly shaped and mediated by oral practices. Literary historians have generally been more interested in the other side of the coin, that is, in how oral practices are shaped and mediated by print. We have tended to treat print as the dominant medium of nineteenth-century British culture and to investigate its power to remake oral media, either by remediating it as content within written texts or by setting the terms in which all expressive culture is conceived, experienced, and promoted. But exciting recent work by scholars such as McCue, Elizabeth Helsinger, and Steve Newman has opened up new ways of approaching the two-way exchange between print and oral cultures. The idea of a unitary, commanding print culture has given way to a picture of multiple, intersecting print cultures and to accounts tracing the prominence of print to its capacity to interface with rather than displace other media such as the Multigraph Collective's ground-breaking *Interacting with Print* (2018).

Romantic music publishing is especially suited to these new paradigms. Published songs enabled Britain's voracious consumers to read song texts, gain access to songs staged elsewhere, learn new tunes and lyrics, and—most importantly—make music themselves.[4] Leaping nimbly across divisions of wealth, gender, and geography, published songs forged links between diverse musical and print cultures. The status and format of song collections, song-sheets, broadsides, hymns, and other such publications were affected by these intermedial uses. Rather than conferring fixity and authority on a particular version of a song, print publication typically multiplied variants and enabled wider circles of singers to make the song their own by performing it.[5] Conventions concerning editorial involvement, authorial attribution, page layout, indexing, and so on were all oriented towards capturing and fostering real musical events.

In this context, Clare's unfinished song collection looks less anomalous. Like other published songs, it belongs simultaneously to several variegated musical and print cultures. What's more, although many of the era's most prestigious, multi-volume song collections featured musical notation, the majority of songs were published without music.[6] Often the title or first line made it clear what the tune was, and, if not, a common practice was to name the air, too.[7] Perhaps surprisingly, cultural as much as commercial considerations seem to explain this pattern.[8] Historians speculate that songbooks and sheets without music signal publishers' expectation that potential customers would already know the tunes and would want to obtain a full set of lyrics, which were more difficult to memorize.[9] Accordingly, Clare's titles and first lines frequently point to specific tunes, and he names particular airs in a few of his songbook drafts.[10] Equally significant, as Steve Roud explains, 'the idea that texts and tunes should be immutably joined is a relatively recent phenomenon'.[11] Not only did both tunes and lyrics change, often significantly, from one publication to another: popular airs were used for many different lyrics, and some lyrics were performed to more than one air.[12] Our inability to definitively match tunes to Clare's song lyrics is on one level simply an extreme instance of a more general feature of the history of song, which is never fully recoverable in the archive.[13] Indeed, Clare's songs may suggest new methodologies for integrating lost and indefinite sounds into the literary history of poetry, answering appeals by critics such as Nick Groom to 'try to listen to the oral and in particular the harmonic and melodic nature of folk song, and to consider its influence on poetry—even, or perhaps *especially*, when it has apparently been excised' or, I would add in relation to Clare, lost or unrecorded.[14]

Clare and his contemporaries were familiar with a wide repertoire of vernacular song that included and blurred the boundaries between popular commercial music, folk songs and ballads, and church music.[15] They would also have been aware of a variety of musical practices by virtue of experiencing singing and music-making in formal and informal settings alike, from chapels and inns to fields, street corners, and private homes.[16] As a 'first rate scraper' (fiddler) with affinities for antiquarianism and gypsy culture, Clare seems to have had an especially broad knowledge of vernacular music.[17] In addition to his transcripts of songs and ballads, he 'prick[ed] down' more than 260 melodies in two hand-ruled music books, one of which he entitled *A Collection of Songs Airs and Dances for the Violin*.[18] But ample contemporary evidence, including Clare's own poetry and autobiographical writings, testifies to impressive levels of popular musical expertise, including memorization.[19] Everyday people sang alone and in groups, for themselves and for others, and song was a vital part of domestic, convivial, spiritual, civic, and work life.

Accordingly, many of the tunes to which he wrote his lyrics may well have been recognizable to his first readers. They may have been reminded of specific melodies by titles, catchy phrases, and choruses in his songs, and they may have enjoyed applying an air they already knew to his words, puzzling out the metre and trying on tunes from similar sorts of songs for size. That Clare took all this for granted is made clear in an early poem about the woodman singing to his children around the evening fire: 'with his singing book he does repair / To humming oer an anthem hymn or psalm' and 'often carrols oer his cottage hearth / "Bold robin hood" the "Shipwreck" or the "storm"'.[20] The woodman knows the melodies of a varied set of songs and 'often' performs them with the help of his 'singing book', a song collection. Clare's term 'singing book' implies that the volume itself warbles and croons along with the woodman, a magical transformation of an inanimate object into a living being accomplished when they make music together. This intimation of magic, like the sounds of singing and humming words to familiar airs, can still be faintly heard, whispering in all Clare's songs.

TAKEN DOWN FROM THE SINGING

The textual record of the song collection and its afterlife in Clare's work is remarkably complete.[21] He began by writing out transcripts and drafting close imitations of songs in two rough-copy manuscripts.[22] These raw materials were then reworked into fair-copy notebooks, most significantly a manuscript containing only 'Old Songs & Ballads' he claims to have collected,[23] and another in which he calls the songbook 'National and Provincial Melodies Selected from the Singing and Recitations of the Peasantry in and about Helpstone and its neighbourhood with some alterations and corrections necessarily required'.[24] Clare gave the songs titles emphasizing their antiquity and identifying his sources, such as 'Taken Down from a Shepherd' (written 1820s) and 'Old Song—Fragments gathered from my Fathers & Mothers singing—& compleated' (written 1819–32). Even at this stage, few of these texts seem to be unedited transcripts, as Clare's titles indicate—they have been altered, corrected, and completed. Most inhabit a murky middle ground, entirely characteristic of the mode, where collecting, amending, redeploying, and inventing all come into play.[25] A few of the pieces from these rough- and fair-copy manuscripts found their way into print, but most were revised again after the song collection floundered. Clare reworked them into two new fair-copy notebooks: the *Midsummer Cushion* manuscript, which served as the basis of his fourth book, *The Rural Muse* (1835)[26]; and a manuscript his modern editors have dubbed the 'guardbook' since it contains poems not yet published but still destined, he hoped, for print.[27] In these new fair-copy manuscripts, these compositions were usually retitled simply 'Song' or 'Ballad' and dispersed among dozens of other poems of the same name.

Clare's proposed titles reveal a lot about his project. First, he was working on a specific kind of songbook: a collection of *National and Provincial Melodies* inspired by works including Moore's *Irish Melodies*, Joseph Ritson's *Select Collection of English Songs* (3 vols., 1783), Robert Tannahill's *Poems & Songs, Chiefly in the Scottish Dialect* (1805), James Hogg's *The Mountain Bard* (1807), and Allan Cunningham's *Songs of Scotland* (4 vols., 1825), all of which were in Clare's library when he died.[28] He notated several tunes from songs collected or written by Cunningham and Moore, as he did with a handful of songs associated with Burns that appeared in James Johnson's *Scots Musical Museum* (6 vols., 1787–1803), suggesting he may have had access to that collection too. In any case, he knew both the words and tunes to numerous Burns songs and owned a copy of James Currie's *Works of Robert Burns* (1800), which contained the texts of more than 135 songs. Clare referred to these poet-songwriters frequently in letters and autobiographical writings. His excitement about collecting and writing songs was encouraged by their example.[29] Like them, he revised and reworked old songs, composed new lyrics for existing tunes, and wrote poems that could easily be set to music.[30] For him, too, these were strategies for marrying his poetic creativity to his 'auditory imagination' and enabling his songs to be sung by others.[31] Like them, Clare was participating in a living song tradition in which words and airs with roots in the past were continually being written, renewed, and performed.[32]

The titles also signal his interest in music history and aesthetics. Many of the song collections mentioned above, as well as others Clare knew, open with weighty prefaces, the most important of which was Ritson's 'Historical Essay on the Origin and Progress of National Song'. These prefaces synthesized works Clare may not otherwise have known such as Charles Burney's *General History of Music* (4 vols., 1776–89) and John Aikin's *Essays on Song-Writing* (1772), and they resonated strongly with other books he admired such as Thomas Percy's *Reliques of Ancient English Poetry* (1765), Hugh Blair's *Lectures on Rhetoric and Belles Lettres* (2 vols., 1783), and James Beattie's *The Minstrel* (2 books, 1771–4).[33] Clare had a full picture of eighteenth- and early nineteenth-century investigations of music—and not only of music but also, as Ritson puts it, of the 'origin and progress' of humanity's enduring urge to express 'a sentiment, sensation or image [...] by words differently measured, and attached to certain sounds, which we call melody or tune'.[34] For these writings interpreted song in terms drawn from philosophies of mind, conjectural histories of language, primitivist veneration of the strength and simplicity of ancient civilizations, and stadial models of history. As Gary Tomlinson writes, song was 'envisaged as the earliest, most immediate, and most passionate of utterances—the form in which language first emerged—and as a modulated and disciplined art of the present day'.[35] Discourses on song promised writers and singers an exhilarating access to powerful and prestigious art forms and to essential aspects of their humanity, stripping away the artificiality and pretence that seemed often to characterize contemporary culture. Clare summed up these discussions in 'Songs Eternity' (written 1832), which McCue calls a 'checklist of Romantic ideas about song'.[36] Associating song with the whole history of western civilization and with the 'Melodys of earth & sky', he says that 'Songs once sung to adams ears' and 'Ballads of six thousand years / Thrive, thrive'.[37]

A handful of texts associated with Clare's song collection, particularly in the rough-copy manuscripts, seem to be faithful transcripts. They correspond substantially to published song texts and contain few alterations, deletions, or signs of revision in their initial drafts. When they represent variants of songs whose tunes are known, they are the easiest of all Clare's compositions to connect with particular melodies, although even here we cannot be certain that he was familiar with specific variants or that tunes collected later were those he heard. For instance, 'Taken from My Fathers Singing' (written 1820s), whose first line is 'The winter it is past', is a version of the 'widely known' song of that name, which appeared in numerous broadsides and collections, including the *Scots Musical Museum*.[38] Similarly, the (a) text of 'Another with a Fine Melody Taken from My Fathers Singing' (written 1820s) is a variant of 'Bushes and Briars', a haunting song collected by Ralph Vaughan Williams in 1903 and still a staple in folk music and choral repertoires.[39]

Clare states that 'Bushes and Briars' has a 'fine melody' and Vaughan Williams agreed, noting, 'It is impossible to reproduce the free rhythm and subtle portamento effects of this beautiful tune in ordinary notation'.[40] Indeed, in both these cases the melodies are essential to the songs. In 'Bushes and Briars' the second and fourth lines of each verse are repeated, something Clare does not indicate in his transcript. When repeated in this way, these plaintive lines convey hopelessness as well as heartache in 'Another with a Fine Melody Taken from My Fathers Singing': 'Long time have I been waiting for the coming of my dear' (line 4). Additionally, both songs develop a rich interplay between syntax, melodic phrasing, and metrical and musical rhythm.[41] In 'Bushes and Briars', long notes and rests divide the words into semantically surprising units: 'Lo-ong time | ha-ave I | been wait | i-ing for | | the coming | of | my-y dear' (line 4). In 'The winter it is past', the music reinforces the basic contrasts that structure the song—between winter and summer, the joy in nature and the suffering of the singer, and so on—by dividing each of Clare's six-line stanzas into two melodic strains. This melodic reverberation heightens the tension between lines such as 'My love is like the sun' and '& his is like the moon' (line

13, line 16). Moreover, the melodies of both songs embellish everyday words and heighten emotional effects, as in these lines from 'The winter it is past': 'The hearts of these [singing birds] are glad / But my poor heart is sad', which quaver over 'the' and 'but' and rise to a high note on 'glad' before falling down to 'sad' (lines 4–5). At a most basic level, too, both songs are to be sung 'very slow', as the *Scots Musical Museum* puts it, making them much slower to sing or hear than to read silently.[42] In all these ways, the pathos, verbal texture, and structure of these songs are shaped by their melodies as much as by their words.

The music changes 'Benbow a Sea Song Take[n] Down from My Fathers Memory' (written 1826?) even more dramatically. The tune is likely the one collected as 'Benbow, the Brother Tar's Song' by William Chappell in *Popular Music of the Olden Time* (2 vols., 1855–59).[43] Clare's version begins:

> Come all you Seamen bold lend an ear lend an ear
> Come all you seamen bold lend an ear
> Its of our Admirals fame bold Benbow called by name
> How he fought on the main you shall hear you shall hear
> How he fought on the main you shall hear.[44]

Here, as throughout the song, each repeated clause is syntactically complete and is reproduced exactly, with no internal variation. But what might look to purely textual analysis like flat, unvaried recurrence acquires momentum, variety, and complex layers of dissonance and resonance when the music is added. Each of the three instances of 'lend an ear' takes a different sequence of notes, and lines 1–2 and 4–5 differ melodically despite adopting the same pattern of repeated clauses. Similarly, while the words 'ear' and 'hear' rhyme every time they occur, they are sung to many different notes. In performance, moreover, this structure opens the song to multiple voices. The repeated clauses invite a pulsing alternation between a lead singer and the whole company, and Chappell designates the final line a chorus. Contemporary accounts, both fictionalized and antiquarian, describe how 'everybody joined lustily in the choruses' during '"folk" singing events', and it is easy to imagine such energetic participation in this song.[45] In all these ways, 'Benbow' does not simply make greater use of exact repetition than most lyric poems do. It uses repetition differently, to coordinate multiple voices and add sonorous complexity.

'I SHALL INSERT SOME IMITATIONS'

In his letter to Taylor about his 'Sea Songs Love Ballads &c &c', Clare writes, 'I shall insert some imitations [...] a specimen of each shall be quickly with you'.[46] Some of these imitations were based on the transcripts of songs from his parents and other local singers. His own take on 'Bushes and Briars', for instance, appears on the very same manuscript page as his transcript. Other imitations seem to have emerged even as he was writing a song down, resulting in drafts that are full of cancelled, rewritten, and original passages. For example, 'Mary Neel A Ballad' (written 1826–7) appears in rough-copy as 'a mass of amendments and deletions', as Deacon writes.[47] Among other revisions, Clare changes the first line from 'O Mary Neil is handsome' to 'O Mary Neil is beautys self' and tests several possibilities for the second line: '& Mary Neil is fair', 'None can her powers withstand', and 'All hearts she might command'.[48] These alternatives offer varying amounts of certainty and poetical abstraction, and they emphasize either Mary herself or her effect on others. Similar processes of revision and invention can be glimpsed in other manuscripts.[49]

Still other imitations make use of floating stanzas, which drift or float across many popular songs. He draws one such stanza from the mournful, even desolate, song 'I Wish, I Wish' into his 'Ballad [A faithless shepherd courted me]' (written 1826–7):

> I wish I wish but its in vain
> I wish I was a maid again
> A maid again I cannot be
> O when will green grass cover me[?][50]

Clare elaborates on the sentiment and format of this stanza in subsequent verses. Similarly, he often takes a line, stanza, or chorus from a vernacular song and spins it in a new direction. The first lines of the following compositions are all drawn from well-known songs whose melodies fit Clare's words perfectly: 'Song Taken from My Mothers & Fathers Recitation & Compleated by an Old Shepherd' (written 1818–20?), 'Song [The week before easter the days long & clear]' (written 1819–32), and 'Ballad [On martinmass Eve the dogs they did bark]' (written 1819–32).[51] In these cases, he retains a verbal tie to an existing song, anchoring his lyrics to a tune and drawing attention to his source, even as he also reworks words, adds his own material, and gives his own emphasis to the story and the setting. Some changes seem to reflect his larger interests, for instance when he substitutes meadows for forests in the line 'I went in the meadow some flowers to find there'.[52] Other alterations seem to signal his fascination with particular aspects of popular song such as the theme of betrayal in love or the technique of using natural images to express undying fidelity, as in the lines 'The dove shall change a hawk in kind [...] Ere I do change my love for thee'.[53]

All these traces of the songs that inspired Clare link his imitations to specific tunes. Such links are more tenuous than with the transcripts, but they are valuable nevertheless, since they enable analysis of how the words and tunes might interact in the songs. The same sorts of dynamics are evident once again. The melodies consistently amplify and, as it were, make more credible the emotional force of the lyrics, and they add layers to the songs' sound patterns and structures. Given how frequently Clare retains the first line of a vernacular song, it seems plausible that in such cases he expected his audience to recognize his source and know its melody. In any event, such verbal echoes establish connections to particular words and tunes in the vernacular musical tradition and underscore the intertextual and intermedial origins and status of Clare's songs.

Nevertheless, many of Clare's imitations cannot be linked to particular tunes by shared lines or stanzas or by a record of textual revision. He may have had an unknown tune in mind while he composed them, or he may have hoped they would later be set to music. Either way, they are compatible with many airs and highly amenable to musical setting. They present themselves as songs to be sung, rather than as representations of acts of singing witnessed by someone else in the manner of William Wordsworth's 'The Solitary Reaper' (1807). They tend to feature three- and four-beat lines and simple rhyme schemes, including the appropriately named 'common meter'. In thematic terms, too, they often explore conventional subjects and sentiments, resonating broadly with existing songs and musical styles. For example, 'Song [Whence comes this coldness pr[a]y thee say'] (written 1819–32) and 'Ballad [Fair maiden when my love began]' (written 1826?), both in common metre, express the despondent feelings of an abandoned lover and draw on natural images of constancy and change. By directly addressing the beloved, they emphasize their first-person voicing. 'The Topers Rant' (written 1819–32), meanwhile, is a drinking song that both thematises and prompts singing in lines such as 'We'll sing racey songs now we're mellow'.[54] Although such songs do not connect themselves to specific tunes, Clare makes it easy for a musician to find, adapt, or create a tune to perform them to, whether in his day or now.

Moreover, imitations that lack ties to specific tunes share with the other imitations an abiding interest in the meaning-making structures of vernacular song. One of the most striking aspects of all his imitations, irrespective of their proximity to their sources, is how consistently he uses them to experiment with the various ways that songs organize themselves, establish the voice of the singer, and situate expressions of feeling within natural and social settings and dramatic situations. Thus he writes imitations in the voices of young women and Scotsmen, not to mention gypsies, soldiers, poachers, thieves, and emigrants.[55] In this way, he explores the generic impersonality of song, which theorists had credited with enabling the expression of authentic, universal feeling and which figures like Burns had shown 'makes available a remarkable range of situations, themes, passions, and attitudes' for the songwriter.[56]

Similarly, Clare seems to have become fascinated with how songs use generative formulas. For instance, in 'Song [Dream not of love to think it like]' (written 1819–32), a singer performs a series of actions—'I put my finger in a bush / […] I threw a stone into the sea', and so on—each of which reveals an aspect of the betrayal she has suffered at the hands of her 'false lover':

> I watched the sun an hour too soon
> Set into clouds behind the town
> So my false lover left & said
> 'Good night' before the day was down[57]

Such formulas involve repetition, but unlike in 'Benbow' the repetition is conceptual and formal, determining the placement of coordinated elements within balanced lines and stanzas.[58] In other songs the singers cycle through the seasons; liken themselves one by one to a series of birds; and express sequences of wishes: 'O I would flye […] O I would rest', 'O would I were the little bird / […] O would I were the golden cage', and so on.[59] At their most subtle, these formulas look like schemes for incremental repetition, as in the lines 'O far is fled the winter wind / & far is fled the frost & snow / […] More cutting then ten winters wind / More cutting then ten weeks of frost'.[60] As Helsinger writes, such formulas 'draw out the music in endless variation' and suggest that the song is 'open to infinite extension in a potentially continuous evolution of expectation, satisfaction, and surprise'.[61] The point, whatever it is, is made when the formula is established, but it always bears making again in a new way. Since heartbreak, say, feels like waking up from a dream, being cut by a thorn, throwing a stone in the water, watching the sunset, and picking a flower, the formula generates a whole series of now-related images, metaphors, and symbols, as well as a potentially infinite stream of patterned sounds orchestrated by rhythm, rhyme, and melody. What's more, because the formulas give rise to highly segmented verses that make 'parallel statements' with little narrative or tonal progression, they ensure that 'the same musical interpretation would be appropriate for all stanzas'.[62] The formulas, in other words, produce distinctly song-like compositions, whether their tunes are known or not. And they testify to Clare's desire to understand what Helsinger calls song's 'formal generativity'.[63]

'THE TALES BALLADS & SONGS THAT I WANT FOR THE VOL.'

In the summer of 1832, Clare told a correspondent, 'I have been very earnest in making up the [Tales] Ballads & Songs that I want for the Vol', by which Clare meant *The Midsummer Cushion*.[64] A few months later, he finished entering texts into the guardbook of poems earmarked for later publication.[65] By this time, then, the transcripts and imitations associated with his songbook project had made their way into print, fallen by the wayside, or, most often, been reworked into one or both of these notebooks. Those that survived had by now been renamed. The generic labels 'Song' and 'Ballad' had replaced titles locating the songs in the past and in the repertoires of particular singers, and references to correcting and completing the texts and to their fragmentary nature had been deleted. For instance, Clare's version of 'The Week before Easter', one of the songs that gestures to its source in its first line, became simply 'Song', having earlier been called 'An old Ballad copied from my mother & fathers memory with some few touches at correction' and 'Old Song—Fragments gathered from my Fathers & Mothers singing—& compleated'.[66] The new titles prioritize genre and classification, present the compositions as finished and whole, and foreground Clare's role as their creator.

As he had reworked these pieces, he had also reordered them and separated them from one another. No longer do they constitute a distinct set of 'Old Songs & Ballads' or 'National and Provincial Melodies'. Instead, they take their places among the many similarly named compositions in the guardbook, including hymns and metrical psalms, and in the 'Ballads & Songs' section of the *Midsummer Cushion* manuscript, explicitly set apart from the 'Tales' and sonnets.[67] The principles for selection and ordering still centrally involve ties to music and to singing, but the texts now belong to a more general song culture that includes church music and that exists in an understated way in the present.

On the one hand, Clare's transcripts and imitations of vernacular music have become poems. The new manuscripts assimilate the songs into volumes that aspire to the status of printed poetry and that appeal to the protocols of private, silent reading. Viewed in this way, his experiments with 'making across media'[68] bear fruit in song-poems, including the many poems in three- and four-beat lines that have long anchored his reputation such as 'A Vision' (written 1844), and 'An Invite to Eternity' (written 1847). Both these poems weave sound patterns within a frame of song-like rhythms and rhymes. And 'An Invite to Eternity' features both a refrain, 'Say maiden wilt thou go with me', and a generative formula: 'Where the path hath lost its way / Where the sun forgets the day / Where there's nor life nor light to see'.[69] As these examples suggest, just as listening carefully to birdsong teaches him to write poems using the human medium of language,[70] nurturing his ear for verbal harmony and mastering song's structure teaches him about poetic sounds and forms.

On the other hand, the presence of Clare's transcripts and imitations in the guardbook and in the *Midsummer Cushion* renders those manuscripts multi-medial products. Like Currie's *Works of Robert Burns* or Tannahill's *Poems & Songs*, they contain both literary poems and songs for singing and are suited to both personal textual encounters and familial and convivial performance. Indeed, for readers who knew the tunes, that knowledge would shape even private, silent reading, synchronizing it to the tempo and cadence of the air, informing judgements about tone, and perhaps calling to mind particular occasions on which the song was performed. Viewed from this angle, Clare never stopped writing songs for his readers to sing, and the 'Songs' and 'Ballads' that he created until the end of his life still invite us to match them to music. He may have assumed, with Ritson, that 'A *tune* is so essentially requisite to perfect the idea which is, in strictness and propriety, annexed to the term *song*' that any experience of a song's 'words or poetical parts' without its tune 'must necessarily be defective and incomplete'.[71]

As he had done in his songbook project, in later works Clare occasionally leaves clues indicating that his lyrics are written to specific airs. Deacon detects several of these in the titles, first lines, and choruses of later compositions, including the 'Child Harold' song '[Heres a health unto thee bonny lassie O' (written 1841), which connects to the lovely song 'Kelvin Grove'; and 'Song [My old Lover left me I knew not for why]' (written early 1850s), a variant of 'My Love has Forsaken Me', the tune to which Clare hoped to collect.[72] I caught echoes in other 'Child Harold' songs, to Burns's 'Auld Lang Syne' and 'I Love my Jean', and to Tannahill's 'Jessie, The Flow'r o' Dumblane', one of Clare's favourite songs, and I am sure that there are many more such links to be discovered.[73] In these cases, unsurprisingly, the melodies add layers of richness and force to Clare's words. For instance, the 'Child Harold' songs 'Kelvin Grove' and 'Jessie' are mellow and harmonious, and as such they add a layer of untroubled tenderness to the poem's often discordant and dissonant tone. Similarly, the music and sentiments of 'Auld Lang Syne' resonate with the poem's searching, mournful investigation of loss and memory. These songs contribute much to the emotional range and subtlety of the poem.

For the most part, though, Clare's song-poems must be read without reference to specific tunes. Poems lacking direct ties to particular songs can be approached in light cast by his theory and practice of songwriting, those of the writers who inspired him such as Burns and Tannahill, and the music-making customs of the age. In this light, too, the titles 'Song' and 'Ballad' come into focus as cues, instructions to his audience to take a leap of faith and sing these compositions to plausible contemporary airs. Ultimately, to do so is not only to restore them to Romantic song and music cultures but also to enliven them in our own reading—and singing—practice.

Acknowledgement An earlier version of this chapter was given at the 'John Clare and Song' symposium hosted by the Centre for John Clare Studies at the University of Cambridge. I am grateful to the participants and audience members for sharing their work and for their many helpful comments and questions.

Notes

1. For Clare's intention to publish a song collection, and his efforts to do so, see Bate, *Biography*, 214–16, 347–50; Deacon, 18–27.
2. See also Trevor Hold, 'The Composer's Debt to John Clare', *JCSJ* 1 (July 1982): 25–9; Simon Kövesi, *John Clare: Nature, Criticism and History* (London: Palgrave Macmillan, 2017), 55–61.

3. *Letters*, 387. I focus on compositions that can reasonably be supposed to have been part of the process by which he transcribed, reworked, and imitated vernacular song with an eye to publishing a collection. In practical terms, this means limiting my data set to compositions that first enter into Clare's writing in the draft-copy manuscripts for the project. Most also appear in Nor. MS 18, a fair-copy notebook that is the closest thing we have to a ready-for-publication song collection by Clare, as I explain below.

4. On British music consumers and publishing, see Cyril Ehrlich and Simon McVeigh, 'Music', in *Oxford Companion to the Romantic Age: British Culture 1776–1832*, ed. Iain McCalman et al (Oxford: Oxford University Press, 1999), 242–50; Kirsteen McCue, 'The Culture of Song', in *The Oxford Handbook of British Romanticism*, ed. David Duff (Oxford: Oxford University Press, 2018), 645. For Clare's experience learning new tunes in Edward Drury's shop, see *By Himself*, 110 and Frederick Martin, *The Life of John Clare* (London, 1865), 80–1.

5. See David Atkinson, 'Folk Songs in Print: Text and Tradition', *Folk Music Journal* 8.4 (2004): 456–83; David Duff, 'The Retuning of the sky: Romanticism and lyric', in *The Lyric Poem: Formations and Transformation*, ed. Marion Thain (Cambridge: Cambridge University Press, 2013) 145; and Maureen N. McLane, *Balladeering, Minstrelsy, and the Making of British Romantic Poetry* (Cambridge: Cambridge University Press, 2008), 84–116.

6. Steve Roud, *Folk Song in England* (London: Faber & Faber, 2017), 10.

7. See, for example, a broadsheet with two ballads digitized on the Bodleian Libraries' Broadside Ballads Online website at http://ballads.bodleian. ox.ac.uk/view/edition/8327, accessed 30 May 2019. The words 'TUNE—"With a helmet on his brow"' are printed under the title of the song 'Peace and Plenty, Love and Liberty', while the title indicates the tune of the well-known song 'We Are All Jolly Fellows Who Follow the Plough'. For Clare's take on this song, see '[The ploughm[e]n are out before the cock crows]', *Middle Period*, 5: 311.

8. Nick Groom, '"The purest English": Ballads and the English Literary Dialect', *The Eighteenth Century* 47.2/3 (Summer/Fall 2006): 188.

9. Claire Lamont, '"The essence and simplicity of true poetry": John Clare and Folk-song', *JCSJ* 16 (1997): 26. For publishers' expectations, see also Leith Davis, 'At "sang about": Scottish song and the challenge to British culture', in *Scotland and the Borders of Romanticism*, ed. Leith Davis, Ian Duncan, and Janet Sorensen (Cambridge: Cambridge University Press, 2004), 188–203; Katherine Campbell and Kirsteen McCue, 'Lowland Song Culture in the Eighteenth Century', in *The Edinburgh Companion to Scottish Traditional Literatures*, ed. Sarah Dunnigan and Suzanne Gilbert (Edinburgh: Edinburgh University Press, 2013), 95.

10. See, for example, 'Ocean Glories—Tune "Old Benbow" A Beautiful Melodie' and 'Peggy Band / Tune—Peggy Band', a poem he also entitles 'Peggy Band / In imitation of the provincial ballad', which also suggests an expectation that the audience will know the tune (*Middle Period*, 4: 90, 57n).

11. Roud, *Folk Song*, 10.

12. Clare frequently noted these phenomena, for instance in *Letters*, 152 and *By Himself*, 212–13. In the tunebooks he notated multiple airs for at least 12 songs, on which see Deacon, 300. For a fascinating 'biography' of a song, showing how the music changes as it is published and republished, see 'Afton Water', Romantic National Song Network website, rnsn. glasgow.ac.uk/Scotland/afton-water, accessed 20 May 2019.

13. On the difficulty of matching texts and tunes in earlier historical periods, see Marisa Galvez, *Songbook: How Lyrics Became Poetry in Medieval Europe* (Chicago: University of Chicago Press, 2012); David Lindley, '"Words for music, perhaps": Early modern songs and lyric', in *The Lyric Poem: Formations and Transformations*, 10–29; Kate Van Orden, *Music, Authorship, and the Book in the First Century of Print* (Berkeley: University of California Press, 2014); and Philip Zumthor, *Toward a Medieval Poetics*, trans. Philip Bennett (Minneapolis: University of Minnesota Press, 1992), 18–39.

14. 'Purest english', 184, italics in original. See also Simon Jarvis, 'Musical Thinking: Hegel and the Phenomenology of Prosody', *Paragraph* 28.2 (July 2005): 70, where he asserts that only by taking seriously our own 'musical and prosodic experiences', even when they are necessarily 'personal, idiosyncratic, or unrepresentative', will scholars be able to investigate the 'musical thinking' that occurs in poetry.

15. For Clare's expertise, see *Biography*, 93–6; Deacon, 10–76; and Lamont, 'Essence'. For Clare's contemporaries, see Valentina Bold and Suzanne Gilbert, 'Hogg, Ettrick, and Oral Tradition', in *The Edinburgh Companion to James Hogg*, ed. Ian Duncan and Douglas S. Mack (Edinburgh: Edinburgh University Press, 2012), 10–20; Campbell and McCue, 'Lowland Song Culture'; McCue, 'Culture of Song'; Roud, *Folk Song*, 273–386; Dave Russell, *Popular Music in England, 1840–1914: A Social History* (Montreal: McGill-Queen's University Press, 1987); and Derek B. Scott, *The Singing Bourgeois: Songs of the Victorian Drawing Room and Parlour* (Milton Keynes: Open University Press, 1989). For the blurred lines between popular, folk, and religious music, see David E. Gregory, *Victorian Songhunters: The Recovery and Editing of English Vernacular Ballads and Folk Lyrics, 1820–1883* (Lanham, Maryland: Scarecrow Press, 2006), 3–5.

16. See Roud, *Folk Song*, 273–386; and Russell, *Popular Music*, 131–248.

17. *Letters*, 138.
18. *Letters*, 153; for descriptions of the notebooks, see Deacon, 300; David Powell, *Catalogue of the John Clare Collection in the Northampton Public Library* (Northampton: County Borough of Northampton Public Libraries, Museums and Art Gallery Committee, 1964), 9.
19. In 'Essence', Lamont draws together Clare's many comments about and depictions of song and singing.
20. *Early Poems*, 2: 294–295, lines 183–84, lines 186–87.
21. For summaries of Clare's process of collecting and revision, see Deacon, 11; Eric Robinson et al., 'Introduction', *Middle Period*, 4: xv–xvii, xxiii–xxv.
22. These are now known as Peterborough Manuscripts B4 and B7.
23. This is Northampton MS 18. For the title, see Powell, *Catalogue*, 10. For descriptions of the notebook, estimates about when Clare used it, and quotations from his introduction, see Powell, *Catalogue*, 10 and Robinson et al., *Middle Period*, 4: 614.
24. *Middle Period*, 3: xvi. Importantly, Clare mentions reciting as well as singing. There is a robust literature about recitation, the relation between the speaking and singing voice, and the distinction between narrative ballads, often recited, and lyrical songs, which dates to this period but which Clare does not usually observe. See Duff, 'Retuning'; Dianne Dugaw, 'On the "Darling Songs" of Poets, Scholars, and Singers: An Introduction', *The Eighteenth Century* 47.2/3 (2006): 100–105; Andrew Elfenbein, *Romanticism and the Rise of English* (Stanford: Stanford University Press, 2009), 108–143; Gregory, *Victorian Songhunters*, 3–12; Elizabeth Helsinger, *Poetry and the Thought of Song in Nineteenth-Century Britain* (Charlottesville: University of Virginia Press, 2015), 1–21; McCue, 'Culture of Song', 645–46; David Perkins, 'How the Romantics Recited Poetry', *Studies in English Literature* 31.4 (Autumn 1991): 655–71; Catherine Robson, *Heart Beats: Everyday Life and the Memorized Poem* (Princeton: Princeton University Press, 2012); Stephanie Kuduk Weiner, 'John Clare's Speaking Voices: Dialect, Orality, and the Intermedial Poetic Text', *Essays in Romanticism* 25.1 (2018): 85–100.
25. See Matthew Gelbart, *The Invention of 'Folk Music' and 'Art Music': Emerging Categories from Ossian to Wagner* (Cambridge: Cambridge University Press, 2007), 162–6; Hamish Mathison, 'Robert Burns and National Song', in *Scotland, Ireland, and the Romantic Aesthetic*, ed. David Duff and Catherine Jones (Lewisburg: Bucknell University Press, 2007) 78–82; Kirsteen McCue, 'Burns's Songs and Poetic Craft', in *The Edinburgh Companion to Robert Burns*, ed. Gerard Carruthers (Edinburgh: Edinburgh University Press, 2009), 74–85; and Murray Pittock, 'The W. Ormiston Roy Memorial Lecture: Who Wrote the *Scots Musical*

Museum? Challenging Editorial Practice in the Presence of Authorial Absence', *Studies in Scottish Literature* 42.1 (2016): 3–27. On Clare's method, see Deacon, 20–34; Elizabeth Helsinger, 'Poem Into Song', *New Literary History* 46 (2015): 674–6; and Roud, *Folk Song*, 62–6.

26. This is now known as Peterborough MS A54.
27. This is now known as Peterborough MS A40. For the title 'guardbook', see Robinson et al., 'Introduction', xxiii.
28. See Powell, *Catalogue*. The years given in parentheses are original dates of publication, but Clare often owned later, revised editions, which are listed in the bibliography of this chapter. Clare's library contained only the first and third volumes of Ritson's *English Songs*.
29. Adam White, *John Clare's Romanticism* (London: Palgrave Macmillan, 2017), 269–93.
30. Hold, 'Composer's Debt', 25.
31. For Moore's 'auditory imagination', see Harry White, *Music and the Irish Literary Imagination* (Oxford: Oxford University Press, 2008), 35–78.
32. On the living song tradition, see Bold and Gilbert, 'Hogg', 12–14; Davis, 'At 'sang about''; Duff, 'Retuning', 143–49; McCue, 'Culture of Song', 653; and White, *Music*, 35–8.
33. Ritson drew extensively on Burney, and Aikin is mentioned by Thomas Park, who enlarged the second edition of *English Songs* with a new preface and additional songs and notes. Clare also had access to extensive discussions of song and music in the *London Magazine*. These included articles on song around the world, both historical and contemporary; regular reports of concerts and music society meetings in London and beyond; and philosophical meditations on music, singing, and the human voice.
34. Joseph Ritson, *A Select Collection of English Songs, with their original airs: and a historical essay on the origin and progress of national song*, 2nd edn, with additional songs and occasional notes by Thomas Park, 3 vols (London, 1813), I.i.
35. 'Musicology, Anthropology, History', in *The Cultural Study of Music: A Critical Introduction*, ed. Martin Clayton, Trevor Herbert, and Richard Middleton, 2nd edn (New York: Routledge, 2012), 61. See also Gelbart, *Invention*.
36. McCue, 'Culture of Song', 643.
37. *Middle Period*, 5: 3, lines 13, 15, and 17–18.
38. *Middle Period*, 2: 258, line 1. Deacon, 121. See James Johnson, *The Scots Musical Museum*, 6 vols (Edinburgh, 1787–1803), 2: 208 (hereafter abbreviated to *SMM*). Jean Redpath's recording of this version of the song is available at www.youtube.com/watch?v=ioJXRVXeetE, accessed 14 May 2019. Another version of the tune, which does not fit Clare's lyrics quite as well, can be listened to via ABC notation at www.folktunefinder.

com/tunes/197639, accessed 14 May 2019. The song is number 583 in the Roud Folk Song Index (hereafter, given as Roud #). Many copies of the broadside, usually under the title 'Cold Winter is past', can be seen on the Bodleian Libraries' Broadside Ballads Online website at ballads.bodleian.ox.ac.uk.

39. *Middle Period*, 2: 278–9. See Vaughan Williams et al., 'Songs Collected from Essex', *Journal of the Folk-Song Society* 2.8 (1906): 143–5, where it is noted that the air is given as the tune for other broadsides, suggesting it was popular. Deacon, 184–6, discusses the song and uses Vaughan Williams's tune. The song, Roud 1027, can be heard in numerous recordings, listed on the Mainly Norfolk website at mainlynorfolk.info/june.tabor/songs/bushesandbriars.html, and via ABC notation at www.folktunefinder.com/tunes/144395, both accessed 14 May 2019.

40. Vaughan Williams et al., 'Songs Collected', 144.

41. On musical rhythm, linguistic phrasing, and metre, see Derek Attridge, *The Rhythms of English Poetry* (London: Longman, 1982); Amittai F. Aviram, *Telling Rhythm: Body and Meaning in Poetry* (Ann Arbor: University of Michigan Press, 1994); Richard D. Cureton, *Rhythmic Phrasing in English Verse* (London: Longman, 1992); Elisa Bickford Jorgens, *The Well-Tun'd Word: Musical Interpretations of English Poetry, 1597–1651* (Minneapolis: University of Minnesota Press, 1982); Zumthor, *Toward*, 67–76; and White, *Music*, 69–74.

42. *SMM* 2: 208.

43. For the music, see William Chappell, *Popular Music of the Olden Time; a collection of ancient songs, ballads, and dance tunes, illustrative of the national music of England*, 2 vols (London, 1855–59), 678 and Cecil Sharp's different tune in *One Hundred English Folksongs* (Boston, 1916), 200–01. For this song and Clare's imitations of it, see Deacon, 124–30. Deacon links Clare's text to Chappell's tune, and both share a final chorus at the end of each verse, but in other respects Sharp's tune works equally well. The popularity of the song, Roud 227, is attested to by the 64 related items in the Vaughan Williams Memorial Library database at www.vwml.org/roudnumber/227, accessed 14 May 2019. Bertrand Bronson traces the stanza pattern through secular and religious songs all the way back to the sixteenth century in *The Ballad as Song* (Berkeley: University of California Press, 1969), 18–36. The same stanza pattern is used with a different tune in Burns's 'Ye Jacobites by Name', *SMM* 4: 383.

44. *Middle Period*, 4: 95, lines 1–5.

45. Roud, *Folk Song*, 337, 321.

46. *Letters*, 387.

47. Deacon, 160.

48. *Middle Period*, 4: 452n.

49. See, for example, the notes to 'Old Song—From My Mothers Singing' in *Middle Period*, 4: 456, where his amendments implicate rhythm and rhyme as well as meaning.
50. *Middle Period*, 4: 370, lines 13–16. 'I Wish, I Wish', Roud 495, also shares other verbal echoes with Clare's song, most explicitly the stanza beginning 'When my apron would hang low' (5). For the tune, see the list of recordings at https://mainlynorfolk.info/folk/songs/whatavoice.html, accessed 30 May 2019. Similarly, the stanza beginning 'I sat my back against an oak' in 'Song [Dream not of love to think it like]', *Middle Period*, 4: 459n, is drawn from the 'Jamie Douglas' variant of 'Waly, Waly', Roud 87, which appeared in the *SMM* 2: 166. The tune, which fits Clare's 'Song' perfectly, can be heard in numerous recordings, many available online, and at folktunefinder.com/tunes/49948, accessed 14 May 2019.
51. The songs are, respectively, 'Turtle Dove', Roud 422; 'The Forlorn Lover', Roud 154; and 'Nobody Coming to Marry Me', Roud 846.
52. *Middle Period*, 4: 417, line 3. For the lyrics of 'The Forlorn Lover', see the broadside digitized by the Bodleian Libraries' Broadside Ballads Online at ballads.bodleian.ox.ac.uk/view/edition/23692, accessed 30 May 2019.
53. *Middle Period*, 4: 439, line 19, line 23.
54. *Middle Period*, 4: 75, line 3.
55. For young women, see *Middle Period*, 2: 258 and *Middle Period*, 4: 355; for Scotsmen, *Middle Period*, 4: 552; for gypsies, *Middle Period*, 4: 52; for soldiers, *Middle Period*, 4: 57; for poachers, *Middle Period*, 4: 378; for thieves, *Middle Period*, 4: 395; and for emigrants, *Middle Period*, 4: 70, a song that he told Taylor 'goes a descent musical poney canter' (*Letters*, 389).
56. Steve Newman, *Ballad Collection, Lyric, and the Canon: The Call of the Popular from the Restoration to the New Criticism* (Philadelphia: University of Pennsylvania Press, 2007), 85. On impersonality, see Newman, *Ballad Collection*, 85–91; Helsinger, *Poetry*, 32, 34, 55–7. On relevant singing practices, see Roud, *Folk Song*, 335–8; Scott, *Singing Bourgeois*, 22–32.
57. *Middle Period*, 4: 458–59, line 9, line 13, line 4, lines 17–20.
58. This coordination is very clear, for instance, in '[O says the linnet if I sing]', *Middle Period* 2: 285–86. The first line of each verse begins 'O says the [bird] […]', and the remaining three lines trace a feature of the bird's plumage or behaviour to the departure of the beloved (1). These formulas often produce what Roger deV. Renwick calls 'catalogue songs' in *Recentering Anglo/American Folksong: Sea Crabs and Wicked Youths* (Jackson: University Press of Mississippi, 2001), 59–91.
59. *Middle Period* 4: 456, line 23, line 25; *Middle Period* 4: 66–7, line 1, line 9. For the seasons, see *Middle Period* 4: 439, lines 13–16. For birds, see *Middle Period* 4: 439–40, lines 19–22, lines 31–2; *Middle Period* 4: 456–7, lines 21–32.

60. *Middle Period*, 4: 455, lines 1–2, lines 5–6.
61. *Poetry*, 51–2.
62. Jorgens, *Well-Tuned*, 15.
63. *Poetry*, 42.
64. *Letters*, 587.
65. Robinson, et al., xxiii, estimate that he used the notebook from spring 1825 until November 1832.
66. *Middle Period*, 4: 417.
67. For the headings, see Robinson, et al., xxv, note 91. For the hymns, see *Middle Period* 4: 464–78.
68. McLane, *Balladeering*, 110.
69. *Early Poems*, 1: 348, line 2, lines 5–7
70. See Stephanie Kuduk Weiner, *Clare's Lyric: John Clare and Three Modern Poets* (Oxford: Oxford University Press, 2014), 23–49.
71. Ritson, *English Songs*, I. xiii–xiv.
72. See Deacon, 197–201 and 21 for Clare's intention. 'Kelvin Grove' (Roud V2124) is tune 23679 in the Folk Tune Finder. Among the many easily available recordings, I especially recommend Jesse Ferguson's performance at youtube.com/watch?v=RfDgVdMMcRw, accessed 19 May 2019. 'My love has forsaken me' (Roud V29405) appears in *SMM* 2: 159 and Allan Cunningham, *The Songs of Scotland, ancient and modern; with an introduction and notes, historical and critical, and characters of the lyric poets*, 4 vols (London, 1825) 3: 5–6.
73. See *Later Poems* 1: 42–3 for 'Jessie' (Roud 15024), which appears in Robert Tannahill, *Poems & Songs, Chiefly in the Scottish Dialect*, 4th ed (London, 1817), 137–8; *Later Poems* 1: 43–4 for 'Auld Lang Syne' (Roud 13892); and *Later Poems* 1: 63 for 'I Love my Jean', *SMM* 3: 244. Clare mentions 'Jessie' in *By Himself*, 58, 185.

BIBLIOGRAPHY

Atkinson, David. 'Folk Songs in Print: Text and Tradition'. *Folk Music Journal* 8.4 (2004): 456–83.
Attridge, Derek. *The Rhythms of English Poetry*. London: Longman, 1982.
Aviram, Amittai F. *Telling Rhythm: Body and Meaning in Poetry*. Ann Arbor: University of Michigan Press, 1994.
Bate, Jonathan. *John Clare: A Biography*. New York: Farrar, Straus and Giroux, 2003.
Bold, Valentina and Suzanne Gilbert. 'Hogg, Ettrick, and Oral Tradition'. In *The Edinburgh Companion to James Hogg*, edited by Ian Duncan and Douglas S. Mack, 10–20. Edinburgh: Edinburgh University Press, 2012.

Bronson, Bertrand Harris. *The Ballad as Song*. Berkeley: University of California Press, 1969.

Campbell, Katherine and Kirsteen McCue. 'Lowland Song Culture in the Eighteenth Century'. In *The Edinburgh Companion to Scottish Traditional Literatures*, edited by Sarah Dunnigan and Suzanne Gilbert, 94–104. Edinburgh: Edinburgh University Press, 2013.

Chappell, William. *Popular Music of the Olden Time; a Collection of Ancient Songs, Ballads, and Dance Tunes, Illustrative of the National Music of England*. 2 vols. London, 1855–59.

Clare, John. *The Later Poems of John Clare, 1837–1864*. 2 vols. Edited by Eric Robinson, David Powell, and Margaret Grainger. Oxford: Clarendon Press, 1984.

———. *The Letters of John Clare*. Edited by Mark Storey. Oxford: Clarendon Press, 1985.

———. *Early Poems of John Clare, 1804–1822*. 2 vols. Edited by Eric Robinson, David Powell, and Margaret Grainger. Oxford: Clarendon Press, 1989.

———. *John Clare by Himself*. Edited by Eric Robinson and David Powell. Manchester: Carcanet Press, 1996.

———. *Poems of the Middle Period, 1822–1837*. 5 vols. Edited by Eric Robinson, David Powell, and P.M.S. Dawson. Oxford: Clarendon Press, 1996–2003.

Cromek, R. H. *Remains of Nithsdale and Galloway Song: with Historical and Traditional Notices Relative to the Manners and Customs of the Peasantry*. London, 1810.

Cunningham, Allan. *The Songs of Scotland, Ancient and Modern; with an Introduction and Notes, Historical and Critical, and Characters of the Lyric Poets*. 4 vols. London, 1825.

Cureton, Richard D. *Rhythmic Phrasing in English Verse*. London: Longman, 1992.

Currie, James, ed. *The Works of Robert Burns*. 8th edn. 5 vols. London, 1814.

Davis, Leith. 'At "sang about": Scottish Song and the Challenge to British Culture'. In *Scotland and the Borders of Romanticism*, edited by Leith Davis, Ian Duncan, and Janet Sorensen, 188–203. Cambridge: Cambridge University Press, 2004.

Deacon, George. *John Clare and the Folk Tradition*. London: S. Browne, 1983.

Duff, David. 'The Retuning of the Sky: Romanticism and Lyric'. In *The Lyric Poem: Formations and Transformation*, edited by Marion Thain, 135–55. Cambridge: Cambridge University Press, 2013.

Dugaw, Dianne. 'On the "Darling Songs" of Poets, Scholars, and Singers: An Introduction'. *The Eighteenth Century* 47.2/3 (2006): 97–113.

Ehrlich, Cyril and Simon McVeigh. 'Music'. In *Oxford Companion to the Romantic Age: British Culture 1776–1832*, edited by Iain McCalman et al., 242–50. Oxford: Oxford University Press, 1999.

Elfenbein, Andrew. *Romanticism and the Rise of English*. Stanford: Stanford University Press, 2009.

Galvez, Marisa. *Songbook: How Lyrics Became Poetry in Medieval Europe*. Chicago: University of Chicago Press, 2012.

Gelbart, Matthew. *The Invention of 'Folk Music' and 'Art Music': Emerging Categories from Ossian to Wagner*. Cambridge: Cambridge University Press, 2007.

Gregory, E. David. *Victorian Songhunters: The Recovery and Editing of English Vernacular Ballads and Folk Lyrics, 1820–1883*. Lanham, Maryland: Scarecrow Press, 2006.

Groom, Nick. '"The purest English": Ballads and the English Literary Dialect'. *The Eighteenth Century* 47.2/3 (Summer/Fall 2006): 179–202.

Helsinger, Elizabeth. 'Poem Into Song'. *New Literary History* 46 (2015a): 669–90.

———. *Poetry and the Thought of Song in Nineteenth-Century Britain*. Charlottesville: University of Virginia Press, 2015b.

Hogg, James. *The Mountain Bard*, 3rd edn. London, 1821.

Hold, Trevor. 'The Composer's Debt to John Clare'. *JCSJ* 1 (July 1982): 25–29.

Jarvis, Simon. 'Musical Thinking: Hegel and the Phenomenology of Prosody'. *Paragraph* 28.2 (July 2005): 55–71.

Johnson, James. *The Scots Musical Museum*. 6 vols. Edinburgh, 1787–1803.

Jorgens, Elisa Bickford. *The Well-Tun'd Word: Musical Interpretations of English Poetry, 1597–1651*. Minneapolis: University of Minnesota Press, 1982.

Kövesi, Simon. *John Clare: Nature, Criticism and History*. London: Palgrave Macmillan, 2017.

Lamont, Claire. '"The essence and simplicity of true poetry": John Clare and Folk-Song'. *JCSJ* 16 (1997): 19–33.

Lindley, David. '"Words for music, perhaps": Early Modern Songs and Lyric'. In *The Lyric Poem: Formations and Transformations*, edited by Marion Thain, 10–29. Cambridge: Cambridge University Press, 2013.

Martin, Frederick. *The Life of John Clare*. London, 1865.

Mathison, Hamish. 'Robert Burns and National Song'. In *Scotland, Ireland, and the Romantic Aesthetic*, edited by David Duff and Catherine Jones, 77–92. Lewisburg: Bucknell University Press, 2007.

McCue, Kirsteen. 'Burns's Songs and Poetic Craft'. In *Edinburgh Companion to Robert Burns*, edited by Gerard Carruthers, 74–85. Edinburgh: Edinburgh University Press, 2009.

———.'The Culture of Song'. In *The Oxford Handbook of British Romanticism*, edited by David Duff, 643–58. Oxford: Oxford University Press, 2018.

McLane, Maureen N. *Balladeering, Minstrelsy, and the Making of British Romantic Poetry*. Cambridge: Cambridge University Press, 2008.

Multigraph Collective. *Interacting with Print: Elements of Reading in the Era of Print Saturation*. Chicago: University of Chicago Press, 2018.

Newman, Steve. *Ballad Collection, Lyric, and the Canon: The Call of the Popular from the Restoration to the New Criticism*. Philadelphia: University of Pennsylvania Press, 2007.

Perkins, David. 'How the Romantics Recited Poetry'. *Studies in English Literature* 31.4 (Autumn 1991): 655–71.

Pittock, Murray. 'The W. Ormiston Roy Memorial Lecture: Who Wrote the *Scots Musical Museum*? Challenging Editorial Practice in the Presence of Authorial Absence'. *Studies in Scottish Literature* 42.1 (2016): 3–27.

Powell, David. *Catalogue of the John Clare Collection in the Northampton Public Library*. Northampton: County Borough of Northampton Public Libraries, Museums and Art Gallery Committee, 1964.

Renwick, Roger de V. *Recentering Anglo/American Folksong: Sea Crabs and Wicked Youths*. Jackson: University Press of Mississippi, 2001.

Ritson, Joseph, *A Select Collection of English Songs, with Their Original Airs: And a Historical Essay on the Origin and Progress of National Song*, 2nd edn, with Additional Songs and Occasional Notes by Thomas Park. 3 vols. London, 1813.

Robson, Catherine. *Heart Beats: Everyday Life and the Memorized Poem*. Princeton: Princeton University Press, 2012.

Roud, Steve. *Folk Song in England*. London: Faber & Faber, 2017.

Russell, Dave. *Popular Music in England, 1840–1914: A Social History*. Montreal: McGill-Queen's University Press, 1987.

Scott, Derek B. *The Singing Bourgeois: Songs of the Victorian Drawing Room and Parlour*. Milton Keynes: Open University Press, 1989.

Sharp, Cecil J. *One Hundred English Folksongs*. Boston, 1916.

Tannahill, Robert. *Poems & Songs, Chiefly in the Scottish Dialect*, 4th edn. London, 1817

Tomlinson, Gary. 'Musicology, Anthropology, History'. In *The Cultural Study of Music: A Critical Introduction*, edited by Martin Clayton, Trevor Herbert, and Richard Middleton, 59–72. 2nd edn. New York: Routledge, 2012.

Van Orden, Kate. *Music, Authorship, and the Book in the First Century of Print*. Berkeley: University of California Press, 2014.

Vaughan Williams, Ralph, Lucy E. Broadwood, Cecil J. Sharp, Frank Kidson, J. A. Fuller-Maitland, and C. T. S. 'Songs Collected from Essex'. *Journal of the Folk-Song Society* 2.8 (1906): 143–60.

Weiner, Stephanie Kuduk. *Clare's Lyric: John Clare and Three Modern Poets*. Oxford: Oxford University Press, 2014.

———. 'John Clare's Speaking Voices: Dialect, Orality, and the Intermedial Poetic Text'. *Essays in Romanticism* 25.1 (2018): 85–100.
White, Adam. *John Clare's Romanticism*. Milton Keynes, Palgrave Macmillan, 2017.
White, Harry. *Music and the Irish Literary Imagination*. Oxford: Oxford University Press, 2008.
Zumthor, Philip. *Toward a Medieval Poetics*. Trans Philip Bennett. Minneapolis: University of Minnesota Press, 1992.

John Clare's Landforms

Sara Lodge

In May 1842, the *Northampton Mercury* published an 'Original Poem, by John Clare, the Northamptonshire Poet'. It reported that Clare was currently an inmate of a lunatic asylum but 'outwardly there is nothing to indicate insanity' about his appearance:

> He writes frequently, and beyond a doubt composes many more poems than he puts upon paper. If indeed his life is not passed in one almost unbroken poetic dream. He may be seen any fine day, walking with a rapid step and an abstracted manner about the grounds of the Asylum, one hand in his pocket and the other in the bosom of his waistcoat, easily distinguishable by the most careless observer as no ordinary man.[1]

The poem that the *Mercury* printed is of particular interest because the contributor observed that Clare 'had been reading Shelley previously to the composition of these verses and his mind was evidently under the

S. Lodge (✉)
University of St Andrews, St Andrews, Scotland
e-mail: sjl15@st-andrews.ac.uk

© The Author(s) 2020
S. Kövesi, E. Lafford (eds.), *Palgrave Advances in John Clare Studies*, Palgrave Advances,
https://doi.org/10.1007/978-3-030-43374-1_5

influence of the lines we have quoted'. The passage from Percy Bysshe Shelley was the 'Dirge' at the end of 'Ginevra', published in 1824:

> Old winter was gone
> In his weakness back to the mountains hoar,
>   And the spring came down
> From the planet that hovers upon the shore
>   Where the sea of sunlight encroaches
> On the limits of wintry night:
>   If the land and the air and the sea
> Rejoice not when Spring approaches,
>   We did not rejoice in thee,
>   Ginevra!

Clare's poem channels Shelley's lines and images, but takes them in a different direction:

> Winter is nearly spent
>   And gone to the deserts of gloom,
> Sweet spring hath her heralds sent,
>   Gay flowers in the valleys bloom;
> When the sun turns to gold on the grass
>   And the flowers turn to stars in the night.
> The land and the sea and the air
> Bid welcome to Spring coming there,
>   And my heart biddeth welcome to thee, its delight,
>   Sweet Jessey.
>
> I knew her in her childhood,
>   In scenes from strife and noise,
> When singing to the wildwood
>   Tales and songs of childish joys;
> Making playmates of flowers as she lay;
>   And talking to birds as they flew
> O'er the molehill of thyme all the day.
> Her voice and her features were known;
>   I went up and called her my own
>   Sweet Jessey.[2]

Most obviously, Clare has turned a choric lamentation over an unhappy bride who expires on her wedding day—the mysterious, mediaeval Italian figure of Ginevra—into a recollection of a native, rural figure who is the speaker's own sweetheart, Jessey. His love lyric is intimate, nostalgic for the springtime of youth as much as for Jessey herself. Where Shelley's poem stages itself as grand opera, Clare's poem aligns itself with folk song. The plangent end of Shelley's dirge, 'Ginevra', becomes 'Sweet Jessey', the kind of recurring chorus familiar in many songs devoted to women: 'Sweet Adeline', 'Sweet Georgia Brown'.

Nonetheless, Clare models the form of his poem on Shelley's. Shelley's dirge has an accordion shape: it begins with a trimeter line, expanding into tetrameter, then diminishing into trimeters and closing with a single vocative cry. Clare's similarly opens with trimeter, expands into tetrameter, then closes with an exclamation naming its subject. Clare, too, experiments with the effect of alternating line length and metrical pattern. From the strong dactylic opening of 'Winter is nearly spent', he moves to the running anapaests 'when the sun turns to gold on the grass / And the flowers turn to stars in the night': lines that evoke the magic of sunlight and starlight, the two-way flow of planetary movement and organic life on earth. Clare's imagined sweetheart is a child of nature, who sings to the birds and makes friends of the flowers, but his poem is grounded on the 'molehill of thyme all the day': a punning vision of space and time as both locally small and infinite. Clare can entertain Shelley's cosmic worldview of 'the land and the sea and the air', but he is less interested in the supernatural and speculative than in what is known, at a physical and local level: 'Her voice and her features were known; / I went up and called her my own / Sweet Jessey'.

It is helpful to have this recorded snapshot of Clare thinking through Shelley when creating his own work, as it underlines the effect of Clare's extensive reading on his approach to poetic form. At his death, Clare's library contained over 500 volumes.[3] He is a responsive writer, who experiments continually with metre, rhyme-scheme and stanza length. But he is also drawn back to traditional poetic modes and subjects (song, ballad, tale), just as he is thematically drawn to documenting local traditions, celebrating seasonal return, invoking anger about 'old ways' lost to modernising forces, and lamenting the loss of childhood innocence and freedom. Clare's literary forms are shaped by the patterns of his lived landscape, which he chooses to reflect, to celebrate and to defend in writing. They are, I shall argue, 'landforms' because they attend and attune themselves so closely to the shapes and rhythms of the natural world, and to their expression in dialect and the patterns of rural life. But Clare's formal designs also respond to the scenes and preoccupations of the literary land-scape he entered, with its rich mix of writers, recently published or revived from older sources, and its proliferation of different literary models and outlets for publication. In formal terms, he is both an embedded writer and an explorer.

The *Northampton Mercury*'s 1842 article illustrates some of the diffi-culties that attend Clare studies. In the picture it presents, Clare is both a Romantic subject and a Romantic object, a figure in whom dignity and pathos merge. His habit of walking with one hand in his waistcoat—a rhetorical pose shared by Napoleon and associated in portraiture of this period with leadership—makes him appear statesman-like.[4] Did he mean to appear thus? Clare is abstracted in thought, in an 'almost unbroken poetic dream', which may ambiguously be a heightened state of composi-tion or one of mental confusion. Since Shelley's 'Ginevra' is a dreamlike poem in which Ginevra is 'absorbed like one within a dream who dreams / that he is dreaming', it is unclear whether Clare's own poem is a con-scious commentary on it or the result of unconscious absorption in Shelleyan thought, or even identity. Analysing Clare's agency in his late work is especially fraught. In his earlier work, too, however, it is often dif-ficult to gauge how 'finished' his unpublished manuscripts are, and how we should approach them. Would he, if given an entirely free choice, have wished them to be punctuated by others and rendered grammatically reg-ular? Would he have wanted his first thoughts to be visible or preferred more polished versions of his poems to supersede them? Any discussion of Clare's formal vision must confront these editorial uncertainties.[5] I shall be using the nine-volume Oxford edition of Clare's poetry, which prefers to present Clare's work in its original, unpunctuated manuscript form. Whether this editorial strategy frees or limits the verse remains, however, a perennial topic of debate that concerns how best to respect Clare's cre-ative autonomy.

MOCK-HEROIC AND SATIRE

An early example of Clare making a spirited sortie in a new form is his 'Sorrows for a Favourite Tabby Cat Who Left This Scene of Troubles Friday Night Nov. 26 1819':

> Let brutish hearts as hard as stones
> Mock the weak muses tender moans

As now she wails oer tittys bones
   Wi anguish deep
Doubtless our parents dying groans
   Theyd little weep […]

Ah mice rejoice yeve lost yr foe
Who watchd yr scheming robberies so
That while she livd twant yours to know
   A crumb of bread
Tis yours to triumph mines the woe
   Poor pusseys dead[6]

Clare's poem, written when he was twenty-five, is a loving response to Burns's 'Poor Mailie's Elegy', a mock-heroic lament for a dead sheep:

Lament in rhyme, lament in prose,
Wi' saut tears trickling down your nose;
Our *Bardie's* fate is at a close,
   Past a' remead!
The last, sad cap-stane of his woes;
   Poor *Mailie's* dead![7]

This six-line stanza is known in Scotland as 'Standard Habbie' and was favoured by Burns. Its rhythm lends itself to comedy, because the short fourth and sixth lines frequently act as 'punch-lines', bringing up short the high-flown sentiment developed in the rhymed tetrameters that precede them. The metre has a histrionic quality—especially when the occasion lacks the gravitas the repeated ejaculations imply. In Clare's poem, the 'anguish deep', 'dying groans' and 'woe' are hyperbolic responses to the death of 'Titty': a cat whose name suggests littleness (a title that is more of a tittle).

Clare successfully incorporates aspects of Burns: not only replicating the mock-heroic occasion—the death of a pet—but also elements of Scots dialect ('No sooner peept ye out your nose / But ye were instant in her claws / Wi squeakings dread'). This is a distinctively 'folk' voice and one that emphasises its closeness to rural life by its attention to physical, animal behaviour. Clare's pouncing rhyme between 'nose' and 'claws' is more Scots than English. It is interesting, however, that his rhyme between 'bread' and 'dead' is more English than Burns's 'remead' with 'dead' (pronounced 'deid' in Scots). His language is straddling the border between Scots homage and Northamptonshire home-page. Clare also develops the idea, present throughout Burns, of the animal as a political figure within a system akin to that of human governance: here the mice are set free from 'tyrant laws' but will be subject to the speaker's 'dreadfull war' if they 'infringe the laws' and plunder his cupboard. Persecuted animals are depicted as akin to hunted persons in many of Clare's later works, from his depiction of moles as executed felons 'sweeing in their chains',[8] to his badger-baiting sonnets, but, in this early sally, its effect is more comic than tragic.

Just as Burns adopts different rhetorical guises and personae, Clare tries on here a voice that appears to be wailing in lamentation and shaking its fist in anger: warning the mice away from his schemes and traps. The effect is consciously absurd. The smallness of the object and the rhetorical ambition of the poet are set at deliberate odds. Clare's title, 'Sorrows for a Favourite Tabby Cat [...]' also includes a nod to Thomas Gray's mock-heroic poem 'Ode on the Death of a Favourite Cat Drowned in a Tub of Goldfishes' (1747). The 'Scene of Troubles' the cat has left recalls Hamlet's 'sea of troubles', while the specific day and date Clare attaches to the poem wink at the habit of poets such as Wordsworth and Coleridge of including precise dates in their poems' titles—inviting the reader's imaginative identification with the poet's personal experience as a trigger to composition. Form here is a tribute to Burns's style and swagger, his ability to alternate between punchy and lyrical approaches to the elegiac mode.

Clare made more than one early excursion in 'Standard Habbie'. Also around 1819, he wrote 'Ale', a poem praising Tant Baker's tavern, the Hole in the Wall, 'in the favourite Scotch metre of Ramsay and Burns it was not good but there are parts of it as I think worthy of a better fate than being utterly lost'.[9] Clare's early reading and listening contained several Scottish sources, including *The Scotch Rogue*, a picaresque novel which includes Scots dialect and which features a hero who engages in bawdy exploits.[10] Although Clare attributes his village tale in tetrameter couplets, 'Robs Terrors of Night or Courting on Ass Back', to stories told by his parents, its direct literary inspiration is Burns's 'Tam O' Shanter'. Just like Tam, who rides home drunk at night glowering round 'wi' prudent cares / lest bogles catch him unawares', Clare's picaresque hero Rob worries about being caught by witches:

How theyd ride out a nights on switches
O whychen wood & willow wicks
On brushes & on beesome sticks
How theyd transform to L—d knows what
T[o] crowing hen or spit fire cat
& scare night trampers most to death
In lonsome ways of wood & heath
Bobbing from bushes unawares
& crossing lanes in form of hares[11]

Like Tam O' Shanter, Rob eventually reaches his sweetheart, but not before his fears of female devilment have made an ass of him.

Recent studies have considered Burns's influence on Clare's lyricism.[12] It is, however, equally worth considering Burns's influence on Clare's early forays into comedy. A strong earthy, satirical, often bawdy vein runs through Clare's writing. He often uses his literary reading as a spade to dig down to his folk roots. Burns is enabling for Clare because he uses dialect with pride, not because it is his only available voice, but because it is one whose pithiness and pawkiness he revels in. When one reads Burns's Scots verse aloud, one has to shape one's mouth to its guttural vowels and terse consonants. In his formal choice to deploy Burns's language as well as his metre, we can see Clare as a Northamptonshire-born, working-class poet of Scots ancestry, experimenting with the power of dialect to be deliberately and productively 'rude' in the sense of unvarnished, grainy, emotionally tactile. However, as Stephanie Kuduk Weiner has suggested, self-conscious use of dialect positions Clare as 'both native informant and antiquarian collector', insisting (through, for example, the glossary in *Poems Descriptive*, which links his dialect usages to Chaucer and the King James Bible) on the antiquity and cultural value of regional varieties of language in a manner that deliberately aligns him with other, learned preservers of folk talk, tale and song.[13] John Barrell has commented that 'Clare's language is [...] purely local—a vocabulary of the names he and his neighbours use for what things are and what they do [...] it reminds us that [...] the rightness of this or that word, is completely dependent on its being used of the things and actions in the place to which that language belongs'.[14] But Clare's familiar use of Scots dialect in poems written throughout his life emphasises the range of vocabulary at his disposal: his language is rooted in love for the land, but his sense of belonging within landscape (as dialect, tradition and vistas seen both literally—as a person present in that place—and figuratively, on the page) encompasses a broad territory that can include Scotland. In 'Robs Terrors of Night', Clare fuses Scots lore, words and rhymes ('what' with 'cat') with Northamptonshire traditions and dialect: the word 'whychen' for 'wych-elm' is not cited by the OED between 1621 and 1820, when Clare brings it back into written use.

COUPLETS AND RHETORICAL FORM

Clare's commitment to celebrating rural life and landscape, like Burns's, is tempered with sharp and witty observation of the faults of his society. His long poem *The Parish* (1820–27) owes an obvious debt to the works of George Crabbe. It is couched in heroic couplets that are deployed to satirical effect in a series of portraits of the local squirearchy, from Farmer Cheetum to Dandy Flint Esquire: a rogue's gallery of exploitative nouveaux riches whose rakish habits of self-aggrandisement contrast with the honest paternalism of what Clare sees as an earlier generation of unpretentious yeoman farmers who shared their table with their co-workers.

Clare's use of form in *The Parish* is noteworthy. While the observations are local and drawn from rustic experience, the heroic couplets showcase a self-conscious wittiness that is in the eighteenth-century neoclassical tradition of balanced epigram. The symmetrical quality of the couplet here draws attention to its own verbal symmetries to emphasise the writer's rational prowess in pronouncing judgement:

> Cant & hypocricy disguise their ways
> Their praise turns satire & their satire praise[15]

Clare's crisp use of antithesis and chiasmus here is repeated throughout the poem. The clever, studied parallelisms show that Clare had been reading Pope as well as Crabbe with attention to their formal wit and how they deploy it to deconstruct others' verbal infelicity. This is especially true when Clare takes down the local rhetorician, Young Brag, who stirs up the crowd with 'bad english' and 'broken speech':

> His fustian wit trots wild on broken feet
> Jostling the readers patience from his seat
> Half prose half verse they stagger as they go
> & after fashions follys dribbling flow[16]

This passage echoes Pope's 'Epistle to Dr. Arbuthnot', where the poet is criticised 'whose Fustian's so sublimely bad, / It is not Poetry, but Prose run mad'.[17] Clare criticised Pope's pastorals, but enjoyed his satirical writing, quoting the 'Satires of Dr. John Donne' in a letter of 1824 to Henry Francis Cary where he claims that his own 'confused stile' falls 'under the censure of Popes "period of a mile"'.[18] This self deprecating remark, suggesting that his own lines are interminably long, shows how attentive Clare is to verbal rhythm and sentence construction. Young Brag in *The Parish* is given to using 'monny syllables' and false appeals to patriotism to inflame the audience:

> Of 'Rotten boroughs—'bribery'—'tyrants'—'slaves'
> Were selfs a patriot & opposers knaves
> To fill the void his lack of words will cause
> He bawls out freedom & expects applause[19]

Clare is adept at using the form of his own verse to mimic the failings of others' rhetorical craft. Here, the 'void his lack of words will cause' is a deliberately long-winded way of conjuring Young Brag's dearth of ideas, which he disguises by shouting 'freedom' and expecting applause to fill the gap, as it fills up the couplet. Brag's words 'in thick disorder flye / & from his mouth like crackers bounce & dye'.[20]

Clare later worried that *The Parish* showed him in a bitter and ungracious light. It is, nonetheless, an important early work, demonstrating his close attention to the mechanics of form and style. The 'monny syllables' that, Clare tells us, Brag has 'spent' make a connection between money and words that hints at how politicians buy their voters, as well as hitting them with verbal barrages. Clare is alert to linguistic irregularity and disorder as markers of political incompetence and stupidity. His own nimble use of the couplet is implicitly contrasted with the hiccupping firecrackers of the stump speaker.

Clare is, however, equally alert from an early stage in his career to the possibility that verse can be too regular, with singsong or 'gingling periods' that enervate the reader by their predictability. In 1824, he remarks that 'the turnpike hackneyisms of sounding rhymes & tinkling periods then in fashion for most of the rhymers of that day seem to catch their little inspirations from Pope'.[21] Clare's coinage of 'turnpike hackneyisms' is typically witty. A turnpike was a spiked barrier in the road, which forced a carriage to stop and pay a toll. Here, Clare takes the original meaning of 'hackney' (a hired cab) and fuses it with its secondary meaning (trite, banal) in an image of a coach that stops for a rhyme at the end of each line, as if to pay a fee. Clare would comment on changing historical values in poetry in a playful sonnet 'Style' (written between 1819 and 1832), which exemplifies the different techniques it discusses. He contrasts John Donne's poetry—'old homely gold' that nonetheless contains 'broken feet'—with 'Popes smooth rhymes that regularly play / In musics stated periods all the way', concluding with a metrical joke about the constraints of form:

> One line starts smooth & then for room perplext
> Elbows along and knocks agen the next
> & half its neighbour—where a pause marks time
> & [the] clause ends. What follows is for ryhme[22]

Clare's later response to Byron's 'Don Juan' makes similar internal jokes about the constraints of rhyme. His early meditations on poetic form underline the conscious choices he makes regarding lexis, syntax, metre and rhyme-scheme. In *The Parish*, he refers to his own poetry as 'plain homespun verse' that 'lets none escape / Nor passes folly in its rudest shape' compared with 'young bards silken lines'.[23] Smoothness in this poem is equated with slipperiness, inauthenticity and flattery. Clare's rougher textual weave deliberately sets out to catch in its net a 'ruder' set of ideas and persons, in a way that will allow him to be provocatively rude about them: alluding, for example, to venereal disease and the sexual exploitation of female domestic workers by the ruling class. Clare's use of 'homespun' couplets in *The Parish* asserts his folk roots and his commitment to the land rather than the landed; his commentary on rhetorical form is also sophisticated and indicative of his sense of cliché and empty phrasing as lazy forms of manipulation.

Although he experiments with many types of stanza, including quatrains, ballad metre and Spenserians, ottava rima and occasional blank verse, Clare will continue to use couplets for the rest of his poetic life: they are his most characteristic formal footwear. He also favours perfect rhyme. The couplet is, I think, central to what many readers value in Clare. It is a form that feels as solid and ancient as walking or ploughing. It relates his poetry to that of Chaucer and other writers with strong links to the oral, folk tradition. It invites the reader to keep step with its regular iterative progress: a progress that is often reflected in the poem's gradual, attentive journey through a landscape. This is true of poems such as 'Pleasures of Spring', 'Hollywell', 'The Holiday Walk' and many fragments, such as ''Tis midsummers eve & the suns shut his eye'. 'Heres the light agile spider a weaving a way', Clare remarks in an untitled poem, as if simply gesturing towards it, and 'Heres the old fairey rings by this dark thickets side / Where the owl roosts in fear & the foxes abide'.[24] Webs, rings, dens: Clare's lines admire forms of return and belonging in nature.

Yet, Clare uses couplets artfully. As we have seen, he is cognisant of the different genre signals that a tetrameter couplet (in the mode of Burns's 'Tam O' Shanter', which imitates Tam's horse-ride home) and a heroic couplet (in the mode of Pope's satirical verse) can send. He is also wary of overly regular, smooth or jingling lines and rhymes that weary through repetition and the constant expectation of toll-rhymes at the turn of each rhythmic road. Clare, then, persistently casts his lines in a manner that plays to and from the possibility of closure. Indeed, in his finest verse, the pleasure the reader experiences in sound and imagery is constantly heightened by the movement created by surprise, waywardness and incompleteness as Clare conjures them through flowing, interrupted and open-ended form.

BOUNDEDNESS AND UNBOUNDEDNESS: WALKING CLARE'S LINE

Clare's poetry invites us to experience rural life and scenery, often without prologue or personal reflection that might situate the poem in time and place or otherwise prepare the reader for the direct encounter it not only conveys but mimics. 'Snow Storm', a delightful pair of sonnets, written sometime between 1832 and 1837, deliberately opens *in medias res*:

> What a night the wind howls hisses & but stops
> To howl more loud while the snow volly keeps
> Insessant batter at the window pane
> Making our comfort feel as sweet again
> & in the morning when the tempest drops
> At every cottage door mountanious heaps
> Of snow lies drifted that all entrance stops
> Untill the beesom & the shovel gains
> The path—& leaves a wall on either side—
> The shepherd rambling valleys white & wide

With new sensations his old memorys fills
When hedges left at night no more descried
Are turned to one white sweep of curving hills
& trees turned bushes half their bodys hide

The boy that goes to fodder with supprise
Walks oer the gate he opened yesternight
The hedges all have vanished from his eyes
Een some tree tops the sheep could reach to bite
The novel scene emboldens new delight [...]^25

Although debate rightly flourishes about whether some of Clare's poetry should be punctuated, this particular poem seems to glory in its lack of punctuation marks. The first line conveys excitement. There is no pause between 'what a night' (presumably the poet's ejaculation) and 'the wind howls hisses'. Grammatically, it could be the wind that is howling 'what a night!' And this rushing, onward sense of continuity between what the wind is doing and what the poet is saying, sweeps us up in its dramatic movement. The poem relishes the snug comfort of being indoors and the simultaneous assault of the 'volly' of snow, its 'insessant batter'. Boundedness and boundlessness become two sides of the window pane of imaginative pleasure.

Clare uses the word 'stops' twice in this poem. The word was often used in his period to mean 'punctuation'.^26 In this largely unpunctuated double sonnet, the word itself both acts as punctuation—suiting its meaning to its place in the line—and resists the closure that actual punctuation would imply. Enjambment carries us on: 'stops / To howl more loud'; 'all entrance stops / Until the beesom & the shovel gains'. Again, here, the poem plays with the effect of the snowstorm. It is unstoppable and it creates stoppage—until the snowdrift can be cleared by human action. 'Stops' makes us think about pausing, only to read on.

Once we are outside, Clare's long, unbroken line leads us to see the way in which snow has levelled large objects in the vista, enabling it to be read continuously: 'turned to one white sweep of curving hills / & trees turned bushes'. Snow has enjambed the landscape. Clare tells us that 'The shepherd rambling valleys white & wide / With new sensations his old memorys fills'. At first glance, this is an odd locution, yet we understand it easily. It is as if the man's memory is the landscape. The snow has filled it, creating visual and tactile sensations that change its contours. Trees and bushes have 'bodys': the physical shape of human experience and of the natural world is essentially identical.

Clare's spelling and syntax here add to the freshness of the vision: the 'mountanious' drifts have a spontaneous hugeness, while the boy's 'supprise' (Clare's customary spelling) is more plosive in its unexpectedness than 'surprise' would be. Whether these markers arise from what Johanne Clare has argued is Clare's general 'indifference' to spelling and punctuation,[27] or are effects consciously preferred by him, they make the poem stronger and more original.

Should we think of this double sonnet as an experiment in seeing form differently? Like snow, a poem can articulate and can make us enjoy transformative experience: its own negotiation between a form we think we know (a hedge; a sonnet) and something less familiar. Boundaries can be buried that allow one to 'walk oer the gate [one] opened yesternight'. This experience, implicitly shared between the boy, the poet and the reader, is liberating.

Clare's snow poems are good examples of how his method of accretion, line by line, often deliberately mirrors natural forms and processes. His many poems about birds nesting also draw attention to the similarity between poem and nest. As various critics have observed, Clare delights in parataxis.[28] No fewer than sixty-four of his poems begin with the word 'And'.[29] In his sonnet 'The Meadow Hay', the speaker lies stretched out, hidden in the hay, a position that places his melody horizontally within the landscape, arising organically alongside the 'weeds' and 'wind':

> I often roam a minute from the path
> Just to luxuriate on the new mown swath
> & stretch me at my idle length along
> Hum louder oer some melody or song
> While passing stranger slackens in his pace
> & turns to wonder what can haunt the place[30]

In this poem, Clare himself becomes the 'genius loci' or spirit of the place, his 'idle length' part of the luxuriant outgrowth of 'buoyant joy' that brings the singing weeds, sweet grass and 'delighted wind' together in 'play' that is both indolent—associated with wandering and slackness—and creative. The '&' of this poem is temporal, but also by implication topographical and affective: an assertion of how being in harmony with a field might feel.

Clare's habitual association between the lie of the land and the poetic line informs what John Goodridge rightly calls the 'righteous anger and elegiac sadness' of the political poems in his 'poetic war against enclosure'.[31] In 'The Mores', one of Clare's masterpieces, one can see the luxuriant poetic line whose uninhibited length he celebrates as a vision of freedom in landscape:

> Far spread the moorey ground a level scene
> Bespread with rush and one eternal green [...]
> Unbounded freedom ruled the wandering scene
> Nor fence of ownership crept in between
> To hide the prospect of the following eye
> Its only bondage was the circling sky[32]

Clare's management of the various possibilities of the couplet here is ingenious. In the opening lines, which dramatise the punning infinity of the 'mores', open vowels and enjambed description throw wide the curtains of the couplet. With delicious paradox, unbounded freedom 'rules' and the 'scene'—normally a static concept—is conceived as 'wandering', free to wander in. When, however, we come to the description of enclosure, Clare brings to bear everything he has learned from Pope and Crabbe about chiasmus, antithesis and parallelism: the end-stopped closure of each heroic couplet becomes a metaphor for the fences erected to privatise common land:

> Each little tyrant with his little sign
> Shows where man claims earths glows no more divine
> On paths to freedom & to childhood dear
> A board sticks up to notice 'no road here' [...]
> As tho the very birds should learn to know
> When they go there they must no further go[33]

When Clare writes 'these paths are stopt—' his syntax conveys the physical experience of being brought up short. The 'notice' says 'no' so that wild creatures (absurdly) may 'know' negation. Clare's monosyllables are powerful comments on the 'little signs' that restrict the 'mores' from free public access. His couplets enact the difference between open country and the restrictions enforced by (that oxymoron so prevalent in modern life) the 'gated community' of wealthy landowners.

Clare's persistent exploration of boundedness and unboundedness in landscape through poetic form and its inherent negotiation between open and closed space is nowhere more apparent than in his sonnets. Sonnets traditionally draw attention to their boundaries and to the poet's nimbleness in performing the 'turn' from quatrain to couplet, or from octave to sestet. Clare's sonnets, however, often deliberately court a more open approach to the landscape of form, where the sonnet itself may hover between a sense of finished and unfinished thought, unitary identity and existing within a continuous, potentially infinite sequence of views.

SONNET AND SEQUENCE

'The Meadow Hay' is—aptly, given its theme of 'being amongst' landscape 'buried in the sweet grass'—an open-ended sonnet entirely composed in couplets. Couplet sonnets were practised by Robert Herrick, whom Clare particularly admired, and by other early poets he valued such as Thomas Carew and Charles Cotton, but by the nineteenth century were widely proscribed as illegitimate models: not sonnets at all. Clare's adoption of couplet form for so many of his sonnets becomes, in this context, a radical choice that reflects his insistence on the validity of early verse forms associated, by him, with the English countryside.

Throughout Clare's period, the Petrarchan sonnet was considered the apogee of sonnet form. As James Noble Ashcroft put it in 'The Sonnet in England':

> The superiority of the true Italian to the Shakspearian or any other sonnet form in unity, weight, and harmony, will be doubted by hardly any competent critic; indeed, with the solitary exception of Ebenezer Elliot, it has not, so far as our knowledge goes, been explicitly questioned by any well-known poet.[34]

The fact that Ashcroft cites Ebenezer Eliot, the 'corn-law rhymer' and protest poet, as the only dissenting voice on sonnet form, suggests the politicisation of the debate. John Clare, like Eliot, refuses to accept that the Petrarchan form of sonnet is 'superior'. The twenty-one sonnets in his first published volume, *Poems Descriptive of Rural Life and Scenery* (1820), favour the Shakespearean form over the Petrarchan. Of the sixty sonnets in his second collection, *The Village Minstrel* (1821), most are hybrid. Clare became adept at fusing two Shakespearean quatrains with a

Petrarchan sestet: a solution that avoids the potentially confining restrictions of the Petrarchan octave (abbaabba) and the tidy sum of the Shakespearean closing couplet. Over time, he developed many experimental approaches to hybrid form. Several of the more successful sonnets in Clare's *The Village Minstrel* play with positioning the couplet(s) before the end of the poem, closing only to open again, like a melody that moves from a perfect cadence into a new theme. In 'The Last of April' (ababb cdcdd efef), a sonnet frequently anthologised by later Victorians, and 'Summer Tints' (ababb cddcd ecec), the schematic units of quatrain and couplet, or octave and sestet, give way to a freer interwoven rhyming pattern: Clare delights in variation. Here, as in so many of his other lyrics, he plays thoughtfully to and from the boundaries of established form.

Clare's intellectual boldness and the surprising range of his reading, given his income and situation, are evident in his views on the sonnet. He lambasted Robert Southey's *Select Works of the British Poets from Chaucer to Jonson* (1831) as 'very slovenly edited' with 'many names left out that ought to be in', such as Herrick, Suckling and Surrey whose 'Sonnets are tender and very poetical there is a breathing of Shakspearian healthfulness about them that is evergreen'.[35] In July 1820, he wrote to James Hessey, the publisher he shared with Keats, that

> I began on our friend Keats new Vol:—find the same fine flowers spread if I can express myself in the wilderness of poetry—for he la[u]nches on the sea without compass—& mounts pegassus without saddle or bridle as usual & if those cursd critics could be shovd out of the fashion wi their rule & compass & cease from making readers believe a Sonnet cannot be a Sonnet unless it be precisely 14 lines [...] he may push off first rate[36]

Clare was writing about Keats's final collection, *Lamia, Isabella, The Eve of St Agnes and Other Poems* (1820), which—by conventional standards—contains no sonnets whatsoever. Evidently, Clare was reading poems such as 'To a Friend', where ten-line stanzas in couplets congregate around one of fourteen lines, 'Lines on the Mermaid Tavern' with its 'broken sonnet' ending, and the odes, with their ten- and eleven-line stanzas composed of two Shakespearean quatrains and two or three rhyme-lines (often a penultimate couplet), as loose variations on sonnet form that adventurously take to the seas without a 'compass': in the double sense of an instrument indicating fixed direction and a set of confining boundaries.

Clare's own experiments with stanza length and rhyming pattern reflect his creative dialogue with Keats and with the evergreen 'old poets' whom they both enjoyed reading. Clare's 'Autumn', which begins 'Syren of sullen moods and fading hues', is an open tribute to Keats's 'To Autumn', which begins 'Season of mists and mellow fruitfulness'. It is almost as if Clare has put on his friend's jacket, but turned it inside out. The metrical pattern (iambic pentameter) of the first lines is the same, but words have changed colour: season to syren; fruitfulness to fading hues.

> & yet sublime in grief thy thoughts delight
> To show me visions of most gorgeous dies
>   Haply forgetting now
>   They but prepare thy shroud
> Thy pencil dashing its excess of shades
> Improvident of waste till every bough
>   Burns with thy mellow touch
>   Disorderly divine[37]

Clare's Autumn is aware of her own approaching death, as Keats was, and her thoughts, 'sublime in grief' become a way of talking simultaneously about the burning intensity of Autumn colours 'gorgeous dyes' and about Keats's own dying shade, whose pencil's dashing excess had left such a rich poetic legacy.

Clare is neither confined by the literary language he uses here (borrowing 'haply', perhaps, from Shakespeare's sonnet XXIX, 'mellow' from Keats), nor by the eleven-line stanza form of Keats's ode. Rather, he experiments with creating eight-line stanzas that flow seamlessly into one another. These recall aspects of the nine-line Spenserian stanza, but choose to alternate freely between unrhymed iambic pentameter and three-stress lines. Clare's poem contains many images of divine disorder: 'lawless floods', 'dishevilled hair', 'disordered scenes'. His ode uses the metrical pattern of the poem to conjure the beguiling, lulling beauty of the 'syren' season, while its formal peculiarity and diminishing line length suggest the restlessness that also preoccupies him: 'Autumn' becomes an elegiac season / poem uneasily meditating its own end, while 'snatching sweet scraps of song'.

Clare was an early practitioner, within what became the nineteenth-century sonnet revival, of what we now call 'sonnet sequences'. By 1824, he was planning an ambitious project akin to Wordsworth's 1820 sequence of sonnets on the River Duddon, to write a hundred sonnets 'as a set of pictures on the scenes & objects that appear in the different seasons'.[38] Form, multiply replicated, here appears as akin to the framing of a 'set of pictures' that one might view in a gallery of landscapes, or the collecting of natural history specimens ('objects that appear in the different seasons'), with natural variation in colour and pattern, but similar size and shape.

In a sequence of sonnets that pay homage to Izaak Walton as well as to his own love of fishing, Clare emphasises the way in which a poem itself is an excursion, dependent on flow and on choosing the right place and moment to angle for the reader's attention. The fisherman 'with the rivers brink…winds his way' until he finds 'a spot half shade half sun / That scarcely curves to show the waters run':

> Right cautious now his strongest line to take
> Lest some hugh monster should his tackle break
> Then half impatient with a cautious throw
> He swings his line into the depths below
> The water rat hid in the shivering reeds
> That feeds upon the slime & water weeds
> Nibbling their grassy leaves with crizzling sound
> Plunges below & makes his fancys bound
> With expectations joy—down goes the book
> In which glad leisure might for pleasure look
> & up he grasps the angle in his hand
> In readiness the expected prize to land[39]

Clare makes us feel the punning analogy between poetic line and fishing line. He uses the medial caesura in his couplets to create movement and surprise. His syntax and management of the line is all the more effective because, in this largely unpunctuated poem, the medial caesura and the long dash are the only breaks. We experience the short gap in time between the angler throwing out his line and its swing into the water; we are 'supprised' by the plunging water rat, which makes the foolish angler jump up in expectation of a fish.

A poet other than Clare would likely say, of the fisherman, that 'jumping up, he grasps the rod'. But Clare's wonderfully free use of language and syntax allows the reader to picture the scene in a fast and fluid manner. Getting up and grasping the 'angle' become one, urgent movement—like the angler, the reader becomes fixated on the float which 'now shakes and

quickens his delight / Then bobs a moment and is out of sight'. We experience the sensuous 'gush of joy' and the landing of the fish, which 'bounds
and flounces mid the new mown hay' and 'pants upon the plain'.
Characteristically, there is more than a hint of erotic pleasure to this sonnet sequence that describes the sun 'mount[ing] up' with 'ruddy face', the
flushed cheeks of milkmaids waking the dewy fields to joy, the dancing
crowd of 'waterflyes… imprinting little rings', the 'stirring float' and 'a
larger yet' [fish implied] that 'from out its ambush shoots'. Clare plays the
reader, tickling our fancy.

This sonnet sequence both gives us a narrative of a day's fishing and a
descriptive account of the way the angler 'winds his way' along the river
'marking its banks how varied things appear'. Like the walk along a meandering stream, the poetic sequence is only ever provisionally ended. There
could easily be a sequel. This can seem a fault in Clare's poetry: the poem
as a unit may have no absolute architectonic sense of finality. Zachary
Leader has claimed that that Clare's poems 'often lack […] balance, shape,
proportion'[40] or, in a word, structure. In fact, a degree of open-endedness
and provisionality is characteristic of Clare's organic sensibility towards
form. Natural forms are continuous. Rivers do not end: they become
other rivers, go underground, flow into the sea. As Stephanie Kuduk
Weiner observes:

> anti-closural strategies place Clare in complicated ways within the history of
> the lyric. His unbounded poems seem to invert the typical effort of the lyric
> to triumph over time […] The fragments of Clare's unclosed sonnets […]
> celebrate the resonance between the poems' permeable edges, the flux of
> time, and the infinite extension of space—celebrating, that is, the poems'
> structural likeness to the unbounded world, whose units of time and space
> are shown to be human impositions, arbitrary and transient.[41]

There is a vital relationship between Clare's loving admiration for form
in nature and the shapes and rhythms of his poems. Clare's verse often
observes change mimetically, attending to incremental developments that
reflect the time of year. His poems and prose pieces embody both specificity and abundance: frequently focusing on a single tree, bird, animal, they
resemble in aggregate an almanac of days spent outdoors. His work also
embraces sauntering, rambling, soodling, progging: modes of serendipi-
tous encounter in landscape that communicate the experience of co-
habiting a space where things occur—such as weather, the seasonal

modulations of plants, the movements of animals—and where human perception of these changes is a product of the cross-hatched texture of labouring rural life, where continuous relationality is inevitable. Both in space and time, Clare invites us to experience waywardness, a directed openness to paths that become the lines that feet may take. In this sense, 'ways by woods & brooks'[42] may be 'secret walks for making rhymes and books': forms that emphasise at once their traditionality and their informality, the way in which they are continually improvised afresh. This way of working does not exclude reflective or philosophical literary strategies. It does not doom Clare to littleness, of scope or of perception. On the contrary, it links him backward in time to the 'old poets', in his own lifetime to fellow Romantic poets, and forward to ecological poets of the twentieth and twenty-first centuries. We should never underestimate the literary craft and range of allusion that underpins Clare's approach to form and sequence. He writes not only from his 'knowledge'—in the sense of his mental map of his locality and its open-field vistas—but from his reading, his politics and his imagination.

Like the hares in his sonnet 'Hares at Play', Clare runs 'through well-known beaten paths' but also 'nimbling [...] sturts' in unexpected directions and finds 'hidden lairs' (and layers) in language. A hare's form is its home, but is also a very slight mark in the landscape; likewise, Clare's work is deep-rooted in form, but simultaneously acutely aware of the vulnerability of landscape and language to change and depredation, and the necessity of adapting to new circumstances. His experiments involve dialogue with a multitude of other authorial voices, from Burns, Crabbe and Pope, to Keats, Byron and Shelley. They are thus vital to the way that he positions himself in the poetic landscape of early nineteenth-century poetry, asserting his literary awareness of tradition at the same time as he asserts his difference, as a labouring poet working in the particular landscape and dialect of Northamptonshire. His poetry digs deep into the well-loved strata of land and literature, while always 'nimbling' into new and unexpected forms.

Notes

1. 'Original Poem by John Clare, The Northamptonshire Poet', *Northampton Mercury* 30 April 1842, 2. The article was reprinted in the *Derby Mercury* 4 May 1842, 4.

2. Ibid. *Later Poems*, 1: 320, lines 1–20 reproduce the Knight transcript of this poem, which has minor variants, for example, 'Jessy' for 'Jessey'.
3. When Clare's collection was offered for sale in 1867, it was advertised in the *Northampton Mercury* as consisting of 'above 500 volumes' (22 June 1867, 5). The collection was bought by subscribers for the Northampton Library. In 1902, some of the more valuable signed presentation copies were sold off, but between 450 and 500 volumes were retained. See *Northampton Mercury* 18 July 1902, 6.
4. See, for example, Jacques-Louis David's portrait of *Napoleon in his Study* (1812) or Robert Home's *Arthur Wellesley, 1ˢᵗ Duke of Wellington* (1804).
5. These textual questions are discussed in Bate, *Biography*, 563–75. The debate also preoccupies many issues of the *John Clare Society Journal* that appraise editions of Clare's poetry: for example, Mark Storey, 'Edward Drury's "Memoir" of Clare', *JCSJ* 11 (1992), 14–16; Jonathan Bate, Review of *Middle Period*, 3 and 4, *JCSJ* 18 (1999), 79–83; Bob Heyes, Review of *John Clare: Flower Poems*, ed. Simon Kövesi, *JCSJ* 21 (2002), 83–6; R. K. R. Thornton, Review of *John Clare: The Living Year 1841*, ed. Tim Chilcott, *JCSJ* 20 (2001), 85–8; R. K. R. Thornton, 'Review Essay: the Raw and the Cooked', *JCSJ* 24 (2005), 78–86; John Goodridge, Review of *John Clare: Poems*, ed. Paul Farley, *JCSJ* 26 (2007), 86–7; Simon Kövesi, 'Beyond the Language Wars: Towards a Green Edition of John Clare', *JCSJ* 26 (2007), 61–75; and Valerie Pedlar, Review of Paul Chirico, *John Clare and the Imagination of the Reader*, *JCSJ* 27 (2008), 81–4.
6. *Early Poems*, 2: 225–6, lines 1–6 and 31–6.
7. Robert Burns, 'Poor Mailie's Elegy', *Poems, Chiefly in the Scottish Dialect* (Kilmarnock: Wilson, 1786), 66, lines 1–6.
8. Clare, 'Remembrances', *Middle Period*, 4: 132, line 39.
9. Clare, *The Prose of John Clare*, ed. J. W. and Anne Tibble (London: Routledge, 1970), 28.
10. 'Donald Macdonald', *The Scotch Rogue, or, the Life and Actions of Donald Macdonald* (London: Gifford, 1722).
11. *Early Poems*, 2: 258, lines 54–62. This poem has another form, 'The Lovers Journey', where Clare credits 'A Hint Taken from the Simply Simple Tales of the Illustrious Bard G.C.—L.L.D.' This refers to George Crabbe (properly denominated LLB), but the style is that of Burns's 'Tam O' Shanter'.
12. Adam White, *John Clare's Romanticism* (Basingstoke: Palgrave Macmillan, 2017) has a chapter on Clare's and Burns's love lyrics. Mina Gorji, *John Clare and the Place of Poetry* (Liverpool: Liverpool University Press, 2008), discusses versions of pastoral in Clare and Burns. For a balanced account of Clare's debt to eighteenth-century poetics, especially Cowper, see Adam Rounce, 'John Clare, William Cowper and the Eighteenth Century' in

New Essays on John Clare, ed. Simon Kövesi and Scott McEathron (Cambridge: Cambridge University Press, 2015), 38–56.

13. Stephanie Kuduk Weiner, 'John Clare's Speaking Voices: Dialect, Orality, and the Intermedial Poetic Text', *Essays in Romanticism* 25, no. 1 (2018): 90 and 99.

14. Barrell, 128.

15. *Early Poems*, 2: 701, lines 71–2.

16. Ibid., 729, lines 843–6.

17. Alexander Pope, *An Epistle from Mr. Pope to Dr. Arbuthnot* (Dublin: Faulkner, 1735), 10, lines 185–6.

18. 30 December 1824, *Letters*, 312. Clare is quoting Pope's 'Satires of Dr. John Donne, Versified', in which Bishop Hoadly is chastised for this fault.

19. *Early Poems*, 2: 729, lines 825–8.

20. Ibid., 728, lines 813–14.

21. Clare's journal, 27 October 1824, *Prose of John Clare*, 116.

22. *Middle Period*, 4: 380, lines 11–14. Lines in 'Style' directly echoing *The Parish* suggest the poems may be close in date.

23. *Early Poems*, 2: 714, lines 418–20.

24. 'Tis midsummers eve & the suns shut his eye' (untitled), *Middle Period*, 2: 202–8, lines 31 and 84–5.

25. *Middle* Period, 5: 213–14, lines 1–19.

26. OED cites the first use of 'stop' to mean 'a mark or point of punctuation' as 1616, and this usage was current until the early twentieth century. *Punctuation Personified; or Pointing Made Easy* (London: Harris, 1824) was, suggestively, taught by a character called Mr Stops.

27. Johanne Clare, *John Clare and the Bounds of Circumstance* (McGill: Queens University Press, 1987), 119–20.

28. Barrell, 157–8, introduced this observation. Stephanie Kuduk Weiner argues that in his mature work 'Clare's central syntactic strategy [...] is parataxis', in *Clare's Lyric* (Oxford: Oxford University Press, 2014), 34.

29. I include poems and fragments beginning with an ampersand in this number, drawn from John Goodridge, *First-Line Index to the Published and Unpublished Poetry of John Clare* (undated). http://www.johnclare.info/flindex.html.

30. *Middle* Period, 4: 253, lines 1–6.

31. John Goodridge offers a brilliant, sustained close reading of the poem in *John Clare and Community* (Cambridge: Cambridge University Press, 2013), 125–31.

32. *Middle Period*, 2: 347–50, lines 1–2, 7–10.

33. Ibid., lines 67–70, 73–4.

34. James Ashcroft Noble, 'The Sonnet in England', *Contemporary Review* 38 (September 1880), 448.

35. 24 July 1831, *Letters*, 549, 548.
36. 29 June 1820, *Letters*, 80.
37. *Middle Period*, 3: 266–7, lines 97–104.
38. 3 January 1824, *Letters*, 288.
39. *Middle Period*, 4: 339, lines 43–54.
40. Zachary Leader, *Revision and Romantic Authorship*, (Oxford: Clarendon, 1996), 252.
41. *Clare's Lyric*, 71–2.
42. 'The Fate of Genius', *Early Poems*, 2: 669, line 85.

Bibliography

Burns, Robert. *Poems, Chiefly in the Scottish Dialect*. Kilmarnock: Wilson, 1786.

Clare, Johanne. *John Clare and the Bounds of Circumstance*. McGill: Queens University Press, 1987.

Goodridge, John, ed. *First-Line Index to the Published and Unpublished Poetry of John Clare* (undated). http://www.johnclare.info/flindex.html.

Goodridge, John. *John Clare and Community*. Cambridge: Cambridge University Press, 2013.

Gorji, Mina. *John Clare and the Place of Poetry*. Liverpool: Liverpool University Press, 2008.

Leader, Zachary. *Revision and Romantic Authorship*. Oxford: Clarendon, 1996.

Macdonald, Donald (pseud.). *The Scotch Rogue, or, the Life and Actions of Donald Macdonald*. London: Gifford, 1722.

Noble, James Ashcroft. 'The Sonnet in England'. *Contemporary Review* 38 (September 1880): 448.

Pope, Alexander. *An Epistle from Mr. Pope to Dr. Arbuthnot*. Dublin: Faulkner, 1735.

Rounce, Adam. 'John Clare, William Cowper and the Eighteenth Century'. In *New Essays on John Clare*, edited by Simon Kövesi and Scott McEathron, 38–56. Cambridge: Cambridge University Press, 2015.

Stops, Mr. (pseud.). *Punctuation Personified; or Pointing Made Easy*. London: Harris, 1824.

Weiner, Stephanie Kuduk. 'John Clare's Speaking Voices: Dialect, Orality, and the Intermedial Poetic Text'. *Essays in Romanticism* 25.1 (2018): 85–100.

———. *Clare's Lyric*. Oxford University Press, 2014.

White, Adam. *John Clare's Romanticism*. Basingstoke: Palgrave Macmillan, 2017.

John Clare's Ear: Metres and Rhythms

Andrew Hodgson

Clare's ear for the natural world was acute. Here he is describing the call of the 'Fern Owl or Goat sucker or Night jar':

> one cannot pass over a wild heath in a summer evening without being stopt to listen & admire its novel & pleasing noise it is a trembling sort of crooing sound which may be nearly imitated by making a crooing [...] noise & at the same time patting the finger before the mouth to break the sound[1]

The passage is a discreet *ars poetica*. Clare thinks of being immersed 'in' a summer evening, rather than out walking 'on' one; 'being stopt' is the phrase of a poet governed by his senses. And while the prose slips and slides around this 'trembling sort of crooing sound' which can be 'nearly imitated' by, well, 'crooing', there is an intuitive felicity in the way its repetitions ('noise [...] sound [...] noise [...] sound') shadow Clare's ululations. Clare's voice, as Stephanie Kuduk Weiner has said, enters into a 'direct and intimate' relation with the world to which he listens.[2]

A. Hodgson (✉)
University of Birmingham, Birmingham, UK
e-mail: a.hodgson@bham.ac.uk

© The Author(s) 2020
S. Kövesi, E. Lafford (eds.), *Palgrave Advances in John Clare Studies*, Palgrave Advances,
https://doi.org/10.1007/978-3-030-43374-1_6

Clare's literary ear is less celebrated, though his poetic mimicry is sure-footed, too:

Styles may with fashions vary—tawdry chaste
Have had their votaries which each fancied taste
From Donns old homely gold whose broken feet
Jostles the readers patience from its seat
To Popes smooth rhymes that regularly play
In musics stated periods all the way
That starts & closes starts again & times
Its tuning gammut true as minster chimes
From these old fashions stranger metres flow
Half prose half verse that stagger as they go
One line starts smooth & then for room perplext
Elbows along & knocks against the next
& half its neighbour where a pause marks time
There the clause ends what follows is for ryhme
('Shadows of Taste', lines 79–92)[3]

The passage is always quoted to prove Clare's metrical skill, and you can hear why. To take just one line, 'Half *prose* | half *verse* | that *stag* | ger *as* | they *go*' is alive to the way momentum may be 'staggered' by the arrangement of words along the pentameter's rise and fall (and how malleably 'Half prose half verse' makes itself available to both the iambic pattern of the verse and a trochaic emphasis of speech).[4] But the lines stand out, too, for their rarity. Clare seldom advertises his prosodic intelligence. In his letters, attention to his own metres extends only to a few early exchanges with John Taylor which show Clare happily yielding to his publisher's metrical emendations.[5] One could be forgiven for thinking that metre was a technical matter, like punctuation, which Clare felt to be of secondary importance. Indeed, part of the attractiveness of the above lines owes to their faint aloofness, an implication in the very panache of the writing that such superficial effects might be carried off by anyone. In the spirit of his imitation of the nightjar, Clare frames his tour of prosodic 'fashions' with an assertion of the more permanent virtues of 'truth to nature' (line 77).

But Clare's poems are metrically subtle and adventurous. Something of their accomplishment is implicit in his comments on the prosody of his late-Romantic contemporaries: Clare praised the 'calm placid manner of the verse' that 'runs smooth and deep' in Beddoes's *The Bride's Tragedy* (phrasing which values a correspondence between surface texture and inner substance); he was drawn to the 'mystical beauty' that 'hangs about' the 'measures & expressions' of Darley's *Labours of Idleness* and 'creates a feeling in one somthing akin to musing or listning to fancys imaginary music'.[6] That sense of rhythm's ability to 'create a feeling' sponsors the impact and intricacy of Clare's own voice. As the paragraphs that follow show, a supple prosodic skill underpins a range of Clare's acknowledged strengths: his fusion of vernacular and literary song traditions; the humane attentiveness and verve of his blank verse; and the isolated self-possession of his later asylum lyrics. Clare's rhythms are crucial to his verse's mimetic power, yes; but beyond that his cadences shape feeling, dramatise thought and calibrate attention. Clare's metrical artistry creates a potent 'imaginary music'.

Song Forms

Clare's art was nurtured by a tradition of actual rather than 'imaginary' music, the lineage of vernacular song 'which mouth to mouth thro ages handles down', as he puts it in 'Rural Morning'[7] ('handles', as opposed to, say, 'hands on', speaks with a touching sense of the duty of care involved).[8] Its influence grants much of his apprentice work a homespun energy—in some cases literally. 'I measured this ballad today wi the thrumming of my mothers wheel if it be tinctured wi the drone of that domestic music you will excuse it after this confession', Clare apologised of one paean to his local landscape, sent in a bid to entice his publishers into commissioning a collection of similar pieces in 1820.[9] 'You would never know that it has been composed to the steady click of a spinning wheel',[10] observes Jonathan Bate, recognising an aural vitality which Clare sells short. Though in fact, you might well guess as much, since the song's spirited localism manifests itself in a four-stress line striking for its 'thrumming' regularity:

> Swamps of wild rush beds & sloughs squashy traces
> Grounds of rough fallows wi thistle & weed
> Flats & low vallies of kingcups & daiseys
> Sweetest of subjects are ye for my reed[11]

Internal echoes and glancing rhymes grant texture, but the rhythm holds steady. Metre serves as the 'co-presence of something regular', as Wordsworth thought of it, though the regularity here is not 'supperadded', but arises from the 'domestic music' of Clare's environment.[12] Variations are kept to modulations of pace and emphasis, as when, having swung from a dactylic to a rising anapaestic pattern, Clare renews his panegyric at the start of the final stanza:

> & long my dear valleys long long may ye flourish
> Tho rush beds & thistles make most of your pride
>   (lines 17–18)

Though the rhythm again keeps to the metre, the words play along the pattern with renewed flair, thanks both to the plangent repetitions of 'long' in the opening line (where 'long long' urges the voice to slow against the anapaestic cadence) and the movement from 'flourish' to 'Tho rush', a lovely, rhyming rise and fall of stresses across the lines, that sets a flourish on the poem's praise for the unspectacular. More downbeat emphasis colours a second 'Ballad' Clare sent in the same letter, a love lyric which adapts his tetrameters to expressions of regret and disappointment. Again, the poem shifts from a falling dactylic pattern into a rising anapaestic one; but as it comes to address the source of its sadness, the dactylic shape of the opening is recalled:

> It grieves me to mark the first open may blossom
> Mary if still the hours 'membered by thee
> Twas just then thou wisht one to place in thy bosom
> When scarce a peep showd itself open to me[13]

On the one hand, the abbreviation of 'remembered' shows how readily Clare's early songs prioritise metrical conformity; on the other, the second line, returning to a falling cadence, shows how intuitively their auditory imagination responds to feeling. The modulation lends urgency to the appeal to 'Mary', and, echoing the rhythm of the start of the poem, intimates that Clare's own memory of this moment of adolescent crisis has not faded.

The early 'ballads' are driven by a youthful eagerness; as Clare said to Taylor, 'I […] want your judgement only either to stop me or to set me off at full gallop'.[14] But if the bold rhythmic strokes of such poems show Clare's art 'moving back into the life of song from which it had come', as Elizabeth Helsinger argues,[15] Clare's best songs balance the urge to return to vernacular roots with a consciousness of the increased craft and sophistication available on the printed page. 'Ballad: Winter Winds', a poem of 1819–20, showcases Clare's ability to infuse folk tradition with literary subtlety. The poem's two-stress lines achieve a bleak dactylic music, a more hollow and haunted timbre than results from Clare's use of the same metre across more elongated lines. (That Clare was toying with metrical possibilities is apparent from an alternate version in Peterborough MS A40, which trials a jogging trochaic rhythm. '*Winter* | *winds* so | *Cold* and | *blea*'.) Burns stands behind the poem's tale of love against the odds, but Clare achieves distinctive tenderness. His downcast rhythms play against a passionate commitment:

> Winter winds cold & blea
> Chilly blows oer the lea
> Wander not out to me
>   Jenny so fair
> Wait in thy cottage free
>   I will be there[16]

Clare controls the emotional temper by varying the pressure on the unstressed syllables. So while '*Wan*der not | *out* to me', say, flows rapidly, '*Win*ter winds | *cold* & blea', where 'winds' and 'blea' almost take a secondary stress within their feet, is more encumbered. In the third and fourth stanzas, attention turns to the anticipated joys of love, and the stilted dactylic pulse relaxes so that the dominant metre becomes interspersed with lines equally amenable to being read with an upbeat iambic swing. 'How sweet can courting prove', he asks at the start of the third stanza (line 13), his line leaning towards an iambic cadence that would lay emphasis on the potential 'sweetness', before he mutes the optimism with a comic reflection on the difficulties of courtship in the snow: 'How can I kiss my love / Muffld i' hat & glove / From the chill air' (lines 14–16). Even as these lines return to a dactylic ripple, though, 'How can I kiss my love' lays itself open to a more yearning iambic emphasis. In the fourth stanza, too, latent iambic possibilities strain beneath the dactyls, as Clare begins to thrill at sexual possibility: 'Lay by thy woolen vest / Rap no cloak oer thy breast' (lines 19–20).

    The poem ends with the poet contemplating his clandestine arrival at his lover's cottage, the atmosphere poised between sexual exhilaration and nervousness of the intrusions of a cold world:

When the latch gis a tink
Who is it ye may think
Wi no feard fancies shrink
    Undo the door
Or at the window blink
    Then yell be sure

Shut from the chilly air
To thee Ill hitch my chair
Snudgd on thy bosom bare
    Lost in thy charms
O how Ill revel there
    Rapt in thy arms
                    (lines 37–48)

Dactylic rhythms underline the tentativeness evoked in the opening triplet of the penultimate stanza, edging each line uncertainly to its brink, and they give point to the verbs that animate the closing scene: 'Snudgd', 'Lost' and 'Rapt' (a favourite Clare spelling, which fuses the shelters and wonders of love). The turn from the beloved's nervous anticipation to the poet's own cosiness caps the poem with a moment of generous surprise: this song seemingly about a protective male lover ends with the speaker 'Snudgd' cosily in the woman's arms.

'Winter Winds' exploits the ambiguities of emphasis made possible by the printed page, but does so to sustain contact with the cadences of breathing human passion. The poem's twinned impressions of spontaneity and artifice typify Clare's conflicted inhabitation of ballad forms. Song is for Clare often the arena for ironic treatment of the claims of the literary, even as he depends upon literary resources to animate that irony. Few poems illustrate his ability to marry seemingly artless impulse with tonal complexity and vocal dexterity so well as 'Songs Eternity', a poem from Clare's mid-1820s maturity. '"Tootle tootle tootle tee!" in a softly-coloured Fenland landscape—that is the sum of John Clare's poetry from boyhood to the grave', Edmund Gosse once remarked, taking a line from the poem, and meaning to praise.[17] And one doesn't have to subscribe to the view that the song's alternating four- and two-stress lines mimic the call of the blue tit to appreciate the deftness with which it harmonises natural and artistic music.[18] Yet as Johanne Clare points out, the poem's 'sing-song rhythm' conceals intricacies of tone and perspective which enable the poem to house ironic commentary on its initial 'premise', that time scorns human aspirations to immortality.[19] Clare's thought is endlessly to-ing and fro-ing, his structure conducting a delicate call-and-response pattern, orchestrated to poignant effect in the opening stanza:

> What is songs eternity
> Come & see
> Can it noise & bustle be
> Come & see
> Praises sung or praises said
> Can it be
> Wait awhile & these are dead
> Sigh sigh
> Be they high or lowly bred
> They die[20]

The verse poses weighty questions in the quietest of accents. Clare begins, in gently ironic mood, by testing the possibility that the 'eternity' of song might rest on the 'noise', 'bustle' and 'praises' of the present, a cacophonous trio which the poem's own light-footed movement floats above. The answer is, of course, 'no', but, for all its firm sense of human delusions, the poem tilts towards this recognition with regret, rather than triumph. The inquisitive a-rhymes are sustained beyond the mid-point of the stanza, their hopeful questioning dispelled only in the final four lines. The rhythms of the last two shorter lines cut affectingly against their earlier equivalents' continuation of a falling, trochaic pattern—first, with a spondee that speaks with poignant passivity in the face of time's passing; next by sealing the stanza with an iambic foot of cold finality. The voice, as Johanne Clare says, is at once 'sweet and ruthless'.[21]

'Songs Eternity' is genuinely questioning as well as tartly ironic. Its second stanza follows the same rhyming and metrical pattern, but deploys it to sunnier effect, as Clare locates the source of 'Songs Eternity' in the 'Melodys of earth and sky':

> What is songs eternity
> Come & see
> Melodys of earth & sky
> Here they be

> Songs once sung to adams ears
> Can it be
> —Ballads of six thousand years
> Thrive thrive
> Songs awakened with the spheres
> Alive
>
> (lines 11–20)

The brightening tone is marked by small changes in the way the poem inhabits the metre. Clare accentuates the stressed syllable of the trochee at the start of the fourth line, as though to mark a moment of discovery ('*Here* they be'); and while he keeps up the spondaic and then iambic pattern of the final two short lines, he reverses their inflection from plangency to exhilaration. The poem joins in unison with the Edenic 'Ballads of six thousand years' which still 'thrive'.

But the song's argument doesn't follow a simple trajectory from lamentation to celebration. The antiphonal quality of Clare's form enables acknowledgements of earthly transience to coexist with glimmers of artistic transcendence. So in the next stanza, the shorter lines move back to underlining the rapidity with which human achievement vanishes ('Crowds & citys pass away / Like a day' [lines 23–4]) and to 'sighing' for the books left 'with the dead' (line 27) by time. Fluid enjambments allow subsequent stanzas to glide free of this deftly handled glimpse into an abyss, whether by pointing attention to nature's music ('Dreamers list the honey be[e] / Mark the tree / Where the blue cap tootle tee / Sings a glee / Sung to adam & to eve' [lines 31–5]), or in rising to more emphatic assertions, as at the close of the penultimate stanza: 'Natures glee / Is in every mood & tone / Eternity' (lines 48–50). 'Eternity' there answers back across the poem to the opening stanza's rhymes on 'sigh' and 'die'; vatic confidence takes over from plangent lament as the word expands the stanza's final line into two iambic feet. In some versions the poem ends here, but a culminating stanza included in Peterborough MS A57 again owes its force to small prosodic variations, as Clare hymns the presence of a song imminent both in the world around, and achieved in his own lines:

> The eternity of song
> Liveth here
> Natures universal tongue
> Singeth here

> Songs is heard & felt & seen
> Every where
> Songs like the grass are evergreen
> The giver
> Said live & be & they have been
> For ever[22]

'Here' rhymes triumphantly through each of the shorter lines; an iambic upswing fuels the joyous crescendo of the final three. Nuanced artistry underlies the song's harmony with the 'evergreen' life it celebrates.

Part of what ensures song's 'eternity' is the tendency of its communal idiom to universalise feelings rooted in private circumstances. In 'Love and Memory', originally titled 'To the Memory of ******' when it was published in *The Gem* in 1829, that balance of the individual and the impersonal is aligned with a phrasing which by turns follows and eludes the constraints of metre and lineation.[23] The poem is an elegy for a young lover, written in a tender second-person voice which endows a quality of intimate address rather than public tribute. Clare deploys an eight-line cross-rhymed stanza with anapaestic dimeter lines, a form which has two principal effects: first, to compress Clare's apprehensions of loss into a slick and memorable lyricism; secondly, to underpin the pathos of the poem with a metre that can seem incongruously buoyant, as though straining to cheer the mood up. The odd mix is apparent from the start:

> Thou art gone the dark journey
> That leaves no returning
> Tis fruitless to mourn thee
> But who can help mourning[24]

Metre prompts memorability: 'to have gone the dark journey' sounds more absolute than to have 'gone on' it—to have set off towards death is to have departed for good. And 'That leaves no returning' is more poignant than, say, 'That none can return from': partly for the way 'leave' catches up in itself both the lover's departure and the absence left behind, and partly for the way 'returning' jangles in a rhyme (and assonance with 'journey') that flaunts the very business of returning. Clare's criss-crossing feminine rhymes answer to the baffled impulses that drive the poem: a conviction of both the fruitlessness of mourning and the urge to grieve and pay tribute. His alternating form channels swirl and counter-swirl of feeling. The third stanza looks quizzically at our tendency to idealise the dead:

> The nearer the fountain
> More pure the stream flows
> & sweeter to fancy
> The bud of the rose
> & now thourt in heaven
> More pure is the birth
> Of thoughts that wake of thee
> Than ought upon earth
>   (lines 17–24)

The back-and-forth rhyming affects straightforwardness. But Clare's argument is slippery. The opening images seem to prepare the ground for a reflection on the beauty of youth taken too young (and Clare pursues this in the stanza that follows), but the thought becomes trickier: now the woman is 'in heaven', Clare asserts in lines of characteristically specious fluency, she seems 'more pure' than anything upon earth, yet whether this is a source of comfort or indicative of a painful tendency to idealise what we have lost is uncertain. Repeatedly, the form conducts an inner struggle about how you ought to feel about loss if you believe that the lost one is now in a happier place:

> I know thou art happy
> Why in grief need I be
> Yet I am & the more so
> To feel its for thee
>   (lines 33–6)

Potential consolation spirals into puzzled grief. The third line, begging a weighty caesura but impelled onward by the lilt of the metre, shows Clare's ability to engender discord between musical flow and emotional weight. Throughout, the poem struggles with a sense that its feelings are not what they should be. 'Who would wish thee from joy / To earths troubles again' (lines 79–80), Clare asks at the end of the penultimate stanza, where 'wish' flickers with a sense that to wish something may be to make it so. What seems a rhetorical question is, in the closing stanza, shown to be a genuine dilemma:

Yet thy love shed upon me
Life more then mine own
& now thou art from me
My being is gone
Words know not my grief
Thus without thee to dwell
Yet in one I felt all
When life bade thee farewell
(lines 81–8)

The gracefulness of the rhythms glosses over a striking honesty. The direction of thought in Clare's songs is often more surprising than their simple
structures would imply. Clare's statement that, thanks to the woman's
loss, his 'being is gone', set in a slight off-rhyme with the second line, and
underscored by the emphasis on '*being*' and '*gone*', hints that he may well
wish her back to 'earths troubles'. The writing grieves as much for vanished selfhood as for the woman. The closing confession of inarticulacy in
the face of feeling is hardly unusual in elegy, but Clare gives it force by
dropping his feminine endings and iambic substitutions to flatten the
cadence of the final three lines, and by joining the lines in a triplet which
leaves 'grief' as the only unrhymed word in the stanza. The compression
of the phrasing, in which words crowd confusingly like the feelings they
describe, testifies to a sorrow that has taken all the poet's heart for speech.

SPOKEN RHYTHMS

Clare's songs blend folk and literary impulses into a seductive 'imaginary
music'. Elsewhere, particularly in the natural history poems that are one
signature of his mature style, Clare's rhythms, mostly running along iambic pentameter lines, suggest the inflections of speech, rather than the
sway of song. But fine metrical artistry remains at the root of the poetry's
affective power. Clare's rhythms 'engage not just the mechanical gears of
a metre' but 'take hold also on the sprockets of our creatureliness',
observes Seamus Heaney.[25] The poetry's technical attunement to the
world is also an emotional one—Clare's rhythms compose an alert and
compelling sensibility.

   In his most contented poems, Clare's rhythms find harmony with a
secure and stable natural world. 'The Robins Nest', one of the happiest
among the assembly of poems on birds' nests, presses home its iambic

pattern with incremental vigour as it speaks of experiencing in nature 'that superior power':

> That guards & glads & cheers me every hour
> That wraps me like a mantle from the storm
> Of care & bids the cold[est] hope be warm[26]

This 'power', says Clare, encouraging us to pay heed to the emotional pressure as well as the semantic content of his own words, 'speaks in spots where all things silent be / In words not heard but felt' (lines 31–2). That is a tricky distinction; and if it suggests the comfort of a pre-verbal eloquence in nature, it also primes us to remain alert to the extra-semantic suggestiveness of Clare's own words. Just fleetingly, one hears in the phrasing of 'The Robins Nest' a nerviness at odds with its explicit meaning. At the poem's heart, as Clare contemplates the special protection the birds enjoy in the woods, his language is at its most celebratory, but his rhythms are at their most apprehensive of disruption:

> Their homes with safetys wildness—where nought lends
> A hand to injure—root up or disturb
> The things of this old place—there is no curb
> Of interest industry or slavish gain
> To war with nature [...]
>
> (lines 51–5)

Nothing threatens the birds' peace, but, as Clare's emphatic caesuras become pivots for clauses which upset the bounds of the pentameter, it is as though in the very act of cherishing what he calls in a characteristically exuberant turn of phrase 'safetys wildness', Clare is disquieted by the possibility of its disturbance. The rhythms channel an unspoken apprehensiveness; as Johanne Clare observes, Clare's descriptions of birds' nests are often flecked with 'Small but sharply felt intimations of distruption and loss'.[27] Ultimately, though, this is a poem whose rhythms delight in imagining mutual comfort and love. Its vision is epitomised by its depiction of the 'wood robin', as

> He sits [&] trembles oer his under notes
> So rich—joy almost choaks his little throat
> With extacy & from his own heart flows
> That joy himself & partner only knows
>
> (lines 72–5)

The lines achieve unison with the bird through a control of sound and rhythm that is better heard than described. To pick one small example, the phrase 'joy *al* | most *choaks* | his *litt* | le *throat*' manages touching sympathy as Clare's voice is choked by the internal rhyme and the 'joy' that threatens to bubble up into a stressed syllable in spite of the iambic pressure. Art and nature are at one.

The flipside of Clare's longing for tranquillity is an anxiety about change. Many poems register indirect tremors of the effects of enclosure upon Clare's home village, Helpston. The sonnet 'Sudden Shower', for instance, plays out a miniature drama of disturbance and recovery:

> Black grows the southern sky betokening rain
> & humming hive bees homeward hurry bye[28]

The lines display the dramatic scope and descriptive tact of Clare's pentameters. The inverted foot with which the poem opens sets an ominous music rumbling through its line, whose stresses fall on the variously inflected 'ou' and 'o' sounds as the rhythm settles back into an iambic pattern. Attention then swaps from the panoramic to the minute. Clare's arrangement of his phrasing along the pentameter ensures that the humming alliterative 'h' words all arrive with a falling emphasis, causing them to zip along with something of the nervous speed of the bees. After a central section in which Clare makes skilful use of caesura to vary momentum, enabling us to 'feel the change' (line 3) stirred up by the coming storm, the sonnet closes on a tentatively rhymed couplet whose rhythms pull against the underlying iambic order:

> That *litt* | le *Wren* | knows *well* | his *shelte* | ring *bower*
> Nor *leaves* | his *dry* | *house* tho | we *come* | so *near*
>   (lines 13–14)

The final line, stalled by its inverted third foot, lingers over the thought of the 'dry house' and mimics the speaker's cautious approach to the bird. Clare's rhythms score a precarious harmony.

But Clare's rhythms are alert to change's capacity to enliven as well as threaten. Another Helpston poem, the triple sonnet 'The Flood', apprehends a more turbulent disruption. 'On Lolham Brigs in wild & lonely mood / Ive seen the winter floods their gambols play', the poem begins,[29] leaving it productively uncertain whether the 'floods', Clare himself or

'Lolham Brigs', the bridge on which Clare stations himself, are in 'wild and lonely mood'. Clare captures the river's surging energies in lines whose metrical violence and syntactic turmoil suggest affinities between outer world and inward apprehension:

> round & round a thousand eddies boil
> On tother side—then pause as if for breath
> One minute—& ingulphed—like life in death
>
> Whose wrecky stains dart on the floods away
> More swift then shadows in a stormy day
>
> (lines 12–16)

It is, one assumes, the 'eddies' whose 'wrecky stains' 'dart away' on the flood; but the coherence of Clare's syntax is so engulfed by the surging life of the scene that it is hard to sustain its central thread, and it might as well be 'life in death' that is seen being washed away. Clare takes that phrase from Coleridge's 'Rhyme of the Ancient Mariner' as he finds in the local disruption the image of a larger cataclysm. The sense that the flood epitomises a world speeding to ruin is emphasised by the slight metrical variations that accelerate the opening of the second sonnet: an inverted third foot that thrusts forward emphasis onto 'dart' in the first line, and the dampening of emphasis in the same foot of the succeeding line. The next settles into a resonant iambic metre that lifts the line out of the evolving descriptive tumult as a slogan for the poem's larger vision: 'Things trail & turn & steady—all in vain' (line 17). Yet Clare's rhythms prove capable of whimsy as well as intensity. As his eye is caught by a 'feather' which '*dan* | ces *flut* | ters *&* | a*gain* / *Darts* through | the *deep* | est *dang* | ers *still* | a*float*' (lines 19–20), Clare gives his own lines a dancing agility by ensuring stresses fall on the first syllables of his verbs. Taken by the feather's incongruous delicacy, the poetry surfs fancy momentarily, entertaining in lightly stressed lines the idea that 'faireys whisked it from the view / & danced it oer the waves as pleasures boat' (lines 21–2), before submerging once more into the immediate tumult to track, in the emphatically staged stresses of the second sonnet's final line, how the flood's debris 'plunges—reels—& shudders out of sight' (line 28). The writing's sketched rapidity cannot help but suggest excitement at the unfolding commotion.

Evocative precision is accompanied by visionary power. The final sonnet presents a nightmarish succession of waves, like 'monsters'

> plunging headlong down & down—& on
> Each following boil the shadow of the last
> & other monsters rise when those are gone
> Crest their fringed waves—plunge onward & are past
>
> (lines 33–6)

The lines again teeter on the symbolic as they envision a series of moments which 'rise and vanish in oblivion's host', as Clare would later put it in 'I Am'.[30] The rhythms enact the waves' descent '*down* | & *down*— | & *on*', curve momentarily into trochees to describe how they '*Crest* their | *fring*ed | *waves*', before submerging at the caesura, via a heavy stress on 'plunge', back into the flow of iambs. At the end of that line, 'are past' works as a characteristically ambiguous piece of grammar, catching a sense that the visions have not only passed by, but have solidly become the substance of 'the past'. The vanishing coincides with the end of the octet of the final sonnet, an intimation of the formal control Clare sustains beneath the chaos. The closing sestet conducts a mysterious and affecting transition into a mood of chilly hopelessness:

> Strange birds like snow spots oer the huzzing sea
> Hang where the wild duck hurried past & fled
> —On roars the flood—all restless to be free
> Like trouble wandering to eternity
>
> (lines 39–42)

The rhythm of the first line answers to Clare's disturbed vision: the monosyllables, while iambic, only hazily follow the demands of the stress, seeming ill at ease like the birds they describe, whose hovering is caught by the inversion at the start of the next line. Then comes a reassertion of the flood's persistence—a final metrical surge as though to say that art can never arrest nature's energies—before the meandering cadence of the final comparison. Fittingly, the final line keeps the iambic pulse only lightly, as the poem's immediacy dissipates to leave a troubled sense of emotional as well as literal desolation, and a simile which, in its quietly counter-intuitive way, mystifies rather than clarifies Clare's vision.

Clare's pentameters might, as Heaney says, 'engage the sprockets of our creatureliness', but they mobilise contemplation as finely as they dramatise action or stir instincts. The way 'The Flood' drifts into sudden dreaminess has affinities with the close of 'The Yellow Wagtails Nest', whose rhythmic fluency fuels uncharacteristic flights of fancy. Clare's discovery of a nest beneath an abandoned ploughshare prompts him to reflect on nature's benevolence:

> So thought I—sitting on that broken plough
> While evenings sunshine gleamed upon my brow
> So soft so sweet—& I so happy then
> Felt life still eden from the haunts of men[31]

Clare's ease shines forth in the way his interjection, strung across the couplets, comes to dwell upon its closing iambs: 'So *soft* | so *sweet*'. Looking upon 'the brook-pond waters spread below / Where misty willows wavered too & fro' (line 34), Clare's iambs ripple with the reflections they depict; and the scene tempts Clare into further Romantic speculation:

> The setting sun shed such a golden hue
> I almost felt the poets fables true
> & fashioned in my minds creating eye
> Dryads & nymphs like beautys dreams go bye
> From the rich arbours of the distant wood
> To taste the spring & try its golden flood
>
> (lines 35–40)

The syntax is beautifully and suggestively fluid. It appears, to begin with, that Clare's conjectures are contained within the 'eye'/'bye' couplet, the opening inversion of whose final line gives boldness to the '*Dry*ads | & *nymphs*' Clare imagines. But as the lines run on, the grammar morphs in a way that suggests Clare's increasing faith in the 'truth' of his speculations. The first part of the sentence, '& fashioned in my minds creating eye / Dryads and nymphs', is overtaken by a description of the nymphs' behaviour which causes our awareness that this is merely an image that Clare has fashioned to fade. The dreamy vitality of Clare's imaginings is underscored by rhythms that, yearningly eluding the underlying metre, evoke 'the *rich* ar*b*ours of the *dist*ant *wood*'. And the closing lines remain seduced by the appeal of imaginative reverie, even as Clare concedes the need to return from dream to normality:

> Thus pleasures to the fancy often shine
> Truest when false when fables most divine
> & though each sweet consception soon decays
> We feel such pleasures after many days

(lines 41–4)

The lines unfold a complex attitude to poetic vision. For 'pleasures' to 'shine' to the 'fancy' might suggest their superficiality, but the strong stress on 'Truest' reverses the suggestion, and seemingly endorses imaginings as a source of pleasure. The development 'Truest when false' puts a check on that impulse, but the chiastic pattern of the line then shifts the balance back in favour of the 'divine' potential of 'fable'. The final couplet leaves the poem with a poised judgement that concedes the unreality of our 'consceptions', but testifies to their lingering imaginative presence. Clare's pentameters engage our creaturely 'sprockets', but remind us that we are creatures of thought as much as sensation as they do so.

Asylum Verse

Many of Clare's most virtuoso metrical accomplishments derive from his years in the asylum between the late 1830s and his death in 1864. The most arresting among these later poems are frequently those which straddle the lyrical and colloquial tendencies I have been tracing so far: 'From these old fashions stranger metres flow / Half prose half verse that stagger as they go', as Clare observes in the lines from 'Shadows of Taste' (lines 87–8). Any 'strangeness' in Clare's late rhythms, though, tends towards a sharpening of vision rather than any 'staggering' of inspiration:

> The Elm tree's heavy foliage meets the eye
> Propt in dark masses on the evening sky
> The lighter ash but half obstructs the view
> Leaving grey openings where the light looks through[32]

The rhythms of this very late fragment respond masterfully to the scene. 'Foliage' weighs its foot down with the possibility of an extra syllable. Stresses gather like the elm's branches in '*Propt* in | *dark mas* | ses'. The closing lines, in which 'Leaving' speaks with understated wit about the patterns made by the leaves, draw contrasting tunes from the same metrical pattern. The first cleaves tightly to the iambic pulse; the second, also iambic, seems to open out: '*Lea*ving | grey *ope* | nings where | the *light* | looks *through*'. The word 'openings' itself, arranged so that its first syllable is the stressed syllable of an iamb, and the second is the first syllable of a pyrrhic foot, or very lightly stressed iamb, asks to be stretched into 'op-en-ings'; lastly, the chiastic sound-patterning of '*th*e *l*ight *l*ooks *th*rough' restores the lyric glint.

The intimacy of the attention is quietly affecting: even as the final image suggests a state of self-enclosure being breached, it is difficult to imagine how one could answer the voice's exactness and self-possession. But such self-assurance is rare among Clare's asylum verse, the main body of which, written in the 1840s when memories of a more fulfilling existence were fresher, speaks in an accent at once alienated and yearning. Metrical 'strangeness' underpins fragile bonds between speaker and audience. Poems are animated by sporadic colloquial bursts, as at the start of 'Spring Violets':

> Push that rough maple bush aside,
> Its bark is all ridgy—and naked beside;
> But it stands in the way of the flowers that engross
> My eye—in bloom, by its stump of green moss:[33]

The urgency is piercing and odd. Why is Clare so impatient with the 'ridginess' of the maple bark? Or does the 'But' indicate a lingering attraction to the tree superseded by the appeal of the flowers? The ghost of an abandoned musicality haunts the abruptness, gradually taking hold as the iambic metre of the first line expands into anapaests, before the jarring enjambment tracks the movement of an eye 'engrossed' by the hidden flowers. The impression is of a voice erratically seeking direction. The remainder of the poem moves less idiosyncratically, though it shows Clare's skill at letting the rhythms flow on beneath irregular turns of thought, as the poem meditates on the overlapping lives of the plants across the years and seasons. The jaunty anapaests of the closing couplet, for instance, garner an unusual pathos in their contemplation of life from the plant's perspective: 'Those sweet *flowers* | that look *up*, | in their *beaut* | iful *bloom* / Will *ne'er* | live to *see* | the bright *map* | le leaves *come*' (lines 17–18). That is a cliché, in its way, but the buoyancy of the metre wreathes the truism with an estranging serenity.

Clare's asylum poems often express an alienated sensibility by puncturing or deviating from song's communal vigour. 'Flowers shall hang on the pawls', dated '11th February 1847' in the Knight transcripts, is, on the face of it, one of Clare's most archetypally Victorian poems.[34] An elegy for an unnamed, possibly imaginary 'maiden' (line 8), the poem achieves florid poignancy in its contemplation of the rituals of grieving. But the voice expresses detachment as much as participation as it negotiates its anapaestic tetrameter couplets. The opening stanza moves with sombre delicacy:

> Flowers shall hang upon the pawls
> Brighter than patterns upon shawls
> And blossoms shall be in the coffin lids
> Sadder than tears on greifs eyelids
> Garlands shall hide pale corp[s]es faces
> When beauty shall rot in charnel places
> Spring flowers shall come in dews of sorrow
> For the maiden goes down to her grave tomorrow
>
> (lines 1–8)

The lines proceed with a lamed elegance, never quite resurrecting the sprightly rhythmic energy that haunts them. The limping cadence with which 'upon shawls' answers 'upon the pawls' across the first two lines, for instance, belies the 'brightness' the lines apparently notice; 'eyelids' forms a mis-stressed rhyme with 'coffin lids' across the third and fourth lines, giving its answer in a saddened, minor key. A florid decorum colours the end of the stanza, its lilting combination of iambs and anapaests combining with the feminine rhymes to allow the verse to move with frail glamour above the macabre spectacle it describes.

The rhythms of the second stanza are more regular, barring a (possibly accidental) extra stress which gives the second line an incongruous dactylic levity ('*Gay* as first | *flowers* of | *spring* or the | *tune* of a | *song*' [line 10]). The verse finds composure in rehearsing platitudes: 'Her eye was as bright as the sun in its calm / Her lips they were rubies her bosom was warm' (lines 12–13). The third stanza recapitulates the phrasing of the first, a suggestive strategy in a poem concerned with patterns of remembrance. Yet at the same time as the poem seeks consolation in repetition, the effect is to accentuate Clare's half-saddened, half-sardonic questioning of the rituals of grief:

> Spring flowers they shall hang on her pawl
> More bright than the pattern that bloom'd on her shawl
> And blooms shall be strewn where the corp[s]es lies hid
> More sad than the tears upon griefs eyelid
>
> (lines 17–20)

The rhythms stay closer to the metre than in the first stanza, but both the forced cheeriness of the internal rhyme ('*blooms* shall be *strewn*') and the limping conclusion to the second couplet remain alert to the gap between outward show and inner feeling. When the stanza does find its metrical stride, it is only to strike up a macabre parody of the sweet song for which its rhythm is appropriate. Clare contemplates, grimly, how the maiden's body, 'ere the return of another sweet May / Shall be rotting to dust in the coffined clay' (lines 21–2), hinging his vision on the discomposed internal rhyme of 'return' into 'rotting'. The closing lines encapsulate the poem's blend of hesitancy and momentum:

> And the grave whereon the bright snowdrops grow
> Shall be the same soil as the beauty below
>
> (lines 23–4)

The final line scans easily, the penultimate one awkwardly. Together, they apprehend a conventional feeling in a unique and peculiar way. It is difficult to say whether we ought to find the thought that new life springs from death consoling or grotesque—or merely specious; and the way the rhythms struggle towards their songlike polish is integral to that uncertainty.

Few asylum poems plait fluency and irregularity with such tonal complexity as 'An Invite to Eternity'. Here rhythmic unsteadiness traces a narrative of apprehension and resolve. The poem extends an invitation to accompany the poet through a desolate mental landscape with a cautious, troubled courtesy underpinned by its hesitant negotiation of a songlike iambic tetrameter. 'Say maiden', it appeals recurrently, the phrase speaking so longingly for the way pleading pressure on the notionally unstressed 'Say' retards the iambic pulse, and finding no answer. Skilled use of catalexis shapes a music that is, by turns, hobbled and encouraging. The opening four lines, for instance, shift between falling and rising emphasis, as though uncertain of the path to take:

> *Wilt* thou *go* with *me* sweet *maid*
> Say *maiden wilt* thou *go* with *me*
> *Through* the va*lley depths* of *shade*
> Of *night* and *dark* obscurity[35]

Then, across the middle of the stanza, the writing tends towards a more bouyant iambic cadence and commits to a more purposeful couplet shape:

> Where the *path* | hath *lost* | its *way*
> Where the *sun* | for*gets* | the *day*
> Where *there's* | nor *life* nor *light* | to *see*
> Sweet *maid* | en *wilt* | thou *go* | with *me*
> (lines 5–8)

Clare's rhythms are under the sway of contradictory urges to drive on into this desolating, visionary landscape and to hesitate, revisit and re-inquire. The tread of the fifth and sixth lines wavers between trochaic (with a lightly stressed first syllable) and the iambic trimeter with an initial ana-paest I have sketched above—the rhythmic path momentarily losing any certain way. As a more vigorous iambic pattern establishes itself in the seventh line the vision darkens and the rhythms slow. And, in its reworking of the stanza's opening, the closing line seems, poignantly, to have got no further forward.

The poem turns over its cadences with sorrowful persistence. It appeals to a 'Sweet maiden', but hears only its own words echoed back to it. The second stanza begins with steady iambic purpose, four lines which summon courage to tread onward into a world 'Where life will fade like visioned dreams' (line 11), before resolving into a defeated fourth line which, though it upholds the iambic pulse, shifts its upstress onto the first syllable of its words: 'And *moun* | tains *dark* | en *in* | to *caves*' (line 12). The images populate a landscape in which nothing has substance, a sur-real hall-of-mirrors in which everything becomes its opposite. The writing is most captivating, however, in its efforts to gain purchase on Clare's hollowed-out state of 'sad non-identity' (line 13), a phrase which acquires quiet pathos as it tempers the iambic pulse it runs along. The third stanza begins with reiterated appeal to the maiden, as though to steady itself, before plunging in to an evocation of Clare's deracinated consciousness. Its last four lines become the most rhythmically unstable in the poem:

> At once to be, and not to be
> That was, and is not—yet to see
> Things pass like shadows—and the sky
> Above, below, around us lie
>
> (lines 21–4)

Adapting Hamlet's 'To be or not to be' to his tetrameter rhythms, Clare takes English poetry's most famous line of iambic pentameter on a disorientating metrical journey. Two chiastic (abba) phrases pattern the language with his sense of inner contradiction: the first straddles a heavy caesura, brandishing its paradox; the second is telescoped into the first half of a line whose phrasing then unmoors itself from the lineation and drifts into a vision of peaceful obsolescence. But if the slowed iambic rhythms of the stanza's close suggest that 'sad non-identity' might be a state of release as much as torment, Clare ends the poem in more ironic temper:

> Say maiden can thy life be led
> To join the living with the dead
> Then trace thy footsteps on with me
> We're wed to one eternity
>
> (lines 29–32)

Clichés are reanimated to unsettling ends: to 'lead one's life' is to be led astray; to 'trace one's footsteps on' envisions a life of endless repetition. Marlowe plays sardonically in the background: 'If these delights thy mind may move, / Then live with me, and be my love'.[36] As the poem retraces its own metrical footsteps, it affirms the intimation in the rhyme of 'dead' and 'wed' that the 'eternity' in which it moves is a purgatory rather than a paradise. Yet there is a resilience to the iambic tread that means the tone eludes mere bitterness or despondency. Even as they contemplate 'eternity', Clare's rhythms keep time with a poignant and spontaneous apprehension of life.

NOTES

1. *Natural History*, 33.
2. Stephanie Kuduk Weiner, *Clare's Lyric: John Clare and Three Modern Poets* (Oxford: Oxford University Press, 2014), 24.
3. *Middle Period*, 3: 303–10.
4. Throughout, I indicate stressed syllables (as I hear them) in *italics*, and divide metrical feet, where pertinent, with a | mark.
5. *Letters*, 145–52.
6. *Letters*, 262, 371.
7. *Early Poems*, 2: 612, line 14.
8. See George Deacon, *John Clare and the Folk Tradition* (London: Sinclair Browne, 1983).
9. *Letters*, 65.
10. Bate, *Biography*, 206.
11. *Letters*, 65, lines 1–4.
12. William Wordsworth, 'Preface to *Lyrical Ballads*', *The Major Works*, ed. Stephen Gill (Oxford: Oxford University Press, 2008), 609. For overviews of Romantic debates about metre, see Susan Stewart, 'Romantic Meter and Form', in *The Cambridge Companion to British Romantic Poetry*, ed. James Chandler and Maureen N. McLane (Cambridge: Cambridge University Press, 2008), 53–75 and Susan J. Wolfson, 'Stressing the Sound of Sound', in *Meter Matters: Verse Cultures of the Long Nineteenth Century*, ed. Jason David Hall (Athens: Ohio University Press, 2011), 53–77.
13. *Letters*, 66, lines 25–8.
14. *Letters*, 64.
15. Elizabeth Helsinger, 'Poem into Song', *New Literary History* 46.4 (2015): 676.
16. *Early Poems*, 2: 228, lines 1–6.
17. *Critical Heritage*, 346.
18. See J. W. and Anne Tibble, *John Clare: A Life*, 1932, rev. edn. (London: Michael Joseph, 1972), 311.
19. Johanne Clare, *John Clare and the Bounds of Circumstance* (Montreal: McGill-Queen's University Press, 1987), 157–8.
20. *Middle Period*, 5: 3, lines 1–10.
21. Clare, *Bounds of Circumstance*, 155.
22. This final stanza appears in the version of 'Songs Eternity' as presented in *John Clare: Major Works*, ed. Eric Robinson and David Powell (Oxford: Oxford University Press, 2004), 124, lines 51–60. In this version, Clare's manuscript '&' is presented as 'and' and the fifth line runs 'Songs Ive heard and felt and seen'.

23. Bate speculates that the poem elegises the death of Betsey Sell, with whom Clare had conducted an affair before his marriage to Patty (*Biography*, 330–1).
24. *Middle Period*, 3: 435, lines 1–4.
25. Seamus Heaney, 'John Clare's Prog', in *Finders Keepers: Selected Prose, 1971–2001* (London: Faber and Faber, 2002), 281–2.
26. *Middle Period*, 3: 533, lines 28–30.
27. Clare, *Bounds of Circumstance*, 180.
28. *Middle Period*, 4: 262, lines 1–2.
29. *Middle Period*, 4: 234, lines 1–2.
30. *Later Poems*, 1: 396, line 4.
31. *Middle Period*, 3: 475, lines 29–32.
32. 'Fragment', *Later Poems*, 2: 1090, lines 1–4.
33. *Later Poems*, 1: 307, lines 1–4.
34. *Later Poems*, 1: 491
35. *Later Poems*, 1: 348, lines 1–4.
36. Christopher Marlowe, 'The Passionate Shepherd to His Love', lines 23–4, in *The Complete Poems and Translations*, ed. Stephen Orgel (Harmondsworth: Penguin, 1971), 207.

Bibliography

Bate, Jonathan. *John Clare: A Biography*. New York: Farrar, Straus and Giroux, 2003.

Clare, Johanne. *John Clare and the Bounds of Circumstance*. Montreal: McGill-Queen's University Press, 1987.

Clare, John. *Poems of the Middle Period, 1822–1837*. 5 vols. Edited by Eric Robinson, David Powell, and P. M. S. Dawson. Oxford: Clarendon Press, 1996–2003.

———. *The Early Poems of John Clare, 1804–1822*. 2 vols. Edited by Eric Robinson and David Powell. Oxford: Clarendon Press, 1989.

———. *The Later Poems of John Clare, 1837–1864*. 2 vols. Edited by Eric Robinson and David Powell. Oxford: Clarendon Press, 1984.

———. *The Natural History Prose Writings of John Clare*. Edited by Margaret Grainger. Oxford: Clarendon Press, 1983.

———. *The Letters of John Clare*. Edited by Mark Storey. Oxford: Clarendon Press, 1985.

———. *John Clare: The Major Works*. Edited by Eric Robinson and David Powell. Oxford: Oxford University Press, 2004.

Deacon, George. *John Clare and the Folk Tradition*. London: Sinclair Browne, 1983.

Gorji, Mina. 'Clare's Awkwardness'. *Essays in Criticism* 54.3 (2004): 216–39.

Heaney, Seamus. 'John Clare's Prog'. In *Finders Keepers: Selected Prose, 1971–2001*, 281–5. London: Faber and Faber, 2002.

Helsinger, Elizabeth. 'Poem into Song'. *New Literary History*, 46.4 (2015): 669–90.

J. W. and Anne Tibble. *John Clare: A Life*. Rev. edn. London: Michael Joseph, 1972.

Kuduk Weiner, Stephanie. *Clare's Lyric: John Clare and Three Modern Poets*. Oxford: Oxford University Press, 2014.

Marlowe, Christopher *The Complete Poems and Translations*. Edited by Stephen Orgel. Harmondsworth: Penguin, 1971.

Sandy, Mark. *Romanticism, Memory, and Mourning*. Farnham: Ashgate, 2013.

Stewart, Susan. 'Romantic Meter and Form'. In *The Cambridge Companion to British Romantic Poetry*, edited by James Chandler, 53–75. Cambridge: Cambridge University Press, 2008.

Storey, Mark. *The Poetry of John Clare: A Critical Introduction*. London: Macmillan, 1974.

———, ed. *John Clare: The Critical Heritage*. London: Routledge and Kegan Paul, 1973.

Wolfson, Susan J. 'Romantic Measures: Stressing the Sound of Sound'. In *Meter Matters: Verse Cultures of the Long Nineteenth Century*, edited by Jason David Hall, 53–77. Athens: Ohio University Press, 2011.

Wordsworth, William. *The Major Works*. Edited by Stephen Gill. Oxford: Oxford University Press, 2008.

John Clare's *The Shepherd's Calendar* and Forms of Repetition

Sarah Houghton-Walker

Clare's *The Shepherd's Calendar: with Village Stories and Other Poems* (1827) is thematically preoccupied with cyclicality: the obvious turning of the calendar, and with it, the farming year; the charting of the perceived decline of a festive year according to which the rural community previously has functioned; the routines and rituals of daily labour and relaxation.[1] Repetition is thus fundamental to the subject matter of a poem which records local knowledge accrued through the experience of many cycles. Itself functioning as an almanac, the *Calendar* celebrates forms of knowledge dependent upon the repetition of these cycles, most strikingly exhibited in habits of prognostication which might seem to suggest foresight but which are themselves dependent upon observing and experiencing, and thus upon repetition in their turn. Alongside its thematic dominance, repetition permeates the *Calendar* through literary conventions: the tradition of the calendar poem and almanac, allusion to specific

S. Houghton-Walker (✉)
Gonville & Caius College, Cambridge, UK

Centre for John Clare Studies, Cambridge, UK
e-mail: sh250@cam.ac.uk

S. Kövesi, E. Lafford (eds.), *Palgrave Advances in John Clare Studies*, Palgrave Advances,
https://doi.org/10.1007/978-3-030-43374-1_7

137

earlier works, the adoption of recognised stanza and other forms and rhymes, and the poem's revisiting of ideas and of words. The various repetitions of the *Calendar*, however, involve subtle negotiations of constancy and change. This chapter looks at some ways in which repetition is important to Clare's *Calendar*, focusing on 'November' in particular. Thinking about the repetition necessary to knowledge, the chapter will suggest that because Clare's understanding of repetition conceptually accommodates alteration, it goes some way to negotiating the problematic tensions between particular and general which trouble the poet's own perception of the possibility of accurate description of the objective world.

Several poems in Clare's *Calendar* depict the handing-down of oral histories and stories at particular moments of the year. In this way, traditional knowledge exists in a symbiotic relationship with the means of its reproduction (a reiterative form of narrative which actually constitutes one definition of 'repetition' in the *OED*, and one in which the shepherd's wife plays a full part in 'January: A Cottage Evening'). In 'June', labourers 'wi scraps of songs & laugh & tale/Lighten their anual toils'[2]; in 'September', storytelling is an inevitable part of the relaxation of harvest supper[3]; in 'December', 'The harmless laugh & winter tale' charm the family gathered '[a]round the glowing hearth at night'.[4] But whereas other months of the poem celebrate and commemorate the songs and stories that villagers recite, 'November' experiments with echoes and allusions which appeal to specifically literary knowledge. The poem appears self-consciously to be exploiting the wider possibilities of literary repetition, in its texture, through its form, and in its relations to convention. It is perhaps not a coincidence that this experimentation takes place in the month of Clare's *Calendar* most obviously tied to a particular formal tradition of verse. Michael O'Neill has argued that poems of the Romantic period became increasingly 'energized and subtilized by their consciousness of themselves as poems'; in 'November', this consciousness is evident in Clare's engagement with convention.[5] Written in Spenserian stanzas, 'November' employs a form borrowed from the *Faerie Queene* and therefore looks directly at the author of the most obvious predecessor of Clare's *Calendar*. As Stephanie Kuduk Weiner puts it, the Spenserian stanza offers Clare 'a prestigious poetic tradition'[6]: Spenser's experimentations with different forms for various months, his use of textual apparatus and deliberate archaisms, and his looking back to earlier literatures all denote a poem interested in its status as a poem. The Spenserian is the most complex stanza form in *The Shepherd's Calendar*, adding to the sense of its being self-consciously, even ostentatiously, 'poetic'. And Clare is obviously indebted to Spenser in other formal ways: his experimentation with alliterative effects, for instance, as Mina Gorji has argued, is distinctly Spenserian (as Clare's own copy of Spenser discusses in its introduction).[7] 'Spenserian', moreover, does not merely denote a series of stylistic choices: Gorji has also situated Clare's *Calendar* within a shared popular antiquarian revival, 'in which poetry and popular culture were intimately linked'.[8] In all of these ways, Clare engages lightly but directly in discourse with his predecessor. Yet beyond the revisiting of familiar forms, structures and ideas, Clare's experiments with Spenserianism more significantly allow him a unique poetic voice, one deliberately resisting the inadequate (as Clare finds them) categories of 'lyric' or 'narrative'.

'November' is particularly interesting as a shepherd's calendar because of its treatment of the eponymous shepherd. A specific character, and also a general 'type', it is never entirely clear to what extent Clare's *Calendar* 'is' the eponymous shepherd's: is it about, by, or for him (or them)? Often, despite his titular role, Clare's shepherd is conspicuous by his absence. Whilst he does appear in Clare's long poem several times, those appearances are irregular, and often only implied (by a description of his dog, or his hut, for instance); when he features explicitly, the habitually shifting perspective of the poem consistently disrupts any emergent sense of confidence or conclusion about these questions. In many of the shepherd's appearances, he is not actually looking after sheep. The role of shepherd was a significant one in the early nineteenth century, usually entailing almost total preoccupation, though shepherds occasionally assisted with other farm work at pinch points in the agricultural year[9]; indeed, in 'August', shepherds 'share the harvests labours with the rest'.[10] However, it is notable throughout the *Calendar* that when he isn't dipping, or shearing, or feeding his sheep, Clare's shepherd usually adopts the posture of observer: he listens; he imagines; he spies; he dreams. In an exemplary passage in 'March', 'as his eye percieves/Sun threads', even the shepherd boy 'Wi fancy thoughts his lonliness beguiles'; a few lines later,

> He hears the wild geese gabble oer his head
> & pleasd wi fancys in his musings bred
> He marks the figurd forms in which they flye
> & pausing follows wi a wondering eye
> Likening their curious march in curves or rows
> To every letter which his memory knows[11]

Observation and reflection inevitably prompt imagination (and in this example, almost literally become writing).[12] In 'November', the shepherd appears explicitly as a forecaster, creating a connection between observation, knowledge, and prediction embedded within the calendar and almanac tradition itself, and wholly relevant to an interest in repetition.

Despite the ostensibly blank sameness with which 'November' opens, the shepherd appears through the gloominess specifically as an observer whose habitual watching is thwarted by the elements:

> For days the shepherds in the fields may be
> Nor mark a patch of sky—blind fold they trace
> The plains that seem wi out a bush or tree
> Wistling aloud by guess to flocks they cannot see[13]

Prized usually for their unremitting attention to their flock, Clare's shepherds (plural here) are depicted in a relentless failure to see (and I'd like to think there's a little shepherding pun in Clare's description of them as 'blind fold', which reiterates the sense of being enclosed by the weather conditions). However, 'mark' can mean to notice, and to remark, or mark down. Such reporting might be directed to others, or be purely a remarking to oneself: either way, in recording a process of reflection, the self-consciousness of Clare-the-poet as a poet is reinforced. The knowledge possessed by the poet is both in the outward looking at, and in the reflection on. In this way, the poem replicates the gentle bivalence of the calendar and almanac, which list the days to come, but which also imply a memorialised or recorded version of the past: almanacs both make predictions, and catalogue anniversaries and archived statistics; a calendar charts future dates, but in its verbal form looks backwards, meaning 'to list'.[14] Moreover, 'marking' suggests another connection between observation and poetry, as the 'trace' in the landscape here blurs by implication with the written mark/trace on the page. The shepherd therefore is both a kind of poet, observing and recording despite his limited prospect, and the subject of the poem, being observed and written about. Throughout the *Calendar*, the shepherd oscillates between sharing the knowledge and vision of the observing poet and being the object of the poet's gaze; between being an almost-lyric subject and the narrative object. In 'February', for example, he is explicitly 'seen' in the very act of close observation, bending over his hook.[15] This oscillation might merely be a consequence of disagreements between Clare and his publishers during the genesis of the poem. In October 1823, Hessey, stumbling over a Johnsonian privileging of generality over specificity, was complaining that Clare's descriptions were

> [...] too personal to excite much Interest—their wants a human interest—a Story or a more particular delineation of character, and this might easily be given from the experience *you* must have had of life as well as from your own power of Invention & Combination.[16]

How to make writing simultaneously less 'personal', and more 'from the experience *you* must have had of life'? Yet the particular subjectivity of the shepherd as I have described it is, I think, the result of something more sophisticated than a confused reaction to Hessey's demands. Rather, it can more positively be seen as a fundamental strength of the poem, a productive resistance to conventional boundaries of lyric or narrative verse correspondent with Clare's shifting vision and focus throughout the *Calendar* more generally, which function to represent as accurately as it is possible to manage the poet's 'knowledge' of the scene. Such knowledge is constituted by the world Clare describes so particularly, but it is inevitably mediated through a sense of limitation, or distance from that which he describes. As his shepherd pivots between specific character and general type, Clare's fluctuating focus manages to represent exactly this.

Responding to Paul Fussell's claim that the Spenserian stanza is not 'used alone for lyric purposes: it is found primarily as a narrative vehicle',[17] Adam White argues that Clare 'makes the Spenserian form over and again serve lyric ends', and decisively separates Clare's Spenserian fragments from conventional Romantic Spenserianism.[18] If we accept Clare's interest in the possibilities Spenserian form might offer for lyric expression, it seems that 'November' develops its implications: the *Calendar* consistently explores the limits of, and traverses the boundaries between, narrative description of figures in the rural landscape, and lyric expression of the response to that landscape. *The Shepherd's Calendar* is not 'about' Clare-the-poet, and we are never supposed to think that Clare-the-poet 'is' the shepherd. Nor is it straightforwardly 'about' a shepherd characterised fully enough to be the source of lyric expression; it isn't, then, straightforwardly a lyric poem. But neither is it straightforwardly narrative. Instead, it adopts a posture of lyricism which yet preserves the sense of narrative distance Clare understands to be the inevitable condition of the poet. In numerous places, Clare records a sense that his own maturity has initiated an awareness of involvement in rural activity which is at odds with the nature of the traditions taking place, and which confers an inability to participate fully in the community; he frequently inscribes in his work an acute consciousness of his consequent, problematic position as observer. This is registered most subtly in those poems in which that sense of distance is acknowledged, and the inability truly to 'know' (or to experience) the subject of the poem therefore recognized: truly to know would entail being totally consumed by the scene in an unselfconscious way that precluded writing about it.[19] But if the nature of things can only be discovered through involvement, how can the observing poet be faithful in his description? Simply to record a sense of distance would be to neglect the accurate representation of the scene in favour of too great an emphasis on the poet. To be truly descriptive, therefore, the poet must acknowledge the struggle to accommodate close description with distance. In the *Calendar,* we can see Clare managing this characteristic dilemma through the figure of the shepherd: whether the poem's focus is on the shepherd (and by extension, the rural community in its widest sense which he inhabits and alongside which he coexists) as a lyric or narrative subject therefore remains necessarily uncertain and shifting. Far from being a deficiency, this resistance to fixed categories of narrative or lyric is one of the work's most significant achievements, and 'November' exemplifies the way in which it is enabled by engagement with poetic convention, through the Spenserian stanzas in which the month is written.

In his history of changes to the habits of attending to poetry, Peter McDonald argues that in the early nineteenth century, 'the capacity for close, attentive listening was taking hold, both in poetry itself and among the admirers of poets like Wordsworth and Keats'; by 1814, Leigh Hunt was '[i]nsisting on 'attention' to the sound of verse'.[20] Clare's own capacity for careful listening to verse is acutely evident in, for example, his parodies and imitations, both of which are specialised forms of repetition, and his recognition of his poetry's foundation in oral forms. Against this background of heightened awareness of aural attention, it is significant that, in the absence of their capacity to see, 'November' establishes its shepherds as attentive listeners. This self-conscious acknowledgement of the significance to the poem of noticing sound (one might say, of being attentive to poetry) edges into the peripheral awareness of the reader as the poem proceeds. Carefully listening, the shepherds of 'November' are almost literally whistling in the wind, trying to grasp animals 'they cannot see' (line 9), hoping that the animals in turn will respond to the sounds they make. From its first lines, this is a poem fascinated by what can't be seen or known directly, and the sense that must be made nonetheless: however much we are dealing in the language of seeming, and guessing, and blindness, the shepherds continue to trace and whistle, and Clare in turn continues to trace them and their activity (though if he were purely recording the scene, Clare would presumably face the same blanketing obscurity as the shepherds, and could depict only his own experience of the bewildering weather). The portrayal of disorientating fog which necessitates the behaviour of the shepherds is surely there because that's what the weather can be like in November. But it facilitates a shift to a more self-conscious type of writing, calling attention to itself as writing (just as the passage on the thatchers in lines 133–135 focuses on their struggle to work, rather than their work itself), and furthermore calling attention to the act of paying attention. In 'November', any reader who takes up the hint to participate in attentive listening is richly rewarded.

The most obvious form of repetition in the poem is rhyme; palpably, as McDonald points out, 'rhyme carries with it inescapably the burden of repetition, for a rhyme does repeat a sound',[21] and the Spenserian rhyme scheme lends a definite, secure sense of repetition through form. However, Clare's rhymes are not confined to line endings. Given the limited number of sounds in English, any analysis might identify some degree of sound-repetition within a whole stanza, but, in 'November', such sound-repetitions repeatedly have particular and discernible effects. In the first stanza, for example, in the very lines which are interested in the idea of not noticing, 'For' (a word which looks forward, and suggests a sense of purpose or meaning) rhymes with 'Nor' (inevitably a negative, pulling backwards), mirroring the sense of thwarted progression which the stanza works to build; these words appear at the start of consecutive lines, further enhancing this effect (just as we think we're getting going, just as for the shepherds, the mist comes down). Producing a different type of effect, [s] sounds susurrate through line 9, to half-enact the 'Whistling aloud by guess to flocks they cannot see' it describes. Then, the final word of the stanza, 'see', is one to which we have been tuning our ears since the first verb in line 1, where 'The village sleeps ...'. As well as in the C rhymes (be / tree /see) of the stanza, the [iː] sound is picked up in 'Beamless' (line 3), 'sleeping' (line 5), and 'seem' (line 8). All of these words oscillate around ideas of a lack of clarity in tune with the bewildering obscurity the stanza portrays, and in contrast with the knowledge which the 'see[ing]' of the final line might confer, if only it were possible. Of course, it isn't possible ('they cannot see'), and so the confusion is further emphasised. Other rhyme effects initiate a more subtle disorientation, entirely fitting to the bewildering mistiness of 'November'. In the first line, for example, '**from mor**n' mirrors a sequence of letters, and thus their sound, in a way peculiarly appropriate to a stanza which describes a day indistinguishable from itself, yet in which clock-time moves ever onwards. Reversal-rhyme exists in the early lines of the next stanza, too: as Clare describes the unusual behaviour of the hare, the vowel sounds of 'grassy **lare**' in line 2 are picked up and swapped round in 'sc**ar**cly st**ar**tles' in line 3; the same inversion also occurs in lines 1 (h**are**/h**alf**) and 4 (b**ar**king/th**ere**). This sense of substitution is similarly appropriate to a stanza about familiar things appearing strange in a muffling climate. Attention to diurnal transit recurs as 'sun' (line 2) is heard behind 'done' (line 4) in stanza 1. But 'done' refers to the moon of line 3; bringing sun and moon together in this way (as well as through their shared 'if the …' constructions) emphasises the diurnal cycle with which Clare's poem is preoccupied.

The oscillation involved in such artfully understated manipulation of rhyming sounds demands a particular kind of aural alertness. More marked is the way in which Clare's rhymes often appear in the middle of lines, and can therefore be disorientating despite the rigidity of the Spenserian form. The hare appears mid-line, but 'hare' rhymes with the second stanza's B end-rhymes (l**are** /th**ere** /st**are**/forb**eer**). Heard, rather than read, when 'lare' throws us back to 'hare', it is easy to blur the structure of the stanza: did a line possibly end on 'hare' after all? Is this really a Spenserian stanza, or are the line divisions to be found in other places? A similar example occurs at the very opening of the poem:

> The village sleeps in mist from morn till noon
> & if the sun wades thro tis wi a face
> Beamless & pale & **round** as if the moon
> When done the journey of its nightly race
> Had **found** him sleeping & supplyd his place
>   (lines 1–5)

The ABABB rhyme here is undemanding. But line 3 demands a pause after 'round' (the clear effect of its ending a tricolonic list and its preceding a simile). 'Round' thus reaches out into the poem, almost as strongly as an end-rhyme word looking for its fulfilment. The instinct to dwell on 'round' is rewarded, its catching at the ear justified, when 'found' is subsequently heard in line 5 (that 'found' carries a connotation of successful seeking might further this sense of satisfaction). Abstracted from lineation on the page, a listener might well hear these as weighted equivalently to end-rhymes. None of these rhymes (and there are many more) necessarily draws attention to itself on a preliminary reading, and of course we can't be certain which are intuitive and which are more deliberatively employed. However, their subtle cumulative effect brilliantly replicates the sense the poem wants to communicate, of a day which is going on, which is progressing, but is doing so with a sense of disorientating sameness—repetition—and reaching backwards, demanding the attention of those participating in it, and of each reader.

Clare often reuses particular words in his poems; rather than suggesting a limited vocabulary, this accretive repetition usually functions productively. For example, the word 'rain' appears three times in stanzas 12–15 (line 109, line 123, line 130), and twice as 'beating rain' (line 123, line 130), where the felicitous rhyme of 'again' follows shortly after each instance, pertinently suggesting a relentless downpour. Taylor's cuts generally reduce the frequency of full repetition in 'November'; in this case, Taylor ensures that only one use of 'rain' remains, though, appropriately enough in a poem fascinated by repetitions, allows a second use of its rhyme word 'again'. It is possible that Clare's full repetition is a slip, and one he might have been glad for Taylor to eliminate. Nonetheless, Taylor's amendment reduces the strength of the deluge. But such repetitions can be more complex. In his 1800 'Note' to 'The Thorn', Wordsworth had urged a revaluation of the apparent tautology assumed to inhere in the repetition of words, insisting that 'cling[ing] to the same words' might be inevitable and desirable in view of the intense difficulty inherent in expressing 'impassioned feelings'.[22] Various more recent and broader studies of repetition have pointed out that perfect repetition is rendered impossible by the very fact of it being a repetition: in text or in life, a second instance cannot be identical to a first by virtue of its status as repetitious and secondary.[23] Despite the thread of nostalgia running through Clare's writing, which might imply a desire to return to a precisely similar previous state, he too repeatedly finds and is apparently content that repetition must accommodate change within it: the comforting 'same again' is often actually slightly different. In 'The Ravens Nest', for example, boys annually attempt to climb up to the inaccessible perch.[24] The ravens participate in a similarly conservative pattern, returning every year to the same tree. Yet just as a new generation of villagers participates in each renewed attempt, so Clare knows that the birds are not really the same birds (even if the poem speaks as if they are when it calls them 'ancient') but descendants of descendants; the nest itself, through its 'repair', is similarly both the same and different. As Jonathan Bate points out, the tradition 'identifies the village as […] constantly evolving but with necessary continuity'.[25] Just like 'The Ravens Nest', *The Shepherd's Calendar* is animated by a preoccupation with 'memorys' and continuity, but it ultimately depicts on textual and thematic levels cyclical repetition containing within itself continual change.

The shepherd's re-entry into 'November' is prefaced by the breaking storm:

> Dull for a time the slumbering weather flings
> Its murky prison round then winds wake loud
> Wi sudden start the once still forest sings
> Winters returning song cloud races cloud
> & the orison throws away its shrowd
> & sweeps its stretching circle from the eye
> Storm upon storm in quick succession crowd
> & oer the samness of the purple skye
> Heaven paints its wild irregularity
>
> (lines 73–81)

Enacted and reiterated by the [^] sound which drags through the line from 'Dull' to 'slumbering', we are rudely awoken from the day's torpor with the present tense violence of 'flings'. The 'in' sound occurs again in the following line, in 'winds'; if the mind expects a restrictive, lasso-like image of *wind*ing to follow 'prison', 'round' and 'flings', the assumed half-rhyme might cause a stumble, but the dominant 'in' sound is reconfirmed with the satisfaction of the end-rhyming 'sings', so that the wind is singing. It is whistling, too, through the abundant [s] and [ʃ] which are interspersed with repeated [w] sounds, not in the form of a pattern, but rather with resonant crescendos and diminuendos which mimic the 'wild irregularity' being described. (This is far stronger an effect on the ear than the eye, because the [s]/[ʃ] sounds sometimes belong to a soft c, and the [w] sounds to a ou.) '[C]loud races cloud'; 'storm upon storm': here again is sameness, repetition, and yet distinction: the storm that comes 'upon' another storm is not exactly the same, because it comes after the first. Read aloud, the stanza comes alive with the gale it is imagining. Writing about just these kinds of 'currents upon currents that wind into one flow by adding layers of anaphora, assonance, and leap-frogging repetition', Clare Jones has argued that 'It is a testament to the adroitness of Clare's manipulation of sound and sense that [...] the reader becomes swept up into the cyclical nature of sound [...] Clare's poetics of repetition are integral to the poetry itself'.[26] If there are no obvious patterns to these sounds in the stanza from 'November', there is a sense of swirling, of circling: even before it really starts, the weather is flinging its murky prison round, though there's no object here: it is a general encircling, picked up later in 'shroud' and most obviously in the sweeping, 'stretching circle' of the orison, but present also in the fact that the 'forest sings/Winters *returning* song' (my emphasis), and that the forest beings to sing in a line stuffed with a sense of change: the 'sudden start' (start is both a beginning and a jump, which renders the line so much more appropriate than Taylor's version, 'sudden stir') points out that previously the forest has been different, and still; 'once still' again recalls the forest's past, but 'still' clings on semantically to that past. This works on the level of subject, as well as its rendering in verse: the 'samness of the purple skye' behind the wild irregularity persists as its backdrop; something is constant here, even as the untamed storm passes over. *The Shepherd's Calendar*, like all almanacs, circulates around ideas of predictability and variability. The climax of 'November' is line 81, 'Heaven paints its wild irregularity', its significance signalled by its scansion (the shortened alexandrine) and the unusually long polysyllabic word, 'irregularity', as well as the punning irregularity of the rhyme itself. Drawing attention to itself metrically, however, the line is also thematically pivotal. 'Wild irregularity' is central to Clare's picturesque, characterising his aesthetic ideal. In this stanza's image of self-conscious artistry (the forest sings; Heaven paints), Clare's epitome of art is found in the natural world which the poet of the *Calendar* can only copy.

Clare's *Calendar* increasingly recognises the difficulties of accuracy, not only in a conventional 'how can I possibly put this into words?' way, but also in a 'how can I really know this in order to put it into words?' way. Clare registers a Johnsonian, enlightenment interest in specifics and generals, and its implications for what it might mean truly to 'know' something, and therefore to be able to represent it accurately. His insistence on precision in natural historical description consistently privileges accuracy over aesthetic fashion or whim. Yet the scientific pedigree of natural history conflicts with immediate, intimate description; it depends on repeated observation of specifics, only to identify generalities. Many critics have been drawn to discuss what 'knowledge' might mean to Clare, and it undoubtedly involves an understanding of the poet's relationship to the things he describes, as well as an objective accuracy. But Clare's desire for precise record in his writing must face the fact that nature, which is ultimately various, is static enough for representation only in a single instant/ instance. The cyclicality of the *Calendar* even more strongly insists on the almost paradoxical combination of repetition with change which life consistently exhibits. Clare's attempt to render the minutely particular (in nature; in life) must survive the demands of a generalising natural history if it is to be accurate, and therefore aesthetically valuable, according to his own terms.[27] Clare's *Calendar* acknowledges that seasonal change is both predictable (to an extent) and irregular (to an extent), facing the impasse between natural history and poetry directly by investing in forms of repetition which suggest repeatability and predictability, but which always ultimately exhibit subtle change. The falling back into the conventional picturesque aesthetic of 'wild irregularity' within a context which predicts the storm and thus renders it regular returns artistic agency, and consequently the ability to draw scientific generalities, to nature itself. Winter's 'returning song' makes the 'wild irregularity' entirely predictable, as well as gloriously unpredictable, and the painterly imagery in the stanza makes the connection between natural event and artistic rendering of it overt.

Clare worried about the effects of governing conventions upon verse, complaining about 'the old thread bare epithets'.[28] His sense of complicating distance from full participation in the community which might allow him properly to 'know' it, described above, amplifies this suspicion of convention: even the best descriptive verse can never accurately capture real experience, due to limitations in language, and in experience itself. Yet convention, in the form of literary allusion, is one of the ways in which Clare asserts his skill as a poet. Allusion is an explicit demonstration of literary self-consciousness, which allows Clare to navigate towards a place within literary tradition but simultaneously problematises his ability to recognise himself straightforwardly as a member of his own community. Allusion is also another form of repetition, and it plays an important part in 'November'. An early echo of *Macbeth* sounds in stanza three:

> The Owlet leaves her hiding place at noon
> & flaps her grey wings in the doubting light
> The hoarse jay screams to see her out so soon [...]
>
> (lines 19–21)

This echo is significantly figured through sound: the jay's scream. The onomatopoeic flap of the owl—actually the shrieker in *Macbeth*—is also sensed by the ear as much as the eye. Again, the lines emphasise the importance of listening to the poem, and thus to the village. Having faith in our own ears is justified when the allusion revives in stanza 10's 'old dame' and her cat, who 'wi fears alarm / Play[s] hurly burly races wi its tale' (lines 87–88): here are *Macbeth*'s witches, transmuted, domesticated; witches' words are tamed into a portrait of woman and frenzied pet. 'Alarm' also calls to Act V Sc 5 of *Macbeth*, where it is followed by Macbeth's imperative: 'blow wind'. In 'November', too, the winds are to blow, though the place of the poet-shepherd is to 'mark', to 'see', and thus to foretell the weather, not to direct it. But the idea of the alarm, which warns of what is about to happen, is changed in the old woman's perception into a present experience. The pain of her corns ('& while she stops her wheel her hands to warm/She rubs her shooting corns & prophecys a storm', lines 89–90), in its richly allusive context, is akin to the pricking thumbs of *Macbeth*'s witches, another indication of portentous events. But the foresight the old woman possesses is no less true because it is typical: the old woman's experience is physical and immediate (she sees the cat; her feet hurt) and also based in repeated experience and knowledge passed on by the community (this means a storm is on its way).

Clare's playful echoes of *Macbeth* support the validity of local prophecy rooted in careful attention. Certain types of prognostication were morally problematic in a period which sought to distance itself from unenlightened superstition,[29] but the kind of foreknowledge entailed in what Eric Robinson calls 'weather-consciousness' recurs in the *Calendar*.[30] In 'November', Clare's shepherd represents a way of knowing which seems prophetic but which actually is built upon the accrued wisdom of ages, amassed through repeated experience which is both individual and collective, formed through personal observation and handed down by stories and anecdotes themselves understood as reiterative. While almanacs undoubtedly formed part of this (and 'January' opens with an affectionate glance at a farmer reading 'old more' [line 13]), for Clare, observation of natural phenomena is primary. When he writes that ants 'lay their eggs to receive the warmth of the sun & the shepherd by observing their wisdom in this labour judges correctly of the changes of the weather in fact he finds it an infallible almanac',[31] the significant knowledge is not the shepherd's, via a figurative almanac; it is primarily the ants'. In the 1820s, agriculture and husbandry were incorporating increasingly scientific methods; contemporary farming books include systematic, evidence-based chapters on subjects including meteorology. Henry Stephens' *Book of the Farm*, for example, dating from the first half of the nineteenth century, remarks on 'the prescience actually attained by people whose occupations oblige them to be much in the open air and to observe the weather. In this way shepherds [...] have acquired such a knowledge of atmospherical phenomena as to be able to predict the advent of important changes of the atmosphere' (though several pages of technical discussion and summary subsequently suggest that a lifetime spent in the fields might easily be replaced by modern gadgets).[32] Nonetheless, Stephens asserts:

> Some writers affect to despise prognostics of the weather, classing them with quackery and superstition; but [...] natural objects may indicate symptoms of change in the atmosphere before any actually takes place in it to the extent to affect our senses.[33]

Stephen's book combines respect for older forms of knowledge with a future-facing faith in technology and science. Clare's poem looks back a lot; he is explicit that he is describing an economy in transition. But as Stephens acknowledges, the old ways of knowing were not suddenly proved wrong. Clare's shepherd watches, and therefore knows what is to come:

> The shepherd oft foretells by simple ways
> The weathers change that will ere long prevail
> He marks the dull ass that grows wild & brays
> & sees the old cows gad adown the vale
> A summer race & snuff the coming gale
> (lines 82–6)

—just as the old dame's knowledge is derived from painful experience and traditional understandings of her undignified corns. Unlike Gay's Cloddipole in *The Shepherd's Week*, who is undoubtedly an influence on the poem, Clare's dame is not ridiculous; these are ancient ways of prophesying weather, but they are no less accurate for their age. Clare's *Calendar* argues that predicting the future depends on careful observation rooted in the past, both on the part of the shepherd and the predictive cows here (who 'gad' despite being notably 'old', and therefore perhaps also possessed of a lifetime's experience). Moreover, the storm in 'November' arrives in the poem before the indications of its imminence: in another form of repetition, which replicates the accrual of general village knowledge over much longer time periods, we are assured of the event before we encounter the symptoms which presage it, so that we never need doubt the validity of the predictive knowledge.

Stanza 11 continues to flirt with half-echoes of *Macbeth*: though Clare's ludicrous, cross turkey seems a long way from Duncan's Scotland, cumulatively, Clare's allusions here (to portents, vapours, a toad, and b[r]oiling) generally reinforce the poem's preoccupation with knowing through foretelling and 'signs'. *Macbeth* hinges on what is known, specifically on apparently supernatural foresight which turns out to be rooted in facts that are perfectly natural (Macduff was born by caesarean; men can carry branches and thereby look like a moving wood). 'November' is also interested in prophecy, and there is certainly a place in the village community for superstition: stanza 3 is stuffed with it. But in the description of the phenomenon of the storm, subsequent events prove foretelling to be scientific knowledge as much as mystic art. That these allusions and echoes of *Macbeth* occur in what I've already described as the most self-consciously 'poetic' month of Clare's *Calendar* is again surely no coincidence. But Clare handles them brilliantly, because the poem never ceases to work entirely successfully on its own terms. Recognising (hearing) them might add something to a reader's experience, but it doesn't change the experience of the turkey or the dame; nor does it alter the status of weather prediction as it is understood by the community. If anything, it only reinforces the bivalence again: the minute specificity of what is going on, here and now, juxtaposed with the sense of *De Rerum Natura* that the possibility of successful allusion, and successful weather prediction, invokes. Because, counter-intuitively, it incorporates change; repetition therefore allows Clare to negotiate the impasse between specific and general which writing about the world otherwise might present.

The storm in 'November' might be disruptive, but it is generally cohesive: villagers, animals, even oaks in the forest, respond together to its shock. Yet whilst the ploughman 'hies for shelter' in 'the shepherds hut' (lines 118–26), the shepherd himself disappears from the poem until the storm is over and he 'hastes to his evening fire his cloaths to dry' (line 115): the prophetic knowledge of the beginning of the storm is replaced by the practical necessity of getting warm after it. Unlike the dame (the other prophetic figure in the poem), who moves from seeing signs to physically feeling her corns and thus being fully within the felt experience of the storm, the shepherd in his peculiar, almost-poet position remains on the edges of knowledge. The shepherd, who whistles, 'marks' signs, and 'foretells' the storm, and is therefore a kind of poet (composing, watching, and recording, even if only to himself), remains an observer. Again, the shepherd isn't Clare, and Clare isn't the shepherd, but because of his position as almost-lyric focus, he remains like Clare on the periphery of experience. Excluded by Clare from the event at the heart of the poem, he knows it will happen, but we can't see him experience it in a pure or unmediated form of perfect, participatory knowledge.

The fact that the shepherd (like many other individuals in the poem) is both a specific character and representative of a general 'type' is important here: the fluctuation between specific and general which this status allows itself articulates some of Clare's interest in different forms of knowledge, and indeed in the idea of 'knowledge' itself. It is therefore telling that in his cuts to the poem, Taylor removed much of the element of prediction: those characters who survived are those who respond to the storm's effects—the ploughman who 'hears' and 'hies'; the boy who shelters, having been transplanted, in Taylor's edition, from earlier in Clare's poem. This matters, because it reduces the particularity of the weather Clare's poem contains. In Taylor's version, getting wet is a consequence of the storm; in Clare's poem, the boy, like several other characters Taylor deletes, is soaked by the dampness of the day which precedes the storm. Taylor does not allow the characters who survive into his version to 'know' the storm in the sense that prediction implies: their knowledge is confined to sensory experience of the immediate moment, rather than being bound up with a historical bank of precedent experience which is both individual and collective.

Clare's writing is studded through with an awareness of the impossibility of simultaneously observing and participating-in. Self-consciousness about this posture precludes perfect repetition (in the sense of representation). If the intimate knowledge of fractional difference in the natural world is an impediment to the generalising tendencies of natural history, forms of repetition enable Clare to explore and to some extent address the resulting difficulties for expression. Poetry is therefore not only a consequence. It is also a source of knowledge itself: the repetitions which are integral to verse demonstrate the accommodation of difference in action. Repetitions in the world, just as in writing, are, Clare's poems register, never the same, but registering within themselves the sameness-with-difference (that is, the sense of approximation which is the best that descriptive writing may ever achieve), repetition allows Clare to record the sense of difference which necessarily attends knowing and experiencing second-hand. It is therefore vital not only to the texture of his verse but also to his writing down of the results of the attention to attention which run through his poems. As Tim Chilcott has suggested (in a more quantitative discussion of Clare's repetitions than mine has been, but one which just as surely argues for the effectiveness of Clare's use of repetition), repetition might instinctively seem to suggest something boring, dull, or lacking in originality.[34] However, in 'November', Clare exploits various forms of predictability, and his sense of the irregularity which necessarily attends it through his manipulation of repetition in various forms to craft a poem is not only a superbly rendered aesthetic object; it also manages to articulate through the poetic self-consciousness constantly exhibited, and with subtle skill, the posture of a poet who sits on the edge of the world he describes, feeling the awkwardness and sometimes the distress of his position even as he delights in the vantage point it lends.

NOTES

1. *John Clare: The Shepherd's Calendar; Manuscript and Published Version*, ed. Tim Chilcott (Manchester: Carcanet, 2006). References in this chapter will be to Clare's (manuscript) version on the verso pages of Chilcott's edition, unless otherwise stated.
2. Chilcott, *Shepherd's Calendar*, 114, lines 67–8.
3. Chilcott, *Shepherd's Calendar*, 156, lines 131–8.
4. Chilcott, *Shepherd's Calendar*, 192, lines 138 and 137.
5. Michael O'Neill, introduction to *Romanticism and the Self-Conscious Poem* (Oxford: Oxford Scholarship Online, 1997). DOI: https://doi. org/10.1093/acprof:oso/9780198122852.001.0001.
6. Stephanie Kuduk Weiner, 'John Clare's Speaking Voices: Dialect, Orality, and the Intermedial Poetic Text', *Essays in Romanticism* 25.1 (2018): 100. For further illustration of Spenser's engagement with literary heritage, see, for example, Lynn Staley Johnson, *The Shepheardes Calender: An Introduction* (University Park: Penn State Press, 2010), and David Norbrook, *Poetry and Politics in the English Renaissance* (London: Routledge and Kegan Paul, 1984).
7. See Mina Gorji, *John Clare and the Place of Poetry* (Liverpool: Liverpool University Press, 2008), 84.
8. Gorji, *Place of Poetry*, 96.

9. See, for example, Jonathan Brown, *Shepherds and Shepherding* (Oxford: Shire Publications, 2013), 11: 'The status of the shepherd was recognized by the nineteenth-century census returns, which gave him an entry in the occupational returns separate from the other agricultural workers'; see also Henry Stephens, *The Book of the Farm*, 3 vols (Edinburgh and London: Blackwood, 1844), 1: 225–6.

10. Chilcott, *Shepherd's Calendar*, 140, line 112.

11. Chilcott, *Shepherd's Calendar*, 60, lines 100–01; 102; 107–12.

12. For further examples of the shepherd's observing and imagining, see Chilcott, *Shepherd's Calendar*, 'March', 56, lines 4–10 and 60, lines 97–112; 'April', 74, lines 41–2, and 80, lines 155–6; 'July', 124 and 126, lines 16–54; and 'August', 142, lines 147–8.

13. Chilcott, *Shepherd's Calendar*, 172, lines 6–9.

14. See, for example, Clare's use of the verbal form, 'to Calendar', when listing the 'perplexd multitude' of women with whom he has had relationships: *By Himself*, 29.

15. Chilcott, *Shepherd's Calendar*, 44, lines 37–8.

16. Hessey to Clare, 13 October 1823, in *Critical Heritage*, 194.

17. Paul Fussell, *Poetic Meter and Poetic Form* (New York: Random House, 1979), 148.

18. See 'John Clare's Spenserian Lyric Fragments', *JCSJ* 33 (2014): 73; 78.

19. One of the best examples of a poem exhibiting this problematic self-consciousness is 'St Martins Eve' (*Middle Period*, 3: 269–78), but similarly, Clare is unable to share in Lubin's 'struck supprise' or to join in the general mirth in 'The Village Minstrel' (*Early Poems*, 2: 123–179 [esp. line 528; lines 596–9]). In *The Shepherd's Calendar* itself, 'December—Christmas' insists that the abandoned 'mirth' shared in 'boyish days' (lines 113–6) is now lost, though not forgotten. For further illustration and discussion of these characteristics, see Sarah Houghton-Walker, 'The 'Community' of John Clare's Helpston', *SEL* 46, 4 (Autumn 2006): 796–97, or Sarah Houghton, 'John Clare and Festivity', *JCSJ* 23 (2004): 30–37.

20. Peter McDonald, *Sound Intentions: The Workings of Rhyme in Nineteenth Century-Poetry* (Oxford: Oxford University Press, 2012), 27.

21. McDonald, *Sound Intentions*, 18.

22. William Wordsworth, 'Note' to 'The Thorn,' in *Lyrical Ballads*, ed. R.L. Brett and A.R. Jones (London and New York: Routledge, 1984), 288–9.

23. See, for example, Bruce F. Kawin, *Telling It Again and Again; Repetition in Literature and Film* (Ithaca: Cornell University Press, 1972); Edward Said, 'On Repetition', in *The World the Text and the Critic* (Cambridge, MA: Harvard University Press, 1983), 111–125, and Gilles Deleuze, *Difference and Repetition*, trans. Paul Patton (London: Bloomsbury, 2014).

24. *Middle Period*, 3: 559–61. See 559, line 2.
25. Jonathan Bate, 'The Rights of Nature', *JCSJ* 14 (1995): 14.
26. Clare Jones, 'John Clare, Rhymer' (M.Phil diss., University of Cambridge, 2018), 32.
27. For recent critical attention to Clare, specificity and generality, see Stephanie Kuduk Weiner, 'Exemplary Figures in Clare's Descriptive Poems', *JCSJ* 36 (2017): 57–66; Michael Falk, '*The nightjar's shriek: nature's variety in the sonnets of John Clare and Charlotte Smith*', *JCSJ* 36 (2017): 31–48, and Kelsey Thornton, 'The Transparency of Clare', *JCSJ* 21 (2002): 65–79.
28. J.W. and Anne Tibble, *The Prose of John Clare* (London: Routledge and Kegan Paul, 1951), 172.
29. See Ian Bostridge, *Witchcraft and its Transformations, c.1650–c.1750* (Oxford: Clarendon Press, 1997), 1–2.
30. Eric Robinson, 'John Clare and Weather Lore', *JCSJ* 14 (1995): 74.
31. Tibble, *Prose*, 200.
32. Stephens, *Book of the Farm*, 1: 230.
33. Stephens, *Book of the Farm*, 1: 292.
34. Tim Chilcott, 'John Clare's Language', *JCSJ* 35 (2016): 7.

BIBLIOGRAPHY

Bate, Jonathan. 'The Rights of Nature'. *JCSJ* 14 (1995): 7–15.
Bostridge, Ian. *Witchcraft and its Transformations, c.1650–c.1750.* Oxford: Clarendon Press, 1997.
Brown, Jonathan. *Shepherds and Shepherding.* Oxford: Shire Publications, 2013.
Chilcott, Tim. 'John Clare's Language'. *JCSJ* 35 (2016): 5–21.
Clare, John. *John Clare By Himself.* Edited by Eric Robinson and David Powell. Ashington: Carcanet/MidNAG, 1996.
———. *The Shepherd's Calendar; Manuscript and Published Version.* Edited by Tim Chilcott. Manchester: Carcanet, 2006.
———. *The Early Poems of John Clare.* 2 vols. Edited by Eric Robinson and David Powell. Oxford: Clarendon Press, 1989.
———. *Poems of the Middle Period.* 5 vols. Edited by Eric Robinson, David Powell and P.M.S Dawson. Oxford: Clarendon, 1996–2003.
Deleuze, Gilles. *Difference and Repetition.* Trans. Paul Patton. London: Bloomsbury, 2014.
Falk, Michael. 'The nightjar's shriek: nature's variety in the sonnets of John Clare and Charlotte Smith'. *JCSJ* 36 (2017): 31–48.
Fussell, Paul. *Poetic Meter and Poetic Form.* New York: Random House, 1979.
Gorji, Mina. *John Clare and the Place of Poetry.* Liverpool: Liverpool University Press, 2008.

Houghton, Sarah. 'John Clare and Festivity'. *JCSJ* 23 (2004): 21–43.
Houghton-Walker, Sarah. 'The 'Community' of John Clare's Helpston'. *SEL* 46. 4 (Autumn 2006): 781–802.
Jones, Clare. 'John Clare, Rhymer'. M.Phil diss., University of Cambridge, 2018.
Kawin, Bruce F. *Telling It Again and Again; Repetition in Literature and Film.* Ithaca: Cornell University Press, 1972.
McDonald, Peter. *Sound Intentions: The Workings of Rhyme in Nineteenth Century-Poetry.* Oxford: Oxford University Press, 2012.
Norbrook, David. *Poetry and Politics in the English Renaissance.* London: Routledge and Kegan Paul, 1984.
O'Neill, Michael. *Romanticism and the Self-Conscious Poem.* Oxford: Oxford Scholarship Online, 1997. https://doi.org/10.1093/acprof:oso/9780198122852.001.0001.
Robinson, Eric. 'John Clare and Weather Lore'. *JCSJ* 14 (1995): 61–79.
Said, Edward. 'On Repetition'. In *The World the Text and the Critic*, 111–125. Cambridge, MA: Harvard University Press, 1983.
Staley Johnson, Lynn. *The Shepheardes Calender: An Introduction.* University Park: Penn State Press, 2010.
Stephens, Henry. *The Book of the Farm.* 3 vols. Edinburgh and London: Blackwood, 1844.
Storey, Mark, ed. *John Clare: The Critical Heritage.* London: Routledge & Kegan Paul, 1973.
Thornton, Kelsey. 'The Transparency of Clare'. *JCSJ* 21 (2002): 65–79.
Tibble, J. W. and Anne. *The Prose of John Clare.* London: Routledge and Kegan Paul, 1951.
Weiner, Stephanie Kuduk. 'Exemplary Figures in Clare's Descriptive Poems'. *JCSJ* 36 (2017): 57–66.
———. 'John Clare's Speaking Voices: Dialect, Orality, and the Intermedial Poetic Text'. *Essays in Romanticism* 25.1 (2018): 85–100.
White, Adam. 'John Clare's Spenserian Lyric Fragments'. *JCSJ* 33 (2014): 73–86.
Wordsworth, William. 'Note' to 'The Thorn'. In *Lyrical Ballads*, edited by R. L. Brett and A.R. Jones, 288–9. London and New York: Routledge, 1984.

John Clare's Dynamic Animals

James Castell

John Goodridge describes 'Little Trotty Wagtail' and 'I Am' as John Clare's 'two most anthologised poems'.[1] It is also worth noticing the striking difference between these two poems, which are among the most widely read of Clare's work. The more critically celebrated poem, 'I Am', struggles with self-definition and longing. For Timothy Morton, it is an exemplar of Clare's potential for thinking a 'dark ecology' without nature.[2] In contrast, 'Little Trotty Wagtail' is more critically neglected and often relegated to anthologies for children.[3] However, I want to suggest that 'Little Trotty Wagtail' is more than an asylum poem of surprising joy and 'childish humour' as Arthur Symons described it at the beginning of the twentieth century.[4] Instead, this poem highlights an important but comparatively undervalued aspect of Clare's poetic engagements with animals: Clare's animals move.

The behaviour of the personified bird in 'Little Trotty Wagtail' is recorded, above all, by its varied movements: 'he went in the rain', 'tittering tottering sideways he near got straight again', 'he stooped to get a

J. Castell (✉)
Cardiff University, Cardiff, UK
e-mail: castellj@cardiff.ac.uk

S. Kövesi, E. Lafford (eds.), *Palgrave Advances in John Clare Studies*, Palgrave Advances,
https://doi.org/10.1007/978-3-030-43374-1_8

157

worm', he 'look'd up to catch a fly', 'he flew away', 'he waddled in the mud', he 'left his little footmarks' and 'waggle went his tail'.[5] These physical movements are accompanied by considerable dynamism in the sound of a poem which is marked by conspicuous repetition and alliteration. Indeed, the language and form of 'Little Trotty Wagtail' are characterised by movement and transformation as much as the eponymous bird. Although comparatively common in Clare's usage, the more conventional adjective 'nimble' is used as a verb in 'you nimble all about' (line 9).[6] The wagtail's unusual epithet 'trotty' inverts the structure and changes what is more customarily a verb into an adjective. Although the *OED* does not record the use in this poem (its first recorded example is in 1891 for something of 'daintily small proportions'), 'trotty' is a striking coinage on Clare's part which, in alluding to quadrupedal and specifically equine motion, gently aggrandises the wagtail at the same time as the word 'little' diminishes it.[7] Inanimate objects also move in this poem: the 'dimpling water pudge' is disturbed by both bird and rain (line 10). Even words that are not conventionally associated with movement are affected in the texture of the poem's loose hexameters. As a result, 'chirrup' is strikingly deployed not to describe the bird's sound, but instead the motion of its wings as the bird 'chirrupt up his wings to dry upon the garden rail' (line 8). As Seamus Heaney put it with respect to a different poem, these linguistic shifts make this poem 'as surely made of words as one by Mallarmé'.[8] In 'Little Trotty Wagtail', Clare's use of language produces a fleetness of foot in both bird and poem that is not incompatible with its simultaneous awkwardness. Indeed, the charm of 'Little Trotty Wagtail' derives at least partly from how it holds an airy, avian deftness and a sodden, terrestrial clumsiness in poetic tension.

Clare's animals move in three senses. Firstly, they move physically in space. Secondly, they move affectively in the responses of those who encounter them. Thirdly, they move in the formal texture of his poetry. Although Clare is frequently praised for his natural historical accuracy and his oeuvre has become central to ecocritical debates, the dynamism of the animals in his poetry has been less frequently addressed. Instead, critics have tended to focus on how Clare's poetic attention is caught by the nests of birds and other animals. There are good reasons for this focus, but there are also consequences to it which skew our perspective on Clare's writing, including the role that his work might play in thinking about our own age of environmental crisis. I will return to some critical examples and these broader concerns at the end of this chapter. For now, I want to start by turning to a few examples of Clare's moving creatures (including a range of birds, a snail and some migrating frogs), before considering a selection of the poetry that he writes about one particularly dynamic animal: the swallow.

The attention which Clare pays to animals has long been central to criticism of his work. In an unsigned review from 1820 in the *New Monthly Magazine*, Clare is described as looking on 'animals with the eye of a naturalist, and his accuracy, in this respect, shews that he has been a watchful observer of their habits'.[9] Nearly two hundred years later, Onno Oerlemans describes Clare as 'the first great animal poet—a poet for whom animals, animality, and the diversity of species were central themes'.[10] The rise of ecocriticism and animal studies has led to more readings of animal encounters in Clare's poetry than it would be possible to list, ranging from an interest in animal rights to work on the acoustics of bird song.[11] Few critics, however, have focused explicitly on Clare's animals in motion.[12] This is surprising since movement is considered a defining—if not universal—characteristic of animals.[13] Furthermore, Clare's poetry is full of moving creatures. A sonnet from the Northborough period—'The wild duck startles like a sudden thought'[14]—is representative. Before it closes with the small birds that 'nestle in the hedge below', it spends thirteen of its fourteen lines evoking the striking manoeuvres of different birds in the air: 'The flopping crows on weary wing go bye', 'The crowds of starnels wiz and hurry', 'The larks like thunder rise and suthy round', 'The wild swan hurrys high', 'the magpie winnows on' (lines 14, 3, 5, 7, 9 and 12).

When Clare describes his boyhood passion for 'watching the habits of birds' and other creatures, he describes to a considerable extent their movements: he explains how he loved to see 'the wood pecker s[w]eeing away in its ups and downs' and how he often pulled his hat over his 'eyes to watch the rising of the lark or to see the hawk hang in the summer sky and the kite take its cycles round the wood'.[15] In this passage, Clare demonstrates impressive sensitivity to the variety of movement in birds which successively swing, ascend, float and circle. The birds move in space and the birds move Clare to observation. The birds also move his language to two compact metaphors which redouble the sense of movement: Clare describes how 'I heard the cuckoo's "*wandering* voise" and the *restless* song of the Nightingale and was delighted while I pausd and mutterd its sweet jug jug as I passd its black thorn bower' (my italics).[16] There are many examples of humans imitating nightingales in Clare's writing, including a celebrated attempt to translate nightingale song into verse, and the effect is frequently to distance the imitation from the animal as much as it is to bring it into closer proximity.[17] In this passage, however, the predominant effect is that the language perpetuates the paragraph's preceding interest not only in sound but also in movement. Clare passes the bower and the songs are restless, but so is his language which is pushed to wander as far as animal imitation and a quotation from Wordsworth.

It is perhaps unsurprising to find a potential for literal and textual travel in the flight patterns of Clare's birds and their song. But Clare also pays attention to more counter-intuitive examples of movement. In a journal entry from April 1825, he describes how 'I observed a Snail on his journey at full speed & I markd on my watch that he went 13 Inches in 3 minutes which was the utmost he could do without stopping to wind or rest'.[18] In one of his natural history letters, he extends an understanding of the snail's pace to the snail itself, which 'has such a knowledge of its own speed that it can get home to a moment to be save from the sun' and can also time its sorties for food:

> when it has divided its time to its utmost by travelling to such a length as will occpoy all the rest of its spare time to return[,] its instinct will suddenly stop & feed on what it finds there & if it finds nothing it will go no further but return homwards & feed on what it chances to meet with[19]

Clare wrote about animal instinct elsewhere, suggesting that 'the instinct of the animal world is a most wonderful faculty', 'its conclusions are nicer than mathematical acurasy' and 'it seems even to be stronger than human reason[,] for the human mind to be perfect in any art which it chuses to follow is obligd to undergo a long & laborius instruction'.[20] Clare's position on the power—rather than the brutishness—of animal instinct is also reflected in his recognition of the snail's capacity to 'travel to the same spot as accurratly as if they knew geography or was guided by a mariners compass'.[21] For Clare, the snail travels further than the comparatively short distances of its physical range. It is transported by comparison ('as if they knew geography or was guided by a mariners compass') to a carto-graphic scale which zooms out capaciously in its evocation of global trans-portation networks. Through movement, the snail is also granted a greater capacity for knowledge than is conventionally attributed to the species. Observation of the snail's motion moves Clare to new natural historical understanding. It also leads him to religious insight: for Clare, 'the power of Instinct in the most trifling insect […] displays the omnipotence of its maker in an illustrus manner' and this proves that 'nature is a fine preacher

& her sermons are always worth attention'.[22] The movement of animals in Clare's writing extends their actions and meanings beyond any singular domain of significance.

Clare's interest in the speed of the snail reflects a broader sensitivity to the movement of diverse creatures from even his earliest verse. 'Summer Evening', for example, describes the motions of various birds heading home for the night: 'Crows crowd quaking over head/Hastening to the woods to bed' and 'Swallows check their rambling flight/ & twittering on the chimney light'.[23] The birds of day are quickly replaced by nocturnal creatures: 'Bats flit by in hood & cowl/ Through the barn hole pops the owl'; the beetle is 'Haunting every bushy place/Flopping in the labourers face'; 'the snail has made his ring'; and the 'moth with snowy wing […]/'Circles round in winding whirls, /Through sweet evening's sprinkled pearls' (lines 20–31). The movement of different animals in space marks the rhythm of diurnal time. Clare then turns to another terrestrial creature:

> From the hay cocks moistend heaps
> Frogs now take their Vaunting leaps
> & along the shaven mead
> Quickly travelling the[y] proceed
> Flying from their speckled sides
> Dewdrops bounce as grass divides
>
> (lines 41–6)

The 'Vaunting leaps' of the frogs interact with an already dynamic physical and linguistic environment: the haycocks have been 'moistend' by evening dew, the mead has been 'shaven' during the day's labour, and drops of moisture fly off the frogs' bodies into the dividing grass, which further recalls the 'sprinkled pearls' in the preceding lines on the moth. The noun 'drops' and the adjectival past participles 'speckled' and 'sprinkled' resonate with the motion of their associated verb forms. Furthermore, the frogs are not simply moving in this passage: they are, to use Clare's word, 'travelling', they are deliberately proceeding from one place to another, they are making a journey. As with the snail, the movement of these frogs becomes transporting in more than one sense. In the sensitivity of this passage to amphibian motion and its interactions with the environment, the capacity of the frogs to 'travel' moves beyond being an anthropomorphic metaphor and extends towards affective motion in both physical space and the literary text.

Similar effects occur in a natural history letter where Clare describes having 'seen thousands of young frogs crossing a common after a shower':

> [...] early in the morning early risers may see swarms of young frogs leaving their birth place & emegrating as fast as they can hop to new colonys & as soon as the sun gets strong they hide in the grass as well as they are able to wait the approach of night to be able to start again but if in the course of the day showers happen to fall they instantly seize the chance & proceed on their journey till the sun looks out & puts a stop to their travelling again[24]

Once again, the movements suggest that Clare thinks of animal instinct as intelligent and responsive to changing environmental conditions rather than a mechanical reflex. Like his comparison of the snail's navigational abilities to the mariner's use of a compass, Clare superimposes a globalising vocabulary of migration and, indeed, empire on these nomadic amphibians: the frogs emigrate 'as fast as they can hop to new colonys'. The analogy is not casually deployed here: indeed, it is repeated at the end of this letter when Clare turns to consider water eels, as well as in a note on the behaviour of ants.[25] Furthermore, Clare's striking lexical choice connects these frogs to his own ambivalent attitude to potential—if never seriously considered—emigration.

In 'Autobiographical Fragments', Clare describes how his 'old love for parted places the heaths and woods and cowcommons around my native place wears out'. Nevertheless, he argues that

> [...] whenever I am surrounded by my family there is my comfort and if I was in the wilds of america with them for my companions there would my home be—but I am too old fashioned for the times I have no taste for the rage for emigration—if I cannot find peace[,] I dare not venture to look for it out of my country and therefore my emigration is but a short way[26]

Clare never went to America, although he said that he did later in his life when he was visited by Dean Dudley at the asylum in 1850.[27] This remains a remarkable passage, however. Firstly, it is unusual in offering a conception of home which is related more to companionship than it is to a particular place. Secondly, it rejects emigration but only to redefine it. Through the gentle assertion of its 'therefore', Clare's claim that 'my emigration is but a short way' turns a lack of power ('if I cannot find peace') into a virtue. But what does he mean by emigration which is 'but a short way'? The phrase is evocative because it is unexplained in the fragment. Still, there are also rich consequences that result from its connection to

Clare's dynamic animals, a connection which is especially convincing because 'emigration' is not a word used by Clare with particular frequency in other contexts.[28] Among other creatures, the travelling frogs enable Clare's writing to countenance a different sort of mobility to actual trans-atlantic crossings, a form of emigration which is physical and textual, which imaginatively transcends the separation of human and nonhuman, and which operates at multiple scales in all those domains. His 'short way' is, in other words, a modest expression of a far more expansive move, a move that is intimately connected to his written encounters with moving animals.

Few animals are more associated with movement and migration than swallows. Angela Turner traces this association across the etymologies of more than one language, pointing out that 'swallows are called birds of freedom, at home in the air' in Hebrew and that the 'Old English name for a swallow is *swealwe*, aptly meaning one that moves to and fro'.[29] Hirundines are remarkably agile and spend an unusual amount of time in the air preying on insects. They are, as Clare puts it, 'birds of passage' characterised by annual migrations across vast distances.[30] Swallows move in space, therefore, but their movement is a marker of time which extends beyond the daily cycles of the creatures that Clare describes in 'Summer Evening'. Turner, for example, highlights how hirundines 'symbolized spring in ancient Greece', an association which forms the proverb 'One swallow doesn't make spring'.[31] Clare's journal registers this significance in its careful recording of the seasonal departure and arrival of swallows: in September 1824, he writes that 'the swallows are flocking to gether in the sky ready for departing & a crowd has dropt to rest on the walnut tree w[h]ere they twitter as if they were telling their young stories of their long journey to cheer & check fears'; in October, he writes that he 'Observd to day that the Swallows are all gone' although by April 1825, he celebrates that the swallows have, once again 'made their appearance'.[32] The cyclical arrival of the swallows marks a temporal sequence which is bigger than any individual being or single species. Nevertheless, Clare is also perceptive about the potential fragility of seemingly permanent cycles: in the third natural history letter, he notes that nightingales, martins and swallows 'seem to diminish but for what cause I know not'.[33] For Clare, the movements of animals mark seasonal and annual change, but they also mark larger temporal periods of decline or plenty.

Clare's poetry, like his prose, is similarly sensitive to the connection between avian migration and the passage of time. In a manuscript from the early 1820s, Clare writes how 'By twittering swallows we pecieve/ That summers on the point to leave'.[34] In that drafting, the departure of the swallows marks the passing of another year. In a complementary, though incomplete, sonnet from the Northborough period, Clare describes the arrival of swallows as signifying the advent of summer: 'Aye once again thou bird of many shores/I mark thee on the hedges gathering awes' and the hedger 'sees the coming summer in thy face'.[35] In Clare's verse, the passage of swallows is often portrayed as a means for humans to tell the time. In a poem which begins with the question 'Whence goes the swallow tribes[?]' (a question answered with 'the pathless main/Neer chronicles their flight'), Clare describes how 'the wandering swallows bring/The plain unerring almanack of spring'.[36] The swallows are granted an almost supernatural agency in these lines which ties them to far greater forces of celestial motion. The poem draws a parallel between the 'aerial wanderers' and the sun which allows 'the sheep boy' to measure his 'lengthening shadow [...], his clock by which the time is told' (line 7, lines 9–11). In this respect, the movement of swallows airily participates in what Heaney describes in Clare's verse as a combination of 'a glutinous, hydraulic at-homeness in the district with a totally receptive adjustment to the light and heat of solar distances', as well as Clare's 'love for the inexorable one-thing-after-anotherness of the world'.[37] In other words, the varied attention that Clare pays to swallows demonstrates his interest in motion at far greater physical and temporal scales than might be suggested by the comparatively limited scope of the actual journeys he made in his lifetime.

Clare's apostrophe to the 'bird of many shores' demonstrates his understanding of swallow migration, but his question—'whence goes the swallow tribes[?]'—also draws attention to its obscurities for the period. As Margaret Grainger, Jonathan Bate and Alan Vardy have discussed, correspondence with James Hessey on swallows led to Clare starting to work on his own natural history.[38] When Hessey wrote to Clare about swallows, he advocated that Clare write a poem on the 'supposed sinking of the Swallow in the water at the approach of Winter'.[39] Whether swallows migrated or overwintered underwater or in caves had been the subject of considerable debate from antiquity. In the eighteenth century, celebrated ornithologists, including Gilbert White, Daines Barrington and Thomas Pennant, offered opinions on the subject.[40] By Clare's time, however, migration was already established as the most likely reason for their disappearance each winter. In 1817, Thomas Forster argued that there 'is sufficient evidence on record to establish the migration of birds of this genus', although, like White and Pennant, Forster continued to believe that 'while it is pretty certain that the greatest number of swallows migrate, it is not impossible that many individuals of each of the species may be concealed during winter near their summer haunts'.[41]

Clare's poetry suggests that he was more interested in the varied dynamics of swallow migration than he was in making the sort of speculations on their 'brumal retreat' that Hessey was proposing. Nevertheless, like Forster, Clare's attention was also attracted by swallows that appeared to linger through the winter in Britain and he writes about them in more than one sonnet. The final couplet of 'Aye once again thou bird of many shores' refers to how 'Nought but an odd one lingers here behind' in winter (lines 12–13). The idea is far more developed in a pair of sonnets entitled 'On Seeing Two Swallows Late in October'.[42] These swallows remain the 'Lone occupiers of a naked sky' in 'desolate november' when 'all your fellow tribes in many crowds/Have left the village with the autumn clouds':

> Forsaking all like untamed winds they roam
> & make with summers an unsettled home
> Following her favours to the farthest lands
> Oer untraced oceans & untrodden sands
>
> (lines 1–4, 9–12)

For a poet frequently figured as limited to a particular locality, this is a striking evocation of nonhuman creatures in exotic and indeed unexplored places. The swallows make an 'unsettled home' in motion as they are left chasing the sun from summer to summer, with a resonance expressed between swallows, 'untraced oceans' and 'untrodden sands' by the repeated negative prefix. The second sonnet begins by contrasting these elusive birds with the 'little lingerers' that remain 'to brave the chilly air'. Nevertheless, when offered hospitality by the speaker of the poem, these birds also have their own dynamic effects:

> I wish ye well to find a dwelling here
> For in the unsocial weather ye would fling
> Gleamings of comfort through the winter wide
> Twittering as wont above the old fire side
> & cheat the surly winter into spring
>
> (lines 24–8)

Like the emigration 'but a short way' described in 'Autobiographical Fragments', the lingering swallows have a capacity to move in their flinging 'gleamings of comfort' and their transforming of 'the surly winter into spring' which is equivalent to those that successfully departed. Clare's swallows demonstrate the capacity of even the same dynamic animal to move in a variety of different ways, at a variety of different scales, and in a variety of different contexts in his verse.

Such a multiplicity of motion and a multiplicity of signification can occur between two explicitly paired sonnets, like 'On Seeing Two Swallows Late in October'. But it can also occur across much greater distances in his writing. In fact, Clare's oeuvre is, in part, constructed by a web of variously dynamic animals with widely varying effects. For example, at the beginning of his poetic career, a powerful sense of nostalgia is created by the thought of absent swallows:

> Emigrating swallows now
> Sweep no more the green hills brow
> Nor in circuits round the spring
> Skim & dip their sutty wing.[43]

Towards the end of his life, however, a similar scenario produces a very different atmosphere of exuberant presence in 'The Swallow', a poem which is situated next to 'Little Trotty Wagtail' in William Knight's asylum transcriptions. Like its better-known counterpart, 'The Swallow' describes the repeated motions of a bird in language which is also marked by considerable repetition. Indeed, the poem begins with the speaker's own repeated request for repetition:

> Pretty Swallow once again
> Come and pass me i' the rain
> Pretty swallow why so shy
> Pass again my window by[44]

The speaker's request is granted not only by the swallow's movement, but also by other elements in the environment which interact with it:

> The horse pond where he dips his wings
> The wet day prints it full o' rings
> The rain drops on his airy track
> Lodge like pearls upon his back

Then agen he dips his wing
In the wrinkles of the spring
Then o'er the rushes flies again
And pearls roll off his back like rain

(lines 5–12)

These quatrains describe a straightforward event: a bird touches a body of water on a rainy day twice in succession. But, like the description of the travelling frogs in 'Summer Evening', the language of the poem produces a series of relationships which entangle the separate parts in a situation of remarkable complexity and reciprocity. The swallow dips his wings in the pond, which creates a ripple, but the rain also imprints its own lines and circles of agitation on the surface of the water. This is itself a repetition from the 'dimpling water pudge' of 'Little Trotty Wagtail' and 'The Swallow' feels in many ways like a repetition of the poem which precedes it in Knight's manuscript. Nevertheless, there are also many differences. In 'The Swallow', there is a greater sense of hirundine gracefulness in the repetitions. The rain lodges 'like pearls' on the swallow's back before the simile becomes reliteralised and the 'pearls roll off his back like rain'. This poem is characterised by avian and hyetal motions which repeat and thus have repeated effects, and such repetition is itself redoubled in the form of the poem. These two quatrains begin with lines that end in the same way, a form of distance epiphora, which also demands the deployment of repeated rhymes for the first couplets of both. Both quatrains also contain the word 'pearls' and end with a simile. Nevertheless, such similarities do not mire this poem in stasis. Instead, each repetition also marks progression. When the 'pearls rolls off his back like rain', they are no longer rain but instead they are literally drops of water off a swallow's back. The word 'pearls' is also used in the penultimate stanza of the poem when 'Pearls that on the red rose hings/[Fall] off shaken by thy wings' (lines 19–20). The repetitive motions of Clare's swallow poems highlight interconnection and transformation more than exact resemblance or unchanging identity.

Repetition is always delicately placed between similarity and difference, continuity and progression. Derek Attridge connects this situation to linguistic signification in general, arguing that 'meaning itself is grounded in repetition; the never-before-experienced, the wholly other, is meaningless, not even available to perception'. At the same time, for Attridge, 'there is actually no such thing, in the temporal movement of a poem, as an exact repetition' since 'every repetition, repeating itself in a specific here and now, freshly contextualised, is different'.[45] In the moving words of a poem, each iteration of a repetition marks progression as much as it marks a return. Attridge's insight is useful for thinking the repetitions of Clare's dynamic animals. Within individual poems and bits of prose, sequences of repetition often evoke movement in a formally dynamic fashion. In Clare's writing more generally, animal movement becomes a repeated trope which both connects a variety of nonhuman actors together and also produces a shifting web of difference between a variety of physical, textual and imaginative situations.

What broader significances can we draw from this variety of animal motion? For Clare studies, looking explicitly and in detail at Clare's dynamic animals provides a complement to an existing critical focus on nesting birds, which has consequences for how we conceive of his work more generally. Considerations of the nest poems often draw an analogy between the exposure of Clare's animals to violence and his own situation as a labouring-class poet situated in a historical context of enclosure and a biography of madness and confinement. Thomas C. Gannon goes so far as to suggest that 'Clare's bird nest poems [...] serve as projective vehicles for the poet's own yearning for a nest, for ontological security in the safety of some ornithic womb'.[46] Roger Sales argues that, in his bird nest poems, 'Clare celebrates the secret, solitary and secluded' and 'nestles down [...] in order to observe other fugitives from the cruel and predatory human world'.[47] More temperately, Onno Oerlemans proposes that Clare's 'concern for the rural poor (figured very often by the poet himself) parallels his concern for animal life':

> The predominant trope in Clare's poetry of mammals and birds is of their desire to remain hidden. [...] In Clare's poetry about human life as well, peace is the ability to hold one's place, to be secure in a secluded spot. It is a profound ecological and ideological insight to see that this peace is an ideal not just of the rural poor whose place in the land is threatened by enclosure, but also of the animals whose homes are shown in Clare's poetry in danger of being usurped by hunters, farmers, and curious seekers.[48]

Such perspectives reflect the centrality of Clare's nest poems to a critical consensus that sees Clare as both ripe for ecocritical attention and as a poet of a particular class concerned above all with 'place and displacement'.[49] They also suggest that animals, ecosystems and labouring-class poets are characterised by a shared fragility which requires shelter or concealment. The nest as both physical object and poetic trope is central to this view. Through being relatively static in changing environmental conditions, nests are creaturely forms of technology which both provide a rooted refuge embedded in place and leave their inhabitants vulnerable to unexpected incursion.

I do not wish to deny the validity of readings focussing on the significance of nests in Clare's work. There are indeed numerous important and beautiful poems about nests, and readings of them have enabled sophisticated biographical, political and ecocritical explorations of Clare's attachment to and alienation from particular places. Many also recognise the considerable variation even within a comparatively small subgenre of Clare's poetry.[50] It is important, however, for us to recognise that—despite the critical prominence of nesting or hidden creatures—there are also multitudes of nonhuman animals in Clare's poetry which are remarkable for straying beyond the bounds of their cosy or threatened dwellings, creatures which possess a greater sense of agility and agency than might be found if we limit ourselves to a concern with nests. I have explored a necessarily incomplete number of Clare's dynamic animals in this piece, but I hope to have shown that they are an active and important presence across his work. Recognising this fact has significant results. Firstly, it refocuses our attention on Clare's technical capability in producing varied effects on varied subjects, especially his virtuosic capacity to create movement in his verse, what Heaney calls his poetry's 'lambency, its skim factor, its bobbing unencumbered motion'.[51] Secondly, it allows us to extend Clare's significance beyond a potentially classist understanding of Clare as a poet not only defined by but also limited to his rootedness in a particular locality and set of social circumstances. Clare's dynamic animals are vigorous exemplars of his writing's capacity to engage with far more expansive physical and imaginative spaces.

Studying the varied motion of Clare's animals also offers an opportunity to break new ground in the ecocritical terrain that his work is often used to fertilise. In the late twentieth and early twenty-first centuries, ecological approaches to Clare focussed to a large extent on ideas of home.[52] James McKusick describes Clare's poetry as 'an ecolect, in the literal sense of a language that speaks for the *oikos*: the Earth considered a home for all living things'.[53] Jonathan Bate opens his rightly influential chapter on Clare's nest poems with the claim that 'Clare's poetry is the record of his search for a home in the world'.[54] Such perspectives reflect a broader dependence in the environmental humanities on a conceptual vocabulary of 'dwelling' and 'care' loosely derived from the philosophy of Martin Heidegger.[55] The sense of 'home' in such readings is admittedly capacious enough to include the domestic, the local, the national and the planetary.[56] Nevertheless, the *oikos* in ecocriticism often associates with a corresponding centripetal vocabulary of shelter, hiddenness, seclusion, enclosure and dwelling. Bate's quotation of Gaston Bachelard's statement that the nest is 'the center—the term is no exaggeration—of an entire universe' is a good example.[57] If focussing on a single dimension of Clare's writing about animals risks skewing our view of his range, an overly narrow vocabulary also limits the conceptual tools available to the environmental humanities to deal with the considerable ecological challenges of our own moment. I am far from alone in suggesting this. There have been a number of influential terminological moves in this domain, including most obviously Timothy Morton's argument that we need an 'ecology without nature'.[58] Rather than deleting an existing concept or introducing another new theory, however, Clare's encounters with animals offer a wide-ranging and flexible lexical palette for engaging with nonhuman others. Clare's animals 'totter', 'nimble', 'swee', 'suthy', 'wiz', 'flop', 'flock', 'rush', 'hop', 'travel', 'emigrate', 'journey' and 'navigate' in movements that are as often centrifugal as they are directed towards a singular location or home. 'Wandering', 'flying away' and 'roaming' are just as typical as 'dwelling' or 'nesting' in Clare's writing about animals. This is true even in some of Clare's nest poems. As Emma Mason has brilliantly suggested, Clare's 'nest poems evoke more than an idealised world of shelter and care' and might be closer to what Donna Haraway 'calls a "knot in motion", in which "beings constitute each other and themselves" through "their reaching into each other" as "companion species"'.[59] Clare's moving creatures reach out, in other words, and they are characterised by varied modes of unsettledness in varying circumstances and with varying affective results.

In 'Little Trotty Wagtail', the poetic atmosphere created by animal motion was joyful. In 'On Finding a Favourite Nook Destroyed', it is both outraged and hopeless. Clare laments the 'Poor outcast refugees of mother earth', the 'birds & beasts' that are 'Condemnd in vain for rest & peace to roam' and 'Forced from the wilds which nature left your home/By vile evasions of encroaching men'.[60] Like the migrations discussed earlier, it is tempting to see the word 'refugees' in this poem resonating across history with the mass movements of humans and animals in our own ecological moment. As Haraway writes elsewhere, 'Right now, the earth is full of refugees, human and not, without refuge'.[61] For Haraway, there is no possibility of emigration for humans or animals from the global consequences of contemporary environmental crises. Instead, she argues that we must learn to 'stay with the trouble', which will require us to make 'unexpected collaborations and combinations, in hot compost piles' and with a 'material semiotics' that is 'entangled and worldly'.[62] For Haraway, 'staying with the trouble' is very different to the ontological exceptionalism and retirement of Heideggerian dwelling. Instead, 'staying with the trouble' requires a recognition of what Haraway calls '*sympoiesis*' or 'making-with' in 'complex, dynamic, responsive, situated, historical systems'.[63] Clare powerfully evokes animals without refuge in 'On Finding a Favourite Nook Destroyed':

> The rabbit has no waste to make his den
> & the coy p[h]easant has not where to rest
> & cawing rook [...]
> Scarce finds a tree whereon to build its nest (lines 7–10)

But, even though the movement of his verse is made alongside the motions of various creatures, I do not want to suggest that Clare himself makes a corresponding call for anything like Haraway's '*sympoiesis*'. Clare's poem offers no statement of advice to counteract the scenario which it describes. Instead, its second half is stubborn in its use of the present tense and in its disgusted response to the 'tyranny' of what 'devours' 'freedoms birthright' (lines 12–14). As Simon Kövesi has recently argued, we risk doing violence to Clare's work if we force it to speak too directly to our own ecological circumstances.[64] The challenges of displacement faced by both humans and nonhumans in Clare's time were vastly different in scale and order to those which are distributed so unequally across the globe today. Nevertheless, Clare's writing does represent a flexible form of making with movement. When responding to the dynamic animals which move through his writing, we also need to turn away from reactively investigating the same themes and tropes. Instead, as readers of Clare, we need to make an attempt to understand a 'complex, dynamic, responsive, situated, historical' system, which—in the methods required for comprehension, if not in directly transferring the content—may give us some insight into the new cognitive tools required to confront the complexities of our own age.

Notes

1. John Goodridge, 'Poor Clare', *The Guardian*, July 22 (2000).
   https://www.theguardian.com/books/2000/jul/22/poetry.books.
2. Timothy Morton, 'John Clare's Dark Ecology', *Studies in Romanticism* 47 (2008): 179–93.
3. It is, for example, included in Seamus Heaney and Ted Hughes, eds., *The Rattle Bag: An Anthology of Poetry* (London: Faber, 1982), 248 and in Neil Philip, ed., *The New Oxford Book of Children's Verse* (Oxford: Oxford University Press, 1998), 25.
4. *Critical Heritage*, 308.
5. *Later Poems*, 2: 705, lines 1–7.
6. *Oxford English Dictionary* Online.
7. *OED*.
8. Seamus Heaney, 'John Clare: A bi-centenary lecture', in *John Clare in Context*, 134.
9. *Critical Heritage*, 69.
10. Onno Oerlemans, *Poetry and Animals: Blurring the Boundaries With the Human* (New York: Columbia University Press, 2018), 105.
11. See, for example, David Perkins, *Romanticism and Animal Rights* (Cambridge: Cambridge University Press, 2003), 89–103; and on animal sound, see Stephanie Kuduk Weiner, 'Listening with John Clare', *Studies in Romanticism* 48:3 (2009): 371–90; Sam Ward '"To list the song & not to start the thrush": John Clare's acoustic ecologies', *JCSJ* 29 (2010): 15–32; Matthew Rowney, 'Music in the Noise: The Acoustic Ecology of John Clare', *Journal of Interdisciplinary Voice Studies* 1.1 (2016): 23–40.
12. An exception is Katey Castellano, 'Moles, Molehills, and Common Right in John Clare's Poetry', *Studies in Romanticism* 56 (2017), 157–76.
13. The *OED* records how animals 'are typically able to move about, though this ability is sometimes restricted to a particular stage in their life cycle'. The movement of animals is, for example, central to Aristotle's biology: see Aristotle, *Parts of Animals, Movement of Animals, Progression of Animals*, ed. A. L. Peck and E. S. Forster, Revised edn (Cambridge: Harvard University Press, 2015).
14. *Middle Period*, 5: 269–70.
15. *By Himself*, 37–8.
16. *By Himself*, 37–8.
17. *Natural History*, 312. For an extended consideration, see Weiner, 'Listening with John Clare': 384–8. As a compliment to Weiner's focus on listening, I discuss the act of voicing in a forthcoming piece entitled 'Voicing John Clare's nonhuman onomatopoeia'.

18. *Natural History*, 237. By Clare's measurements, the snail is travelling at 0.00410354 miles per hour. Clare was aware of other methods for measuring animal movement. For example, he describes 'a man curious to know how far his bees travelld in a summers day' who dusted them with flour and 'having to go to the market that day he passd by a turnip field in full flower about 5 miles from home & to his supprise he found some of his own in their white powderd coats' (60).
19. *Natural History*, 66.
20. *Natural History*, 92.
21. *Natural History*, 66.
22. For excellent work on the relationship between religion and nature in Clare, see Sarah Houghton-Walker, *John Clare's Religion* (Farnham: Ashgate, 2009), 133–72, and Emma Mason, 'Ecology with religion: kinship in John Clare' in Simon Kövesi and Scott McEathron, eds., *New Essays on John Clare: Poetry, Culture and Community* (Cambridge: Cambridge University Press, 2015), 97–117.
23. *Early Poems*, 1: 5–7, lines 5–6, line 13.
24. *Natural History*, 69.
25. *Natural History*, 69–70, 111–13.
26. *By Himself*, 161. I am grateful to Erin Lafford for bringing this passage to my attention.
27. Bate, *Biography*, 483–4. Dudley's visit led Clare to complain that he wanted to be 'a free man again and go where I please. I am sick of this place, where I have no companions but mad-men'. See also Clare, *Letters*, 670.
28. Even when writing about the disappearance of liberty from England, Clare uses the word in an avian simile: 'Like emigrating birds thy freedom's flown'. See *VM*, 1: 50.
29. Angela K. Turner, *Swallow* (London: Reaktion, 2015), 8. Reflecting a contested etymology, she adds that 'the name is probably originally from the earlier Proto-Germanic *swalwo*, meaning a cleft stick, alluding to the barn swallow's forked tail'.
30. *Natural History*, 38.
31. Turner, *Swallow*, 92.
32. *Natural History*, 175, 188, 235. The swallows and martins also make their appearance at the end of 'April' and the beginning of 'May' in *The Shepherd's Calendar*, ed. Eric Robinson, David Powell and Geoffrey Summerfield, 2nd edn (Oxford: Oxford University Press, 2014), 44, 46.
33. *Natural History*, 38.
34. *Early Poems*, 2: 545, lines 1–2.
35. *Middle Period*, 5: 337, lines 1–2, line 11.

36. *Middle Period*, 2: 208–9, lines 1–2, lines 13–14. Elsewhere, Clare is sceptical about the usefulness of almanacs, describing the 'fresh budget of wonderful predictions' in 'Moors Almanack' as merely 'pretending truth' (*By Himself*, 201; see also 171).
37. Heaney, 'A bi-centenary lecture', 134, 137.
38. *Natural History*, xxxvii; Bate, *Biography*, 277; Alan Vardy, *John Clare, Politics and Poetry* (Basingstoke: Palgrave Macmillan, 2003), 136–7.
39. Letter from Hessey, 7 September 1824, Egerton MS 2246, fol. 377–8, quoted in Vardy, *Clare, Politics and Poetry*, 136–7.
40. For a summary, see Turner, *Swallow*, 50–4.
41. Thomas Forster, *Observations on the Brumal Retreat of the Swallow*, 5th edn (London: printed for Thomas and George Underwood, 1817), 28–9. See also a summary of Forster's position in William Hone, *The Every Day-Book, or, The Guide to the Year* (London: printed for William Hone, 1825), 505–12.
42. *Middle Period*, 4: 328.
43. *Early Poems*, 1: 374–5, lines 41–4.
44. *Later Poems*, 2: 705–6, lines 1–4.
45. Derek Attridge, *Moving Words: Forms of English Poetry* (Oxford: Oxford University Press, 2013), 48.
46. Thomas C. Gannon, *Skylark Meets Meadowlark: Reimagining the Bird in British Romantic and Contemporary Native American Literature* (Lincoln: University of Nebraska Press, 2009), 184.
47. Roger Sales, *John Clare: A Literary Life* (Basingstoke: Palgrave, 2002), 6.
48. Onno Oerlemans, *Romanticism and the Materiality of Nature* (Toronto: University of Toronto Press, 2002), 79, 81. Oerlemans acknowledges that the analogy is complicated by 'the continuous harassment' of animals by 'these same working poor'.
49. Tom Paulin, 'John Clare: A Bicentennial Celebration', in Richard Foulkes, ed., *John Clare: A Bicentenary Celebration* (Northampton: University of Leicester, Department of Adult Education, 1994), 69–78 (74), quoted by Simon Kövesi in *John Clare: Nature, Criticism and History* (London: Palgrave Macmillan, 2017), 3, 62n.
50. See, for example, John Goodridge's claim that, 'while Clare's nest poems have important elements in common, they also possess far more variety' than might have been allowed for if they had been concentrated in one collection, in *John Clare and Community* (Cambridge: Cambridge University Press, 2013), 135.
51. Heaney, 'A bi-centenary lecture', 143. For an excellent and detailed study which focuses on Clare's formal capability, see the first half of Stephanie Kuduk Weiner, *Clare's Lyric: John Clare and Three Modern Poets* (Oxford: Oxford University Press, 2014).

52. Sara Guyer also offers a sophisticated reading of and challenge to this concern with home in the final chapter of *Reading with John Clare: Biopoetics, Sovereignty, Romanticism* (New York: Fordham University Press, 2016), 78–100.

53. James C. McKusick, *Green Writing: Romanticism and Ecology* (Basingstoke: Macmillan, 2000), 89.

54. Jonathan Bate, *The Song of the Earth* (London: Picador, 2000), 153.

55. Most influential are the English translations of the essays 'Building Dwelling Thinking' and '"… Poetically Man Dwells …"' in Martin Heidegger, *Poetry, Language, Thought*, trans. Albert Hofstadter (New York: Harper & Row, 1971), 141–59 and 209–27.

56. For more on this widening scale of significance specifically in Clare's work, see David Higgins, 'John Clare: The Parish and the Nation' in *Romantic Englishness: Local, National and Global Selves, 1780–1850* (Basingstoke: Palgrave Macmillan, 2014), 86–108.

57. Gaston Bachelard, *The Poetics of Space*, trans. Maria Jolas (Boston: Beacon Press, 1994), 94; Bate, *The Song of the Earth*, 158.

58. Timothy Morton, *Ecology Without Nature: Rethinking Environmental Aesthetics* (Cambridge, MA.: Harvard University Press, 2007).

59. Mason, 'Ecology with religion', 106; Donna Haraway, *The Companion Species Manifesto: Dogs, People, and Significant Otherness* (Chicago: Prickly Paradigm Press), 6.

60. *Middle Period*, 2: 34, lines 1–5.

61. Donna Haraway, *Staying with the Trouble: Making Kin in the Chthulucene* (Durham, NC: Duke University Press, 2016), 100. I am grateful to Aidan Tynan for reminding me of this passage.

62. Haraway, *Staying with the Trouble*, 4.

63. Haraway, *Staying with the Trouble*, 58.

64. Kövesi, *John Clare: Nature, Criticism and History*, 1–77.

BIBLIOGRAPHY

Aristotle. *Parts of Animals, Movement of Animals, Progression of Animals*. Edited by A. L. Peck and E. S. Forster. Revised edn. Cambridge, MA: Harvard University Press, 2015.

Attridge, Derek. *Moving Words: Forms of English Poetry*. Oxford: Oxford University Press, 2013.

Bachelard, Gaston. *The Poetics of Space*. Translated by Maria Jolas. Boston: Beacon Press, 1994.

Bate, Jonathan. *The Song of the Earth*. London: Picador, 2000.

———. *John Clare: A Biography*. London: Picador, 2004.

Castellano, Katey. 'Moles, Molehills, and Common Right in John Clare's Poetry'. *Studies in Romanticism* 56 (2017): 157–76.

Clare, John. *The Village Minstrel, and Other Poems.* 2 vols. London: Taylor and Hessey, 1821.

———. *The Natural History Prose Writings of John Clare.* Edited by Margaret Grainger. Oxford: Clarendon Press, 1983.

———. *The Later Poems of John Clare, 1837–1864.* 2 vols. Edited by Eric Robinson, David Powell and Margaret Grainger. Oxford: Clarendon Press, 1984.

———. *The Letters of John Clare.* Edited by Mark Storey. Oxford: Clarendon Press, 1985.

———. *The Early Poems of John Clare, 1804–1822.* 2 vols. Edited by Margaret Grainger, David Powell and Eric Robinson. Oxford: Clarendon Press, 1989.

———. *John Clare By Himself.* Edited by Eric Robinson and David Powell. Manchester: Carcanet, 1996.

———. *Poems of the Middle Period, 1822–1837.* 5 vols. Edited by Eric Robinson, David Powell and P. M. S. Dawson. Oxford: Clarendon Press, 1996–2003.

———. *The Shepherd's Calendar.* Edited by Eric Robinson, David Powell and Geoffrey Summerfield. 2nd edn. Oxford: Oxford University Press, 2014.

Forster, Thomas. *Observations on the Brumal Retreat of the Swallow.* 5th edn. London: printed for Thomas and George Underwood, 1817.

Gannon, Thomas C. *Skylark Meets Meadowlark: Reimagining the Bird in British Romantic and Contemporary Native American Literature.* Lincoln: University of Nebraska Press, 2009.

Goodridge, John. 'Poor Clare'. *The Guardian.* July 22, 2000. https://www.theguardian.com/books/2000/jul/22/poetry.books.

———. *John Clare and Community.* Cambridge: Cambridge University Press, 2013.

Guyer, Sara. *Reading with John Clare: Biopoetics, Sovereignty, Romanticism.* New York: Fordham University Press, 2016.

Heaney, Seamus and Ted Hughes, eds. *The Rattle Bag: An Anthology of Poetry.* London: Faber, 1982.

Heaney, Seamus. 'John Clare: A Bi-Centenary Lecture'. In *John Clare in Context,* edited by Geoffrey Summerfield, Hugh Haughton and Adam Phillips, 130–47. Cambridge: Cambridge University Press, 1994.

Haraway, Donna. *The Companion Species Manifesto: Dogs, People, and Significant Otherness.* Chicago: Prickly Paradigm Press, 2003.

———. *Staying with the Trouble: Making Kin in the Chthulucene.* Durham, NC: Duke University Press, 2016.

Heidegger, Martin. *Poetry, Language, Thought.* Translated by Albert Hofstadter. New York: Harper & Row, 1971.

Higgins, David. *Romantic Englishness: Local, National and Global Selves, 1780–1850*. Basingstoke: Palgrave Macmillan, 2014.
Hone, William. *The Every Day-Book, or, The Guide to the Year*. London: printed for William Hone, 1825.
Houghton-Walker, Sarah. *John Clare's Religion*. Farnham: Ashgate, 2009.
Kövesi, Simon. *John Clare: Nature, Criticism and History*. London: Palgrave Macmillan, 2017.
Mason, Emma. 'Ecology with Religion: Kinship in John Clare'. In *New Essays on John Clare: Poetry, Culture and Community*, edited by Simon Kövesi, and Scott McEathron, 97–117. Cambridge: Cambridge University Press, 2015.
McKusick, James C. *Green Writing: Romanticism and Ecology*. Basingstoke: Macmillan, 2000.
Morton, Timothy. *Ecology Without Nature: Rethinking Environmental Aesthetics*. Cambridge, MA.: Harvard University Press, 2007.
———. 'John Clare's Dark Ecology'. *Studies in Romanticism* 47 (2008): 179–93.
Philip, Neil, ed. *The New Oxford Book of Children's Verse*. Oxford: Oxford University Press, 1998.
Oerlemans, Onno. *Romanticism and the Materiality of Nature*. Toronto: University of Toronto Press, 2002.
———. *Poetry and Animals: Blurring the Boundaries With the Human*. New York: Columbia University Press, 2018.
Perkins, David. *Romanticism and Animal Rights*. Cambridge: Cambridge University Press, 2003.
Rowney, Matthew. 'Music in the Noise: The Acoustic Ecology of John Clare'. *Journal of Interdisciplinary Voice Studies* 1.1 (2016): 23–40.
Sales, Roger. *John Clare: A Literary Life*. Basingstoke: Palgrave, 2002.
Storey, Mark, ed. *Clare: The Critical Heritage*. London: Routledge & Kegan Paul, 1973.
Turner, Angela K. *Swallow*. London: Reaktion, 2015.
Vardy, Alan. *John Clare, Politics and Poetry*. Basingstoke: Palgrave Macmillan, 2003.
Ward, Sam. '"To List the Song & Not to Start the Thrush": John Clare's Acoustic Ecologies'. *JCSJ* 29 (2010): 15–32.
Weiner, Stephanie Kuduk. *Clare's Lyric: John Clare and Three Modern Poets*. Oxford: Oxford University Press, 2014.
———. 'Listening with John Clare'. *Studies in Romanticism* 48.3 (2009): 371–90.

Multispecies Work in John Clare's 'Birds Nesting' Poems

Katey Castellano

In even his most despondent poems about enclosure, John Clare invites readers to reimagine the commons by thinking with unenclosed wild animals that continue to fly over, burrow under, and roam across private property. The enclosure elegy, 'The Mores', for example, nostalgically elegizes the former commons and decries the effects of enclosure while gesturing towards potential animal resistance. The speaker laments by pointing to a sign stating 'No Road Here' that curtails freedom of movement and common right: 'The hated sign by vulgar taste is hung / As tho the very birds should learn to know / When they go there they must no further go'.[1] The 'No Road Here' sign displays 'vulgar taste', which indicates decisions about land use will be made by an individual who 'tramples thoughtlessly' and 'plods his way to the end of his intentions with a mechanic impulse of uninterrupted selfishness'.[2] The poem's speaker,

K. Castellano (✉)
James Madison University, Harrisonburg, VA, USA
e-mail: castelkm@jmu.edu

however, considers the sign from a commoner's point of view, which reveals that birds and other wild animals will never 'learn to know' property boundaries. Although 'The Mores' is a despondent elegy for the commons in which 'All the poor have left is pride in the nobility of their former vision',[3] I argue that 'Each little tyrant with his little sign' (line 67) is nonetheless surrounded by birds and animals that amount to ubiquitous and fugitive commons that ignore the fences of enclosure.

By juxtaposing the sign of ownership and exclusion next to the creaturely forces that ignore it, 'The Mores' gestures towards non-human resistance to enclosure. Ron Broglio argues that 'the life and liveness' of animals and animality 'resists and exceeds the frameworks used to render subjects units of operation within the *dispositif* of capital and the state'.[4] It is the very liveliness of the birds, mentioned in 'The Mores' and explicitly outlined in Clare's many poems about birds' nests, that embodies resistance and alternative modes of dwelling in the land. During privatization, Rob Nixon argues, 'the environment itself is not a predictably quiescent victim. Resistance may assume not just human forms but also arise from an unanticipated recalcitrance on the part of the targeted resource'.[5] Clare's birds exhibit this unpredictable recalcitrance to enclosure. At the same time, wild birds inspire humans to challenge private property rights because birds are 'fugitive' resources that cannot be appropriated and improved, but rather can only be 'captured'. Emma Griffin argues:

> Despite centuries of game laws restricting and removing the once universal right to hunt wild animals, most rural inhabitants still held to the common law principle of *ferae naturae*—that wild animals were without an owner. They simply disagreed that small birds and mammals living in the wild could be owned by any but he with the wit or skill to catch them.[6]

Clare's poetry makes use of the principle of *ferae naturae*; wild animals emerge as fugitive commons in themselves, and to poetically record such commons is to engage in the work of commoning alongside the birds. By observing and making visible animals that continue to work within territories that defy private property boundaries, Clare's birds nesting poems invite readers to think with wild animals about continuing the work of commoning after enclosure.

'Commoning' refers to work that creates and maintains commons. Peter Linebaugh emphasizes that commons are not merely places, but are also human traditions and practices on the land: 'Commoning is embedded in a labour process: it inheres in a particular praxis of field, upland, forest, marsh, coast'.[7] One might expect then more intense nostalgia for former modes of agricultural work in Clare's poetry, but instead, I argue, the work of wild animals becomes a heuristic for reimagining the work of commoning after enclosure. Clare's poetry obsessively details the 'secret toils' ('Thrushes Nest', *Middle Period*, 4: 186–7, line 6) of birds and other wild animals to revise the georgic mode, which depicts humans working to subdue land in order to make it more productive. Clare's bird poems instead suggest animal work undermines the Lockean idea that human work in improving land's productivity entitles appropriation.[8] Although Elisabeth Helsinger argues that 'Clare never, even in his most utopian moments, imagines that physical labour might be happiness, the natural expression of human capacities' and instead 'sees labour as a curse', I argue Clare's attention to the labour of birds and other wild animals revises the georgic mode into shared multispecies work without ownership.[9] Onno Oerelemans argues, 'Clare is the first great animal poet—a poet for whom animals, animality, and the diversity of species were central themes—because of his belief in the fundamental relation between natural beauty and language'.[10] I would add that Clare's belief in the relationship between the natural world and poetry is mediated by the activity of work. In Clare's post-enclosure poetry, animals emerge as agentive figures working within larger lively multispecies assemblages (material commoning) while their activity is celebrated in the work of writing poetry (cultural commoning).

The ungovernable, commoning birds of 'The Mores' arise from Clare's larger poetic interest in the natural history of birds in the 1820s. In the following, I argue Clare's critically neglected 'Birds Nesting' depicts the work of birds as a revelation of multispecies assemblages that resist the imagination of private property. Then I argue that Clare's birds' nest poems further depict birdsong as an auditory experience of unlocatable origin that deterritorializes the space and time of enclosure. In his history of common rights in England, Richard Mabey mentions that until the eighteenth century, work on the commons was negotiated by 'The slow, tentative, often quarrelsome, jostling for position between commoner and landowner, commoner and commoner, [which] is reminiscent of the way animals work out their territorial claims over a piece of land'.[11] For precisely this reason, Clare is interested in bird territories that are revealed by their nests and songs. After enclosure, although signs and fences mark private property, Clare's poetry draws a countermap of how birds' work marks the continuing common.

BIRDS' NESTS

In the 1820s, Clare planned to create an innovative volume of poetry called 'Birds Nesting' and a collection of natural history letters, the 'Biographies of Birds and Flowers'.[12] Clare's interest in natural history may seem to be apolitical, especially when compared to his enclosure elegies. Johanne Clare argues about his bird poems: 'Celebration rather than protest appears to be their formal motive, and the subject of their celebration is not only birds in particular and nature in general, but Clare's retreat from society into nature'.[13] I argue, however, that the joyful, celebratory observations of birds' nests do not retreat from society, but rather map out what Anna Lowenhaupt Tsing calls the 'latent commons', those 'fugitive moments of entanglement in the midst of institutionalized alienation' that exist on the margins of industry. Tsing calls for developing 'arts of noticing' to discern the fugitive entanglements of the latent commons.[14] Clare deploys a poetic 'arts of noticing' in 'Birds Nesting' (*Middle Period*, 2: 163–84), a poem that has been largely neglected by scholars, perhaps because 31 species of birds, 25 types of plants, 15 kinds of animals other than birds, and 3 categories of humans emerge together in its 606 lines. The poem was found in an unpublished notebook (ca. 1825–30), and it is so long and digressive that J. W. Tibble's edition of Clare's poetry (1935) divided the poem into smaller ones. In the second volume of *Poems of the Middle Period* (1996), the poem was finally published in its full form, faithful to the now lost manuscript notebook.[15] The intact poem 'Birds Nesting' maps a continuing multispecies common by simultaneously highlighting certain bird species such as the redcap, green woodpecker, or blackbird, while outlining how the birds' work in nesting is always bound up with other humans, animals, and plants.

Tibble's editorial decision to break up 'Birds Nesting' into smaller, cohesive lyric poems is understandable given its wide-ranging paratactic structure, yet this structure intentionally resists coherent, progressive narrative. Simon Kövesi argues that Clare's overuse of the ampersand in his poetry amounts to intentional parataxis in which 'tactical lines of relation and response engage in ongoing processes' without subordination.[16] The long list-like structure of 'Birds Nesting' suggests just such ongoing yet contingent interrelations. In the poem, the nests themselves are assemblages of materials related explicitly to other animals (hair, webs, wool) and plants (straw, moss, thistledown) that are gathered and woven together in the process of nesting. The nests are situated not only within an assemblage of other living things, but also within or alongside both natural and human-made structures (rocks, streams, barns, houses). John Barrell notes, Clare's 'poems are concerned to express not only his sense of the particularity of things in a landscape, but his sense also of the multiplicity of them'.[17] In highlighting certain species of birds only to subsume them immediately within a larger assemblage, Clare's extended parataxis in 'Birds Nesting' calls attention to the emergent, commoning work of birds after enclosure.

'Birds Nesting' not only focuses on bird behaviour; as a lyric poem, it further attends to the perspective and affective response of the speaker in encountering these commoning assemblages that allow birds to continue nesting. The poem begins:

> It surely is a pleasant thing
> & much delight a ramble yields
> To go birds nesting in the spring
> & hunt about the woods & fields
> To mark the nests of many sorts
> & which in building most excells
> The number of their eggs to note
> & curious colour of the shells (lines 1–8)

In these introductory lines, Clare points out the two forms of labour suggested in the title. First, birds nesting can mean the human activity of a 'ramble' while looking for birds' nests in order to 'mark' their nests and eggs. Yet the human activity of birds nesting is merely to follow the birds' work as they build homes that claim space for a season, take care of their eggs and young, and thereby ensure a future. Clare's play on the double meaning of birds nesting entangles human poetic perception with the non-human material world.

In 'Birds Nesting', the poem's speaker takes the reader nesting alongside schoolboys, who 'peep in every bush / & eager as for money stoop / To hunt the grass & bunch of rush' (lines 9–11). To take the reader nesting alongside schoolboys further complicates the activity of nesting. While the schoolboys in the poem 'Birds Nesting' are not featured throughout the poem, they are added at the beginning as one of many paratactic 'ands' that contribute to the overall picture of birds nesting. Clare recalls his own boyhood pastime of 'birds nesting' on the commons: 'I was very fond of "birds Nesting" as we us'd to call it when I was a Child but this hard hearted practise of Robbing Poor birds was soon laid aside as I grew up'.[18] Why would Clare choose to draw attention to a childhood game that was often condemned as cruel in this poem, his autobiography, and in his letters to Elizabeth Kent (a naturalist with whom he hoped to collaborate on a natural history)?[19] As an adult, Clare perceives the way human activity negatively impacts wildlife. Mina Gorji suggests, he 'celebrates the sanctuary of the wilderness, far from "mans haunts", but retains a troubling sense of himself as a presence that disturbs'.[20] Yet Clare is not a modern ecologist but a commoner. Just as he refuses to outright condemn the rural commoners who engage in or watch badger-baiting in 'The Badger' (*Middle Period*, 5: 360–2), he refuses to condemn or hide the violence of children taking nests or eggs, perhaps because taking those eggs would be permitted by traditional common right. Nonetheless, the boys in 'Birds Nesting' do not engage in violent forms of nesting. In this poem, childhood nostalgia is infused with Clare's post-enclosure sensibility that attends to the vulnerability of birds and other wildlife in the age of improvement.

Hugh Haughton argues that Clare's project for a volume of 'birds nesting' poems aspired to be 'a poetic equivalent of [Thomas] Bewick's marvelously illustrated *History of British Birds*'.[21] However, Bewick's wood engravings of birds are not marvellous merely because of their faithful representation of different species of birds, but rather, as I have argued elsewhere, because they evoke wonder through their 'politics of the miniature' that embed seemingly unlimited multispecies activities within circumscribed place.[22] Bewick's engravings foreground the birds while featuring miniaturized humans, buildings, landscapes, and other plants and animals interacting in the background. A similar perspective takes shape when Clare's nesting schoolboys experience the church and school being left in the background:

> Thus on & on they go & guess
> Their way through fields till now unknown
> The village spire grows less & less
> & leaves them to the world alone
> The school forgot when out of sight
> They further trace the woodland glooms (lines 17–22)

The nesting boys are guided not just by their eyes but also by their ears, because birdsong also territorializes space. As the boys become more and more engrossed in finding a bird's nest, they come across previously unknown fields that defamiliarize their local village. The boys leave the village behind, the spire of the church 'grows less', and the school is 'forgot[ten]'. The focus on the birds and their nests 'leaves them to the world alone'. All the trappings of their individual identities taught in the town, the church, and the school are thrust into the background and then disappear while observing another form of worlding. Such defamiliarization cultivates the art of noticing birds' labouring into animal commons that persist after enclosure.

The boys drop out of the poem at this point, but as the reader continues with the speaker throughout 'Birds Nesting', the emotion associated with observing birds' nests continues to be child-like wonder. The poem's speaker repeatedly expresses surprise in finding the location of a nest or observing the individual behaviour of a bird. The speaker exclaims: 'But never did I see till now' (lines 31 and 43), 'Ive never seen or known yet' (line 66), or 'My wonder I could scarce conseal / & what supprised me more then all' (lines 99–100). The speaker not only describes known birds, but also the ones that he does not know: he describes a bird that the woodmen call willowbiters while acknowledging, 'But what they are in learnings way / Is all unknown to them or me' (lines 171–2). Later, the speaker pursues a mysterious bird in woods but cannot observe it, 'So all enquirey ends in vain' (line 490). Even after reading natural histories and talking with those with more birding skill, 'all remains a mystery still' (line 502).

When the species is known, species characteristics are laid aside as insufficient when it comes to understanding the profoundly singular behaviour of birds that are constantly 'on the wing' making do on private property. The blackbird in particular has a 'thousand whims' (line 83) in choosing places to nest. While the poem records what is typical of species behaviour, at the same time it includes individual variation. The process of natural history becomes one of revealing the limits of human categorization:

> In marking leaves of natures book
> Its varied pages quickly show
> The more enquiring minds may look
> The less enquirery seems to know (lines 503–6)

Clare undermines the discourse of species classification by emphasizing both singular birds within a species and by subsuming those birds within a larger assemblage of living things. He was suspicious of Linnaean taxonomy and associated it with enclosure.[23] Linnaean species classification focused on morphology instead of ecological habitat and thereby excluded knowledge of the embedded locality and singularity of entangled human and non-human worlds. Theresa M. Kelley argues that Clare uses 'the "vulgar" glossary of common names' as part of his larger ethos of 'commonability'.[24] Both linguistically and through their focus on nests, Clare's bird poems are situated within local culture and habitus.

Clare differs from other Romantic poets in 'the frequency with which he writes about the most "lowly" element of the bird world, namely, the nest', Tom Duddy argues.[25] Clare describes lowly nests because they are the products of birds' work, and as the title implies, in 'Birds Nesting', birds are always working. For example, the redcap is 'searching thistles brown & bare' (line 36), while the blackbird is 'chusing places for her nest' (line 84). Kingfishers artfully dig nests in the sides of the riverbank: 'Their holes a full arms length is made / Turned at last with sudden bend' (lines 213–4). Meanwhile, the frenetic hermit swallow attaches its nest to stone so quickly that 'Thoughts hardly can the pace maintain' (line 236). Likewise, observations of the nests themselves demonstrate intricate, painstaking labour, such as the hay chat's nest, which is made of 'Dead airiff stalks & horses hair / & glued or sewed with spiders thread' (lines 257–8). Anne-Lise François argues that 'ongoing expropriation and enclosure entail the loss of another kind of uncertainty or openness to circumscribed improvisation'.[26] I argue 'Birds Nesting' aims to outline just such circumscribed improvisation in bird behaviour after enclosure. Birds constantly use resources and claim space, repurposing gleaned materials and waste in building homes so intricate 'That hands may spoil but not replace' (line 458).

Birds' nests and songs provide an impetus for humans to follow birds and ignore the boundaries of private property in order to 'hunt about the woods & fields' (line 4). In Clare's personal life, the activity was fraught with the contradictory emotions of the joy of discovery and the fear of punishment. In his journals of 1825, the same year that he was working on 'Birds Nesting', Clare describes an encounter:

> Took a walk in the field a birds nesting and botanizing and had like to have been taken up as a poacher in Hillywood by a meddlesome consieted keeper belonging to Sir John Trollop he swore that he had seen me in act more then once of shooting game when I never shot even so much as a sparrow in

> my life—what terrifying rascals these wood keepers and gamekeepers
> are they make a prison of the forrests and are its joalers[27]

It appears that Clare, like the birds in 'The Mores', may have inadvertently
ignored private property signs. By following the birds' nests, private property is directly experienced in its etymological sense: to make something
private is to 'deprive' others of access to it.[28] The activity of birds nesting
further allows Clare to critique the way private property transforms social
relations and the idea of work itself. The woods are now guarded by
gameskeepers, those 'terryfying rascals' whose work amounts to an exercise of power that criminalizes Clare's poetic natural history as poaching.

After over 500 lines detailing 18 birds' nests and marking the birds
unceasing improvisation in building with diverse materials from other animals and plants, the speaker has an epiphany:

> But now no ownership I fear
> Nor path to keep nor stile to climb
> I feel myself a monarch here
> My very fancies grow sublime (lines 523–6)

After observing birds making do in and around private property, the
speaker courageously no longer fears the boundaries of 'ownership', so his
imagination grows sublime and without limits. Goodridge and Thornton
outline Clare's self-consciousness as a 'trespasser' into environmental,
social, and literary territory that excluded him as a landless commoner.[29]
The birds-nesting-sublime allows the speaker to transcend the commoner's constant fear of trespass after enclosure: this is not a revolutionary
overthrow of property but rather an observation of how the birds' improvised nests on and around private property reveal the latent commons. In
this form of poetic natural history, the speaker makes it clear that he is
learning *from* the birds rather than simply *about* them. Thus, as a response
to enclosure, instead of abandoning the idea of agricultural work to its
new form of wage labour, Clare's poetry obsessively details forms of wild
animal work that continue on private land and escape the wage nexus.

BIRDSONG

While 'Birds Nesting' demonstrates that careful visual observation of birds' nests reveals a latent commons, at the same time, the poem's attention to birdsong additionally deterritorializes enclosed space. At the beginning of the poem, the speaker observes: 'Where ever birds but make a noise / Anticipation sees a nest' (lines 15–6). To suggest the need for ongoing work in imagining the commons, 'Birds Nesting' does not end with the epiphany of the birds-nesting-sublime. After the epiphany, two more birds are described in detail, but these two birds are elusive, so they must be described by their songs. The speaker mentions the cuckoo, whose sound is disorienting: '& oftentimes Ive listening stood / & thought ten singing when but one' (lines 557–8). The poem then ends with an extended description of the song and search for the most disorienting bird of all, the land rail. In spite of many attempts to follow its 'craiking noise', the speaker admits he 'never once' has visually observed the mystical 'fairey thing' (lines 586, 591). After hearing the bird in the morning, the speaker looks for the land rail all day, until the evening, when the crepuscular bird calls again. However, it is now too late for the speaker to continue the search: it is 'As though it teazed me with the call / & knew I dare not follow then' (lines 605–6). My reading of the mystical land rail experience that concludes 'Birds Nesting' resonates with Alan Bewell's argument that in Clare's nature poetry 'the present is seen as being haunted by the natures it has displaced, natures that have been violently uprooted yet refuse to leave'.[30] Through the experience of birdsong, the long, paratactic poem ends with defamiliarization and limitation, thus becoming a natural history infused with negative capability and uncertainty that assures the reader of wily animal persistence after enclosure.

In many of Clare's bird poems of the 1820s, birdsong is experienced by the speaker as a sound of unknown origin that indicates non-human territories. Andrew Whitehouse explains, 'For birds, sound-making is also place-making; it is an act of territorializing space, of making relations with other birds and continually reweaving the context of their lives'.[31] Clare's interest in describing birdsong is intrinsically tied to the work of bird nesting. The work of nesting includes singing to create territory and to mediate animal relationships. Birdsong then is part of the birds' fugitive commoning or territorialization of privatized spaces. To suggest birdsong is part of the continuing work of commoning, moreover, resonates with Clare's own project of using poetry to map out the continuing common.

Challenging the poetic conventions that celebrate birdsong, the speaker in 'The Nightingales Nest' delights in the confusion caused by the nightingale's sounds. Noting the difference between the birds' song and the actual appearance of the bird, the speaker notes that the nightingale 'Hath made me marvel that so famed a bird / Should have no better dress than russet brown' (*Middle Period*, 3: 456–61, lines 20–1). The poem further confronts the difficulty that the speaker's visual observation of the bird will likely preclude his aural experience of it. The speaker laments, 'But if I just touched a bush or scarcely stirred / All in a moment stopt' (lines 28–9), and he also recognizes 'our presence doth retard / Her joys' (lines 65–6). Sarah Zimmerman argues that Clare's bird poems exhibit a 'conspiratorial poetics' in which 'a speaker and a companion embark on a search for birds' nests, find them, and then pause to describe these vulnerable sites before walking away—agreeing to keep schtum and implicitly enlisting the reader's silence'.[32] This relationship with animals reflects what Sue Donaldson and Will Kymlicka call 'wild animal sovereignty', which 'means that if and when we humans visit their territory, we do so not in the role of stewards and managers, but as visitors to foreign lands'.[33] Similarly, the speakers in Clare's bird poems call themselves a 'guest' ('The Yellow Wagtails Nest', *Middle Period*, 3: 474–5, line 12) or even an 'intruding guest' ('The Thrushes Nest', *Middle Period*, 4: 186–7, line 5) on bird territories. If birdsong reterritorializes space, then silently listening to and recording it is an act of solidarity with the birds' commons that proposes wild animal sovereignty. Yet for Clare, wild animals *share* their sovereignty in common with humans. Instead of proposing wild animal territories in one place and humans in another, Clare proposes that humans and non-humans are co-producers of the continuing common. In this view, humans are not outside the animal commons, but are always responsible for their impact on a shifting assemblage of many other species.

Clare's poems about birds' nests differ from other poets of the Romantic period because they focus not only on prized songbirds, but also on birds whose vocalizations are not song-like or pleasing to human sensibilities, such as the land rail's 'craiking' (*Middle Period*, 3: 553–4, line 29) or the wryneck's 'hissing noise' (*Middle Period*, 4: 290–1, line 11). Birds with startling or ugly songs nevertheless serve the purpose of disorienting humans, as I argued earlier about the land rail at the end of 'Birds Nesting'. Another poem, 'The Land Rail' (*Middle Period*, 3: 553–4), continues to explore the effect of the birds' loud 'craiking' sounds that echo across the grassy fields and have no obvious origin. If birdsong announces territory, land rail territory seems to reverberate everywhere during the summer months. The bird arrives seasonally: the speaker hears its call only in 'summers prime' when 'knee deep waves the corn', giving cover to the ground-nesting birds below (lines 7, 6). Finding the precise location of the land rail perplexes even those who know the fields intimately. The poem describes farmers using their dogs to search for the source of the noise without success. Even boys who know many birds due to their summer game of 'bird nesting' cannot find the bird and end up marvelling in 'wonder' (lines 24 and 30). Because of the combination of a loud call and camouflage in the fields, the bird seems almost supernatural. Clare explains:

> Tis like a fancy every where
> A sort of living doubt
> We know t'is something but it ne'er
> Will blab the secret out
>
> If heard in close or meadow plots
> It flies if we pursue
> But follows if we notice not
> The close & meadow through (lines 13–20)

As a 'living doubt' that haunts the fantasy of total biopolitical control of the field, the land rail's song is unsettling because it is simultaneously inescapable and unable to be located through human effort. Stephanie Kuduk Weiner argues, 'Listening without seeing keeps Clare listening'. I would add listening with Clare prompts the reader to start attending to the sounds of other more-than-human assemblages as well.[34]

In the late summer, the land rail's nest is occasionally found by hay mowers, and even then, they do not see the bird, and wonder at the bird's vulnerability and resilience because it is noisy, lays eggs directly on the ground, and yet remains undiscovered in the summer months. The nest can be found only through 'accident' or 'chance' but never direct effort (lines 45, 50). Thus, the land rail remains:

> A mystery still to men & boys
> Who knows not where they lay
> & guess it but a summer noise
> Among the meadowhay (lines 57–60)

Instead of elegizing the loss of the commons, the speaker insists on the birds' continuing mystery. Its 'undiscovered song' (line 34) becomes a 'pleasant wonder tale' (line 35) that asserts enclosed space still hosts and is in many ways still subject to unruly creaturely lives.

That the land rail can only be heard in the summer points to another dimension of listening to birdsong: the listener experiences what François calls 'unenclosed time'. François makes a distinction between the standardized, progressive time of capitalism and the repetitive and seasonal nature of unenclosed time. Unenclosed time can function in a myriad of ways, one of which is that 'tasks are only achieved or undertaken when certain environmental conditions are met' such as daybreak.[35] Birdsong resonates at certain times of day, whether diurnal, nocturnal, or crepuscular, and at certain seasons, because some birds are summer migrants and others are year-long residents. Birdsong reveals that animal time is not enclosed, even if space is enclosed and humans increasingly feel beholden to the clock-time of capitalism. Clare's poems describe birds arriving in spring or leaving in autumn, demonstrating the seasonal abundance of summer. Some birds, however, become overwinter companions, such as the heron, crow, wood cock, field fare, and bumbarrels that crowd into the sonnet 'Emmonsails Heath in Winter' (*Middle Period*, 4: 286). Clare wrote at least 85 'birds nesting' poems; taken together, they demonstrate that different species engage in multiple scales of time and that the daily and seasonal temporalities of birds reveal a world that exists for something other than human activity conceived of as a progressive, linear trajectory. Patrick Brenishan argues that Clare's poems depict a 'manifold commons' because 'there was no single "nature", rather there were ongoing relations that constituted many different natures'.[36] The multiple temporalities of the many different kinds of birds that populate Clare's poems suggest that future commons must attend to and cultivate more-than-human understandings of time.

In addition to daily and seasonal time, birdsong embodies the intergenerational time of the commons that remain even after privatization has shifted human consciousness to progressive clock-time. Whereas Clare claimed he was 'out of my knowledge' if he left the spatial boundaries of his village, he was able to imagine intergenerational spans of time within that circumscribed space.[37] His bird poems anticipate the insights of conservation ethicist Thom van Dooren, who argues that birds embody an 'intergenerational world' in which 'any individual bird is a single knot in an emergent lineage: a vital point of connection between generations—generations that do not just happen, but *must be achieved*.[38] Spanning from before enclosure and into the future of emergent commons, the birds' intergenerational time is accomplished through the work of nesting and singing. For example, in 'The Robins Nest', the robins 'court & build & sing their under song' in an ancient place 'Where old neglect lives patron & befriends / Their homes with safetys wildness (*Middle Period*, 3: 532–6, lines 46, 51–2). Likewise, in 'The Ravens Nest', the nest becomes a scene of intergenerational work:

> Up the old monstrous oak where every spring
> Finds the two ancient birds at their old task
> Repairing the hugh nest—where still they live
> Through changes winds & storms & are secure (*Middle Period*, 3: 559–61, lines 42–5)

As the birds continue their fugitive multispecies commoning in spite of immense vulnerability, they embody intergenerational time, thereby suggesting modes of perception for commoning futures.

After observing birds' nests and listening to their songs, the speaker in 'Birds Nesting' declares, 'Ive listened as to school Ive gone' (line 583). In other bird poems, Clare compares nests to human thought: the yellow wagtail's nest is 'nestled like a thought forgot by toil' (line 10) and the nightingale's nest 'seemed as hidden as a thought unborn' (line 16). Clare's attention to bird-work enables him to think freely because it escapes what Vandana Shiva calls a 'monoculture of the mind', a way of thinking that 'disappears' any knowledge that is not useful in the current economy.[39] Thus improvised nests prompt thought that is yet 'unborn', potential commoning futures that challenge the social imaginary of private property. By meticulously recording the place-making signs of birds through their nests and songs, Clare's bird poems mark unenclosed physical and mental territories. Tobias Menely argues that poets who listen to creaturely voices and are 'called to speak by a voice that has no authorized meaning' open the political realm radically to account for the suffering of animals.[40] Clare, however, reverses this formula. He does not wish to draw the birds into the politics of liberal rights, but he rather longs to be drawn into birds' work and worlding, as they build nests and sing songs that provide a commoning counternarrative to the encroaching discourse of private property.

NOTES

NOTES

1. *Middle Period*, 2: 347–50, lines 72–4.
2. From Clare's essay on 'Taste' in *Natural History*, 284.
3. John Goodridge and R.K.R. Thornton. *John Clare: The Trespasser* (Nottingham: Five Leaves, 2016), 64.
4. *Beasts of Burden* (Albany: SUNY Press, 2017), 8.
5. Rob Nixon, *Slow Violence and the Environmentalism of the Poor* (Cambridge, MA: Harvard University Press, 2011), 20–1.
6. *Blood Sport* (New Haven: Yale University Press, 2009), 114–15. Christiana Payne also argues that commoners resisted seeing wild animals as private property. *Toil and Plenty* (New Haven: Yale University Press, 1993), 9–10.
7. *The Magna Carta Manifesto* (Berkeley: University of California Press, 2008), 45.
8. Johanne Clare argues that the georgic 'is diametrically opposed to the tactful, unpossessive attitudes Clare brought to the act of natural observation'. *John Clare and the Bounds of Circumstance* (Kingston: McGill-Queen's University Press, 1987). See also Gary Harrison's 'John Clare's Agrarian Idyll: A Confluence of Pastoral and Georgic', in *A History of British Working Class Literature*, eds. John Goodridge and Bridget Keegan (Cambridge: Cambridge University Press, 2017), 195–207.
9. *Rural Scenes and National Representation* (Princeton: Princeton University Press, 1996), 153–4.
10. *Poetry and Animals* (New York: Columbia University Press, 2018), 105.
11. *The Common Ground* (London: Hutchinson, 1980), 170.
12. Bate, *Biography*, 277–8.
13. *John Clare and the Bounds of Circumstance*, 165.
14. *The Mushroom at the End of the World* (Princeton: Princeton University Press, 2015), 255.
15. Thanks are due to James Madison University's Special Collections librarian, Kate Morris, for her resourcefulness and dedication in procuring a copy of the rare book, *Birds Nesting: The Lost Manuscript*, ed. Eric Robinson (Shropshire: Tern Press, 1987). This limited edition was the only text version of 'Birds Nesting' before its second publication in volume 2 of Robinson, Powell, and Dawson's *Middle Period* in 1996. In the introduction to *Birds Nesting*, Robinson states that the original manuscript of 'Birds Nesting' was checked out from the Peterborough Museum and left in a railway compartment somewhere between Peterborough and Cambridge. The manuscript has remained missing. Bate discusses 'Birds Nesting' briefly in relation to Clare's other prose natural history projects in Bate, *Biography*, 278. Three additional books have been published that anthologize John Clare's poetry and prose about birds: *Birds Nest*, edited

by Anne Tibble (Newcastle: Mid Northumberland Arts Group, 1973); *John Clare: Bird Poems*, edited by Peter Levi (London: Folio Society, 1980); *John Clare's Birds*, edited by Eric Robinson and Richard Fitter (Oxford: Oxford University Press, 1982).

16. *John Clare: Nature, Criticism, History* (London: Palgrave Macmillan, 2017), 115.

17. Barrell, 151.

18. *By Himself*, 32–3.

19. This correspondence with Kent is discussed in Bate, *Biography*, 278.

20. *John Clare and the Place of Poetry* (Liverpool: Liverpool University Press, 2008), 97.

21. 'Progress and Rhyme: "The Nightingale's Nest" and Romantic Poetry', in *John Clare in Context*, 55.

22. *Ecology of British Romantic Conservatism, 1790–1837* (Basingstoke: Palgrave Macmillan, 2013), 65–90.

23. See Eric Miller, 'Enclosure and Taxonomy in John Clare', *SEL* 40.4 (Autumn 2000): 635–57.

24. *Clandestine Marriage* (Baltimore: Johns Hopkins University Press, 2012), 147.

25. 'John Clare and the Poetry of Birds', *Poetry Ireland Review* 104 (September 2011): 64.

26. 'Taking Turns on the Commons', in *River of Fire: Commons, Crisis, and the Imagination*, ed. Cal Winslow (Arlington, MA: Pumping Station, 2016), 378.

27. Journal entry for Saturday, 16 April 1825, *By Himself*, 222.

28. Raymond Williams, *Keywords* (Oxford: Oxford University Press, 1983), 242.

29. *John Clare: The Trespasser*, 16.

30. *Natures in Translation* (Baltimore: Johns Hopkins University Press, 2017), 293.

31. 'Listening to Birds in the Anthropocene: The Anxious Semiotics of Sound in a Human Dominated World', *Environmental Humanities* 6 (May 2015): 58.

32. 'John Clare's Conspiracy', in *New Essays on John Clare*, ed. Simon Kövesi and Scott McEathron (Cambridge: Cambridge University Press, 2015), 57.

33. Sue Donaldson and Will Kymlicka, *Zoopolis* (Oxford: Oxford University Press, 2013), 170.

34. 'Listening with John Clare', *Studies in Romanticism* 48.3 (Fall 2009): 383.

35. 'Taking Turns on the Commons', 363. Emma Mason argues that Clare's spiritual leanings can be located in his contemplative 'aural imagining of nature'. Comingled biophony and church bells facilitate the imagination of cross-species kinship. I would add that church bells, like birdsong, depict

daily, seasonal, and ritual time instead of progressive time. 'Ecology with Religion: Kinship in John Clare', in *New Essays on John Clare*, ed. Simon Kövesi and Scott McEathron (Cambridge: Cambridge University Press, 2015), 98.
36. 'John Clare and the Manifold Commons', *Environmental Humanities* 3.1 (2013)· 74.
37. *By Himself*, 40.
38. *Flight Ways* (New York: Columbia University Press, 2014), 27
39. See *Monocultures of the Mind* (Basingstoke: Palgrave Macmillan, 1993).
40. *The Animal Claim: Sensibility and the Creaturely Voice* (Chicago: University of Chicago Press, 2015), 131.

BIBLIOGRAPHY

Barrell, John. *The Idea of Landscape and the Sense of Place 1730–1840*. Cambridge: Cambridge University Press, 1972.
Bate, Jonathan. *John Clare: A Biography*. New York: Farrar, Straus and Giroux, 2003.
Bewell, Alan. *Natures in Translation: Romanticism and Colonial Natural History*. Baltimore: Johns Hopkins University Press, 2017.
Bresnihan, Patrick. 'John Clare and the Manifold Commons'. *Environmental Humanities* 3.1 (2013): 71–91.
Broglio, Ron. *Beasts of Burden: Biopolitics, Labor, and Animal Life in British Romanticism*. Albany: SUNY Press, 2017.
Castellano, Katey. *The Ecology of British Romantic Conservatism, 1790–1837*. Basingstoke: Palgrave Macmillan, 2013.
Clare, Johanne. *John Clare and the Bounds of Circumstance*. Kingston and Montreal: McGill-Queen's University Press, 1987.
Clare, John. *Birds Nest: Poems by John Clare*. Edited by Anne Tibble. Newcastle: Mid Northumberland Arts Group, 1973.
———. *Birds Nesting: The Lost Manuscript*. Edited by Eric Robinson. Shropshire: Tern Press, 1987.
———. *John Clare: Bird Poems*. Edited by Peter Levi. London: Folio Society, 1980.
———. *John Clare By Himself*. Edited by Eric Robinson and David Powell. New York: Routledge, 2002.
———. *John Clare's Birds*. Edited by Eric Robinson and Richard Fitter. Oxford: Oxford University Press, 1982.
———. *Poems of the Middle Period, 1822–1837*. 5 vols. Edited by Eric Robinson, David Powell and P. M. S. Dawson. Oxford: Clarendon Press, 1996–2003.
———. *The Poems of John Clare*. Edited by J. W. Tibble. London: J. M. Dent, 1935.
———. *The Natural History Prose Writings of John Clare*. Edited by Margaret Grainger. Oxford: Clarendon Press, 1983.

Donaldson, Sue, and Will Kymlicka. *Zoopolis: A Political Theory of Animal Rights*. Oxford: Oxford University Press, 2013.

Duddy, Tom. 'John Clare and the Poetry of Birds'. *Poetry Ireland Review* 104 (September 2011): 60–73.

François, Anne-Lise. 'Taking Turns on the Commons (or Lessons in Unenclosed Time)'. In *River of Fire: Commons, Crisis and the Imagination*, edited by Cal Winslow, 361–89. Arlington, MA: Pumping Station, 2016.

Goodridge, John and R.K.R Thornton. *John Clare: The Trespasser*. Nottingham: Five Leaves Publications, 2016.

Gorji, Mina. *John Clare and the Place of Poetry*. Liverpool: Liverpool University Press, 2008.

Griffin, Emma. *Blood Sport: Hunting in Britain since 1066*. New Haven: Yale University Press, 2009.

Harrison, Gary. 'John Clare's Agrarian Idyll: A Confluence of Pastoral and Georgic'. In *A History of British Working Class Literature*, edited by John Goodridge and Bridget Keegan, 195–207. Cambridge: Cambridge University Press, 2017.

Haughton, Hugh. 'Progress and Rhyme: 'The Nightingale's Nest' and Romantic Poetry'. In *John Clare in Context*, edited by Hugh Haughton, Adam Phillips, and Geoffrey Summerfield, 51–86. Cambridge: Cambridge University Press, 1994.

Helsinger, Elisabeth. *Rural Scenes and National Representation: Britain, 1815–1850*. Princeton: Princeton University Press, 1996.

Kelley, Theresa M. *Clandestine Marriage: Botany and Romantic Culture*. Baltimore: Johns Hopkins University Press, 2012.

Kövesi, Simon. *John Clare: Nature, Criticism, History*. London: Palgrave Macmillan, 2017.

Linebaugh, Peter. *The Magna Carta Manifesto: Liberties and Commons for All*. Berkeley: University of California Press, 2008.

Mabey, Richard. *The Common Ground: A Place for Nature in Britain's Future?* London: Hutchinson, 1980.

Mason, Emma. 'Ecology with Religion: Kinship in John Clare'. In *New Essays on John Clare: Poetry, Culture, and Community*, edited by Simon Kövesi and Scott McEathron, 97–117. Cambridge: Cambridge University Press, 2015.

Menely, Tobias. *The Animal Claim: Sensibility and the Creaturely Voice*. Chicago: University of Chicago Press, 2015.

Miller, Eric. 'Enclosure and Taxonomy in John Clare'. *SEL* 40.4 (Autumn 2000): 635–57.

Nixon, Rob. 'Neoliberalism, Genre, and "The Tragedy of the Commons"'. *PMLA* 127.3 (May 2012): 593–9.

———. *Slow Violence and the Environmentalism of the Poor*. Cambridge, MA: Harvard University Press, 2011.

Oerlemans, Onno. *Poetry and Animals: Blurring the Boundaries with the Human.* New York: Columbia University Press, 2018.

Payne, Christiana. *Toil and Plenty: Images of the Agricultural Landscape in England, 1780–1890.* New Haven: Yale University Press, 1993.

Shiva, Vandana. *Monocultures of the Mind: Perspectives on Biodiversity and Biotechnology.* Basingstoke: Palgrave Macmillan, 1993.

Tsing, Anna Lowenhaupt. *The Mushroom at the End of the World. On the Possibility of Life in Capitalist Ruins.* Princeton: Princeton University Press, 2015.

VanDooren, Thom. *Flight Ways: Life and Loss at the Edge of Extinction.* New York: Columbia University Press, 2014.

Weiner, Stephanie Kuduk. 'Listening with John Clare'. *Studies in Romanticism* 48.3 (Fall 2009): 371–90.

Whitehouse, Andrew. 'Listening to Birds in the Anthropocene: The Anxious Semiotics of Sound in a Human Dominated World'. *Environmental Humanities* 6 (May 2015): 53–71.

Williams, Raymond. *Keywords: A Vocabulary of Culture and Society.* Rev. ed. Oxford: Oxford University Press, 1983.

Zimmerman, Sarah M. 'John Clare's Conspiracy'. In *New Essays on John Clare: Poetry, Culture, and Community,* edited by Simon Kövesi and Scott McEathron, 57–76. Cambridge: Cambridge University Press, 2015.

Biosemiosis and Posthumanism in John Clare's Multi-Centred Environments

Scott Hess

John Clare has long been celebrated as an ecological poet and poet of place; he should now be recognized also as an important early poet of the posthuman. Clare's poems often shift rapidly from one point of view to another, including not only human but also various other-than-human beings, thus decentring the human as a focus of meaning and perception. Unlike the more familiar Romantic mode of the 'egotistical sublime', in which poets represent a single environment or 'nature' around an individualized self, Clare's multi-focal poetics offers a relational, many-centered environment, constituted by multiple, overlapping agencies and networks of perception and cognition.[1] In much of Clare's poetry (to quote from his poem 'Shadows of Taste'), 'minds spring as various as the leaves of trees'. This proliferation of minds and points of view, both human and more-than-human, defines nature and place in posthuman terms as interactive, relational ecologies of selves.[2]

S. Hess (✉)
Earlham College, Richmond, IN, USA
e-mail: hesssc@earlham.edu

199
S. Kövesi, E. Lafford (eds.), *Palgrave Advances in John Clare Studies*, Palgrave Advances,
https://doi.org/10.1007/978-3-030-43374-1_10

Take, for example, the following poem, one of a large number of sonnets that Clare wrote shortly after his 1832 move to Northborough:

The old pond full of flags & fenced around
With trees & bushes trailing to the ground
The water weeds are all around the brink
& one clear place where cattle go to drink
From year to year the schoolboy thither steals
& muddys round the place to catch the eels
The cowboy often hiding from the flies
Lies there & plaits the rushcap as he lies
The hissing owl sits moping all the day
& hears his song & never flies away
The pinks nest hangs upon the branch so thin
The young ones caw & seem as tumbling in
While round them thrums the purple dragon flye
& great white butterflye goes dancing bye.[3]

Like most of Clare's Northborough sonnets, this one is relentlessly paratactic, piling up one description after another in mostly self-contained heroic couplets. The poem is held together not by a single subjectivity or point of view, but by the unity of the place itself, constituted by multiple subjectivities and their interactions. The opening four lines present a seemingly picturesque vignette of an 'old pond full of flags & fenced around/With trees & bushes' and an encircling line of 'water weeds', observed as if from a single viewpoint stationed outside the scene. Already in line 4, however, this relatively static picture is broken by the subjectivity and agency of the 'cattle', who 'go to drink' at 'one clear place' along the shore, actively shaping the place. From there, the poem shifts rapidly through a catalogue of various other subjectivities that engage, interact with, and shape both the place and one another: first the 'schoolboy', then a 'cowboy', a 'hissing owl', young 'pinks' or birds, and finally the 'purple dragon flye' and 'great white butterflye'.

As the poem shifts with each new couplet from one agent and perspective to another, it creates not only a series of paratactic descriptions but also paratactic focalizations. This multiplication of agency is further emphasized by the poem's strong, active verbs—'muddys', 'plaits', 'hears', 'caw', thrums', and so on. There is no single, dominant perspective here and no clear line of demarcation or hierarchy between human and other-than-human agents, as points of view shift rapidly across species boundaries and overlap freely with one another. These points of view, moreover, are not self-contained but defined by the relations between various agents. The schoolboy 'muddies round the place' to catch eels; the cowboy does not just 'lie' by the pond as a passive observer, but 'plaits the rushcap' as he goes there to escape the 'flies'; and the 'hissing owl' responds in turn to the cowboy's unwanted presence. The introduction of this owl who 'hears [the cowboy's] song' shifts the focalization not only from ground level to its perch above, but also from the human to the more-than-human world. The phrase 'never flies away' emphasizes the owl's ongoing agency in deciding to stay on its perch, even as its ultimate purposes for doing so remain unknown to us (perhaps it guards a nest?). The following lines then shift focalization again, to the nest of 'pinks' (Clare's term for chaffinches)[4] in which 'the young ones caw & seem as tumbling in'. While the initial description of the pinks' nest seems focalized from an external viewpoint, the poem's final couplet shifts perspective and scale once again, so that we observe the agency of insects intimately as if from inside the nest, as the 'purple dragon flye' 'thrums' round and a 'great white butterflye goes dancing by'.

Erica McAlpine describes Clare's tendency to undermine the 'spatial positioning of the observer', so that 'each spot in the complex web of images is as central, or un-centred, as the next'.[5] McAlpine evocatively characterizes how in this same sonnet 'perceptions gather around the pond', as 'objects [that] gaze back and forth at each other—and occasionally look back at [the narrator]' (92). She interprets this decentring of perception in the sonnet and across Clare's poetic oeuvre, however, not in posthuman or ecological terms, but as an example of 'transitional' space in Winnicottian Object Relations psychology: a projection of the poet's subjectivity into the surrounding environment so that the description seems to hover 'somewhere directly between the human eye and what it sees' (85–6). Clare's creation of this transitional space between subject and object, according to McAlpine, reflects his need for distance from nature, his 'fear of self-exposure' and 'reticence about participating in the world around him' (99), as his decentred descriptions allow him 'both to identify with and separate himself from his subject simultaneously' (88).

While McAlpine's characterization of Clare's descriptive technique is compelling, her theorization in terms of Winicottian transitional space depends on an implicit humanist ontology. That humanist ontology assumes the human subject as the centre of all meaning and representation, separated from an objective, material world. McAlpine thus approvingly asserts Paul de Man's theorization of all poetry of the natural world as 'pastoral', in that it evidences the 'eternal separation' between 'the mind that distinguishes' and an 'originary' nature.[6] Invoking de Man's categories in this way, however, profoundly misrecognizes and distorts the multi-subjective, relational quality of Clare's poetics by imposing an absolute subject/ object barrier, the very distinction that so much of his poetry works to break down. Based on her humanist assumptions, which centre all representational agency in the individual human subject, McAlpine forces everything in Clare's poetry to refer back to his own separate, internalized psychology. Clare as a human poet must of course represent environments through his own human forms of perception and language, but the forms of his poetics deliberately decentre the human, representing instead a multi-centred, richly relational, and profoundly more-than-human world. Nature here is not a single fixed entity or field of objects, constructed around a singular human self, but a fluid and dynamic network of agencies channelled through multiple overlapping centres of perception, cognition, and action.

Clare's multi-agential, relational poetics resonates powerfully with recent theorizations of the posthuman. Posthumanism both challenges the centrality of the human in representing and defining the 'real' and at the same time reveals how the human is itself constituted by and dependent upon ongoing ecological as well as social relationships. Posthuman theory understands not only material and biological agency but also language, discourse, and representation as distributed throughout the more-than-human world, reconceptualizing environment, in Serpil Opperman's words, as 'a dynamic commingling of discursive and material flows, […] a multiplicity of complex interchanges between innumerable agentic forces'.[7] Subjects and their environments co-emerge with one another, with humans just one of many subjectivities that relationally constitute the world. The individual self is recast, in Rosi Braidotti's terms, as a

> moveable assemblage within a common life-space that the subject never masters nor possesses but merely inhabits, crosses, always in a community, a pack, a group or a cluster. For posthuman theory, the subject is a transversal entity, fully immersed in and immanent to a network of non-human (animal, vegetable, viral) relations.[8]

Humans and human selves are no longer the centre of all things, but as Braidotti puts it, 'an instantiation of a network of connections, exchanges, linkages and crossings with all forms of life'. Posthuman theorists such as Anna Tsing and Donna Haraway describe this necessary entanglement of subjectivity in a surrounding environment, including other subjectivities, as a process of 'multispecies worldmaking' or 'becoming-with'.[9]

This chapter will focus specifically on Clare's relation to biosemiosis, a form of posthumanism that reconceptualizes semiosis (the use and interpretation of signs) as not just an exclusively human activity, but instead as characteristic of and fundamental to all life. Biosemiosis understands environments, in Charles Peirce's suggestive phrase, as 'perfused with signs'.[10] Peirce defines signs in ways that go beyond the intentional communicative expressions of individual agents, to include anything that conveys information: in biological terms, anything that orients an organism to its environment and to its potential future actions. Semiosis in this model includes not only the conventional symbolic signs of human language, as in Saussurean linguistics, but also what Peirce designates as 'iconic' signs (in which the sign resembles that which it signifies, as a picture represents its object) and 'indexical' signs (in which the sign is directly associated with what it represents, as smoke with fire).[11] Any organism, in order to exist, must continually interpret and respond to such iconic and indexical signs from its environment; hence, in Wendy Wheeler's words, 'all life, not just human life and culture, is semiotic and interpretive'. Through this biosemiotic process, Wheeler claims, all living beings are 'bearers of purposes and readers of meaning' in 'constant creative semiotic interaction with their environments: each makes the other in a continual process'.[12] Semiotic communication thus according to Winfried Nöth 'occurs not only among humans but also between all other organisms throughout the whole biosphere'.[13] Semiosis and representation, in other words, are not centred on the human alone but fundamental to all life.

Eduardo Kohn describes signs in these terms as 'ongoing relational processes', which neither originate in the mind nor stand outside the world but exist instead at the interface of mind and world, enabling the mind to function through semiotic participation in its surroundings. Kohn writes, 'Signs don't come from the mind. Rather, it is the other way around. What we call mind, or self, is a product of semiosis'. Selves do not pre-exist this semiotic activity but emerge from it, as 'outcomes of semiosis as well as the starting point for new sign interpretation', forming nodal 'waypoints in a semiotic process'.[14] Human language and mind, in other words, actively emerge out of and depend on ongoing semiotic relations with our environment. These signs are neither exclusively material nor ideational but both at once, orienting minds and bodies to one another. As Timo Maran puts it, 'in every sensation, cognition or contemplation of nature, the subject (the human being) and the object (nature) become indissolubly intertwined'.[15]

Jacob von Uexküll's influential idea of the *umwelt* illustrates these semiotic processes and how they distribute semiotic agency and representation throughout the environment. For von Uexküll, environment is not a single, pregiven entity; instead, all living beings actively create their own *umwelts*, or semiotic representations of environment, as each one registers and represents its surroundings and orients itself in relation to them through its own particular embodied forms of cognition and ways of life. Von Uexküll uses the metaphor of the 'soap bubble' to signal the way in which 'every living thing is a subject that lives in its own world, of which it is the centre'.[16] Instead of imagining an environment, such as a meadow, as a single objective reality that is fundamentally equivalent for every creature, we must understand each creature as actively constructing its own version of the meadow, as objects take on form and meaning only in relation to the life, purposes, and perceptive and cognitive faculties of that particular being. These creature-specific processes of representation create the unique *umwelt* or cognitive 'bubble' that it inhabits. There is no singular 'objective' world, but instead a shared field of relations that each being represents and engages in terms of its own subjective experience and purposes. The shared 'semiosphere', constituted through the interaction of various semiotic agents and signs, is as fundamental to life as the biosphere, constituted through the interaction of material and biological bodies.

From this biosemiotic perspective, human language, knowledge, and culture in its various forms—including both science and poetry—must be understood as necessarily embedded in these semiotic environments that we share and mutually constitute with other living creatures. Our human language and forms of representation do not give us special access to a universal, 'objective' reality, but instead enact our particular human ways of engaging with our semiotic environments, in terms of our own specific forms of perception, cognition, and purpose. In other words, our representations help to produce our own specifically human *umwelts*. At the same time, this process of human semiotic 'world-making' is always shared with and dependent on many other beings, with their different *umwelts* and forms of semiotic agency, all of which collectively constitute the semiosphere.

Clare's poetry often enacts this multi-species, biosemiotic worldmaking, especially during his middle period from the late 1820s through the late 1830s. Many of Clare's poems in this period shift rapidly from one point of view to another, registering how each creature constructs and inhabits its *umwelt* as an active agent through its own perceptions and purposes. John Barrell has described Clare's descriptive poetics as an 'aesthetic of disorder', a multiplicity and particularity of description that offers 'one complex manifold of simultaneous impressions', not subordinated to any single dominant composition or perspective.[17] These 'simultaneous impressions', however, are not just a series of various objects, but also various subjects, focalizing their shared environment in simultaneous yet different ways. These overlapping subjective *umwelts* entangle productively with one another to create the shared, multi-subjective environments of Clare's poems.

Michael Falk links Clare's paratactic descriptive tendencies to his preference for the unusual sonnet form of seven successive couplets.[18] This formal structure is particularly prominent in the sonnets Clare wrote after his move to Northborough in 1832; Simon White associates it with the comparatively flat, open fen environment around Northborough, which provided less visual stimulation and variety than the 'hilly pastureland and woodland' of the Helpstone area.[19] While it may respond in part to Clare's new sense of place, the fundamentally paratactic form of these sonnets also enables Clare to represent multiple semiotic agents and points of view within each environment. Often these poems conclude with a sudden shift of direction in the final couplet to a new and unexpected perspective, in many cases that of an other-than-human being. These final shifts of perspective emphasize the open-ended multiplicity of agencies within any environment, and hence the impossibility of closure in representing those environments.

As an example of Clare's biosemiotic poetics, consider the following sonnet, 'Sudden Shower', part of Clare's manuscript for the *Midsummer Cushion* that he put together in 1831–2 and so roughly contemporaneous to the Northborough sonnets. While this sonnet does not use the seven-couplet form, it demonstrates in other ways Clare's paratactic, multi-focal, and biosemiotic poetics:

> Black grows the southern sky betokening rain
> & humming hive bees homeward hurry bye
> They feel the change—so let us shun the grain

& take the broad road while our feet are dry
Aye there some dropples moistened in my face
& pattered on my hat—tis coming nigh
Lets about & find a sheltering place
The little things around like you & I
Are hurrying through the grass to shun the shower
Here stoops an ash tree—hark the wind gets high
But never mind this Ivy for an hour
Rain as it may will keep us dryly here
That little wren knows well his sheltering bower
Nor leaves his dry house though we come so near.[20]

The poem begins with the darkening of the southern sky 'betokening rain'—in Peirce's terms, an indexical natural sign—and with the various creatures, both human and other-than-human, who interpret and act on that sign. Significantly the bees, not humans, are the initial subject and agent of the poem, who 'feel the change' and 'homeward hurry bye'. These bees hurrying back to the hive then become a sign in turn to the human subjects, who join them in seeking shelter as the first rain 'dropples moistened in my face/ & pattered my hat', another signal of the coming storm. The bees, humans, and many other creatures who inhabit this environment together—'the little things around like you & I'—share this same semiotic environment and react to its and each other's signs in similar ways, thus dissolving the ontological priority and centrality of the human. Even the 'ash tree' under which the speaker and his companion(s) shelter is represented in the poem with an active verb, 'stoops', signalling its own particular form of agency. The concluding lines of the poem then enact Clare's characteristic shift, in this case away from a human perspective to that of the 'little wren', another creature who inhabits this 'sheltering bower' as its 'house'. The wren also actively 'knows' its environment and acts through its own forms of cognition and purpose, making a decision to stay there even though the humans 'come so near'.

Invoking Deleuze and Guattari, Simon Kövesi characterizes the horizontal dynamism of Clare's environments as rhizomatic. As Clare shifts paratactically from one description to another, he breaks down binary oppositions between humans and nature and subjects and objects, representing environments instead in terms of interconnection and relationality as 'ongoing processes which deny fixed subject positions, which are always becomings and never happenings, and which are forever shifting, never still, never resolved, never done, never completed'.[21] Kövesi interprets Clare's Northborough sonnet 'The shepherds almost wonder where they dwell' (p. 67) in these terms as a rhizomatic defamiliarization of place, as the mist that permeates the poem isolates each individual point of view and erases distinctions until 'the place we occupy seems all the world' (line 14). Clare in this way enacts an ontological 'levelling', Kövesi claims, that focuses not on the 'bodies, but the links between' them, including but decentring the human.[22]

While Kövesi persuasively identifies Clare's rhizomatic tendencies, those tendencies in most of his poems do not so much dissolve subjectivity as multiply and proliferate it. Instead of ontologically levelling environments, Clare tends to represent them in terms of multiple subjectivities and centres: the many living beings who 'know' and inhabit those environments in terms of their own subjective *umwelts*. In shifting from description to description, Clare also typically shifts from subjective agent to subjective agent, creating environments in which (to repeat an earlier quotation) 'minds spring as various as the leaves of trees'.[23] Each being and mind establishes its own centre, but no specific centre can define or organize the whole environment. Instead, as the concluding shift of perspective in so many of Clare's poems dramatizes, each being represents and inhabits its own particular version of environment, or *umwelt*, while at the same time sharing and collectively constituting each other's environments as well.

Even in 'The shepherds almost wonder where they dwell', the mist does not so much level various subjectivities as highlight their distinctiveness, as the scene shifts among the disparate focalizations of 'shepherds', 'old dog', 'maiden', and 'ploughman'. The unusual separation of these subjectivities by the fog, as in von Uexküll's metaphor of the 'soap bubble', draws attention to the way that each being constitutes its own *umwelt* or representation of the world. Yet at the same time, the 'wonder' each being experiences is more a sign of habitual interconnection than of separateness, for they are accustomed to inhabiting a shared, multi-subjective environment, in which each being's perception, subjectivity, and agency depend on the presence and semiotic activity of others. Hence the uncanny and defamiliarizing emptiness each feels, isolated by the fog from one another. Even in that separation, these subjects remain bound together by their shared environment and experience, as for each of them in the fog 'the place we occupy seems all the world' (line 14).

These multi-subjective focalizations inform even many of Clare's most seemingly objective or ontologically levelling poems. The Northborough sonnet about the nursing mouse that Clare finds among a 'ball of grass among the hay', for instance—somewhat of a *cause célèbrè* for objectivist readings of Clare with its final image of 'broad old cesspools glitter[ing] in the sun'—focuses primarily on the mother mouse's agency as she first 'hurried from the crawling brood' to hide, and later 'found her nest again among the hay'.[24] Seamus Heaney points out the 'complete absorption' of the poem's final image, its 'combination of deep-dreaming in-placeness and wide-lens attentiveness'.[25] This 'absorption', however, involves not only the putting off of self but also positive recognition of various forms of otherness. The poem's power inheres not only in the irreducible material otherness of the glittering cesspools, but also the irreducible otherness of the mouse's subjectivity, through which the narrator refocalizes the poem after he imagines his departure in its final shift of perspective.

'Shadows of Taste', part of Clare's *Midsummer Cushion* collection, illustrates this extension of subjectivity and agency beyond the human by distributing the faculty of 'taste' throughout the natural world. The poem begins by extending 'taste' not only to animals and birds but even flowers and insects:

Not mind alone the instinctive mood declares
But birds & flowers & insects are its heirs
Taste is their joyous heritage & they
All choose for joy in a peculiar way
Birds own it in the various spots they chuse[26]

'Taste' in this sense, of course, is not just a sensory but also an aesthetic faculty, through which organisms semiotically discriminate their environments in terms of their own functions, meanings, and purposes. Even the flowers in this way exercise 'the wisdom of creative choice/Seem blest with feeling & a silent voice' (lines 23–4). The poem makes no firm distinction between the taste of these birds, insects, and flowers in discriminating, selecting from, and acting on their environments and that of the 'man of science & of taste' (line 107) after which Clare clearly models himself. Clare's widespread use of the term 'wonder' for both humans and other creatures throughout his poetry further illustrates this posthuman decentring of the aesthetic: in the Northborough sonnets, for instance, he describes horses (p. 51) and a dog (p. 110) who 'wonder', as well as shepherds (p. 67), maidens (p. 67), 'boys & shepherds' (p. 100), a passing traveller (p. 98), and the narrator himself (p. 84) (among others). The widespread and repeated experience of 'wonder' throughout Clare's oeuvre dramatizes the uncapturable open-endedness of environments and the multiple agencies within them, which retain a capacity to surprise even the most habituated and knowing agents.

John Coletta characterizes Clare's poetry as enacting a 'non-representational ecology' that challenges the claims of science and other forms of human representation and knowledge to capture a single 'objective' reality.[27] Instead of closure and objectivity, Clare represents 'natural communities as *ironic agents*' (256), composed not just of knowable objects but of multiple subjects whose various forms of semiotic agency surpass our capacities for knowledge and can even deliberately deceive us. Coletta interprets Clare's 'The Skylark' in these terms, as the 'semiotic irony' of the skylark's soaring leads the boys to believe its nest must be high in the air, before it circles back and unbeknownst to them returns to its vulnerable nest site on the ground: a 'lovely irony' through which 'animal life takes advantage of human abstract thought' (263) to enact its deception. Clare's Northborough sonnets include many other accounts of such semiotic deception, such as a fox who plays dead only to spring up and run away once its captors' attention is distracted (p. 25); or a partridge who pretends it has a broken wing to lure a human walker away from its nest (p. 43). This partridge poem ends delightfully with the line '& old cows snorted when they passed the place' (line 14), another of Clare's characteristic shifts to an unexpected and new point of view at the end of a poem. This ending suggests that the cows have some purpose for 'snorting' but leaves that purpose ultimately unspecified: do they snort in knowing acknowledgement at the partridge's successful decoy of the human away from its nest, or for their own independent, unknown reasons? In presenting this final hidden purpose, the poem dramatizes an environment full of other semiotic agencies that elude our knowing.

Other Northborough sonnets present a chicken (p. 86) and turkey (p. 34) who hide their nests and succeed in hatching their young, despite humans' and other creatures' best efforts to find and plunder those nests. These poems again dramatize the independent purposes of other semiotic agents and how they resist our full knowledge. The semiotic construction and hiding of nests is a major theme throughout Clare's poetry, evoking not only his shared sense of vulnerability with other creatures as a labouring-class poet,[28] but also the semiotic agency distributed throughout nature. The sonnet in which the turkey lays its nest includes a long catalogue of potential predators of many species—'old dogs' who see the turkey but 'g[o] away' (line 5); the 'old dame' who 'calls & wonders where they lay' (line 6); the 'fox' who 'unnotices & passes bye' (line 8); the 'old crow' who 'trys to steal the turkeys eggs away' (lines 11–12); and the 'cunning' blackbird who makes its own nest above but 'hides the shells cause none should find the nest' (lines 9–10), engaging in its own form of semiotic deception. Each of these creatures functions as a semiotic agent in its own right, as they observe one another's behaviour, interact with one another, and together make up an environment. Characteristically, the poem again ends with a sudden shift of perspective and agency in the final lines, describing how 'The magpie cackles round for any prey/& finds the wounded snake & flys away' (lines 13–14). We have no idea how the snake was wounded or why it came to be there (perhaps it was also trying to steal the eggs?), but the final shift to these new perspectives and agencies again dramatizes the open-ended subjectivity and multiplicity of this environment.

Isabel Karreman insightfully characterizes Clare's poems in this sense as '"contact zones" in which the relations between humans, animals and environment are reimagined as "material-semiotic nodes or knots in which diverse bodies and meanings co-shape one another", and in which animals exercise "a semiotic competence and ironic agency of their own"'.[29] Patrick Bresnihan similarly describes Clare's creation of a 'manifold commons', in which there is 'no single "nature"', but rather 'ongoing relations that constitut[e] many different natures', in a series of open-ended encounters 'through which self and world unfold together'. This manifold commons for Bresnihan is 'best understood as a verb, a movement, rather than a "thing": commons are produced through commoning—the ongoing, productive relations of people, animals and things'. Within this field of relations, Clare's 'experiences did not spring from his mind alone, but were constituted with and through the force of the world acting upon him', as 'together a world unfolds'.[30] While Clare does to some extent distribute agency throughout material environments, this chapter demonstrates how he focalizes it primarily on other creatures: especially humans, animals, birds, and insects, through whose interdependent semiotic as well as material activities Clare's environments unfold.

The sense of strangeness and dislocation that many critics have recently found in Clare's poetry registers in part this semiotic openness and proliferation of subjectivity: the defamiliarizing multiplicity of perspectives in any environment and their irreducible capacity to surprise or even shock. Joseph Albernaz represents Clare in this sense as presenting not just a singular environment or world, but 'worlds in the plural—local worlds brimming and bustling with their own networks of coexistence and inter-dependence, of sharing and shared being-in-common'.[31] Katey Castellano explores how the figure of the mole in Clare's poetry with its hidden, underground agency evokes 'a multispecies commons that is not subject to single-minded control by humans', but instead emerges out of a 'larger multispecies community'.[32] Enclosure in this sense not only imposes indi-vidualized human ownership on the land, it also destroys the multiplicity and particularity of those environments and their 'shared relational space'.[33] It levels the commons ontologically as well as physically, destroy-ing or rendering invisible the multiple creaturely subjectivities and rela-tions that constitute them. The haunting image of hanging the moles as 'traitors' in Clare's poem 'Remembrances' evokes in this sense not only the physical destruction of rich ecological communities of flora and fauna, but also the ontological destruction of Clare's richly multi-subjective worlds.[34]

In celebrating the multiple subjectivities in Clare's poetry, it is impor-tant to remember also Clare's own semiotic agency in actively construct-ing and representing these environments. Simon Kövesi has recently challenged the critical tendency to define Clare as a poet of place in ways that elide or suppress his agency, as if his poems grew organically from their places or offered a kind of documentary lens that simply records his surroundings.[35] Instead, as a number of other critics have recently pointed out, Clare exercised considerable agency in his poetic choices and in how he negotiated his identity in relation to patrons, publishers, editors, and readers.[36] Clare's environmental imagination was significantly shaped by his own poetic reading as well as his direct experience, for instance,[37] and by his deliberately acquired expertise as a natural historian.[38] Clare's social position, as a 'labouring-class' or 'peasant' poet, certainly shaped his expe-riences and enabled his aesthetic choices, but it did not determine them. Clare's particular vulnerability and the limits of his agency, in relation to enclosure, patronage, and the print market alike, may have predisposed him to identify with the correspondingly vulnerable birds, animals, and insects he wrote about, just as it informed his resistance to universalizing hierarchies and authorities in grammar, economics, and politics alike.[39] His social situation did not, however, predetermine his ontology or the forms his poetry would take. Clare's recognition of the active semiotic agency and taste of other creatures, in this sense, must be understood also as an expression of his own.

Summing up, what lessons can we learn by coming to Clare from a posthuman and specifically biosemiotic perspective? Clare's poems never claim or try to escape human language and meaning or his human subjectivity as a poet. By representing multi-focal environments through sudden and repeated shifts of perspective, however, his poems represent a multi-subjective, biosemiotic process of worldmaking that cannot be reduced to any one form of agency or knowledge or centred around any one subject, human or otherwise. Human subjectivity does not exclusively define these environments, but instead participates in their collaborative, multi-species processes of worldmaking. The unity of so many of Clare's Northborough sonnets, in this sense, comes not from a single unifying human narrative or perspective, either explicit or implicit—such as a series of impressions along a walk[40]—but from the place or environment itself as focal point for various beings' semiotic activities and their overlapping subjectivities and purposes. Such a poetics enacts meaning as always relational and positional, part of not only a social but also a more-than-human ecology.

Clare's relational, multi-centred environments address a specific challenge for a posthuman ecology: how to decentre the human while at the same time acknowledging the humanness of our own specific forms of semiotic agency and representation. Clare's multi-focal poetics can lead to the recognition that our human selves exist only within a wider 'ecology of selves' (to invoke Kohn's term),[41] both human and more-than-human. The richness of our human selves, environments, and meanings (not to mention ultimately our survival), depends in this sense on the continuing flourishing and diversity of these other selves, with which we share our semiosphere as well as biosphere. Our language and representations do not divide us from these other-than-human beings, but instead emerge out of and depend on our relations with them. At the same time, Clare's biosemiotic poetics reminds us of the limits of how we can know, making us realize that we cannot simply reduce the semiotic agency of these other creatures to our own human ways of knowing or representing, either 'objective' or aesthetic, but must continue in ongoing, creaturely dialogue with them. We are always co-authors, never the sole or solitary author, of our environments, our selves, and our cultures. In alerting us to the irreducible multiplicity of the environments we inhabit, this posthuman poetics has the capacity to foster an ongoing sense of wonder that can resist a wide variety of dangerous forms of reductionism: ontological, ethical, economic, and political. Clare's biosemiotic poetics allows us to recognize how ecological catastrophe, in impoverishing the semiosphere, will have catastrophic consequences not only for our biological and material lives but also for our subjectivities and our meanings.

In Clare's later, asylum poetry, much of this multi-subjective richness fades into the more abstracted and stripped-down environments of poems such as 'I Am', 'A Vision', and 'An Invite to Eternity'. Timothy Morton interprets 'I Am' as an exemplum of 'dark ecology', claiming that the poem offers 'the stunning moment at which [...] otherness is perceived as intrinsic to the self, at a terrible cost'.[42] In contrast to Morton, I find very little 'otherness' of any kind in the poem, stripped as it is of the multiple subjectivities and rich particularities that animate so much of Clare's earlier poetry. 'I am—yet what I am, none cares or knows', the poem begins, isolating the poet from both his social and ecological environments as the 'self-consumer of my woes'.[43] The complete social estrangement and emptying out of the self that the poem records is matched by a corresponding estrangement and emptying out of environment, as all of Clare's formerly rich and variegated description is reduced to only two abstract strokes in the final line: 'The grass below—above the vaulted sky' (line 18). This line centres all of nature around a single, isolated human subject. Instead of epitomizing ecological awareness, 'I Am' in this way dramatizes the impoverishment of both self and world in an environment stripped of multi-subjective semiotic agencies and relationships: the poverty of an enclosed self in an enclosed world. The poem reflects Clare's alienation in the asylum from the various relations that provided him with meaning and identity, even as it testifies in other ways to his continuing imaginative power. It enacts the ontological reductionism of modernity in the Romantic mode of the egotistical sublime, in which an isolated self centres an abstracted and semiotically impoverished nature around its own supposedly autonomous imagination.

Yet even in the relative isolation and enclosure of his asylum years, Clare often continues to engage environments in richly multi-subjective ways. In what may be his final poem, 'Birds Nest', he writes:

Tis Spring warm glows the South
Chaffinchs carry the moss in his mouth
To the filbert hedges all day long
& charms the poet with his beautifull song
The wind blows blea oer the sedgey fen

But warm the sunshines by the little wood
Where the old Cow at her leisure chews her cud[44]

Here again the 'warm glow' of spring impacts many different beings and subjects, who intertwine with one another as they each engage their shared environment through their own distinctive perceptions, representations, and purposes. These multiple agents include not just 'the poet' who writes but the 'chaffinches' who build their nest and sing and the 'old Cow' who 'chews her cud' at 'leisure' in the final line, a kind of dramatic echo of the poet's aesthetic leisure. Once again the poem reveals 'taste' as more-than-human, as each creature aesthetically discriminates and inhabits its own *umwelt*. The final line of Clare's final poem concludes his oeuvre with one last suggestive shift of perspective, opening into the subjectivity and 'leisure' of the cow in a way that reaffirms the multiplicity and open-endedness of multi-species worldmaking: its many subjectivities irreducible to any single viewpoint or 'objective' reality. The human self is only one node in this wider 'ecology of selves', whose multiple centres interact with one another to represent and constitute their shared while different worlds.

NOTES

1. See, for instance, Scott Hess, 'John Clare, William Wordsworth, and the (Un)Framing of Nature', *JCSJ* 27 (2008): 27–44; Scott Hess, *William Wordsworth and the Ecology of Authorship: The Roots of Environmentalism in Nineteenth-Century Culture* (Charlottesville: University of Virginia Press, 2012).
2. John Clare, *The Midsummer Cushion*, ed. Anne Northgrave Tibble and R. K. R. Thornton (Ashington, England: Mid Northumberland Arts Group and Carcanet Press, 1990), 131, line 54.
3. John Clare, *Northborough Sonnets*, ed. Eric Robinson, David Powell, and P. M. S. Dawson (Ashington, England: Mid Northumberland Arts Group and Carcanet Press, 1995), 40. Subsequent references to poems from this edition will be cited parenthetically by page number.
4. John Clare, Eric Robinson, and Richard Sidney Richmond Fitter, *John Clare's Birds* (Oxford: Oxford University Press, 1982), 35.
5. Erica McAlpine, 'Keeping Nature at Bay: John Clare's Poetry of Wonder', *Studies in Romanticism* 50, no. 1 (2011): 92. Subsequent references to this source are cited parenthetically by page number.

6. McAlpine, 99–100. Quoted from Paul De Man, *Blindness and Insight: Essays in the Rhetoric of Contemporary Criticism*, 2nd ed., rev. (Minneapolis: University of Minnesota Press, 1983), 239.

7. Serpil Opperman, 'From Ecological Postmodernism to Material Ecocriticism: Creative Materiality and Narrative Agency', in *Material Ecocriticism*, ed. Serenella Iovino and Serpil Oppermann (Bloomington: Indiana University Press, 2014), 28.

8. Rosi Braidotti, *The Posthuman* (Cambridge, England: Polity Press, 2013), 193.

9. Pramod K Nayar, *Posthumanism* (Cambridge, England: Polity Press, 2014), 5; Donna Haraway, *Staying with the Trouble: Making Kin in the Chthulucene* (Durham: Duke University Press, 2016), 12–13, 97; Anna Lowenhaupt Tsing, *The Mushroom at the End of the World: On the Possibility of Life in Capitalist Ruins* (Princeton: Princeton University Press, 2015), 21–2.

10. Peirce quoted from Wendy Wheeler, 'Natural Play, Natural Metaphor, and Natural Stories: Biosemiotic Realism', in *Material Ecocriticism*, ed. Serenella Iovino and Serpil Oppermann (Bloomington: Indiana University Press, 2014), 67. On the equivalence of biosemiotics and life, see Marcello Barbieri, ed., *Introduction to Biosemiotics: The New Biological Synthesis* (Dordrecht, Netherlands: Springer, 2007), esp. 102, 109.

11. For a comparison of Saussurean and Peircean semiotics, see Winfried Nöth, 'Ecosemiotics and the Semiotics of Nature', *Sign Systems Studies* 29, no. 1 (2001): 71–81; Eduardo Kohn, *How Forests Think: Toward an Anthropology Beyond the Human* (Berkeley: University of California Press, 2013).

12. Wheeler, 'Natural Play, Natural Metaphor', 69; Wendy Wheeler, '"Tongues I'll Hang on Every Tree": Biosemiotics and the Book of Nature', in *The Cambridge Companion to Literature and the Environment*, ed. Louise Hutchings Westling (Cambridge: Cambridge University Press, 2014), 122.

13. Nöth, 'Ecosemiotics and the Semiotics of Nature', 72.

14. Kohn, *How Forests Think*, 33–4.

15. Timo Maran, 'Where Do Your Borders Lie? Reflections on the Semiotical Ethics of Nature', in *Nature in Literary and Cultural Studies: Transatlantic Conversations on Ecocriticism*, ed. Catrin Gersdorf and Sylvia Mayer (New York: Rodopi, 2006), 466.

16. Jakob von Uexküll, *A Foray into the Worlds of Animals and Humans: With A Theory of Meaning*, trans. Joseph D. O'Neil (Minneapolis: University of Minnesota Press, 2010), 45; see also 69–70 on the 'soap bubbles'.

17. Barrell, 152, 157.

18. Michael Falk, 'The Nightjar's Shriek: Nature's Variety in the Sonnets of John Clare and Charlotte Smith', *JCSJ*, no. 36 (2017): 31–48. See also

Sara Lodge, 'Contested Bounds: John Clare, John Keats, and the Sonnet', *Studies in Romanticism* 51, no. 4 (2012): 533–54.
19. Simon J. White, 'John Clare's Sonnets and the Northborough Fens', *JCSJ* 28 (2009): 56.
20. Clare, *Midsummer Cushion*, 433.
21. Simon Kövesi, *John Clare: Nature, Criticism and History* (London: Palgrave Macmillan, 2017), 115.
22. Kövesi, 110–17, qtd. 116.
23. See note (2), above.
24. Clare, *Northborough Sonnets*, 54, lines 1, 14, 10, 12.
25. Seamus Heaney, 'John Clare—A Bicentenary Lecture', in *John Clare in Context*, 133–4.
26. Clare, *Midsummer Cushion*, 130, lines 3–7.
27. W. John Coletta, 'Literary Biosemiotics and the Postmodern Ecology of John Clare', *Semiotica* 127, no. 1–4 (1999): 242.
28. Chase Pielak, *Memorializing Animals during the Romantic Period* (Burlington, Vt.: Ashgate, 2015), 37–53.
29. Isabel Karremann, 'Human/Animal Relations in Romantic Poetry: The Creaturely Poetics of Christopher Smart and John Clare', *European Journal of English Studies* 19, no. 1 (2015): 97–8.
30. Patrick Bresnihan, 'John Clare and the Manifold Commons', *Environmental Humanities* 3, no. 1 (2013): 74, 78, 87, 80, 84.
31. Joseph Albernaz, 'John Clare's World', *European Romantic Review* 27, no. 2 (2016): 192.
32. Katey Castellano, 'Moles, Molehills, and Common Right in John Clare's Poetry', *Studies in Romanticism* 56, no. 2 (2017): 163, 171. See also Castellano's chapter in this volume, 'Multispecies Work in John Clare's "Birds Nesting Poems"'.
33. Albernaz, 'John Clare's World', 198. See also Bresnihan, 'John Clare and the Manifold Commons', 87.
34. Clare, *Midsummer Cushion*, 369–71, lines 37, 69. See Castellano, 'Moles, Molehills, and Common Right', esp. 163–5.
35. Kövesi, *John Clare*, ch. 1, see esp. 1–10.
36. Sarah M. Zimmerman, 'Accounting for Clare', *College English* 62, no. 3 (2000): 317–34; Paul Chirico, *John Clare and the Imagination of the Reader* (New York: Palgrave Macmillan, 2007); Mina Gorji, *John Clare and the Place of Poetry* (Liverpool: Liverpool University Press, 2008).
37. Gorji, *John Clare and the Place of Poetry*; John Goodridge, *John Clare and Community* (Cambridge: Cambridge University Press, 2013).
38. Robert Heyes, 'John Clare's Natural History', in *New Essays on John Clare: Poetry, Culture and Community*, ed. Simon Kövesi and Scott McEathron (Cambridge: Cambridge University Press, 2015), 169–88; M. M. Mahood, *The Poet as Botanist* (Cambridge: Cambridge University Press, 2008), 112–46.

39. Barrell; *John Clare in Context*, 1–27, 87–129; Kövesi, *John Clare*, 79–117.
40. Robin Jarvis, *Romantic Writing and Pedestrian Travel* (New York: St. Martin's Press, 1997), 184–7.
41. Kohn, *How Forests Think*, 16, 78, 116, 119.
42. Timothy Morton, *Ecology without Nature: Rethinking Environmental Aesthetics* (Cambridge, Mass.: Harvard University Press, 2007), 200.
43. *Later Poems*, 1: 396–7, lines 1, 3.
44. *Later Poems*, 2: 1106.

Bibliography

Albernaz, Joseph. 'John Clare's World'. *European Romantic Review* 27.2 (2016): 189–205.
Barbieri, Marcello, ed. *Introduction to Biosemiotics: The New Biological Synthesis*. Dordrecht, Netherlands: Springer, 2007.
Barrell, John. *The Idea of Landscape and the Sense of Place 1730–1840: An Approach to the Poetry of John Clare*. Cambridge: Cambridge University Press, 2010.
Braidotti, Rosi. *The Posthuman*. Cambridge, England: Polity Press, 2013.
Bresnihan, Patrick. 'John Clare and the Manifold Commons'. *Environmental Humanities* 3.1 (2013): 71–91.
Castellano, Katey. 'Moles, Molehills, and Common Right in John Clare's Poetry'. *Studies in Romanticism* 56.2 (2017): 157–76.
Chirico, Paul. *John Clare and the Imagination of the Reader*. New York: Palgrave Macmillan, 2007.
Clare, John. *Northborough Sonnets*. Edited by Eric Robinson, David Powell, and P. M. S. Dawson. Ashington, England: Mid Northumberland Arts Group and Carcanet Press, 1995.
———. *The Later Poems of John Clare, 1837–1864*. Edited by Eric Robinson and David Powell. 2 vols. Oxford: Clarendon Press, 1984.
———. *The Midsummer Cushion*. Edited by Anne Northgrave Tibble and R. K. R. Thornton. Ashington, England: Mid Northumberland Arts Group and Carcanet Press, 1990.
Clare, John, Eric Robinson, and Richard Sidney Richmond Fitter. *John Clare's Birds*. Oxford: Oxford University Press, 1982.
Coletta, W. John. 'Literary Biosemiotics and the Postmodern Ecology of John Clare'. *Semiotica* 127.1–4 (1999): 239–71.
De Man, Paul. *Blindness and Insight: Essays in the Rhetoric of Contemporary Criticism*. 2nd ed., rev. Minneapolis: University of Minnesota Press, 1983.
Falk, Michael. 'The Nightjar's Shriek: Nature's Variety in the Sonnets of John Clare and Charlotte Smith'. *JCSJ* 36 (2017): 31–48.
Goodridge, John. *John Clare and Community*. Cambridge: Cambridge University Press, 2013.

Gorji, Mina. *John Clare and the Place of Poetry*. Liverpool: Liverpool University Press, 2008.

Haraway, Donna. *Staying with the Trouble: Making Kin in the Chthulucene*. Durham: Duke University Press, 2016.

Hess, Scott. 'John Clare, William Wordsworth, and the (Un)Framing of Nature'. *JCSJ* 27 (2008): 27–44.

———. *William Wordsworth and the Ecology of Authorship: The Roots of Environmentalism in Nineteenth-Century Culture*. Charlottesville: University of Virginia Press, 2012.

Heyes, Robert. 'John Clare's Natural History'. In *New Essays on John Clare: Poetry, Culture and Community*, edited by Simon Kövesi and Scott McEathron, 169–88. Cambridge: Cambridge University Press, 2015.

Jarvis, Robin. *Romantic Writing and Pedestrian Travel*. New York: St. Martin's Press, 1997.

Karremann, Isabel. 'Human/Animal Relations in Romantic Poetry: The Creaturely Poetics of Christopher Smart and John Clare'. *European Journal of English Studies* 19.1 (2015): 94–110.

Kohn, Eduardo. *How Forests Think: Toward an Anthropology Beyond the Human*. Berkeley: University of California Press, 2013.

Kövesi, Simon. *John Clare: Nature, Criticism and History*. London: Palgrave Macmillan, 2017.

Lodge, Sara. 'Contested Bounds: John Clare, John Keats, and the Sonnet'. *Studies in Romanticism* 51.4 (2012): 533–54.

Mahood, M. M. *The Poet as Botanist*. Cambridge: Cambridge University Press, 2008.

Maran, Timo. 'Where Do Your Borders Lie? Reflections on the Semiotical Ethics of Nature'. In *Nature in Literary and Cultural Studies: Transatlantic Conversations on Ecocriticism*, edited by Catrin Gersdorf and Sylvia Mayer, 455–76. New York: Rodopi, 2006.

McAlpine, Erica. 'Keeping Nature at Bay: John Clare's Poetry of Wonder'. *Studies in Romanticism* 50.1 (2011): 79–104.

Morton, Timothy. *Ecology without Nature: Rethinking Environmental Aesthetics*. Cambridge, Mass.: Harvard University Press, 2007.

Nayar, Pramod K. *Posthumanism*. Cambridge, England: Polity Press, 2014.

Nöth, Winfried. 'Ecosemiotics and the Semiotics of Nature'. *Sign Systems Studies* 29.1 (2001): 71–81.

Opperman, Serpil. 'From Ecological Postmodernism to Material Ecocriticism: Creative Materiality and Narrative Agency'. In *Material Ecocriticism*, edited by Serenella Iovino and Serpil Oppermann, 19–36. Bloomington: Indiana University Press, 2014.

Pielak, Chase. *Memorializing Animals during the Romantic Period*. Burlington, Vt.: Ashgate, 2015.

Summerfield, Geoffrey, Hugh Haughton, and Adam Phillips, eds. *John Clare in Context*. Cambridge: Cambridge University Press, 1994.

Tsing, Anna Lowenhaupt. *The Mushroom at the End of the World: On the Possibility of Life in Capitalist Ruins*. Princeton: Princeton University Press, 2015.

von Uexküll, Jakob. *A Foray into the Worlds of Animals and Humans: With A Theory of Meaning*. Translated by Joseph D. O'Neil. Minneapolis: University of Minnesota Press, 2010.

Wheeler, Wendy. 'Natural Play, Natural Metaphor, and Natural Stories: Biosemiotic Realism'. In *Material Ecocriticism*, edited by Serenella Iovino and Serpil Oppermann, 67–79. Bloomington: Indiana University Press, 2014a.

———. 'Tongues I'll Hang on Every Tree': Biosemiotics and the Book of Nature'. In *The Cambridge Companion to Literature and the Environment*, edited by Louise Hutchings Westling, 121–35. Cambridge: Cambridge University Press, 2014b.

White, Simon J. 'John Clare's Sonnets and the Northborough Fens'. *JCSJ* 28 (2009): 55–70.

Zimmerman, Sarah M. 'Accounting for Clare'. *College English* 62.3 (2000): 317–34.

Common Distress: John Clare's Poetic Strain

Michael Nicholson

CLARE has here an unhappy advantage over other poets. The most miserable of them were not always wretched […] In the 'annals of the poor' want occupies a part of every page, except the last, where the scene changes to the workhouse, but then the burthen which is taken from the body is laid upon the spirit: at least it would be so with CLARE; for though the contemplation of parochial relief may administer to some minds a thankless, hopeless sort of consolation, under the pressure of extreme distress, yet to the writer of the following lines it must be the highest aggravation of affliction:—

John Taylor, 'Introduction' to John Clare's *Poems Descriptive of Rural Life and Scenery* (1820)

CLARE has […] contributed so much to our gratification, what ought we to render in return to him?—He deserves […] something more substantial than mere pity, because he is placed in circumstances, grievous enough to vulgar minds, but to a man of his sensibility more than commonly distressing;—

Taylor, 'Introduction' to Clare's *The Village Minstrel, and Other Poems* (1821)

M. Nicholson (✉)
Department of English, McGill University, Montreal, QC, Canada
e-mail: michael.nicholson@mcgill.ca

© The Author(s) 2020   221
S. Kövesi, E. Lafford (eds.), *Palgrave Advances in John Clare Studies*, Palgrave Advances,
https://doi.org/10.1007/978-3-030-43374-1_11

Long before his asylum years, John Clare was introduced by John Taylor as a poet whose first volume found its origins in 'distressing circumstances' and an 'exclamation of distress':

> Taking a view […] of my parents' distresses at home, of my labouring so hard and so vainly to get out of debt, and of my still added perplexities of ill-timed love,—striving to remedy all, and all to no purpose,—I burst out into an exclamation of distress, "What is Life!" […] I hastily *scratted* down the two first verses of it, as it stands, as the beginning of the plan which I intended to adopt.[1]

Taylor's introductions to Clare's first two published volumes, *Poems Descriptive of Rural Life and Scenery* (1820) and *The Village Minstrel, and Other Poems* (1821), figure the poet's distress as exceptional. According to Taylor, Clare would also experience relief from 'the pressure of extreme distress' in an uncommon way, as 'the highest aggravation of affliction'. As these selections imply, Taylor constructs his case for Clare's 'more than commonly distressing' circumstances by means of the poet's verse. The introduction to *Poems Descriptive* famously concludes:

> If the expectations of 'better life', which he [Clare] cannot help indulging, should all be disappointed, by the coldness with which this volume may be received, he can
> ——put up with distress, and be content.[2]

Taylor takes a line from the first poem appearing in *Poems Descriptive* out of context. In Clare's 'Helpstone', the phrase applies to the collective activity of 'little birds in winters frost and snow' and is preceded by an ampersand: 'they went / & put up with distress & be content—'.[3] Taylor's removals of Clare's represented birds and coordinating conjunction provide the grounds for the present essay, which considers the ways in which, despite his reputation for descriptive and particular poetry, Clare theorizes general and ubiquitous forms of distress that exceed his editor's more circumscribed and singular uses of the term.

The word 'distress'—insofar as it signifies '[t]o subject to severe strain or pressure (physical, financial, or other); to put to sore straits, to embarrass'; '[t]he overpowering pressure *of* some adverse force, as anger, hunger, bad weather; stress (of weather)'; and '[t]he sore pressure or strain of adversity, trouble, sickness, pain, or sorrow; anguish or affliction affecting the body, spirit, or community'[4]—historically encompasses financial and cultural forms of capital, atmospheres and affects under pressure, and bodies and minds in pain. As several writers across the eighteenth and nineteenth centuries were quick to point out, whether understood in terms of organic or mechanical metaphors, the poet's voice and body—like all bodies—could be understood in terms of distress. Oliver Goldsmith notes that like 'all things', human bodies 'sustain a very great weight of air; and although, like men walking at the bottom of the sea, we cannot feel the weight which presses equally round us, yet the pressure is not the less real'.[5] Henry Brooke's *Universal Beauty* (1728–36), reprinted in Alexander Chalmers's revised edition of Johnson's *Works of the English Poets* (1810), figures the human form as a weather system whose breath derives from the distress of respiring lungs:

> Subsiding Lungs their lab'ring *Vessels* press,
> *Affected* mutual with severe Distress,
> While tow'rds the Left their confluent Torrents gush,
> And on the Heart's *sinister Cavern* rush,[6]

Pairing 'severe Distress' with 'press' and figuring human organs, '*Vessels*', as collectively 'lab'ring' under duress, Brooke's poem anticipates some of Clare's favourite tropes and forms of word play. After the fashion of Brooke's alignment of embodied and atmospheric pressures, 'confluent Torrents' of blood and air, Clare sees distress as universally permeating diverse dynamic systems.

As Clare and his predecessors also distinguished, like the term 'stress' ('probably an aphetic form of distress'),[7] the word 'strain' applies as much to weather conditions and personal anxieties as to poetic craft ('strain' can signify 'a musical sequence of sounds' and a 'passage of song or poetry').[8] The second edition of English lawyer George Crabb's *English Synonymes, Explained in Alphabetical Order* (1818) ties the term 'strain' to the same forms of injury and damage associated with distress: the words 'strain', 'sprain', and 'stress' are 'variations of the same word, namely, the Latin *stringo*, to pull tight, or to stretch'; 'figuratively we speak of *straining* a nerve, or *straining* a point'.[9] Susan Stewart traces the term 'distress' to the same etymology: originating in 'distrain', 'distress' stems from 'the Latin root *dis* (apart) + *stringere* (to draw tight and stretch)'.[10]

In the opening lines of his antipastoral poem *The Village* (1783), English poet George Crabbe experiments with these etymological links:

> The village life, and every care that reigns
> O'er youthful peasants and declining swains [...]
> No shepherds now in smooth alternate verse,
> Their country's beauty or their nymphs' rehearse;
> Yet still for these we frame the tender strain,
> Still in our lays fond Corydons complain,[11]

Rhyming 'strain' and 'complain', Crabbe plays on the amorous complaint of a shepherd's 'tender strain' and the strained nature of such 'smooth alternate verse'.[12] By juxtaposing real and idealized shepherds—the 'swain' who rhymes with and is pressed by 'every care that reigns', and the 'Corydons' who 'complain' and chime with 'strain' (but are also bound by rhyme to the impoverished 'swain')—Crabbe is able to translate the sweet distress of the pastoral's idyllic 'strain' into a laboured poetic practice: 'rehearse', 'Yet still'. Emphasizing authentic rural work,[13] *The Village* returns us to the material definition of poetic strain appearing in Crabb's dictionary: 'a person [...] *strains* his throat or his voice when he exercises the *force* on the throat or lungs so as to extend them'.[14]

Clare's universal poetics of distress reworks the insights of these earlier poets, representing not only precariously extended strains and songs, but also images and views. In a sonnet entitled 'A Scene' from *Poems Descriptive*, for example, Clare envisions an elastic, ever-widening perspective: 'The landscapes stretching view that opens wide / With dribbling brooks & rivers wider floods'.[15] Attending to these 'stretching', strained images—the 'dribbling brooks' that expand into 'rivers wider' and discover infinity in the sonnet—this essay argues for a new understanding of Clare as a distressed poet who uniquely reconciles the formal, physical, meteorological, and professional dimensions of stress.[16] Focusing primarily on his first two published volumes—which appeared in the period of general agricultural distress defined by the continued effects of the Corn Laws and the looming return to the gold standard (approved in 1819 and completed the year *The Village Minstrel* appeared in 1821)[17]—my research explores the connections between harmony and harm as they specifically apply to Clare's poetic imagination of a new concept of community defined by common distress.

'CRACKS AND FISSURES': CLARE AS DISTRESSED POET

Following Taylor, countless readers and critics have understood distress to be constitutive of Clare's biographical identity and literary personae. Sarah M. Zimmerman traces how 'as "peasant poet" Clare has often had his works read as the poetic articulations of his distressed circumstances, rather than as the carefully crafted products of his extensive reading, and sustained poetic experimentation'.[18] While it is a critical commonplace to say that Clare was understood as distressed, few scholars have conceptualized him as a 'distressed poet'.[19] Turning to the social role of the distressed poet, however, allows us to better account for the ways in which his poetics, interlocutors, circumstances, and public presentation often exceed the bounds of the labouring-class poet and what Roger Sales terms the 'brand-name of peasant'.[20]

While Taylor repeatedly comments on Clare's unparalleled distress, he is also careful to fit him into existing literary histories. By means of allusion he discovers community—distress in common—in Clare's ostensibly singular situation; after contending that 'no Poet of our country has shewn greater ability, under circumstances so hostile to its development', he states that 'all this is found here without any of those distressing and revolting alloys, which too often debase the native worth of genius, and make him who was gifted with powers to command admiration, live to be the object of contempt or pity'.[21] Taylor here reworks Capel Lofft's preface to the labouring-class poet Robert Bloomfield's *Farmer's Boy* (1800), which itself seeks to allay fears about Bloomfield's delineation of 'RURAL SCENERY':

> [...] I had to encounter a prepossession not very advantageous to any writer: that the Author was treading in a path already so admirably trod by THOMSON; and might be adding one more to an attempt already so often, but so injudiciously and unhappily made, of transmuting that noble Poem [*The Seasons*] from Blank Verse into Rhime;...from its own pure native Gold into an alloyed Metal of incomparably less splendor, permanence, and worth.[22]

Although it does not explicitly reference Bloomfield, Taylor's introduction transforms the 'pure native Gold' that Lofft assigns to Thomson into a description of Clare's unalloyed 'native worth'.

Clare's lyric practice, like the poetic mythos that Taylor constructs, originates and ends in distress. As John Goodridge has shown, the poet was deeply interested in the lives, careers, iconography, and aesthetics of so-called distressed poets, from the tragic life of Thomas Chatterton, to 'Pope's scribbling dunces' and 'Hogarth's image of the 'Distressed Poet' (1736/7)'; Chatterton in particular functioned 'as a clear warning to the new poet, a *memento mori* [...] to be joined later by other favourites who died in melancholy circumstances'.[23] As Paul Chirico contends, Clare's 'conception of a literary community' includes both readers and texts.[24] Continually reading and composing verse about poets in dire straits, Clare was an avid collector of poetry written by and about distressed poets. In a 30 December 1824 letter to Henry Francis Clay, Clare recounts poring over 'a collection of Poems which was lent me calld 'Distress' written by a Robert Noyes'.[25] In addition, the poet's journal entry for 10 October 1824 reads: 'A wet day have finished the life of Savage in Johnsons Lives of the Poets'.[26] In *Lives*, Johnson casts Richard Savage in the role of 'merit in distress',[27] a phrase that would later appear in the preface to Bloomfield's *Farmer's Boy* (Taylor's introduction similarly refers to Clare's 'merit' and 'circumstances'). According to Sales, Clare also 'planned to write a life' of Bloomfield,[28] a poet whose 1823 passing *The Remains of Robert Bloomfield* (1824) describes as leaving his family 'in distress'.[29]

As Goodridge also shows, in 'The Poets Wish' Clare 'wishes himself into the community of English poetry, while figuring it as a tradition of ill-luck and poverty'.[30] Here Clare's poetics of stress carefully balances lyric and labour:

> Poor trembling tenants of the quill
> —'Here sir I bring my masters bill—
> He heavd a sigh & scratchd his head
> & Credits mouth wi' promise fed
> Then Set in terror down again
> Invok'd the muse & scrig'd a strain[31]

As this passage demonstrates, Clare's early works draw on and reshape the urban Grub Street imagery of the tortured muse, the strained couplet, and the unfortunate poet that Pope's *Dunciad* famously tied to the rise of a competitive print marketplace in which 'Some strain in rhyme; the Muses, on their racks, / Scream like the winding of ten thousand jacks'.[32] Apropos of Pope and the etymology of distress, the glossary entry for 'Scrigg'd' in

Poems Descriptive reads 'forced, or squeezed'.[33] Clare's reference to poetic production as 'forced or squeezed' suggests pressing circumstances and strained bodies; 'scrig'd a strain' again recalls the strain (labour) inhering in any poetic strain (song).

As Clare was surely also aware, long before Pope another famously distressed poet, Stephen Duck, had portrayed the toil and sweat of field labour in terms of poetry's streams and strains in *The Thresher's Labour* (1730):

> With rapid Force our well-whet Blades we drive,
> Strain every Nerve, and Blow for Blow we give [...]
> And Streams of Sweat run trickling down a-pace;[34]

Duck's poem cannily bookends these agricultural distresses, 'Strain every Nerve' and 'Streams of Sweat', with various sonic strains: the pastoral shepherd's easeful songs, 'The Shepherd well may tune his Voice to sing', and the confused chat of the Haymakers, 'By quick degrees so high their Notes they strain'.[35]

These examples reveal the ways in which Clare's poetics of distress participates in an expansive literary tradition of distressed works and lives. Clare revelled in what Walter Scott, in his critique of Chatterton's poetic forgeries, termed the capacity to 'imitate the cracks and fissures produced by the hammer upon the original'.[36] Throughout his career, 'cracks and fissures' defined Clare's aesthetic and compositional methods; his speakers are most at home when, like the poetic voice of *The Village Minstrel*, they find themselves 'haply sheltering in some lonley nook'.[37] Taylor's introduction to *Poems Descriptive* memorably describes 'a hole in the wall of his room, where he stuffed his manuscripts'.[38] Moreover, his introduction also stresses the poet's proximity to Pickworth's ruins, associating him with fragment writing; according to Taylor, since Clare could not immediately transcribe his 'imperfect memorials', 'several of his poems are quite lost, and others exist only in fragments'.[39] While Clare at times composed self-consciously distressed Romantic forms, including 'Fragments' (1820–2), his poetics of distress also encompasses the fractures that so often accompany traumatic experience. An early poem entitled 'Effusion' (1819–20) is instructive:

> Who that has feelings woud not wish to be
> A friend to parents such as mine to me

>   Who in distress broke their last crust in twain
>   & tho want pincht the remnant broke again[40]

'Effusion' stages a revision of the Eucharist in which a 'last crust' replaces the Last Supper; here breaking of bread marks material want rather than sacramental spirit. Under pressure, Clare's speaker aligns distressed bodies, 'want pincht', with the recurrent stretching and tearing of 'their last crust': 'the remnant broke again'.

Clare effectively comprehends distress as a pervasive milieu affecting mind and body; while the parents of 'Effusion' are 'in' distress, elsewhere his poetic voices labour under or amid it. He at times represents distress as generally characteristic of the careers and conditions of all poets. Clare's 1821 poem 'The Fate of Genius', for example, reimagines an unsigned popular prose list of calamities, also entitled 'The Fate of Genius' (1821), which recounts the ways in which distress has affected the most renowned classical and modern poets: 'HOMER was a beggar; [...] Tasso was often distressed for five shillings; [...] Milton sold his copy-right of Paradise Lost for fifteen pounds, [...] Dryden lived in poverty and in distress; [...] Savage died in prison at Bristol, [...] Chatterton, the child of genius and misfortune, destroyed himself!'[41]

Revising this catalogue, Clare's 'Fate of Genius' alternatively locates distress, after Thomas Gray, 'Far from the life of market towns'.[42] Clare's represented 'rustic genius' ultimately haunts the landscape from beyond the grave:

>   The damps of dissapointment provd too much
>   & warm hopes witherd at the chilly touch
>   Shrinking from life & hopes emblazoned noon
>   (lines 25–7)

By means of Gray's verse and one of his own favourite images, 'damp'—whose multiple meanings encompass atmospheric moisture, depressed energy, noxious fumes, and, most relevant to the poetic voice, stifling or choking[43]—Clare here presents a version of himself as a distressed poet. The poet's connection of psychological distress to material dampness also again notably reimagines the poetics of Crabbe's *Village*, which literally represents the mists facing English field labourers as stifling and distressing:

Thro' fens and marshy moors their steps pursue,
When their warm pores imbibe the evening dew;
Then own that labour may as fatal be
To these thy slaves, as luxury to thee.[44]

'The Fate of Genius' therefore exhibits the ways in which Clare simultaneously writes himself into the list of distressed poets (including Homer, Milton, and Chatterton), extends prior poetic visions of distress, and focuses on the specific material and psychological conditions that *Poems Descriptive* represents labouring-class poets as facing: 'Want, thy confinement make[s] me scrany'.[45]

'*ALL* COMPLAIN': CLARE AND GENERAL DISTRESS

Clare's biography, both as he and Taylor constructed it, also happened to resonate with the severe agricultural distress that followed the institution of the Corn Laws and the return of the gold standard (by way of the so-called Peel's Act). Taylor's metallurgical reference to 'distressing' alloyed genius in the preface to *Poems Descriptive* takes on an additional resonance in the era of financial distress marked by anticipations of the return of the gold standard (1819–21). Although a historical contingency, Clare's cultural moment clearly paralleled his life experience. His first literary productions capitalized on the ways in which his biography resonated with what Matthew Rowlinson has termed a 'cash poor' period during which money itself was scarce and impoverished as a result of 'the exceptionally dilapidated state of the legal tender coinage and the poor design of early banknotes'.[46] Taylor thus possibly feared that if Clare were to be cast as a debased genius, his works would be read as the aesthetic equivalent of the unreliable currency that defined Britain's transition to the gold standard.

As these pecuniary concerns exhibit, the publication events of Clare's first two volumes participated in and were shaped by significant cultural conversations about distress. In May of 1820, the British Parliament appointed a 'committee on the agricultural distress'[47] after Holme Sumner presented '218 protectionist petitions'.[48] Speaking on the necessity of such a committee, Sumner found it 'unnecessary to occupy the time of the House in exhibiting the distressed state of the agricultural interests; [...] from 1814 to the present time [1820], its deterioration had been most rapid and alarming'.[49] Although Sumner's account of the particularly 'disturbed state of the agricultural mind' carried the day, his colleagues variously critiqued his emphasis on the sufferings of landowners over manufacturers and rural labourers during 'a moment when general distress pressed upon every class of society'.[50] A pseudonymous 1823 treatise accordingly draws attention to 'the overwhelming distress of the Agricultural body', recounting how, from 1820 to 1822, 'the Agricultural Distress has advanced with a rapidly-accelerating pace'.[51] The radical journalist William Cobbett's *Weekly Political Register*, while not neglecting the exponential growth of farmers' distress in the wake of the Corn Laws and Peel's Act—from 1815–22 'their distress, with a short interval of tardy pace, has proceeded rapidly increasing'[52]—figured distress as a common ailment and unemployment as a symptom. The 27 May 1820 edition of Cobbett's periodical lists an array of failed diagnoses of the body politic—including 'a *sudden transition from war to peace*', 'a *superabundant produce*', 'a *surplus population*', and 'the *use of machinery*'—before recounting a dizzying array of failed state 'remedies'.[53] In Cobbett's view, the condition of England under Peel's Act is one of universal distress and elemental outcry: 'The *land* sends forth its uncouth complainants, who howl like the winter blast through the forest [...] *All* complain. *All* are in distress. All call upon the parliament to do *something* for them'.[54]

In order to more fully comprehend the ways in which Clare's first volumes shaped and were shaped by these cultural discourses of general distress, it is worth noting that, in the wake of the 1819 Peterloo Massacre, Cobbett's rhetoric of '*All* [...] in distress' had itself become ubiquitous. The 3 November 1819 editions of the radical periodicals *The Black Dwarf* and *The Cap of Liberty*, for example, reprinted the following petition drafted in a public meeting of 'non-represented People of the Metropolis': 'the universality of distress in all parts of the United Kingdom of Great Britain and Ireland cry aloud for instant relief to stay the flood of misery from overwhelming society in one common scene of confusion'.[55] Considered alongside this 'common scene of confusion', the rural scenery that memorably defines Clare's first volume often adopts a different attitude; *Poems Descriptive* represents distress by practising a version of what Kevis Goodman identifies as poetry's mediation of the news 'as *unpleasurable* feeling: as sensory discomfort, as disturbance in affect and related phenomena'.[56]

Parliamentary reports during the post-Peterloo period included speculation that distress might be a transnational phenomenon capable of being communicated across borders. Discussions of the so-called Six Acts considered the possibility that Britain's financial depression had originated 'from the distress of America'; the mobility, opacity, and generality of distress, it seemed, exceeded the policing power of the state: 'distress might arise from causes which the government could not control'.[57] During these debates Robert Waithman argued that a distressed public would ultimately become a calamity in its own right: 'Distress, discontent, and irritation [...] would burst forth like a volcanic eruption, sweeping every thing along, and destroying all in their course, if that House did not apply a sufficient remedy'.[58] Such accounts represent popular distress as a universal cataclysmic tide 'sweeping every thing along', an eruptive force resonating with both the energies of ecological catastrophe and political revolution. Moreover, they suggest the strong resonance between calamity's etymological associations, 'Latin writers associated [the term] with *calamus* straw, corn-stalk [...] in the sense of damage to crops from hail, mildew', and the disastrous effects of the Corn Laws.[59]

As the titles of texts such as *Proofs of Existing Agricultural Distress* (1820) and Cobbett's references to the prevailing 'universal distress' of 1820 make clear, distress was ubiquitous and urgent during the time of Clare's first two volumes.[60] The term's breadth and scope, along with its uncanny ability to transgress all apparent bounds, can also be glimpsed in the era's dictionaries and medical textbooks. Romantic writers from a broad range of backgrounds commonly represented distress as a general term, distinguishing it from adjacent (and in many accounts, more specific) terms such as anxiety, depression, and melancholy.[61] In his 1806 treatise on insanity, for example, Thomas Arnold states: 'I make use of the word *distress* in a general and comprehensive sense, as implying grief, dejection, despondency, anxiety, and in short every depressing affection with which the mind may be permanently afflicted'.[62] According to Crabb's dictionary, '*Anguish* and *agony* are species of distress'; '*anxiety* respects that which is future', 'that pain which one feels on the prospect of an evil', while distress is an ineluctable environmental force 'produced by the present' and 'some outward cause': '*Distress* is the pain felt when in a strait from which we see no means of extricating ourselves'.[63]

'Beneath Life's Pressure': Clare, Atmosphere, and the Nature of Distress

As Clare understood, the commonness of distress during his time also engaged the term's unique ability to represent climatological concerns. By way of the obsolete meteorological definition of distress capturing the barometric pressure of 'bad weather', Clare relates environmental and cultural (affective, medical, aesthetic, and political) forms of pressure. While it has long been commonplace to articulate the ways in which his economic circumstances and ecological surroundings bear on his poetry, his early poems themselves appear to invite such readings; in 'A Hunt for Dobin or the Force of Love' (1808–19), for example, the abundant constraints of poverty encircle the metaphorical wealth of nature:

> But who more dearly loves alone to prye
> In Natures gambols—Wild Variety
> To such a one (and many such abounds
> In the low path which poverty surrounds)[64]

A metaphorical atmosphere, 'poverty' here 'surrounds' the environment and itself; moreover, Clare formally reinscribes this representational phenomenon by means of a parenthesis.

Like Clare's 'A Hunt for Dobin', the opening line of Taylor's introduction also focuses attention on milieu: 'The following Poems will probably attract some notice by their intrinsic merit; but they are also entitled to attention from the circumstances under which they were written'.[65] Playing on privilege, 'entitled to attention', Taylor relates the power of entitlement—which so often derives from owning property—to Clare's lack of possessions and the land itself (insofar as it defines the peasant poet's 'circumstances'). Here again Taylor reworks Lofft's preface to Bloomfield's *Farmer's Boy*, particularly the proverb '"*it is not easy* for those to emerge to notice whose circumstances obscure the observation of their Merits"'.[66] His introduction transforms Lofft's 'circumstances' that 'obscure the observation' into a depiction of authorizing environs.

Considering the ways in which Clare's poetics of distress accounts for adverse and benevolent correspondences of mind and matter calls for a return to Mary Favret's influential observation that 'the mind was part of the weather' during the Romantic period.[67] Popular repositories such as *The British Encyclopedia* not only stressed the intensity and universality of atmospheric pressure, 'It is surprizing that such weights should be able to be borne without crushing the human frame', but also associated 'the weight of the air' with mood and mind: 'In Great Britain, for instance, the barometer varies from 28.4 to 30.7 [...] but when the weight of the air diminishes, the weather is often bad, and we feel listlessness and inactivity'.[68]

On the one hand, atmospheric pressure regularly signals psychological distress in Clare's poetry. On the other hand, the poet often figures moods and thoughts in meteorological terms, rendering human nature and climate by means of the same tropes. As a result, Clare's verse conveys what Marjorie Levinson terms the Spinozan sense that 'affection is synonymous with "idea," underscoring that the mind is an unmediated registration of the impact of other bodies on our own'.[69] Clare's early unpublished elegy 'Lines on the Death of Mrs Bullimore' (1809–19), for example, deftly coordinates human and nonhuman influences and impressions:

> [...] the first impressions made
> On the young plant its tender shoot to aid
> Must give the promise of a statley tree
> And the first cause of its perfections be
> In the same sence of her it may be said
> Who's guiding hand my infant foot-steps led
> To learning path—that her impressing plan
> First laid the basis of the future man
> And by imbibing what she simply taught
> My taste for reading there was surely caught[70]

The speaker's 'same sence', one of Clare's many lyric reflections on resemblance, coordinates material and linguistic forms of pressure; these 'impressions' also link the living and the dead. Clare's poetic voice represents learning as a material process of 'impressing' resembling agriculture—as a phenomenon coordinated by the 'guiding hand' of the gardener. Rhyming 'be' with 'tree', he aligns two forms of continual pressure, the organic 'impressions made / On the young plant' and the teacher's 'impressing plan'. Reading is a corporeal experience governed by 'taste', while knowledge derives from 'imbibing what she simply taught'.

Clare, however, most often registers the downwardly pressing atmospheric energies associated with depression. In poems such as 'An Effusion to Poetry' (from *Poems Descriptive*), we do not find flowing strains; we instead encounter broken, iterative poetic voices seeking to defy the threat of being 'Dampt despisd or scorn'd again'.[71] John Barrell's account of Clare's egalitarian poetic craft registers this aesthetic under pressure: 'no sooner does one object enter the poem than it is pushed aside by the next; so that we have the sense always that outside the poem are hundreds of images hammering to be admitted'.[72] The speaker of Clare's 'Native Scenes', a sonnet from *Poems Descriptive*, laments that 'vanishd pleasures crowd my swimming eyes'.[73] This 'hammering' lyric practice, which Barrell elsewhere terms 'images [...] crammed together' and a 'continuum of related impressions',[74] constitutes a poetics of distress insofar as it draws together various vocabularies: the press of the urban crowd; the weight of the air; the impressions of affect; the pressures of mass print; and the urgency of the lyric image.

The winter scene from Clare's 'Helpstone' simultaneously addresses barometric, poetic, and cultural pressures by means of Thomson's distressed weather. The 'little birds' of 'Helpstone' sing

> Visions like mine that vanish as they flye
> In each keen blast that fills the higher skye [...]
> & like to me these victims of the blast
> (Each foolish fruitless wish resign'd at last)
> Are glad to seek the place from whence they went
> & put up with distress & be content—[75]

Clare here notably rewrites the final lines of Thomson's 'Winter' from *The Seasons*:

> [...] Ye good distrest!
> Ye noble few! who here unbending stand
> Beneath life's pressure, yet a little while,
> And what you reckon evil is no more;
> The storms of WINTRY TIME will quickly pass,
> And one unbounded SPRING encircle all.[76]

In Clare's hands, the distress that Thomson ties to both 'life's pressure' and the stress of weather, 'storms of WINTRY TIME', does not 'quickly pass'. Besides intensifying Thomson's tempest and rehearsing the final lines of 'Winter' in the middle of 'Helpstone', Clare expands the bounds of his predecessor's universalizing atmosphere ('Beneath life's pressure') and dignified figures ('good distrest'; 'noble few'), creating cross-species affiliations between the ostensibly local distresses of 'little birds' and a labouring-class speaker. The poem following 'Helpstone' in *Poems Descriptive*, 'Adress to a Lark Singing in Winter', further extends the scope and duration of Thomson's represented weather while also re-emphasizing the surprising durability of distressed human and ornithological life. Rhyming 'freezing' with 'season' and 'sing' with 'sting', the opening stanza of Clare's 'Adress to a Lark' concludes by ironizing the valedictory optimism of *The Seasons*.[77] Clare's poem artfully revises Thomson's 'Winter' by extending the winter scene of 'Helpstone':

> [...] these victims of the blast
> (Each foolish fruitless wish resign'd at last)
> Are glad to seek the place from whence they went
> & put up with distress & be content—
>   ('Helpstone', lines 43–6)

> Drop were thou was beforehand seated
> In thy warm nest
> Nor let vain wishes be repeated
> But sit at rest

> Tis winter let the cold content thee
>   ('Adress to a Lark Singing in Winter', lines 15–19)

Thomson's celebrated images of distressing weather exerted poetic pressure on the young Clare. Clare's early winter poems emphasize not only striking and originary Romantic forms but also the ways in which distressed allusions and detached images (from one's own poems and the works of others) can simultaneously persist without becoming tired and trite.

In 'Address to Plenty in Winter: A Parody' (from *Poems Descriptive*), Clare again returns to Thomson's *Seasons*, this time coordinating class-based and climatological visions of distress:

> In convulsive eddies wreath
> & as in oppresion proud
> Peals his howlings long & loud
> & as tyrant like the storm

> Takes delight in doing harm
> To their uttermost extent
> Gives his rage & fury vent
> Down before him crushing all[78]

Rhyming 'harm' and 'storm' while associating 'oppresion proud' with the 'convulsive eddies' of meteorological activity, Clare constructs a common lexicon of distress—'crushing all', 'uttermost extent'—which simultaneously critiques economic and ecological forms of violence. While Favret finds war riding on the Romantic storm winds,[79] Clare's poem discovers a more ordinary 'oppresion proud' in the atmosphere. 'Address to Plenty in Winter' resonates with Thomson's 'Autumn', a work which renders the 'mad tumult' of hunting horns, shouts, and 'The gun thick-thundering' indistinguishable from the wild weather of a distressing 'tempest'.[80] By 1661, the term 'climate' itself had taken on the figurative sense suggested by phrases such as 'climate of opinion' and 'economic climate', which capture the 'prevailing' attitudes of 'a body of people, a nation'.[81]

While Thomson's 'Autumn' represents a human storm, Clare's unpublished 'Lamentations of Round-Oak Waters' (1818) reduces the human speaker to a metaphorical 'worm' that rhymes poorly with the grand 'storm':

> (For when my wretched state appears
>   Hurt friendless poor and starv'd [...]
> To think how money'd men delight
>   More cutting then the storm
> To make a sport and prove their might
>   O' me a fellow worm)[82]

Clare's 'poor and starv'd' speaker envisions the financial forms of distress caused by 'money'd men' as exceeding those of the turbulent atmosphere: 'More cutting then the storm'. As this comparison of the speaker to a 'worm' intimates, Clare's poetry often imagines distress as extending beyond the limits of the human. In 'Adventures of a Grass Hopper', the eponymous protagonist 'limped on his crutches in sorrow & pain / With neer a hope left to indulge his distress',[83] while the speaker of *The Shepherd's Calendar* likens a 'badgers shrieks' to the cries of a 'shrieking woman in distress', and memorably comments that the bustling insects 'seem partakers in the toil'.[84]

A fourth winter poem appearing towards the end of *Poems Descriptive*, the sonnet 'To a Winter Scene', again finds Clare experimenting with extensive forms of distress. Eliding the boundaries between body and environs, subjectivity and weather, his speaker self-consciously incorporates himself into the winter landscape:

> Hail scenes of Desolation & despair
> Keen Winters over bearing sport & scorn
> Torn by his Rage in ruins as you are
> To me more pleasing then a summers morn
> Your shatter'd scenes appear—despoild & bare [...]
> The ice-bound floods that still with rigour freeze
> The snow clothd valley & the naked tree
> These sympathising scenes my heart can please
> Distress is theirs—& they resemble me[85]

Clare's poetic voice yokes impoverishment and aesthetics, equally distributing distress across 'shatter'd scenes' and lyric utterance: 'Distress is theirs—& they resemble me'. The speaker's 'Hail scenes', a pun on icy weather and courtly norms, appears to performatively address Clare's volume, whose title also includes the term 'scenery'. Moreover, these 'sympathising scenes' of wintry 'Distress' evoke the poetic revisions of *The Seasons* that Clare assembles in *Poems Descriptive*. Representing remarkable lyric observers capable of being moved by 'scenes' while remaining in place, Clare discovers in distress a potentially heightened form of poetic attention that he extends to the reader. This embedded, involved, and potentially overwhelming view combining pressure and vision resonates with Timothy Brownlow's discussion of the ways in which Clare adopts the 'comprehensiveness', the 'circular all-at-onceness', of the low-lying, 'kaleidoscopic' perspective defined by 'moving pictures' whose 'details are in constant mutation'.[86]

Considered in light of the anti-reformist writings published during his lifetime—which railed against 'vehement speeches [...] calculated only to aggravate the pressure of distress'—and radical oratory's 'turning to mischievous purposes that susceptibility which distress had created,'[87] Clare's poetic project participates in a broader cultural conversation about the ways in which distress might produce more open and susceptible subjects. Clearly anticipating these anxieties, Taylor's introduction ties the poet's famed receptivity to natural pleasures rather than 'mischievous purposes':

'CLARE, it is evident, is susceptible of extreme pleasure from the varied hues, forms, and combinations in nature'.[88] While Taylor's appreciative comments resonate with Amanda Jo Goldstein's descriptions of Lucretian Romantic writers who 'cast life as dependent upon context, contact, and combination: a contingent *susceptibility* rather than an autonomous *power*',[89] the introduction to *Poems Descriptive* ultimately fails to capture the visionary ways in which Clare's lyric sensitivity to distress marks both pleasure and pain.

'DESERTS FOR HIS GAINS': CLARE AND DISTRAINT

As the 'shatter'd scenes' of 'To a Winter Scene' indicate, Clare's land-scapes, speakers, lines, and soundscapes are continually cut up, fragmented, and tattered. His works repeatedly point to the origins of the term 'dis-tress' in 'distrain' (a word whose Latin etymology denotes 'to draw asun-der, stretch out, detain, occupy').[90] The poet's verse notably employs the legalistic definition of 'distrain', a term whose earliest recorded use in the *OED* relates to legal seizure: 'To constrain or force (a person) by the sei-zure and detention of a chattel or thing'; 'to punish by such seizure and detention'.[91] The speaker of 'The Moorehens Nest' (ca. 1825–6), for example, figures agricultural labour itself as a distraining force:

> I hate the plough that comes to dissaray
> Her holiday delights—& labours toil
> Seems vulgar curses on the sunny soil
> & man the only object that distrains
> Earths garden into deserts for his gains[92]

Satirically coupling 'distrains' and 'gains', Clare's poetic voice casts the furrowing of the soil as a seizure of wild, open, and paradisiacal land ('Earths garden'). According to the speaker, rent, debt, and property pro-duce only 'deserts' and 'dissaray'. Similarly challenging the legal basis of distraint, Clare's 'Lament of Swordy Well' (1832–7) interrogates the 'pound'[93]: 'an enclosure maintained by authority, for detaining stray or trespassing cattle, or for keeping distrained cattle or goods until redeemed'.[94]

In works such as 'The Moorehens Nest' and 'The Lament of Swordy Well', Clare draws on his own biography; the poet experienced distraint from an early age. In an autobiographical fragment, Clare recounts how his disabled father, Parker Clare, suffered distraint after 'every misfortune as it were came upon him to crush him at once [...] as soon as he went to the parish for relief they came to clap the town brand on his goods and set them down in their parish books because he shoud not sell or get out of them'.[95] Published in 1820 and instituted on 19 April 1821, a new 'Act to Amend the Law respecting the inclosing of Open Fields, Pastures, Moors, Commons and Waste Lands, in *England*' worsened the situation by extending the reach of distraint; the revised law allowed 'Landlords or Persons acting under their Orders' to 'enter upon Land allotted and demised by them, and seize and distrain for Rent' even while 'the Commissioners' Award' permitting enclosure was still pending execution.[96]

Famously surveying the literary resonances of legal seizure through distraint, Stewart conceptualizes the 'distressed genre' as a deliberately 'distressed' work of art.[97] In her view, the distressed genre rises to prominence during the long eighteenth century as an antiqued artefact manifesting manufactured 'effect[s] of wear' intended to accrue pecuniary and cultural capital.[98] To be sure, Clare's poems, in extent, historicity, and construction, transcend Stewart's concept of the distressed genre. Yet the poet's oeuvre also engages the aesthetic stretching and tightening that Stewart memorably associates with distress by means of the term's origin in distrain ('*dis*' and '*stringere*').

Experimenting with these etymological connections, Clare's poems manifest a version of the universality that Crabb discovers in stress: '*Stress* is applicable to all bodies, the powers of which may be tried by exertion; as the *stress* upon a rope, upon a shaft of a carriage, a wheel or spring in a machine'.[99] *The Village Minstrel*'s frowning skies and furrowed landscapes make the ubiquity of distress present and visible (Crabbe's verse similarly employs these metaphors). At the same time, Clare locates the continuous, liquid songs of his and nature's poetic voice in the pre-enclosed past: 'While oft in beautys praise the while he hummd full many a strain'; '& heard em there sing each delightful strain'.[100] The poet's lyric soundscapes typically rely on rhyming and punning to signal the simultaneous impoverishment and plenitude that distressed poetic voice affords. As this essay has shown, Clare's verse incessantly capitalizes on the linguistic contingency that 'distress' and 'stress' rhyme with both terms of affliction— 'oppress', 'repossess', 'press', and 'depress'—and comfort—'rest', 'blessed', and 'progress'. In a similar way, the poet's corpus commonly recalls how 'strain' and 'distrain' chime with 'pain' and 'complain' and 'gain' and 'swain'. Yet the poet's sonic experiments were themselves distressed as, according to Gerard Cohen-Vrignaud, in the wake of the Peterloo Massacre rhyme was 'increasingly viewed as a lowbrow poetic effect, either generated by or aimed at the labouring classes' since 'rhyme's involuntary phonic impressment turns the reader's body against his mind'. By reclaiming such ostensibly 'lowbrow' forms of 'phonic impressment', Clare worked to reanimate the alternative labouring-class tradition of the distressed poet.[101]

The present essay has sought to rediscover the visionary connections that Clare drew between ostensibly separate concepts of stress. Clare's poetics of common distress—of particular interest in a present-day moment in which '*All* complain'—speaks to us across the ages, moving as it does beyond human bounds. Far from marginal or anomalous, the voice of the distressed poet stretches—reaches out and opens itself to the human and nonhuman communities (labourers, birds, insects, trees, and rocks) commonly subject to strain. Never 'more than commonly distressing', Clare's unlimited concept of poetic stress involves rather than excludes shared experiences, atmospheres, and expressions.

NOTES

1. *VM*, 1: x–xi.
2. *PD*, 53.
3. *Early Poems*, 1: 158, lines 45–6.
4. *Oxford English Dictionary Online*, v. sense 1a; n. senses 1b, 2a.
5. Oliver Goldsmith, *An History of the Earth, and Animated Nature* (London: J. Nourse, 1774), 1: 300.
6. Henry Brooke, *Universal Beauty: A Poem, Part IV* (London: J. Wilcox, 1735), 13, emphasis Brooke's. Clare's library lists several volumes by Johnson, including an 1818 edition of *Lives of the Poets*, making it possible that he had access to Brooke's poem as well.
7. *OED*.
8. *OED*, senses 13a, 13b.
9. George Crabb, 'Strain, Sprain, Stress, Force', in *English Synonymes, Explained in Alphabetical Order* (1816), 2nd ed. (London: Baldwin, Cradock, and Joy, 1818), 850–1.
10. Susan Stewart, *Crimes of Writing: Problems in the Containment of Representation* (Oxford: Oxford University Press, 1991), 67.
11. George Crabbe, *The Village: A Poem* (London: J. Dodsley, 1783), 1–2.

12. Eliza Emmerson's 1820 tribute to Clare not only similarly couples 'strain' with 'swain', but also rhymes 'Clare' with 'care'. See 'Lines Written by a Lady, and Presented with a Volume of "Clare's Poems" to a Noble Friend (30 January 1820)', *Morning Post* (8 February 1820), in *Critical Heritage*, 57.

13. Clare famously questioned Crabbe's authenticity, 'whats he know of the distresses of the poor'. See *Letters*, 137.

14. Crabb, 'Strain, Sprain, Stress, Force', 850.

15. *Early Poems*, 1: 413, lines 1–2.

16. On Romanticism's 'multiplied' forms of attention, see Lily Gurton-Wachter, *Watchwords: Romanticism and the Poetics of Attention* (Stanford: Stanford University Press, 2016), 1, 11.

17. Matthew Rowlinson, *Real Money and Romanticism* (Cambridge: Cambridge University Press, 2010), 12.

18. Sarah M. Zimmerman, 'Accounting for Clare', *College English* 62.3 (2000): 318.

19. Sidney Colvin refers to Clare as a 'distressed peasant poet' in *John Keats: His Life and Poetry, His Friends Critics, and After-Fame* (London: Macmillan and Co., 1917), 475n1.

20. Roger Sales, *John Clare: A Literary Life* (Basingstoke: Palgrave Macmillan, 2002), 26. Sales discusses Clare's early rejection of publication by subscription, the precarious politics of publishing as a peasant poet during a time defined by 'the suppression of working-class vice', and the poet's participation in 'a tradition of writing that merited attention, as much for philanthropic as for literary reasons'; see 20, 26.

21. Taylor, Introduction to *PD*, in *Critical Heritage*, 53. Sales traces the connections between so-called Cockney and peasant poets by way of the *London Magazine* edited by Taylor 'between 1820 and 25'; see *Clare: A Literary Life*, 35–6, 70.

22. Capel Lofft, Preface to Robert Bloomfield, *The Farmer's Boy: A Rural Poem* (London: Vernor and Hood, 1800), ii.

23. John Goodridge, *John Clare and Community* (Cambridge: Cambridge University Press, 2013), 12–13, 41–2.

24. Paul Chirico, *John Clare and the Imagination of the Reader* (Basingstoke: Palgrave Macmillan, 2007), 19. Chirico also explores Clare's and Taylor's dedication to 'the reclamation of earlier neglected writers'.

25. *Letters*, 312.

26. *Natural History*, 189.

27. Samuel Johnson, 'Savage', in *The Lives of the English Poets* (Dublin: Whitestone et al., 1779), 3: 55.

28. Sales, *Clare: A Literary Life*, 10.

29. *The Remains of Robert Bloomfield*, ed. Joseph Weston (London: Baldwin, Cradock, and Joy, 1824), 1: xxviii.

30. Goodridge, *Clare and Community*, 41. On 'Clare's extreme self-consciousness about his literary debts', see Chirico, *Clare and the Reader*, 27.

31. *Early Poems*, 1: 491–2, lines 77–82.

32. Alexander Pope, *The Dunciad*, in *The Works of Alexander Pope, Esq.* (London: L. Gilliver and J. Clarke, 1736) 4: 196.

33. *PD*, 221.

34. Stephen Duck, *The Thresher's Labour*, in *Poems on Several Subjects* (London: J. Roberts, 1730), 19.

35. Duck, *Thresher's Labour*, 17, 21.

36. Walter Scott, *Minstrelsy of the Scottish Border* (1802–3), ed. T. F. Henderson (Edinburgh: Oliver and Boyd, 1932); qtd. in Stewart, *Crimes of Writing*, 88.

37. *Early Poems*, 2: 126, line 61.

38. Taylor, Introduction to *PD*, in *Critical Heritage*, 50.

39. Taylor, Introduction to *PD*, in *Critical Heritage*, 50.

40. *Early Poems*, 2: 35, lines 27–30.

41. 'The Fate of Genius', in *The Scrap Book*, ed. John McDiarmid (Edinburgh: Oliver and Boyd, 1821), 288–9. This piece appeared in several other Romantic compendia of anecdotes.

42. *Early Poems*, 2: 666, line 1.

43. *OED*, senses 1a, 3a, 5a. The term thus resonates with the etymology of 'anxious', a word derived from '*angere*', to choke, strangle, and associated with a 'physical feeling of discomfort or tightness in the chest' and 'shortness of breath'. See *OED*, senses 3, 4.

44. Crabbe, *The Village*, 11.

45. *Early Poems*, 1: 144, line 51.

46. Rowlinson, *Real Money*, 31.

47. 'Agricultural Distress—Committee Appointed' (31 May, 1820), in *The Parliamentary Debates* (London: T. C. Hansard, 1820), 1: 705.

48. David Spring and Travis L. Crosby, 'George Webb Hall and the Agricultural Association', *Journal of British Studies* 2.1 (1962), 126.

49. 'Agricultural Distress' (30 May, 1820), *Parliamentary Debates*, 1: 637.

50. 'Agricultural Distress—Committee Appointed' (31 May, 1820), *Parliamentary Debates*, 1: 727, 730.

51. Vindex, *Observations on the Present Agricultural and National Distress*, 2nd ed. (London: Sherwood and Co., 1823), 39.

52. Cobbett, 'Sussex Journal' (January 12, 1822), in *Cobbett's Weekly Register* (London: C. Clement, 1822), 41: 109.

53. Cobbett, 'To Mr. Baron Garrow' (May 27, 1820), in *Cobbett's Political Register* (London: William Benbow, 1820), 36: 760–1.

54. Cobbett, 'To Baron Garrow', *Political Register*, 36: 761–2.

55. 'Finsbury Meeting' (3 November, 1819), in *The Black Dwarf: A London Weekly Publication*, ed. T. J. Wooler (London: T. J. Wooler, 1819), 3: 720. Mary Fairclough's discussion of this passage emphasizes 'the power of the diffusion of information' and the importance of print media in communicating distress. See *The Romantic Crowd: Sympathy, Controversy and Print Culture* (Cambridge: Cambridge University Press, 2013), 161.

56. Kevis Goodman, *Georgic Modernity and British Romanticism: Poetry and the Mediation of History* (Cambridge: Cambridge University Press, 2004), 3–4.

57. 'Seditious Meetings Prevention Bill' (6 December, 1819), *Parliamentary Debates*, 41: 762, 770.

58. 'Seditious Meetings Prevention Bill' (6 December, 1819), *Parliamentary Debates*, 41: 773.

59. *OED.*

60. Cobbett, 'A Second Letter to Mr. Alderman Wood' (24 June, 1820), in *Cobbett's Political Register*, 36: 1074.

61. On Romantic anxiety, 'transport', and the mobile affects that this essay discovers in distress, see Miranda Burgess, 'Transport: Mobility, Anxiety, and the Romantic Poetics of Feeling', *Studies in Romanticism* 49.2 (2010): 241.

62. Thomas Arnold, *Observations on the Nature, Kinds, Causes, and Prevention of Insanity*, 2nd ed. (London: Richard Phillips, 1806), 1: 29.

63. Crabb, 'Distress, Anxiety, Anguish, Agony', in *English Synonymes*, 380.

64. *Early Poems*, 1: 75, lines 192–5.

65. Taylor, Introduction to *PD*, in *Critical Heritage*, 43.

66. Lofft, Preface to Bloomfield's *Farmer's Boy*, xiv; emphasis Lofft's.

67. Mary Favret, *War at a Distance: Romanticism and the Making of Modern Wartime* (Princeton: Princeton University Press, 2010), 120.

68. 'Atmosphere', in *The British Encyclopedia, Or Dictionary of Arts and Sciences*, ed. William Nicholson (London: Longman, Hurst, Rees, and Orme, 1809), 1: np.

69. Marjorie Levinson, *Thinking Through Poetry: Field Reports on Romantic Lyric* (Oxford: Oxford University Press, 2018), 121.

70. *Early Poems*, 1: 199, lines 41–50.

71. *Early Poems*, 1: 546, line 30.

72. Barrell, 151.

73. *Early Poems*, 1: 301, line 13. On the 'unstoppable momentum' of Clare's lyric subjects, see my essay, 'The Itinerant 'I': John Clare's Lyric Defiance', *ELH* 82.2 (2015): 640.

74. Barrell, 152, 155. In Barrell's view, Clare's rural scenes crowd and press upon the reader: '*The Village Minstrel* [...] speaks of "every form that *crowds* the circling round"' (152–3).

75. *Early Poems*, 1: 158, lines 39–40 and 43–6.
76. James Thomson, *The Seasons, A Poem* (London: J. Millan and A. Millar, 1730), 302.
77. *Early Poems*, 1: 99, lines 1–6.
78. *Early Poems*, 1: 319, lines 238–45.
79. See Favret, *War at a Distance*, 121.
80. Thomson, *The Seasons*, 186–93.
81. *OED*, sense 2b.
82. *Early Poems*, 1: 228, lines 17–18 and 21–4.
83. *Middle Period*, 3: 126, lines 125–6.
84. *Middle Period*, 1: 46, lines 190–2; 110, line 12.
85. *Early Poems*, 1: 417, lines 1–5 and 11–14.
86. Timothy Brownlow, *John Clare and Picturesque Landscape* (Oxford: Clarendon Press, 1983), 22–3, 116.
87. Roger Therry, *The Speeches of the Right Honourable George Canning* (London: James Ridgway, 1828), 1: 106.
88. Taylor, Introduction to *PD*, in *Critical Heritage*, 49.
89. Amanda Jo Goldstein, *Sweet Science: Romantic Materialism and the New Logics of Life* (Chicago: University of Chicago Press, 2017), 22.
90. *OED*.
91. *OED*, sense 7a.
92. *Middle Period*, 3: 469, lines 32–6.
93. See *Middle Period*, 5: 113, line 227.
94. *OED*, sense 1a.
95. *By Himself*, 117.
96. *The Statutes of the United Kingdom of Great Britain and Ireland: 60 Geo. III. & 1 Geo. IV. 1819–20. And 1 Geo. IV. 1820* (London: J. Butterworth, 1820), 24.
97. Stewart, *Crimes of Writing*, 67, 88.
98. *OED*, 'distress', sense 7.
99. Crabb, 'Stress, Strain, Emphasis, Accent', in *English Synonymes*, 852.
100. *Early Poems*, 2: 152, lines 679–80; 171, line 1133.
101. Gerard Cohen-Vrignaud, 'Rhyme's Crimes', *ELH* 82.3 (2015): 998, 1003.

Bibliography

'Agricultural Distress'. *The Parliamentary Debates*. Vol. 1, 635–93. London: T. C. Hansard (30 May 1820).
'Agricultural Distress—Committee Appointed'. *The Parliamentary Debates*. Vol. 1, 705–42. London: T. C. Hansard (31 May 1820).

Arnold, Thomas. *Observations on the Nature, Kinds, Causes, and Prevention of Insanity.* 2nd edn. 2 vols. London: Richard Phillips, 1806.

Barrell, John. *The Idea of Landscape and the Sense of Place, 1730–1840.* Cambridge: Cambridge University Press, 1972.

Brooke, Henry. *Universal Beauty: A Poem, Part IV.* London: J. Wilcox, 1735.

Brownlow, Timothy. *John Clare and Picturesque Landscape.* Oxford: Clarendon Press, 1983.

Burgess, Miranda. 'Transport: Mobility, Anxiety, and the Romantic Poetics of Feeling'. *Studies in Romanticism* 49.2 (2010): 229–60.

Chirico, Paul. *John Clare and the Imagination of the Reader.* Basingstoke: Palgrave Macmillan, 2007.

Clare, John. *Poems Descriptive of Rural Life and Scenery.* London: Taylor and Hessey, 1820.

———. *The Village Minstrel and Other Poems.* 2 vols. London: Taylor and Hessey, 1821.

———. *The Natural History Prose Writings of John Clare.* Edited by Margaret Grainger. Oxford: Clarendon Press, 1983.

———. *The Letters of John Clare.* Edited by Mark Storey. Oxford: Clarendon Press, 1985.

———. *The Early Poems of John Clare, 1804–1822.* 2 vols. Edited by Eric Robinson, David Powell and Margaret Grainger. Oxford: Clarendon Press, 1989.

———. *John Clare By Himself.* Edited by Eric Robinson and David Powell. Manchester: Carcanet, 1996.

———. *Poems of the Middle Period, 1822–1837.* 5 vols. Edited by Eric Robinson, David Powell, and P. M. S. Dawson. Oxford: Clarendon Press, 1998–2003.

Cobbett, William. 'A Second Letter to Mr. Alderman Wood'. *Cobbett's Political Register.* 36 (24 June 1820a): 1033–80.

———. 'Sussex Journal'. *Cobbett's Weekly Register.* Vol. 41 (12 January 1822): 91–121.

———. 'To Mr. Baron Garrow'. *Cobbett's Political Register.* 36 (27 May 1820b): 753–73.

Cohen-Vrignaud, Gerard. 'Rhyme's Crimes'. *ELH* 82.3 (2015): 987–1012.

Colvin, Sidney. *John Keats: His Life and Poetry, His Friends Critics, and After-Fame.* London: Macmillan, 1917.

Crabb, George. *English Synonymes, Explained in Alphabetical Order* (1816). 2nd edn. London: Baldwin, Cradock, and Joy, 1818.

Crabbe, George. *The Village: A Poem.* London: J. Dodsley, 1783.

Dalbiac, J. G. *Proofs of Existing Agricultural Distress.* Lewes: Sussex Advertiser Office, 1820.

Duck, Stephen. *The Thresher's Labour. Poems on Several Subjects.* London: J. Roberts, 1730.

Emmerson, Eliza Louisa. 'Lines Written by a Lady, and Presented with a Volume of 'Clare's Poems' to a Noble Friend'. In *John Clare: The Critical Heritage*, edited by Mark Storey, 57–8. London: Routledge & Kegan Paul, 1973.

'The Fate of Genius'. *The Scrap Book*. Edited by John McDiarmid, 288–89. Edinburgh: Oliver and Boyd, 1821.

Favret, Mary. *War at a Distance: Romanticism and the Making of Modern Wartime*. Princeton: Princeton University Press, 2010.

'Finsbury Meeting'. *The Black Dwarf*. Vol. 3, 720–04 (3 November 1819).

Goldsmith, Oliver. *An History of the Earth, and Animated Nature*. 8 vols. London: J. Nourse, 1774.

Goldstein, Amanda Jo. *Sweet Science: Romantic Materialism and the New Logics of Life*. Chicago: University of Chicago Press, 2017.

Goodman, Kevis. *Georgic Modernity and British Romanticism: Poetry and the Mediation of History*. Cambridge: Cambridge University Press, 2004.

Goodridge, John. *John Clare and Community*. Cambridge: Cambridge University Press, 2013.

Gurton-Wachter, Lily. *Watchwords: Romanticism and the Poetics of Attention*. Stanford: Stanford University Press, 2016.

Johnson, Samuel. 'Savage'. *The Lives of the English Poets*. 3 vols. 29–186. Dublin: Whitestone, et al., 1779.

Levinson, Marjorie. *Thinking Through Poetry: Field Reports on Romantic Lyric*. Oxford: Oxford University Press, 2018.

Lofft, Capel. Preface. Robert Bloomfield. *The Farmer's Boy: A Rural Poem*, I–XVI. London: Vernor and Hood, 1800.

Nicholson, Michael. 'The Itinerant "I": John Clare's Lyric Defiance'. *ELH* 82.2 (2015): 637–69.

Nicholson, William. 'Atmosphere'. *The British Encyclopedia, Or Dictionary of Arts and Sciences*. 6 vols. London: Longman, Hurst, Rees, and Orme, 1809.

Pope, Alexander. *The Dunciad*. *The Works of Alexander Pope, Esq*. 4 vols. London: L. Gilliver and J. Clarke, 1736.

The Remains of Robert Bloomfield. Edited by Joseph Weston. 2 vols. London: Baldwin, Cradock, and Joy, 1824.

Rowlinson, Matthew. *Real Money and Romanticism*. Cambridge: Cambridge University Press, 2010.

Sales, Roger. *John Clare: A Literary Life*. Basingstoke: Palgrave Macmillan, 2002.

Scott, Walter. *Minstrelsy of the Scottish Border* (1802–3). Edited by T. F. Henderson. 4 vols. Edinburgh: Oliver and Boyd, 1932.

'Seditious Meetings Prevention Bill'. (6 December 1819). *The Parliamentary Debates: From the Year 1803 to the Present Time*, Vol. 41, 757–805. London: T.C. Hansard, 1820.

Spring, David and Travis L. Crosby. 'George Webb Hall and the Agricultural Association'. *Journal of British Studies* 2.1 (1962): 115–31.

The Statutes of the United Kingdom of Great Britain and Ireland: 60 Geo. III. & 1 Geo. IV. 1819–20. And 1 Geo. IV. 1820. London: J. Butterworth, 1820.

Stewart, Susan. *Crimes of Writing: Problems in the Containment of Representation.* Oxford: Oxford University Press, 1991.

Storey, Mark, ed. *John Clare: The Critical Heritage.* London: Routledge & Kegan Paul, 1973.

Therry, Roger. *The Speeches of the Right Honourable George Canning.* 6 vols. London: James Ridgway, 1828.

Thomson, James. *The Seasons, A Poem.* London: J. Millan and A. Millar, 1730.

Vindex. *Observations on the Present Agricultural and National Distress.* 2nd edn. London: Sherwood and Co., 1823.

Zimmerman, Sarah M. 'Accounting for Clare'. *College English* 62.3 (2000): 317–34.

'fancys or feelings': John Clare's Hypochondriac Poetics

Erin Lafford

In his essay 'Beghosted Bodyhood', Steven Connor suggests that 'only if you are ill will you have a definite idea of how you are—and, for the hypochondriac, perhaps, of who you are'.[1] Whilst this statement speaks to the complex interplay of representation and self-fashioning in relation to imaginary illness that this essay will explore, it is at the same time not easily applied to John Clare. Roy Porter staged a key intervention in the reception of Clare's madness in particular (the most critically discussed aspect of his illness) when he argued that the poet's asylum writings, and behaviours Clare purportedly displayed in High Beach and Northampton General asylum, could not be read straightforwardly as diagnostic evidence. By asking 'Was Clare actually mad? If so, from which psychiatric disorder was he suffering?' but then dismissing 'the parlour game of retrospective diagnosis', Porter opened up a new critical conversation in relation to Clare's madness that could accommodate the possibilities of subversion and performance in the face of clinical power.[2] No longer is it the case that the

E. Lafford (✉)
University of Derby, Derby, UK
e-mail: e.lafford@derby.ac.uk

© The Author(s) 2020   249
S. Kövesi, E. Lafford (eds.), *Palgrave Advances in John Clare
Studies*, Palgrave Advances,
https://doi.org/10.1007/978-3-030-43374-1_12

competing suggestions of schizophrenia or bi-polar disorder made by Geoffrey Grigson and John and Anne Tibble, respectively, govern how Clare's 'madness', and its manifestations in his verse, can be read.[3] Frederick Burwick and Roger Sales, for example, have argued variously for Clare's self-conscious engagement with a Romantic tradition of poetic 'madness' that colours his identification with Byron and De Quincey in his asylum verse, and for the inherently 'theatrical' elements of asylum culture.[4] Clare emerges from these non-diagnostic readings not simply as the poor suffering peasant eventually estranged from his faculties that early biographers favoured,[5] but as an accomplished, self-aware poet for whom madness is just one mask he might put on.

   If the result of scholarly developments surrounding Clare's madness is that critics are more willing to read pathology as performance, or even to suggest that Clare's disorder might not have been straightforwardly 'real', then this essay asks what can be gained from returning to some fleeting claims about Clare's mental and physical health that express a struggle between reality and imagination, but have not yet received sufficient attention. I refer here to suggestions, both from his contemporary moment and from his subsequent critical reception, that Clare was a hypochondriac. Romantic poets such as Coleridge, Shelley, and Byron continue to attract attention for their intensive scrutiny of their own physical and mental health and its manifestation in their writing.[6] George C. Grinnell's study of hypochondria in this period also asserts that writers such as Mary Shelley, Thomas Beddoes, Thomas De Quincey, and Mary Prince were key figures who evidenced hypochondria's shaping influence on Romantic culture.[7] Clare has so far been overlooked in these critical conversations, even though his propensity for hypochondria was suggested at the beginning of his poetic career by Edward Drury (the bookseller who first introduced Clare's poetry to John Taylor): Drury, supposedly concerned about the consequences of Clare's 'talent' being 'forced' after his initial success, worried about the poet's coping methods: 'he has no other mode of easing the fever that oppresses him after a tremendous fit of rhyming except by getting tipsy [...] Then he is melancholy and completely hypochondriac'.[8] Jonathan Bate argues that Drury's assessment of Clare's writing habits and their effect on his mental and physical health is 'as good as, if not better than, those of the doctors who entered the story in later years',[9] but there is yet to be a sustained discussion of how hypochondria might have shaped Clare's relationship to his own poetry and pathologies, as well as to a wider Romantic culture of imaginary illness.

Contemporary critical studies of Clare have engaged with hypochondria in a suggestive but fleeting fashion. Porter claimed that the poet, in worrying about frequent 'psychosomatic' symptoms, such as headaches, stomach-aches, and digestive problems, 'turned into a hypochondriac' and in doing so 'reflected ruefully on the power of the imagination'.[10] Simon Kövesi, too, in his discussion of Clare's fixation on what he often felt was his imminent death, remarks that the poet's frequent worries over having contracted venereal disease were the 'exaggerated product of a guilt-ridden hypochondriac'.[11] These comments read either as an offhand way of saying that Clare was worrying over nothing, or else leave much more to be said. Hypochondria, I suggest, should be taken seriously as a conceptual lens through which to read Clare's wider poetic imagination in relation to illness and disorder. Instead of choosing between the critical apparatuses of diagnosis on the one hand, or the dismissal of pathology as clinical power on the other, hypochondria occupies a distinct interpretative space of uncertainty and of literary associations that, this essay argues, are better able to approach Clare on his own terms. My concern in this essay is not to debate whether Clare was a hypochondriac or not. Instead, I approach hypochondria in two interrelated ways: as a social and literary culture that Clare wanted to participate in and that also framed some of his writing, and as a form of poetic imagination and attention that emerged from Clare's anxious scrutiny of his own body and mind. I also explore, through a final reading of a sonnet Clare published in the *London Magazine* in 1821, how hypochondria can become an important lens through which to consider Clare's lyric subjectivity, uncovering as it does the ambiguously pathological experiences or registers that might disrupt his observation of the natural world.

Clare's mental distress and eventual institutionalisation are much discussed by critics, but the poet also complained of various physical symptoms throughout his life. His letters mention headaches and stomach-aches frequently; many of the former seem to have been the result of alcohol ('Ive more to say but my head aches after Burghley ale'),[12] but some are described as extremely debilitating: 'my head is so stupid & my hand so feeble & trembling'.[13] There were also other strange and persistent sensations. Clare wrote of how his 'insides feels sinking & dead', as well as of a 'sensation as if cold water was creeping all about my head'.[14] He complained of 'prickly pains in my head arms & shoulders', and a more alarming 'sort of numbing through my private parts which I cannot describe'.[15] There were also episodes of what Clare called 'Fever with frequent

Faintings', recorded especially in his earlier letters at the start of his poetic career. He wrote about these with embarrassment, urging one confidant 'besure dont say nothing to none of my friends respe[c]ting my alarm of the fit or rather swooning'.[16]

There is an ineffable quality to many of these symptoms, as Clare struggles to describe wandering sensations that seem to alienate him from his own body. Clare referred to his susceptibility to both physical and mental affliction more generally as his 'indisposition', a suitably vague term that skirts around any concrete diagnosis. An early passage from his 'Sketches in the Life of John Clare', for example, shows him trying to pinpoint the origins of his 'week' constitution:

> my indisposition, (for I cannot call it illness) origionated in fainting fits, the cause of which I always imagined came from seeing when I was younger a man name Thomas Drake after he had fell off a load of hay and broke his neck the gastly palness of death struck such a terror on me that I coud not forget it for years and my dreams was constantly wanderings in church yards, digging graves, seeing spirits in charnel houses etc etc[17]

The early trauma described here is pitched as a key turning point in Clare's life, marking an uneasy transition from well to unwell, even as he skirts hesitantly around a recognition of true 'illness'. Yet what is offered as a sure sense of the cause of his 'indisposition' is in fact besieged with uncertainty; this is an origin story rooted in what was 'always imagined' rather than confidently known. As such, it is possible to uncover a language of hypochondria in Clare's attempts to describe and locate his suffering. Clare writes of an 'indisposition' that manifests in 'dreams' and 'spirits' in this passage; whether he was conscious of their connotations or not, such experiences of haunting and a fixation on death can also be read in terms of the anxieties of hypochondria as a form of disorderly or over-active imagination. As Grinnell and others have traced, hypochondria transitioned from being understood as a physical illness with a specific location in the body (the liver or spleen), to a 'disorder of imagined infirmity' in the eighteenth century and the Romantic period.[18] With this transition came, according to Grinnell, an unsettling of the hypochondriac's knowledge of their own body, as the imagination was deemed capable of producing symptoms and sensations that may not really be there at all.[19]

Although Clare complained of various physical and mental symptoms throughout his life, there were key periods during which his suffering

peaked. One period in particular was during the years that Clare was trying to compose and publish his 1827 volume *The Shepherd's Calendar* (ca.
1822–1827). This was a fraught time during which both Clare and his
publisher, Taylor, endured severe illness. Another crisis occurred in the
years following 1832, when Clare moved a short distance from his home
in Helpston to Northborough, a 'flitting' that is often interpreted as a tip-
ping point in the poet's mental and physical health.[20] Alienated from his
new surroundings and with his mind and body in seeming decline, Clare
wrote frequently to friends and his publishers after the move to utter his
distress and seek advice. A succession of letters drafted and sent by Clare
from May to July 1834 expressed a persistent wish to see Dr. George
Darling especially, his London-based physician who had also attended
John Keats:

> I feel so little better in fact I feel so ill that I feel an inclination to come to
> London to see Dr Darling he has prescribed for me & the things he sent has
> done me no good but I think if I could get up he would do me good & that
> directly[21]

> I am scarcely able to write to tell you that I am anxious to hear from you &
> to have your advice I want to get up to London if I can for I feel if I could
> see Dr Darling I should get better[22]

> I am in such a state that I cannot help feeling some alarm that I may be as I
> have been. You must excuse my writing; but I feel if I do not write now I
> shall not be able. What I wish is to get under Dr. Darling's advice, or to have
> his advice to go somewhere; for I have not been from home this twelve-
> month, and cannot get anywhere. Yet I know if I could reach London I
> should be better, or else get to salt water. Whatever Dr. Darling advices I will
> do if I can.[23]

Clare's anguish in these letters is unmistakeable, and his consistent appeals
to medical authority shape a pervasive sense of contingency. Everything
feels conditional: if Clare 'could get up' to or 'could reach' London, if he
'could see' Dr. Darling, then he might recover, making his present condition one of suspension. He 'may be' as ill as he claims to have been in the
past, but until he can have this suspicion confirmed by his physician,
Clare's sense of his own state hangs in the balance.

Clare shows a dependency on Dr. Darling's advice to stir him into
action in these letters, which he elsewhere described as 'such a stubborn

opinion of his skill'.[24] Looking to Darling's replies in this period of exchange, however, introduces a new dynamic to their relationship. Prior to the appeals sent about seeing Darling in May–July, the doctor had written to Clare with his own take on the situation:

> I am very sorry to hear that you are so much out of health and the more so as you appear to be aggravating the ordinary ills of life of which you must expect your share as well as common mortals by imaginary—purely imaginary—apprehensions.[25]

Instead of the promise of a prescription or practical advice about how to alleviate his symptoms (which Darling had offered frequently in the past), here is a suggestion that Clare's worries about his health are 'purely imaginary'. Darling's response articulates some of the key dynamics of hypochondria as understood from contemporary medical and cultural perspectives. Catherine Belling's suggestion that hypochondria 'can exist only in the presence of doctors' is alive to how medical discourse (in the vein of Foucauldian power relations) might create the problem of hypochondria in the first place, but also to the clinical encounter as a space capable of fostering doubts and uncertainties as much as clear diagnoses.[26] As a 'problem of knowing, telling, and anxious imagining', hypochondria describes a failed meeting point between the patient's subjective experience and the physician's knowledge, where individual feeling brings this knowledge into question and tests its limits, or the difference between 'feeling' and 'knowing' becomes difficult to discern.[27] Clare's response to Darling's letter is not to find assurance in the suggestion that his illness is imaginary, but to ask increasingly for more clinical attention, showing a simultaneous distrust of and need for medical authority when faced with a body and mind that he cannot make sense of.

Alongside a tracing of the kind of doctor-patient dynamic (and the unsettling of knowledge within it) that hypochondria engenders, however, is also Darling's sense of the 'ordinary ills of life' that Clare must reconcile himself to. Here emerges the potential for illness to be considered as a cultivated marker of difference—what John Mullan refers to as both the 'burden' and the 'privilege' of a rhetoric of sensibility in eighteenth- and nineteenth-century culture.[28] Darling implies that, through his imaginary 'apprehensions', Clare is not only *not* ill (or at least not ill enough to warrant his attention), but also trying to escape the realms of the 'ordinary' and the 'common' by adopting illness as a state that separates him from mere 'mortals'; this letter is an attempt to bring him back down to earth. What does it mean, then, to say that Clare was a hypochondriac? Where can he be placed in the slippage between anxious uncertainty and artful awareness that colours so much of the discussion and reception of hypochondria in the eighteenth and nineteenth centuries? If Clare was a hypochondriac, he was certainly in good company amongst the numerous Romantic poets and writers who fretted over their health and channelled these worries into their writing. With the turn to nervous sensibility as a marker of creative excellence being so oft-discussed in studies of eighteenth-century and Romantic medical and literary culture, it is now almost taken for granted that, as George Rousseau suggests, 'illness was a necessary hallmark of all Romantic writers'.[29] Yet Rousseau is also careful to qualify how, within this pervasive literary culture of illness, hypochondria was 'ultimately, an exclusionary strategy'.[30] That Clare has been left out of sustained discussions of hypochondria in the period is telling of the lines along which these exclusions were drawn. Definitions and discussions of hypochondria from the period insist almost invariably on a scholastic, sedentary lifestyle as one of its main causes. John Hill (whose botanical writings Clare greatly admired) wrote in 1766 of how 'the finer spirits are wasted by the labour of the brain: the Philosopher rises from his study more exhausted than the Peasant leaves his drudgery'[31]; John Reid suggested in 1816 that 'the labour of the poor man relieves him at last from the burden of fashionable ennui, and the constant pressure of physical inconveniences, from the more elegant, but surely not less tolerable distresses of a refined and romantic sensibility'.[32] As a disorder of the 'fashionable' and 'refined', and the burden of the scholar and the over-thinker, hypochondria is framed along class and occupational boundaries.[33]

To call Clare a hypochondriac is to return initially to his unsettled status as a labouring-class poet, and to think about hypochondria as a social and literary culture that Clare sought actively to participate in even as its definitions excluded a large part of his identity. In the language of eighteenth- and nineteenth-century treatises on hypochondria and nervous disease, Clare the *labourer* should not have been susceptible to hypochondria, with neither the time nor apparently the sensitive, imaginative capacity to cultivate the 'fashionable ennui' as Reid saw it. The association of labour with physical robustness and vitality is vexed for Clare. It is an idea that, whilst it appears frequently in his poetry, is not usually celebrated straightforwardly. In a poem like 'The Woodman' (1819),[34] for example, there lies a critique of idle privilege that is couched in terms of health and illness: the speaker comments on the excess that 'does paul the idly great/As rich & sumptious foods does surfeitings create' (lines 98–9) as a way to elevate the sparer existence of the woodman who, with access to 'hardy labour & the freshing air/Should'crease his strength & keep entire his health' (lines 101–2). Clare knows, though, that this health is also hard won; the joys of the woodman and his family are still but a 'glimpse' (line 95), and he does not shy away from critiquing the shortcomings of parish relief and its 'scouts benevolence' (line 107) in the poem. In another poem, 'The Wish' (1808–19),[35] Clare discounts the narrative of the healthy labourer (what Raymond Williams would later call a 'slanted association'[36]) altogether, declaring that 'Be as it will I hold in spite of strife/That health ne'er rises from a labouring life' (lines 201–2). Instead, he announces a wish to spend his days in studious occupation, and covets the kind of lifestyle where hypochondria could potentially flourish: 'The other hours I'd spend in letterd ease/To read or study just as that might please' (lines 212–13). Granted, this is a scene of studious 'ease' rather than of the feverish application that could supposedly provoke hypochondria (Bernard Mandeville warned against 'Men that continually fatigue their Heads with intense Thought and Study' [1711; 1730][37]), but nevertheless it shows Clare yearning for the freedom to indulge fully in intellectual activity instead of physical labour.

Poems like 'The Wish' reveal a tension in Clare's identity as a labouring-class poet. Richard Cronin has written of how Clare's poetic ambitions placed him in an awkward relationship to his labouring-class community, where he was not at ease with a labouring life nor free to break away from it.[38] The poet was acutely aware of feeling at odds with his local community—of being wired differently somehow, or at least of representing himself as such. He recalls in his autobiographical reflections how 'I thought somtimes that I surely had a taste peculialy by myself and that nobody else thought or saw things as I did', and having to pursue in 'secresey' his early forays into poetry because his parents 'began to dislike my love of books and writing, thinking it of no longer use since I had determind to stick at hard labour'.[39] Aware of the accusations of idleness or even pathology surrounding his poetic sensibilities, a poem like 'Labours Leisure' (1819–32)[40] shows Clare trying to negotiate his identity as a labourer and a poet, especially along the lines of striking a healthy balance between physical and mental exertion. A series of three sonnets, the first opens with a fond call to the kinds of feeling that ostensibly only labour can offer: 'O for the feelings & the carless health/ That found me toiling in the fields—the joy/ I felt at eve with not a wish for wealth' (lines 1–3). The 'carless' kind of health that comes from toil here resonates with the freedoms begot by bodily exhaustion described in treatises on hypochondria; to be employed in physical 'drudgery' (to use Hill's term) is to be free, supposedly, from mental 'care'. What is important in this poem, however, is what this 'carless' feeling of bodily health prepares Clare's speaker for. He goes on to describe how the 'joy' of labour not only emerges in the repose *after* physical activity (it is significant that it is 'eve' in the moment of this poem and the working day is at an end), but also that it precedes the time when he 'homeward used to hie/ With thoughts of books I often read by stealth' (lines 5–6). The feeling of secrecy confessed in the word 'stealth' is suggestive of Clare's sensitivity to how the pleasures of reading are not considered as salubrious as those of physical work; that 'stealth' is rhymed with 'health' in the poem only compounds this sense of his having chosen to pursue a potentially unhealthy indulgence (which is perhaps part of the enjoyment). However, the scene of reading that unfolds in the rest of the sonnet is depicted in terms reminiscent of the healthy labour Clare has left joyfully behind. Describing himself as a voracious reader, he recalls how 'bending oer my knees I used to read/ With earnest heed all books that had the power/To give me joy in most delicious ways' (lines 11–13). Here, reading is presented as a vigorous physical activity, with Clare 'bending oer' his books in a manner reminiscent of his earlier toil. Hill's treatise on hypochondriasis advised that the 'stooping posture of the body, which most men use, though none should use it, in writing and in reading' was a contributing cause to the disorder.[41] Clare, however, takes an opportunity to forge parallels between the posture of reading and the posture of labour. By lending a physicality to the 'earnest' mental exercise of reading, he is able both to enjoy his furtive intellectual pursuits and to reclaim them as a healthy pastime.

If reading in 'Labours Leisure' could be pitched as a route to the kinds of 'delicious' joy that the exhaustion of a hard day's physical work could provide, then Clare shows elsewhere that he was also sensitive to its more morbid pleasures. A later poem, 'The Winters Come' (1842–64),[42] for example, is focused around another scene of reading, again tucked away indoors, but this time as a deliberate choice to retreat from the elements. After two stanzas that observe the signs of the changing season, where the landscape and its wildlife have become 'Naked, and bare' (line 14) and 'Sluggish, and dull' (line 16), the speaker suddenly declares:

> 'Tis winter! and I love to read in-doors,
> When the moon hangs her crescent upon high:
> While on the window shutters the wind roars,
> And storms like furies pass remorseless by,
> How pleasant on a feather bed to lie,
> Or sitting by the fire, in fancy soar,
> With Milton, or with Dante to regions high,
> Or read fresh volumes we've not seen before,
> Or o'er old Bartons 'melancholy pore.'
>   (lines 19–27)

In this cosy scene of escapism, reading is transportive, and the state of 'fancy' it induces a means of retreating from a less desirable reality. Although Clare greets his volumes of Milton and Dante as old, reliable companions in these lines, Jeffrey C. Robinson has noted how fancy could also be perceived as a faculty that was 'destructively, dangerously, uncontrollable' in the eighteenth century and the Romantic period.[43] Whilst Robinson is careful to distinguish between fancy and the imagination (in line with Coleridge) in order to reclaim the particular work and values of this faculty within Romanticism, it was also often synonymous with imagination and, importantly, both were suspect faculties in writings about hypochondria. Reid, for example, wrote of how 'a diseased fancy will not unfrequently produce nearly all the symptoms, or at least all the sensations of bodily disease'.[44] If fancy offers transcendent recuperation from the 'storms' outside in this poem, there is also the hint of less restorative flights of fancy taking place in its closing lines.

The turn to 'old Bartons 'melancholy'' at the end of the poem is a misspelled reference to Robert Burton's *The Anatomy of Melancholy* (1621), and evokes a habitual pleasure not entirely in-keeping with the book's subject matter. Invoking Burton's encyclopaedic study of melancholy—of both its causes and cures—suggests the reader in this scene has had need to return frequently to its pages and 'pore' over them in search of either diagnosis or remedy, but has also found forms of delight in doing so. In many respects, Clare's choice of reading material here is a means of harmonising the internal and external weather of the poem's subject. Jonas Cope argues that Clare's 'autumn verse' is consistently 'informed by his own physical and psychological responses to the season';[45] Clare himself wrote in his correspondence how every 'Spring & Fall' saw the return of a 'confounded lethargy of low spirits' upon him.[46] Clare may be both playing on the literary trope of autumn and the waning of the year as a time of melancholy moods (the poem begins with a reference to the now 'paled sky' that 'in the Autumn seem'd to burn' [line 3]), and reflecting on his own psychophysiological state in 'The Winters Come'. Yet the leisurely pleasure taken in self-anatomisation also turns into a more anxious 'poring' over Burton's *Anatomy* (with this word carrying connotations of intense scrutiny and focus[47]) that surely uncovers a hypochondriacal tendency in the poem, too.

Burton's *Anatomy* persisted as an influence on eighteenth-and nineteenth-century understandings of hypochondria, even as conceptions of the disorder began to shift towards considering it a 'nervous' affliction instead of a somatic complaint. For Burton, 'hypochondriasis' was a species of melancholy itself, known otherwise as 'windy melancholy'.[48] Influenced by Hippocrates and Galen, Burton classed this form of melancholy primarily as a bodily disorder, locating it in the bowels, liver, and spleen that produced 'wind and rumbling in the guts' alongside other digestive complaints, as well as concurrent emotional states of 'fear and sorrow'.[49] Stephanie Shirilan, however, traces how Burton's insistence on the fear and delusions that attend the hypochondriacal melancholic has also 'come to bear a closer resemblance […] to modern representations of hypochondria as an imaginary illness'.[50] Samuel Johnson's definition of 'hypochondriack' in his dictionary as 'Melancholy; disordered in the imagination' certainly shows the persistence of a slippage between hypochondria and melancholy, even as it grounded its definition in the disorder's more 'modern' iteration in the imagination.[51] 'The Winters Come' is, however, not solely significant as an index of Clare's familiarity with a key text in the medical history of hypochondria. In its alertness to reading as an activity that gives permission to 'fancy', it is also sensitive to the enjoyment that can be taken in imagined infirmity. Shirilan reminds readers of an early warning in Burton's text that 'reading the descriptions of melancholy detailed in his book could worsen the symptoms of a reader'; Burton anticipated readers of a certain temperament 'applying that which hee reads to himself'.[52] By poring over 'Bartons 'melancholy'', then, the poem's subject opens themselves up willingly to more morbid forms of fancy than this scene of cosy, domestic retreat seems initially to suggest.

Adam White's examination of Clare's particular strain of 'Romanticism' argues for him as a poet who reclaims and reinvigorates 'fancy' as 'central to a serious apprehension of the world', in contrast to other Romantic poets who instead valorise the imagination.[53] White sees Clare's investment in fancy in particular as an opportunity to 'reveal one of the fundamental tensions of his verse: that between a descriptive, attentive impulse and a more fanciful, more abstracting tendency'.[54] This reading speaks to a growing critical approach that seeks to debunk the conception of Clare as simply a poet of immediacy and direct observation of the natural world.[55] Whilst White looks to the wealth of Clare's poetic explorations of the natural world to uncover the many moments of fancy and reverie that govern them, Clare's letters in which he frets over the state of his body and mind are also, I would add, an important index of his poetic disposition. The letter from George Darling to Clare discussed earlier is significant not only for its direct suggestion that the poet's illness may have been imaginary but also for how belated this advice was in the face of the poet's own self-awareness. Clare shared his publishers with another sickly Romantic poet: John Keats. The two never met but exchanged comments about each other's work via letters to Taylor.[56] Keats's departure for Italy in 1821 affected Clare greatly, giving him yet another opportunity to dwell on what he felt must be his own hastening end. He wrote to Taylor:

> Give my respects to *Keats* & tell him I am a half mad melancholly dog in this moozy misty country he has latly cast behind him but I feel somthing better at least I fancy which I believe to tell truth is the whole of my complaint which I am so fussy over bytimes[57]

There is a striking self-consciousness about the dynamic of his own 'complaint' here. It is at once a confession of hypochondria and an acknowledgement of the unstable relationship to knowledge that it fosters. The slippage between feeling, 'fancy', belief, and 'truth' creates a position willing to entertain multiple interpretations and to dwell in both the real and the unreal, the physical and the imagined. It is fitting that Clare strikes upon this language of indeterminacy in a letter where Keats, the poet of 'negative capability' who valued a temperament that was 'capable of being in uncertainties, Mysteries, doubts', is his main subject of address.[58] Hypochondria is sympathetic with a poetic disposition here, becoming rooted in Clare's propensity for 'fancy' as much as in an anxious fussing over the body and its errant, potentially fanciful, symptoms.

The slippage between 'fancy' and 'feeling' became something that Clare returned to again and again to describe the mode he was in when worrying about his health:

all I regret is that I cannot describe my feelings sufficiently to benefit from our friend Dr Darlings kind advice in whom I always had the greatest confidence—my fancys & feelings vary very often but I now feel a great numbness in my right shoulder[59]

I am sorry that I am but little better though to all appearance as well as ever I was in my life & though I have had a goodnights rest I feel little better I am still troubled & fancy[60]

I fear I shall get worse & worse ere you write to me for I have been out for a walk & can scarcely bear up against my fancys or feelings[61]

These moments from his correspondence speak to an anxiety of interpretation that Clare found frightening and burdensome; he holds here a constant suspicion of illness that must lurk beneath an 'appearance' of wellness. Even if his 'feelings' were the product of 'fancy', that is not to say they were not also experienced vividly; here, they exert a physical presence that the poet feels he has to 'bear up' against. Yet Clare was also able to translate this distressing indeterminacy into poems that appear to revel in the space between fancy and feeling. There are two early works in particular that indulge the kind of morbid fancy hinted at in 'The Winters Come', but push it to a gothic extreme. 'Supersitions Dream' (1821–7)[62] (also referred to as 'The Dream') and 'The Night Mare' (1821–7)[63] were both composed during the time Clare was working on the manuscript for *The Shepherd's Calendar* (1827), and 'Supersitions Dream' went on to be included in that volume. Mark Storey suggests that both poems 'have their relevance to his emotional predicament in these years'.[64] They are certainly works full of turmoil and despair: 'Superstitions Dream' recounts 'A dream of staggering horrors & of dread' (line 9), full of 'shadows' (line 10), 'demons' (line 46), and 'spirits' (line 39) that transform a once beautiful natural world into a scene of desolation, where 'The pleasant hues of fields & woods was past/& natures beautys had enjoyd their last/The colord flower the green of field & tree/What they had been forever ceasd to be' (lines 61–4). 'The Night Mare' similarly tells a chilling tale of a dream that 'began in bliss & lifted high/My sleeping feelings into fancys joy' (lines 1–2), only to descend into wild confusion where anything once familiar becomes 'strange' (line 40) and a beautiful female figure (referred to once as 'Mary' [line 141]) transforms into 'The ugliest pictures fear coud ever make' (line 147). What unites these poems beyond their ghoulish subject matter, however, is their representation of a subject who cannot tell if the dream (or nightmare) is real or not. 'Superstitions Dream' announces in the first few lines that this is a recollection of a dream 'Whose shadows lingerd when the dream had fled/Clinging to memory with their gloomy view/Till doubt & fancy half believd it true' (lines 10–12). 'The Night Mare' similarly figures an experience of reasonable awareness amongst unbelievable horror: 'I coud not move or speak yet reasons power/Seemd wide awake in that spell prisoning hour' (lines 117–18).

It is possible, then, to hear the register of Clare's bewildered attention to his own ailing body in these gothic reveries and episodes of frightened half belief. Indeed, he would often turn to a language of dreams and nightmares when recounting the phantom-like quality of symptoms that he could not pin down. Writing to Hessey in 1824, he claimed that 'to be in this waking dream is almost unbearable I am certain its somthing more then nervous'.[65] To Darling in 1834–5 he wrote that 'I am very unwell & though I cannot describe my feelings well I will tell you as well as I can […] I feel chills <&cold> come over me & a sort of nightmare awake'.[66] In 'The Night Mare' in particular, the speaker recoils as 'awful symtoms rousing gatherd near' (line 86). The poem dramatises a form of hypochondriac fancy as these 'symtoms' are both acknowledged to be imagined or dreamt, and experienced as palpably real. Clare was aware that these two poems were out of the ordinary in comparison to the close studies of the natural world and rural customs that made up his compositions for *The Shepherd's Calendar*, but also that they articulated a vital aspect of his poetic imagination as sourced from his own confusing bouts of suffering: when he wrote to Taylor to tell him of his latest work, he stated 'I have begun one of my terrible experiments agen "The NightMare or Superstitions Dream" youl only laugh at its bombast when I send it but my vanity must have its way—the Night Mare is a thing Ive been very much subject too'.[67] As a confession of 'vanity', Clare wraps his poems in a form of self-obsession or self-interest here that further belies the hypochondriac beginnings of his craft.

If 'The Night Mare' and 'Supersitions Dream' offered Clare a means of forging a poetic imagination out of his own psychosomatic distress, then such poems also attest to the forms of literary influence and community that he found, and cultivated deliberately, in the register of hypochondria. Editors Eric Robinson, David Powell, and P. M. S. Dawson provide a note about the manuscript of 'The Night Mare' that details a footnote Clare included alongside the poem:

I wish to acknowledge that what ever merit this & "Superstitions Dream" may be thought to posess they owe it in part to the "English Opium Eater" as they were written after (tho actual dreams) the perusal of that singular & interesting production'.[68]

Clare was a keen admirer of Thomas De Quincey's *Confessions of an English Opium Eater* (1821). He read it in serialised form when first published in the *London Magazine* and, later, requested a copy of its printed version from Taylor, stating 'he is a great favourite of mine'.[69] In seeking to imitate the nightmarish spectres that pour forth from De Quincey's examination of opium addiction and both its pleasures and pains, Clare declares an affinity with a mode of literature that willingly treads the darker regions of fancy at the same time that he is able to embed his own hypochondriac distress in his verse. He can speak to the truth (or perhaps the frightening and confusing un-truth) of imagined illness, whilst also keeping hypochondria at bay as a 'terrible' literary 'experiment' and examination of disordered imagination in the vein of another author.

Although Clare acknowledged outright the influence of De Quincey's *Confessions* on 'The Night Mare' and 'Superstitions Dream', this text also frames and illuminates the hypochondriac imagination present in another, more unlikely, poem by way of proximity. The October 1821 issue of *The London Magazine* published two pieces that were concerned with the uncertain and unruly nature of the imagination: Charles Lamb's 'Witches, and Other Night-Fears', and the second instalment of De Quincey's 'Confessions'.[70] Lamb's is an essay fascinated by the moveable boundary between imagination and reality. Its opening discussion of witchcraft sets the question of how we are to 'distinguish the likely from the palpable absurd', leading to an acknowledgement that the imaginative realm demands to be taken on its own terms: 'I see no reason for disbelieving one attested story of this nature more than the other on the score of absurdity. There is no law to judge of the lawless, or canon by which a dream may be criticised'.[71] De Quincey's 'Confessions' also traces the seemingly 'lawless' visions that arise from the subject's opium-induced dreams, as part of the 'pains of opium' is an increasing inability to govern the imaginative faculty and keep reality and unreality separate: 'as the creative state of the eye increased, a sympathy seemed to arise between the waking and the dreaming states of the brain in one point—that whatsoever I happened to call up and to trace by a voluntary act upon the darkness was very apt to transfer itself into my dreams'.[72] David Higgins discusses the importance of attending to the original publication context of Lamb's 'Witches' and De Quincey's 'Confessions', in order to appreciate fully how mutually-informing their imaginative projects are in relation to their conception of the 'exotic' in particular.[73] Amongst the fruitful opportunities for thinking about how these two texts speak to each other, however, there has been no acknowledgement yet of how their imaginative register of spectres and phantoms might also speak to and inform another text published in the same issue: a sonnet by Clare.

Clare's sonnet 'A Reflection on Summer' appears a few items after De Quincey's 'Confessions' and Lamb's 'Witches' in the October 1821 issue of the *London Magazine*. Originally titled 'A Reflection in Summer', it is collected with the manuscripts for Clare's second volume *The Village Minstrel* (1821),[74] although the poem was not included in that volume. The sonnet reflects ostensibly on the arrival of summer, but in so doing is immediately drawn back to the wintry scenes that contrast with the present season:

> We well may wonder o'er the change of scene,
>   Now Summer's contrast through the land is spread,
>   And turn us back, where Winter's tempest fled,
> And left nought living but the ivy's green.
>   The then bare woods, that trembled over head
> Like Spectres, 'mid the storm, of what had been,
>   And wrecks of beauty ne'er to bloom again,—
> Are now all glory. Nature smiles as free,
>   As the last Summer had commenced its reign,
> And she were blooming in Eternity.
>   So in this life, when future thoughts beguile,
> And from past cares our spirits get relieved,
>   Hope cheers us onward with as sweet a smile
> As if, before, she never had deceived.[75]

Here, the abundant 'glory' that summer brings is all the more emphatic for the 'wrecks' of winter that came before it. Yet with this sense of 'contrast' as being fundamental to the enjoyment of summer comes also a mistrust of its pleasures. The speaker cannot revel in the present season, but is pulled back instead to 'what had been', as the wondrous scene before them is haunted by the 'Spectres' of winter. The sonnet's final quatrain orchestrates an unshakeable unease through Clare's choice of rhymes: 'beguile' rhymed with 'smile' and 'relieved' with 'deceived' marries a surface contentment, or moment of amelioration, with the disconcerting knowledge that this cannot last, or might have been a deception all along. For a poem that ends with a turn to hope, its outlook is decidedly pessimistic, unable to look away from the winter that is always lurking round the corner.

As a poem that has trouble with accepting surface appearances, 'A Reflection on Summer' has more in common with Lamb and De Quincey's works than might be assumed. With the threat of decay that lingers behind apparent vitality figured as a 'spectre', Clare's sonnet strikes a register of haunting that chimes with the phantoms lurking in 'Witches' and 'Confessions'. Both 'Witches' and 'Confessions' figure a subject highly attuned to their own nervous sensibility or constitution, either past or present. Lamb writes of a younger self who was 'dreadfully alive to nervous terrors', whilst De Quincey concerns himself with tracing the 'subtle links of suffering' that connect episodes in the Opium-Eater's life.[76] It is not surprising, therefore, that both Lamb and De Quincey have also been discussed for their exploration of the hypochondriac figure. For Grinnell, De Quincey's *Confessions* is a text 'unable to look away from hypochondria'[77] in its anxious exploration of the body and mind of its subject, while, for Simon P. Hull, Lamb 'deflates' the 'unhealthily self-absorbed tendency' of the hypochondriac in another essay, 'The Convalescent', so that it becomes a 'mode of behaviour to be affectionately humoured'.[78] The concern with spectres, phantoms, and the reliability of the senses and credibility of seeming realities in both 'Witches' and 'Confessions' certainly speaks to the concerns of hypochondria. The *London Magazine* also published Bryan Waller Procter's two-part series 'The Memoir of a Hypochondriac' in 1822, in which the subject bewails how their 'imagination is sick and haunted', and states that to have hypochondria is to have 'the phantom of fear [...] always about you'.[79] With its inability to shake off the 'spectre' of winter even in the face of summer, it is possible to hear in 'A Reflection on Summer' the fearful suspicion of the hypochondriac that becomes amplified by the other writings surrounding its original publication context. What seems on the surface to be a sonnet reflecting on a change in season—a frequent occurrence in Clare's body of work— becomes drawn in to, as Hull has it, the 'metropolitan' discourse of hypochondria, as a fretful analysis of the body and mind translates into a mode of looking at the natural world.[80]

Indeed, when Clare sent his copy of 'A Reflection on Summer' to John Taylor ahead of its publication in the *London Magazine*, he included a remark that hints even further at the hypochondriacal register lurking within the poem:

> I merely send this letter to hitch off[f] the sonnet as I am began to scribble agen vehemently […] I am agen recruiting from my complaints & shall wait till the book is publishd ere I start so when it is you may let me know & send me what copies you think fit—you will then hear no more of me for a time[81]

In his admission that he is 'agen recruiting from my complaints', Clare offers illness (or at least his conviction that he is ill) as both the occasion and the source material for his poetic compositions. By declaring that when he is finally free to properly indulge this period of 'recruitment' (i.e. after his forthcoming volume is at last in print) Taylor will 'hear no more' of him for some time, Clare also implies the all-consuming nature of this self-attention. There is an invitation here to read 'A Reflection on Summer' as having been written up to send to Taylor during Clare's returning creative focus on his illness. This reading is not meant to overtly pathologise the poem but rather to attend, again, to how Clare's poetic attention is inflected, even latently, with the forms of hypochondriac 'fussing' bestowed on his body and mind. Hypochondria is not only, therefore, a crucial framework that uncovers the literary, medical, and cultural influences behind Clare's attitude to his own 'indisposition'. It can also shape a way of reading Clare's poetry that refuses to lose sight of the pervasive influence his mental and physical suffering had on his verse, becoming alive instead to the spectres of illness that haunt and shape his writing.

NOTES

1. Steven Connor, 'Beghosted Bodyhood: Hypochondria and the Arts of Illness' (2009). http://stevenconnor.com/hypo.html.
2. 'all madness for writing: John Clare and the asylum', in *John Clare in Context*, 264.
3. Geoffrey Grigson, *Poems of John Clare's Madness* (London: Routledge & Kegan Paul, 1949); J. W. and Anne Tibble, *John Clare: A Life*, 2nd edition (London: Michael Joseph, 1972). Other diagnostic approaches to Clare's madness include Evan Blackmore, 'John Clare's Psychiatric Disorder and Its Influence on His Poetry', *Victorian Poetry* 24.3 (1986): 209–28; Arthur Foss and Kerith Trick, *St Andrew's Hospital Northampton The First 150 Years (1838–1988)* (Cambridge: Granta, 1989); Sean Haldane, 'John Clare's Madness', *PN Review* 30.6 (2004): 42–6.

4. Frederick Burwick, *Poetic Madness and the Romantic Imagination* (University Park, PA: Pennsylvania State University Press, 1996), 258–69; Roger Sales, *John Clare: A Literary Life* (Basingstoke: Palgrave Macmillan, 2002), 104.
5. See, for example, Frederick Martin's description of Clare as being 'led away from his wife and children, by two stern-looking men' when discussing his admission to High Beach Asylum in 1864, in *The Life of John Clare* (London and Cambridge: Macmillan, 1865), 269.
6. See in particular George C. Grinnell, 'A Portrait of the Artist as a Dead Man: Coleridge's Hypochondria', in *The English Malady: Enabling and Disabling Fictions*, ed. by Glen Colburn (Newcastle: Cambridge Scholars Publishing, 2008), 177–99; George Sebastian Rousseau and David Boyd Haycock, 'Framing Samuel Taylor Coleridge's Gut: Genius, Digestion, Hypochondria', in *Framing and Imagining Disease in Cultural History*, ed. by George Sebastian Rousseau, Miranda Gill, David Haycock and Malte Herwig (Basingstoke: Palgrave Macmillan, 2003), 231–65; Jonathon Shears, 'Byron's Hypochondria', in *Byron's Temperament: Essays in Body and Mind*, ed. by Bernard Beatty and Jonathon Shears (Cambridge: Cambridge Scholars Publishing, 2016), 100–17; Nora Crook and Derek Guiton, *Shelley's Venomed Melody* (Cambridge: Cambridge University Press, 1986).
7. *The Age of Hypochondria: Interpreting Romantic Health and Illness* (Basingstoke: Palgrave Macmillan, 2010).
8. See Bate, *Biography*, 146.
9. Bate, *Biography*, 147.
10. 'all madness for writing', 260.
11. 'John Clare's Deaths: Poverty, Education, and Poetry', in *New Essays on John Clare: Poetry, Culture and Community*, ed. Simon Kövesi and Scott McEathron (Cambridge: Cambridge University Press, 2015), 148.
12. *Letters*, 203.
13. *Letters*, 304.
14. *Letters*, 294.
15. *Letters*, 537, 615.
16. *Letters*, 44–45.
17. *By Himself*, 18.
18. *Age of Hypochondria*, 4. See also German E. Berrios, 'Hypochondriasis: History of the Concept', in *Hypochondriasis: Modern Perspectives on an Ancient Malady*, eds. Vladan Starcevic and Don R. Lipsitt (Oxford; New York: Oxford University Press, 2001), 3–20.
19. *Age of Hypochondria*, 12.
20. See Barrell, 174; Tim Chilcott, *'A real world & doubting mind': A Critical Study of the Poetry of John Clare* (Hull: Hull University Press, 1985), 108;

Roger Sales, *John Clare*, 65; *Middle Period*, 3: xxii; Eric Robinson, David Powell and P.M.S. Dawson, 'Introduction', *John Clare: Northborough Sonnets*, ed. Eric Robinson, David Powell and P.M.S. Dawson (Manchester: Carcanet, 1995), x.

21. *Letters*, 613.
22. *Letters*, 616.
23. *Letters*, 616.
24. *Letters*, 350.
25. Darling to Clare, February 1834, British Library MSS, Egerton 2249, fol. 180.
26. *A Condition of Doubt: The Meanings of Hypochondria* (New York; Oxford: Oxford University Press, 2012), 5.
27. *A Condition of Doubt*, 1.
28. *Sentiment and Sociability: The Language of Feeling in the Eighteenth Century* (Oxford: Clarendon Press, 1988), 213.
29. 'Coleridge's Dreaming Gut: Digestion, Genius, Hypochondria', in *Cultures of the Abdomen: Diet, Digestion, and Fat in the Modern World*, ed. Christopher Forth and Ana Carden-Coyne (Basingstoke: Palgrave Macmillan, 2005), 109.
30. 'Coleridge's Dreaming Gut', 109.
31. *Hypochondriasis, A Practical Treatise on the Nature and Cure of that Disorder* (London, 1766), 6.
32. *Essays on Insanity, Hypochondriasis, and Other Nervous Affections* (London: Longman, Hurst, Rees, Orme, and Brown, 1816), 6.
33. See also Heather R. Beatty, *Nervous Disease in Late Eighteenth-Century Britain: The Reality of a Fashionable Disorder* (London: Routledge, 2016) for a sustained study of how 'disordered nerves' (including hypochondria) 'were laden with cultural meaning by the middle of the eighteenth century' (5), and of the need to account more fully for the 'constellation of "ordinary" citizens' (4) who suffered from them within a cultural landscape of 'fashionable' disease.
34. *Early Poems*, 2: 287–96.
35. *Early Poems*, 1: 43–50.
36. *The Country and the City* (London: Chatto and Windus, 1973), 116.
37. *A Treatise of the Hypochondriack and Hysterick Diseases* (London: J. Tonson, 1730), 107.
38. 'In Place and Out of Place: Clare in The Midsummer Cushion', in *John Clare: New Approaches*, ed. John Goodridge and Simon Kövesi (Helpston: John Clare Society, 2000), 133–48.
39. *Letters*, 17, 15–16.
40. *Middle Period*, 4: 331.
41. *Hypochondriasis*, 20–21.

42. *Later Poems*, 2: 928–29.
43. *Unfettering Poetry: Fancy in British Romanticism* (Basingstoke: Palgrave Macmillan, 2006), 3.
44. *Essays on Insanity*, 250.
45. 'Autumnal Affect in the Poetry of John Clare', *Studies in English Literature 1500–1900* 58.4 (2018): 864.
46. *Letters*, 234.
47. *OED*, 'pore', v., senses 1a–1c.
48. 'The First Partition', in *The Anatomy of Melancholy* (1621), ed. Holbrook Jackson (New York: New York Review of Books, 2001), 175.
49. *The Anatomy of Melancholy*, 411.
50. *Robert Burton and the Transformative Powers of Melancholy* (London: Routledge, 2016), 125.
51. 'Hypochondriacal; Hypochondriack, adj.', senses 1 and 2, in *A Dictionary of the English Language: A Digital Edition of the 1755 Classic by Samuel Johnson*, ed. Brandi Besalke. https://johnsonsdictionaryonline.com/.
52. *Robert Burton and the Transformative Powers of Melancholy*, 127.
53. *John Clare's Romanticism* (London: Palgrave Macmillan, 2017), 68.
54. *John Clare's Romanticism*, 68.
55. See in particular Erica McAlpine, 'Keeping Nature at Bay: John Clare's Poetry of Wonder', *Studies in Romanticism* 50.1 (2011): 79–104; Michael Nicholson, 'The Itinerant 'I': John Clare's Lyric Defiance', *ELH* 82.2 (2015): 637–69.
56. See John Goodridge, 'Junkets and Clarissimus: the Clare-Keats Dialogue', in *John Clare and Community* (Cambridge: Cambridge University Press, 2012), 59–82, for a sustained discussion of the connections and communications between Clare and Keats.
57. *Letters*, 132.
58. Letter to George and Tom Keats, December 21–7 1817, in *Keats's Poetry and Prose*, ed. Jeffrey N. Cox (New York; London: W. W. Norton & Co., 2009), 109.
59. *Letters*, 513.
60. *Letters*, 613.
61. *Letters*, 615.
62. *Middle Period*, 1: 325–31.
63. *Middle Period*, 1: 332–38.
64. *The Poetry of John Clare: A Critical Introduction* (Basingstoke: Macmillan, 1974), 58.
65. *Letters*, 298.
66. *Letters*, 615.
67. *Letters*, 222.
68. *Middle Period*, I, 371.

69. *Letters*, 269.
70. Charles Lamb, 'Witches, and other Night-fears', *London Magazine* 4.22 (October 1821): 384–7; Thomas De Quincey, 'Confessions of an English Opium-Eater, Being an Extract from the Life of a Scholar Part II', *London Magazine* 4.22 (October 1821): 353–79.
71. 'Witches', 384–5.
72. 'Confessions', 372.
73. 'Imagining the Exotic: De Quincey and Lamb in the London Magazine', *Romanticism* 17.3 (2011): 288–98.
74. See *Early Poems*, 2: 600.
75. 'A Reflection on Summer', *London Magazine* 4.22 (October 1821): 400, lines 1–14. I quote here from the edited version of the poem printed in the *London Magazine*. The manuscript version can be found in *Early Poems*, 2: 600 and in *Letters*, 214.
76. 'Witches', 386; 'Confessions', 353.
77. *Age of Hypochondria*, 121.
78. *Charles Lamb, Elia, and the London Magazine: Metropolitan Muse* (London; New York: Routledge, 2010), 84.
79. 'The Memoir of a Hypochondriac', *London Magazine* 6.33 (September 1822): 250.
80. *Charles Lamb, Elia, and the London Magazine*, 84.
81. *Letters*, 214.

Bibliography

Bate, Jonathan. *John Clare: A Biography.* New York: Farrar, Straus & Giroux, 2003.
Barrell, John. *The Idea of Landscape and the Sense of Place, 1730–1840: An Approach to the Poetry of John Clare.* Cambridge: Cambridge University Press, 1972.
Baur, Susan. *Hypochondria: Woeful Imaginings.* Berkeley and Los Angeles: University of California Press, 1988.
Beatty, Heather R. *Nervous Disease in Late Eighteenth-Century Britain: The Reality of a Fashionable Disorder.* London: Routledge, 2012.
Belling, Catherine. *A Condition of Doubt: The Meanings of Hypochondria.* Oxford: Oxford University Press, 2012.
Berrios, German E. 'Hypochondriasis: History of the Concept'. In *Hypochondriasis: Modern Perspectives on an Ancient Malady*, edited by Vladan Starcevic and Don R. Lipsitt, 3–20. Oxford; New York: Oxford University Press, 2001.
Blackmore, Evan. 'John Clare's Psychiatric Disorder and its Influence on his Poetry'. *Victorian Poetry* 24.3 (1986): 209–28.
Burton, Robert. *The Anatomy of Melancholy.* Edited by Holbrook Jackson. New York: New York Review of Books, 2001.

Burwick, Frederick. *Poetic Madness and the Romantic Imagination.* University Park, PA: Pennsylvania State University Press, 1996.

Chilcott, Tim. *'A real world & doubting mind': A Critical Study of the Poetry of John Clare.* Hull: Hull University Press, 1985.

———., ed. *John Clare: The Living Year, 1841.* Nottingham: Trent Editions, 1991.

Clare, John. 'A Reflection on Summer'. *London Magazine* 4.22 (October 1821): 400.

———. *The Later Poems of John Clare, 1837–1864.* Edited by Eric Robinson, David Powell and Margaret Grainger. 2 vols. Oxford: Clarendon Press, 1984.

———. *The Letters of John Clare.* Edited by Mark Storey. Oxford: Clarendon Press, 1985.

———. *The Early Poems of John Clare, 1804–1822.* Edited by Eric Robinson, David Powell and Margaret Grainger. 2 vols. Oxford: Clarendon Press, 1989.

———. *Northborough Sonnets.* Edited by Eric Robinson, David Powell and P.M.S Dawson. Manchester: Carcanet, 1995.

———. *John Clare By Himself.* Edited by Eric Robinson and David Powell. Manchester: Carcanet, 1996.

———. *Poems of the Middle Period, 1822–1837.* Edited by Eric Robinson, David Powell and P. M. S. Dawson. 5 vols. Oxford: Clarendon Press, 1996–2003.

Colburn, Glen. *The English Malady: Enabling and Disabling Fictions.* Newcastle upon Tyne: Cambridge Scholars Publishing, 2008.

Connor, Steven. 'Beghosted Bodyhood: Hypochondria and the Arts of Illness' (2009). http://stevenconnor.com/hypo.html.

Cope, Jonas. 'Autumnal Affect in the Poetry of John Clare'. *Studies in English Literature 1500–1900* 58.4 (2018): 855–75.

Cronin, Richard. 'In Place and Out of Place: Clare in The Midsummer Cushion'. In *John Clare: New Approaches*, edited by John Goodridge and Simon Kövesi, 133–48. Helpston: John Clare Society, 2000.

———. 'John Clare and the *London Magazine*'. In *New Essays on John Clare: Poetry, Culture and Community*, edited by Simon Kövesi and Scott McEathron, 209–27. Cambridge: Cambridge University Press, 2015.

Crook, Nora and Derek Guiton. *Shelley's Venomed Melody.* Cambridge: Cambridge University Press, 1986.

De Quincey, Thomas. 'Confessions of an English Opium-Eater, Being an Extract from the Life of a Scholar Part II'. *London Magazine* 4.22 (October 1821): 353–79.

Foss, Arthur and Kerith Trick. *St Andrew's Hospital Northampton The First 150 Years (1830–1988).* Cambridge: Granta, 1989.

Goodridge, John and Simon Kövesi, eds. *John Clare: New Approaches.* Helpston: The John Clare Society, 2000.

Goodridge, John. *John Clare and Community.* Cambridge: Cambridge University Press, 2012.

Grigson, Geoffrey. *Poems of John Clare's Madness*. London: Routledge & Kegan Paul, 1949.

Grinnell, George C. 'A Portrait of the Artist as a Dead Man: Coleridge's Hypochondria'. In *The English Malady: Enabling and Disabling Fictions*, edited by Glen Colburn, 177–99. Newcastle: Cambridge Scholars Publishing, 2008.

———. *The Age of Hypochondria: Interpreting Romantic Health and Illness*. Basingstoke: Palgrave Macmillan, 2010.

Haldane, Sean. 'John Clare's Madness'. *PN Review* 30.6 (2004): 42–6.

Higgins, David. 'Imagining the Exotic: De Quincey and Lamb in the London Magazine'. *Romanticism* 17.3 (2011): 288–98.

Hill, John. *Hypochondriasis, A Practical Treatise on the Nature and Cure of that Disorder*. London, 1766.

Hull, Simon P. *Charles Lamb, Elia, and the London Magazine: Metropolitan Muse*. London, New York: Routledge, 2010.

Johnson, Samuel. *A Dictionary of the English Language: A Digital Edition of the 1755 Classic by Samuel Johnson*. Edited by Brandi Besalke. https://johnsons-dictionaryonline.com/. Accessed 3rd January 2020.

Keats, John. *Keats's Poetry and Prose*. Edited by Jeffrey N. Cox. New York; London: W. W. Norton & Co., 2009.

Kövesi, Simon. 'John Clare's Deaths: Poverty, Education and Poetry'. In *New Essays on John Clare: Poetry, Culture and Community*, edited by Simon Kövesi and Scott McEathron, 118–45. Cambridge: Cambridge University Press, 2015.

Kövesi, Simon, and Scott McEathron, eds. *New Essays on John Clare: Poetry, Culture and Community*. Cambridge: Cambridge University Press, 2015.

Lamb, Charles. 'Witches, and other Night-fears'. *London Magazine* 4.22 (October 1821): 384–7.

Letters to John Clare. Egerton Manuscript 2249. The British Library, London.

Martin, Frederick. *The Life of John Clare*. London and Cambridge: Macmillan, 1865.

McAlpine, Erica. 'Keeping Nature at Bay: John Clare's Poetry of Wonder'. *Studies in Romanticism* 50.1 (2011): 79–104.

Mullan, John. *Sentiment and Sociability: The Language of Feeling in the Eighteenth Century*. Oxford: Clarendon Press, 1988.

Nicholson, Michael. 'The Itinerant 'I': John Clare's Lyric Defiance'. *ELH* 82.2 (2015): 637–69.

Porter, Roy. '"all madness for writing': John Clare and the asylum'. In *John Clare in Context*, edited by Hugh Haughton, Adam Phillips and Geoffrey Summerfield, 259–78. Cambridge: Cambridge University Press, 1994.

Porter, Roy, and Dorothy Porter. *In Sickness and in Health: The British Experience, 1650–1850*. London: Fourth Estate, 1988.

Procter, Bryan Waller. 'The Memoir of a Hypochondriac'. *London Magazine* 6.33 (September 1822): 249–61.

Robinson, Jeffrey C. *Unfettering Poetry: Fancy in British Romanticism*. Basingstoke: Palgrave Macmillan, 2006.
Rousseau, George Sebastian and David Boyd Haycock. 'Framing Samuel Taylor Coleridge's Gut: Genius, Digestion, Hypochondria'. In *Framing and Imagining Disease in Cultural History*, edited by George Sebastian Rousseau, Miranda Gill, David Haycock and Malte Herwig, 231–65. Basingstoke: Palgrave Macmillan, 2003.
Rousseau, George. 'Coleridge's Dreaming Gut: Digestion, Genius, Hypochondria'. In *Cultures of the Abdomen: Diet, Digestion, and Fat in the Modern World*, edited by Christopher Forth and Ana Carden-Coyne, 105–26. Basingstoke: Palgrave Macmillan, 2005.
Reid, John. *Essays on Insanity, Hypochondriasis, and Other Nervous Affections*. London: Longman, Hurst, Rees, Orme, and Brown, 1816.
Sales, Roger. *John Clare: A Literary Life*. Basingstoke: Palgrave Macmillan, 2002.
Shears, Jonathon. 'Byron's Hypochondria'. In *Byron's Temperament: Essays in Body and Mind*, ed. by Bernard Beatty and Jonathon Shears, 100–17. Cambridge: Cambridge Scholars Publishing, 2016.
Shirilan, Stephanie. *Robert Burton and the Transformative Powers of Melancholy*. London: Routledge, 2016.
Storey, Mark. *John Clare: The Critical Heritage*. London: Routledge & Kegan Paul, 1973.
———. *The Poetry of John Clare: A Critical Introduction*. Basingstoke: Macmillan, 1974.
Tibble, J. W. and Anne, *John Clare: A Life*. London: Michael Joseph, 1972.
White, Adam. *John Clare's Romanticism*. London: Palgrave Macmillan, 2017.
Whitehead, James. *Madness & the Romantic Poet: A Critical History*. Oxford: Oxford University Press, 2017.
Williams, Raymond. *The Country and the City*. London: Chatto and Windus, 1973.

'A Song in the Night': Reconsidering John Clare's Later Asylum Poetry

James Whitehead

'John Clare has always been a poet known for his commitment to a particular place', Simon Kövesi begins his recent monograph on Clare, reflecting keenly at length on the class politics, difficulties, and possibilities of the rhetoric of rural 'placedness' in Clare criticism to date.[1] However, Clare is also known for his *commitment* to another particular place: the asylum. The purpose of this chapter is to reflect briefly on the equally difficult topic of the place of the asylum in Clare studies, and to consider how the reading and critical discussion of Clare's later poetry, the poetry from his many years in the asylum, might now be most fruitfully advanced. Ultimate interpretative questions for the study of late Clare may include: how should we read these poems, collectively as well as individually? Which is the most appropriate frame, or frames, for their poetics, and what assumptions or habits of interpretation might now be best avoided? Finally, to what extent do we need reading practices or expectations that allow or

J. Whitehead (✉)
Liverpool John Moores University, Liverpool, UK
e-mail: j.r.whitehead@ljmu.ac.uk

compensate for Clare's mental health and situation in the asylum, and how should we develop these? Only the beginnings of answers to these difficult questions are attempted or suggested here, and the context for Clare's asylum poetry is reconsidered in relation to one particular poem, his lyric 'To Jenny Lind' (1849).

In particular, I am interested in the poetry produced by Clare after his committal at the end of 1841 to the Northampton General Lunatic Asylum.[2] Over two decades of Clare's life remained, almost a third of it, and the poetry he wrote at Northampton constitutes a significant portion of his surviving poetic work, at least in terms of quantity; also roughly a quarter to a third, going by John Goodridge's index.[3] Clare's long final spell in the asylum also looms large in the popular perception of the poet, and accounts for much of the emotional appeal of some of his most well-loved work, such as 'I Am' (ca. 1846), which even in 1949, when Geoffrey Grigson published the first separate edition of Clare's asylum writing, was 'of all his poems, the most celebrated'.[4] Yet the later poetry in the asylum has attracted much less critical, and creative, attention than the work of the High Beach period, from 1837 to 1841. 'Don Juan' and 'Child Harold' have now received quite extensive critical commentary, and Clare's departure from Matthew Allen's private asylum and moving account of his 'Journey out of Essex' has provoked several original acts of creative reinterpretation and adaptation. But Clare's later poetry remains critically neglected, on the whole, or is quietly passed over: certainly, there have been few sustained treatments of the later asylum period, as such, in important recent monographs on Clare, or in the handful of landmark edited collections on him, excepting Roy Porter's ebullient but largely biographical and medical historical account from 1994, now a quarter of a century ago.[5]

Indeed, Clare criticism has sometimes deliberately declared its exclusive concentration or focus on his 'pre-asylum' poetry, as if it were necessary to create a cordon sanitaire between early achievement and later decline.[6] The first order of business should be to suggest that this is really not necessary. Many of the recent modes that have been delineated and celebrated in Clare's earlier poetics, especially the centrality of his sense of the 'communitarian tradition' (Goodridge), or 'communitarian nodes' (Kövesi) in his later writings more broadly, and his earlier modes of 'repetitive creativity' and sense of 'sociable texts' (Paul Chirico) as 'friendship's offerings' (Bate), are crucial to understanding his later poetry too.[7] Part of the future work of reading and teaching the later poems will surely be to extend these critical frames to include the later work, mutatis mutandis. They are as much needed here, in the later poems, as redress to an earlier critical tradition that privileged isolation, visionary 'unity' or dissolution, or idiosyncratic explorations of mental heaven and hell, as they were to balance myths of solitary genius or green innocence in Clare's earlier life. In some instances at least, this sort of extension has been effected to the asylum period, by Kövesi, or in Tim Fulford's acute analysis of Clare's lyric 'personations' in the context of his 1845 notebook (Northampton MS 19) as a mode of coterie publication.[8] But a larger job of critical integration, rather than the separation of particular aspects of Clare's poetics within the silos of different 'sane' and 'mad' periods in his life, remains to be done.

The second main point is that no single frame will do, any more than it would do for such a large and various amount of any writer's work, or such a long period of any person's life. One of the dangers of writing about 'madness' in literature, or as an idea in general, is that it often imposes a totality or teleology on a human experience which can be as varied and variable from person to person, and from period to period in a person's life, as any other.[9] This totality too easily reduces a complex life to myth, the symbolic pattern of a pathology, or of inevitable decline, or social defeat or resistance, or psychic dissolution and renewal, or primitivistic purity, or simply the pathos of second childishness and mere oblivion. This is not to say that none of these themes can be read into Clare's later life; but all are easily overplayed to the detriment of a more variegated picture. Much older critical work on late Clare, valuable in many respects, is limited by treating his madness as a singularity. For example, this is one of the problems with Grigson's fifty-page introductory essay to his edition, still in some ways the most sustained discussion of the asylum poetry as such. Grigson has a 'trough and wave' theory of Clare's late-life creativity, plausibly so given the likelihood of mood disorder or another chronic illness with a relapsing-remitting pattern in Clare's life. But he is also determined to find the moment when Clare was finally pushed or jumped over the edge, never to return. Grigson persistently looks for a 'natural sequence' with a 'climax' or an 'essence and a summary'.[10] Sometimes he pessimistically, 'evidentially', traces the degenerative 'parallel course' of Clare's disease and his poetry, and is drawn here towards a medically much more dated sense of Clare's 'paraphrenic' and hence irreversible 'confirmed psychosis'.[11] Elsewhere, he looks for the one moment (e.g. in 'A Vision') where Clare 'completed the discovery of his true feeling, he had pushed his exploration to its horizon, metaphysically, to that edge beyond which he saw only the eternal'; Grigson seems disappointed when he does not find the 'consequences of derangement' in poetry after this, and is embarrassed to have to account for how Clare continued to write poetry into the final year of his life, despite having completed his journey to communion with the infinite almost twenty years earlier in 1844.[12] Later critical attempts to use his madness to enlist Clare into the visionary company have run into similar or analogous issues. (Romanticists nowadays are more likely to write with a revisionary gleam in their eyes, anyway, even about madness.)

One way of reconsidering Clare's later poetry is to think more carefully about the site of its production: the asylum. There is probably still a prevailing tendency among cultural and literary historians to think of the Victorian asylum as simply a site of solitary suffering and oppression, a memory hole into which Clare, like other economically unproductive or non-conforming paupers, was unceremoniously dropped, and where his individuality and agency were inevitably effaced. More specifically, our sense of Clare's confinement (or 'enclosure') within this sort of regime probably owes something to the historical coincidence that Clare was recovered and championed in literary history, partly as a quintessential subject of the alienation of industrialised society, at the same mid-century or post-war point that Foucault, Erving Goffman, and other critics of the 'total institution' were brought to bear on such locations historically. Certainly the standard references on Clare's madness reflect a basic and longstanding divide in the historiography of psychiatry between this kind of position, as in Porter's account, which is mildly inflected with such revisionism, or the more broadly celebratory narratives of 'character, enterprise, and dedication' which characterise the earlier medical and institutional histories of psychiatric institutions, often written by their clinicians, and here represented by Arthur Foss and Kerith Trick's anniversary history of the Northampton Asylum.[13] The latter have also sometimes overlapped with the retrospective diagnoses that have made up the rest of the go-to references on Clare and madness.[14] Yet much recent research on the history of psychiatric institutions, some of it only published in the last decade, has fundamentally challenged both narratives of benevolent medical progress and the *leyenda negra* of nineteenth-century asylum as oppressive total institution; and retro-diagnosis is no longer the primary pursuit of historians of medicine. The upshot of much of this recent research is that Victorian asylums, in any case, were certainly not oubliettes. They were highly visible, in many ways public, and even often social and sociable locations, and a better sense of this may partly help to underpin a re-socialised account of Clare's later poetry.

The convergence of earlier institutional historiography and critical attitudes on Clare can be seen sharply in Eric Robinson and Geoffrey Summerfield's first edition of Clare's later poetry, published in 1964, at the point at which the Canadian sociologist Goffman's account of the total institution was at the height of its Penguin disseminated influence. Robinson and Summerfield's (somewhat notorious) claim that they sought to reproduce 'John Clare in his natural state and not John Clare scrubbed and spruced up for inspection by the Board of Guardians' surely diffusely reflects Goffman's incisive account from 1961 of institutional processing, the 'undressing, bathing, disinfecting, haircutting, issuing institutional clothing' and other 'admission procedures [that] might better be called "trimming" or "programming" because in thus being squared away the new arrival allows himself to be shaped and coded into an object that can be fed into the administrative machinery of the establishment, to be worked on smoothly by routine operations'.[15] Yet their institutional metaphor, which has largely been discussed in the context of the lively debate about editing Clare and 'textual primitivism', is also askew in one crucial, hitherto unnoticed respect: 'inspection by the Board of Guardians' was a feature of the workhouse, not the asylum. The Northampton Asylum was run by a Management Committee, which was subject to (some) oversight by the Commissioners in Lunacy, who were there to inspect the people who ran the asylum, rather than its patients; neither acted as an inquisitory tribunal. The elision of the two institutions here may reflect an equally Goffman-esque position, that all total institutions are nevertheless similar in their normative or punitive functions, or a more specific historical sense that mid-century asylums, many of which were created in the wake of the 1845 County Asylum and Lunacy Acts, were nevertheless entangled in the kinds of structures, such as Boards of Guardians, inaugurated slightly earlier by the 1834 Poor Law, as historians such as Peter Bartlett indeed argue.[16]

However, recent work specifically on the Northamptonshire system shows how this metaphor is nevertheless inapt. Catherine Smith has demonstrated that the Northampton Asylum's early history (before 1876) was not that of a typical county asylum at all. It was originally, and remained, a philanthropic subscription asylum, with a varied mix of paupers, and private patients, as in fact Clare was. Its management resisted various attempts to bring admissions under the control either of the Poor Law officials, or the new county system mandated by the 1845 Acts, in a complex case of how that national legislation interacted with 'considerable local power and autonomy'.[17] The Northampton Asylum remained, at least over the course of Clare's residence there, a decidedly mixed environment. For instance, Smith describes how medical managers like Dr. Edwin Wing (remembered partly for his role in and rather bathetic case notes of Clare's final treatment) 'felt it necessary to point out in the 1860 annual report that the mixing of different social classes of patients gave a "greater resemblance to life out-of-doors." He dismissed the "theoretical objection" that private patients felt demeaned or degraded if mixed with pauper patients, arguing that he had never witnessed this in practice; moreover, not all those classified as pauper lunatics were necessarily of the same class as "those met with in our Union workhouses": some had "education and refinement"'.[18] Certainly, there is little sense of the aggressive gaze of inspection or the scrubbing up of paupers in these aspects of the Northampton Asylum, or in Smith's broader account of its management. It is also useful to remember how *new* an institution it was, as most other asylums of the 1840s were. This will only take us so far, of course. Smith points out that class-based segregation was still practised in the Northampton Asylum, despite Wing's claims, and the social constitution of the asylum only tells us so much about its actual sociability. And is any of this important for Clare, even with 'his being a private patient [...] the fees for which were covered by his trust fund'?[19] Whatever the fine details of the asylum's administration, he experienced it, or certainly repeatedly described it, as an English Bastille, a site of 'no government at all but prison disapline where every body is forced to act contrary to their wishes'.[20] It is at once both absolutely necessary and rather difficult to take such statements entirely at face value. Even taking into account Clare's bleakest and most hopeless expressions of his self-identity as incarcerated lifer, recent research into the very gloomiest of nineteenth-century institutions, including prisons and workhouses as well as the more punitive or overcrowded asylums, has emphasised a varied picture of patient or inmate activity and sociability, and the complicated affective dynamics of 'kindness and reciprocity' that could be involved in relationships between staff and their charges, especially in the soliciting of patient writing. Clare's relationship to W. F. Knight must be seen in this light, in particular. As Helen Rogers has argued, 'we cannot evaluate [such institutional] philanthropy solely in terms of class discipline or normalization [...] if we wish to understand the often intimate relationships binding agents and recipients of charity, even in the prison'; in the asylum, too, patient writing holds the key to how those at the receiving end managed to negotiate identity in relation to 'philanthropic' intervention, through their own 'laboring-class ethics of kinship and neighborliness'.[21]

Along with the general character of the institution, then, another fresh line of inquiry would be to think more deeply about the relationships involved in the production and transmission of Clare's asylum writing. For example, is there is any figure who has played so great a part in the survival of so much of a now canonical poet's work, approximately 800 poems in his transcripts, in whom so little real interest has been taken, as William F. Knight? Knight was the house steward at the Northampton Asylum from 1845–50, and the prompter of the transcripts which survive in two copies in the Northampton Library archive as the main, often the only source for almost all of the later poetry, which continued to be added to them after his departure. Clare's editors have discussed the issues involved in working from these transcripts, and Clare's biographers have also used the correspondence that survives in the archive between Clare, Knight, Knight's friend Joseph Stenson, and Thomas Inskip, to describe Knight's kindness in general towards Clare, and his attempts to keep Clare's public profile alive.[22] But even Jonathan Bate's biography, the most recent and fullest, does not go beyond a smattering of references to Knight drawn from this correspondence. Readers may easily be left with an overall impression of a sympathetic man, but ultimately just another avatar of middle-class values who attempted to promote but also censored Clare under cover of kindliness. Or they might see Knight as the last in a long line of patrons who encumbered Clare with their 'help', in Johnsonian phrase, or more conspiratorially, as the benevolent face of the controlling institution, the 'enlightened Superintendent of the Northampton Asylum', as Robinson and Summerfield call him.[23] Even if there are no further extant sources that will illuminate Knight's attitudes and motivations in eliciting poetry from Clare, and there may not be, we can do a little more than this, drawing on the historiography on institutional roles in the asylum, and the scattered newspaper reports of Knight's career after 1850, as the clerk and steward at the Birmingham Lunatic Asylum.

To begin with, Robinson and Summerfield again misconstrue institutional power to make Knight more of an authority figure than he was. He was not the superintendent, a senior medical role held by a qualified physician, but house steward, a member of the domestic staff.[24] This was a difference of an order of magnitude financially. Knight's salary at the

Northampton Asylum was £60 with board, just above average, the income of a well-to-do servant or clerk; the superintendent's salary was £500, the income of a middle-class professional. Even at the end of his career, almost half a century later, Knight's income was less than half of this.[25] Economically, then, he was much closer to Clare's situation than a middle-class medical officer would be, even if £60pa was still more than Clare ever managed to reliably make from his poetry. Socially too, Knight was closer to Clare than the top brass; the census shows that he was a local man from a rural background, from the village (then) of Rushden, a few miles down the River Nene from Northampton. As steward it is unlikely that he had any direct responsibility for Clare's care, or control over his treatment, as his rueful reflections on Clare's confinement to quarters for occasional intoxication in the letters to Stenson indicate.

Arthur Foss and Kerith Trick, in their chapter on Clare, note Knight's 'keen interest' and 'sympathy and encouragement'; similar terms, still smacking somewhat of noblesse oblige, are used by others. But in an earlier part of their institutional history, perhaps less likely to be read by Clare scholars, they note that Knight's own position was precarious and class-bound. When he was officially appointed in 1845, the local press worried whether his social background and religious principles were respectable enough; he was obliged to provide a bond of surety.[26] He was then in his early thirties; when he left in 1850, the local press again commented on the appointment of his successor, a married man of a similar age; two younger men were rejected.[27] Qualifications were presumably irrelevant for what was a practical role, albeit one that came with significant organisational responsibility. Indeed, across the new asylum system, there were anxieties about how accounting or financial responsibility had to be entrusted to junior and unqualified members of staff acting as clerks and stewards, which reflected broader class tectonics across rapidly changing Victorian professional structures.[28] So Knight, and anyone who was in his position, would be under as much pressure as Clare to be 'scrubbed and spruced up for inspection'. Perhaps we can understand the 'tidying' in his transcripts with this in mind, and as a more genuine and complicated act of kindness and social solidarity, rather than seeing him simply as a censor, or as one more person among the many who 'thought that they knew better than [Clare] did'.[29] The circumstances of his life may remain obscure, but Knight surely deserves further research, and more serious consideration from Clare scholars, rather than being condescended to himself.

A sense of the broader culture of patient or inmate writing in Victorian institutions is useful for understanding Clare's asylum productivity, and the collection of his poetry by Knight. Sarah Chaney has recently argued that in later nineteenth-century asylums, not only did patients have a 'changing and fluid role', but that 'in some instances, representations of madness [...] were the product of a two-way process of negotiation between alienist and patient. Patients, in other words, were not always mere victims of "psychiatric power"; they participated in the construction and circulation of medical notions by serving as active intermediaries between medical and lay perceptions of madness'. Crucially, in the cases she examines, this participation hinged on in-house asylum magazines. Via the authorial identities they might create by writing in such coterie publications, patients could even be credited as friends, advisers, or contributors in the textbooks written by the asylum's medical officers. Another point that Chaney makes is that in socially mixed Victorian asylums, in her case Bethlem, or indeed Northampton, patients and staff sometimes had 'similar backgrounds and shared a world view'; friendship and even identification with staff was much more common than earlier pessimistic accounts would assume, and was a 'conscious strategy that helped patients to cope with asylum life'.[30] In terms of writing, Chaney looks at a slightly later period, when asylum magazines were common across Britain, but there are certainly examples as early as the 1840s, especially in Scotland, some of which are now coming to light because of increasing contemporary interest in recovering patient voices and writings. For example, the Wellcome Library has recently digitised a volume from the Glasgow Royal Lunatic Asylum, *The Gartnavel Minstrel* (1845). Immediately suggestive in relation to Clare if only because of its title, this self-published volume was the production of a single (former) inmate at Gartnavel, J. R. Adam, containing an autobiographical sketch, followed by a miscellany of comic and sentimental songs, some original, some imitations, of Burns and others, and some commonplace-book texts, which should begin to suggest its broader possible relevance to Clare's asylum writings. No similar publication at the Northampton Asylum is apparent, nor an institutional magazine at this point, but the cultural model existed, and such enterprises are a suggestive context for Knight's collecting activity, linked perhaps by the general climate of enthusiasm for gift annuals and keepsake volumes in the 1840s, forms of sociable publication that have interested Romanticists and Victorianists in recent years, and of course a medium which had previously been an outlet for Clare's writing, for example in the annual *Friendship's Offering* in the late 1820s and early 1830s.

The models of domesticity associated with such forms of writing have also been central to recent accounts of Victorian institutions, which have turned increasingly to material culture or popular taste and aesthetics to add substance and nuance to the formerly bleak picture of the county asylum system in particular—and domesticity is no longer assumed to mean 'conformity'. It now seems increasingly as likely in these contexts to have been chosen by patients themselves as dictated or imposed by 'the rules and pressed social smartness of the asylum'.[31] So when Clare is seen in the asylum 'dressed as a plain but respectable farmer in drab or stone-coloured coat and smalls [...] altogether as clean and neat as if he had just been fresh brushed up for market or fair' (or again 'scrubbed and spruced up' later) we may still see this image through Foucauldian eyes attuned to 'the symbolism of institutional clothing' imposed 'as a means to render inmates subject to a manipulative regime', as docile subjects; but we should also be aware of how recent historical work has been interested in how clothes 'could also serve as a means with which patients could undermine therapeutic intentions and even claim control of their own lives' or 'some of the small ways patients could use dress to express their identity or exert agency within the restricted world of the institution'.[32]

Much interesting research has also been done in landscape and garden history about the ideas of 'therapeutic landscapes' that lay behind much mid-century asylum and hospital design, including at Northampton. Any reader with a pre-conceived idea of the Northampton Asylum as a utilitarian environment, alien in all respects to sweet pastoral scenes, should turn for a corrective to the illustration reproduced by Clare Hickman of the 'cottage orné with a thatched roof [...] built in the grounds' of the asylum in the 1850s, or her reference to the management's remodelling of the external areas, which took into account a discussion of the value for patients of different visual experiences of the picturesque landscape.[33] This may seem like a thin philanthropic parody of the real rural home that Clare had lost, of course, or, Hickman adds, could merely 'feel like a gilded prison'.[34] And yet the right to roam in the real surrounding countryside that Clare was usually permitted at Northampton was also not the privilege allowed to an individual, idiosyncratic minor-celebrity patient, but squarely in line with many contemporary medical accounts of the curative value of unhindered access to a natural landscape, rather than bricked-in 'airing courts'. Indeed, the 'hallucinations of fear' of 'the vague danger that exuded through the walls of confinement', the subsequently very real stigma and terror of the escaped madman, and fantasy of confinement and sequestration attached to the asylum and its patients which Foucault writes so vividly about, is often strikingly absent from mid-Victorian discourse about their asylums. It begins to look more like a later efflorescence, just as our sense of the Victorian asylum as dumping ground for inconvenient people is in some ways the back projection of attitudes from the early to mid twentieth century, the years of the eugenic panic, and a much more likely and dangerous time for a disabled or mentally ill relative to be forgotten in a total institution, as Deborah Cohen has persuasively shown.[35]

Perhaps most important for Clare's poetry among these softer faces of the asylum, however, is music and theatrical performance. Victorian asylums were surprisingly musical places. Stef Eastoe, in another account of an asylum which seeks to supplant the older picture of the 'gloomy, isolated, and totalizing' institution with a sense of its richer and kinder 'inner life', describes programmes of 'Amusements' that were important enough to occupy their own sections in asylum annual reports. These might be composed of 'a diverse range of theatrical performances and musical concerts provided by professionals, volunteers, and in many cases by asylum staff themselves'. Much of the repertoire was minstrel shows and comic songs, and the plays were usually farces, but she also reports performances of lieder and operatic arias. Asylums were even designed with dedicated music rooms.[36] At the Northampton Asylum, by the early 1860s, there was a brass band, a glee club, and a similar programme of twice-weekly 'dancing, singing, music, magic lantern shows, lectures and readings— sometimes by the Chaplain—from Shakespeare, Dickens, and other authors'.[37] This has two consequences for Clare's poems. The first is that the performativity of much of his poetry in the asylum, its adoption of roles and alter-egos, while highly distinctive to Clare, also sat in a context where this was one of the primary forms of sociable entertainment.[38] Clare himself called his poems 'Prison Amusements'.[39] The second is that the predominance of songs in the later oeuvre might be framed slightly differently, slightly less as unaccompanied plangency, resounding only with the dying fall of Clare's past, and slightly more as the refrains of an ongoing life. This may help to move past earlier critical disappointment at their apparently derivative (perhaps a better word would be 'familiar') voicing or diction, and disparagement of them as 'traditional jingles'.[40] 'Clare had a "song in the night"', his fellow inmate William Jerom reported in his reminiscences of the last part of Clare's life.[41] In this setting, 'a song in the night' might sound a little less like a voice crying in the wilderness, with no language but a cry, and a little more like something convivial, companionable, communal.

A note of caution: there is no getting around the fact, evident if only from his surviving writing in letters, that Clare's experience in the asylum was not primarily a happy one; from any angle, it is still mostly a melancholy story of personal and familial loss and estrangement. Wherever there is a sense of fellowship or community, it is, as elsewhere in Clare's writing, 'invariably edged with an unblinking awareness of its limits'.[42] Moreover, the dynamics surrounding social and behavioural roles based on domesticity in institutions, or in quasi-familial networks of friendship and reciprocal obligation, are not straightforward. Claiming to find patient agency here, or in any of the more idiosyncratic aspects of the institution, has become a given in the recent social history of medicine, and in medical humanities generally, but it is hard to say that personal relationships are simple alternatives to power relations in social institutions, in the wake of psychoanalysis, or the *Genealogy of Morals*, or structuration theory, or Foucault read properly, for that matter. The dynamics of restriction, dependency, and autonomy at work are delicate. We might see this, by way of a conclusion, in a poem by Clare with a strong sense of curtailment, yet also a sociable exchange of music voices, finding support and relief from pain in musical performance, in shared refrain and repertory:

To
Jenny Lind

I cannot touch the harp again
   And sing another idle Lay
To cool a maddening burning brain
   And drive the midnight fiend away
Music own sister to the soul
   Bids roses bloom on cheeks all pale
And sweet her joys and sorrows roll
When sings the Sweedish Nightingale

The Lilies of the field are fair
   Nought on their whiteness emulates
Nature in pleasure says they are
   Words cannot musics charms create
Nor musings of an idle lay

With music magic e'er prevail
Voice of the soul they steal away
From the young Sweedish Nightingale

I cannot touch the harp again
    No chords will vibrate on the string
Like broken flowers upon the plain
    My heart e'en withers while I sing
Eolian harps have witching tones
    On morning or the evening gale
No melody their music owns
As sings the Sweedish Nightingale

Feby 12th/49.[43]

This is neither Clare's most celebrated nor his most obscure asylum poem; neither the most original, nor the most 'familiar'. It has appeared in most selections of his asylum verse since J. L. Cherry's in 1873, where the difficult to parse second verse was cut, but has drawn little critical attention. Its mixture of emotional intensity—the 'maddening burning brain' and the 'midnight fiend', the sort of line that for later poet-critics like Yeats or Arthur Symons aligned Clare with Blake and Tom o' Bedlam— with the cooler, much more conventional diction of its refrain, is perhaps characteristic; or let it be provisionally illustrative at least, bearing in mind the need to see Clare's asylum poetry as varied and not just one 'mad song'. Contextually, the poem can support the revisionist account of the sociability and permeability of Victorian asylums: popular and worldly voices from the society outside could be heard drifting through their windows; here that of the soprano Jenny Lind, the Swedish Nightingale. (Clare's 'Sweedish', a felicitous spelling whether his own or Knight's, deliciously suggests 'sweetish' with a hint of operatic piping on the vowel and a Garbo drawl on the consonant). It is very unlikely that Clare would have heard of Lind before he entered the asylum, as she was still a teenager in 1837, and only became widely known in Britain after the sensation of her London debut in May 1847. And of course, he never actually heard her sing, which is part of the pathos of the poem's 'audition'. But he probably read about her in the newspapers and periodicals supplied weekly to the asylum by the Northampton Mechanic's Institute.[44] The poem betrays no diffidence about detachment, in this respect, from high culture or fashion.

Moreover, while the poem seems a private fantasy, it is also public, in that it participates in the wider public culture of Lind's celebrity, during the height of her fame. When she took her celebrity to America in 1850, famously sponsored by P. T. Barnum, Lind inspired many 'To Jenny Lind' or 'To the Swedish Nightingale' type poems in the American press; there was even a competition for them. Clare may have read and been responding to similar poems in the British newspapers. Yet the bootstrap of conventional laudatory verse allows Clare subtler affinities and identifications. At the time of the poem's dating, Lind had already intimated her early retirement at twenty-eight from the operatic stage, overwhelmed by the demands of a celebrity sustained through two punishing years of constant performances, many of them in exhausting roles portraying the 'mad' heroines of the bel canto repertoire, such as Amina in Bellini's *La sonnambula* (1831). The religious-minded Lind gave a series of benefit concerts in 1848–9, often at public institutions such as hospitals, before her operatic retirement was announced in May 1849, at which point there was feverish speculation about her eloping or going into a convent. Whatever the level of Clare's awareness of this, his sense of Lind's voice seems fraught both with the anticipation of its silence, a 'string' resonating with his own situation, a 'sister to the soul', and with sympathetic identification towards another artist wounded by being the 'comet of a season', in Byron's phrase, who, damaged and 'stilted up to madness', could not bear to 'touch the harp again', but who kept on singing all the same. Somewhere in the background too is the motif of the caged bird, a common symbol in asylum writings, although often in a more 'pleasant and whimsical form' than we might assume, or used as an image of home and domestic comfort as much as of captivity and yearning.[45]

Lind attracted this kind of identification from other poets, too, a virtual sodality of 'broken flowers'. Clare was not the only male asylum inmate who wrote verses addressed 'to Jenny Lind'.[46] Furthermore, readers of Emily Dickinson, a famed shut-in of a rather different sort, will remember the significance of her attending Lind's concert in July 1851, in another Northampton, in Massachusetts: a nice piece of synchronicity, but more importantly also a threshold encounter between the poet not wholly confident of liberty, and 'the most public of public women'.[47] Also across the Atlantic, and the fences of historical periods, another semi-outsider artist and semi-recluse, Joseph Cornell, became fascinated with Lind. In the words of Octavio Paz, translated by Elizabeth Bishop, arranging scores of 'the solos of Jenny Colonne and Jenny Lind' alongside the dolls and birds who populate his vitrines, Cornell made spaces of confinement which also lovingly protected and displayed a faded or disappeared world: 'Minimal, incoherent fragments:/the opposite of History, creator of ruins,/out of your ruins you have made creations'.[48] This may be pulling away from Clare, or drifting back towards the religiose rhetoric of the infinite and ineffable. But the aesthetics of the minimal or the fragmentary can help us to read Clare's asylum poems in a more modest way than this, too, aligning their 'etiolated life' with what recent critics have posited as 'Rcsm' rather than Romanticism, 'the down-tuning of an aspirational form to its not-quite-barest minimum'.[49] We can see that here in the nightingale and the Aeolian harp, no longer the symbols of prepotent creativity (as they never really were for Charlotte Smith, Coleridge, or Keats), but singing or playing on still, owned by or owning no individual melody, but a common chord.

Clare's poem, finally, may complicate our existing sense that, 'for the last twenty-three years of his life, incarcerated in Northampton General Lunatic Asylum, Clare had no audience'.[50] Some of its audience is imagined, or a virtual community of fellow-feeling stretching into the future, but its outward address is certainly made pointed by Knight's arrangement of the title (To/Jenny Lind), and it was produced with more than one flesh and blood recipient in mind: 'You tell me you write the Swedish Nightingale to please me', Inskip wrote to Clare in April 1849, probably having received the poem in a copy, which is not extant. He added to Knight a month later, in the same week as all the hue and cry surrounding Lind's official retirement: 'I think of trimming up Johns Swedish Nightingale and uncaging her to the public'.[51] 'Trimming' may again make us think of Goffman, and the death by a thousand tiny cuts of Clare's censorious 'improvers'. But we should remember that the etymology of the word 'trim' in English is in addition and increase, rather than subtraction. Originally it meant to 'make firm or strong; to strengthen, confirm', 'to comfort, exhort', and 'to repair, restore, put right'; later 'trimming up', specifically, meant to fit out and dress one's person and appearance, 'so as to give it a finished appearance'.[52] Hilary Mantel has written movingly of being 'so mauled by medical procedures, so sabotaged and made over, that sometimes I feel that each morning it is necessary to write myself into being [...] How then can you create a narrative of your own life? Janet Frame compares the process to finding a bunch of old rags, and trying to make a dress. A party dress, I'd say: something fit to be seen in. Something to go out in and face the world'.[53] The dynamics of 'uncaging'

Clare's asylum poems are not simple; they have always involved compromise and social mediation, and such 'dressing up'. The ambiguity of the word 'trimming' might remind us of this, and remind us to look a little more carefully at the decidedly mixed picture of control, correction, comfort, and sociable concord that early Victorian mental health care aimed at, as well as looking a little more kindly on those individuals who preserved and dressed Clare's poems and sent them out fit to face the public world and to please others, to be both seen and heard. As indeed they still are.

NOTES

1. *John Clare: Nature, Criticism and History* (Basingstoke: Palgrave Macmillan, 2017), 1, 54.
2. Hereafter 'Northampton Asylum'.
3. 'A First Line Index to the Poetry of John Clare: Introduction' (1999), at http://www.johnclare.info/firstlineintro.html, accessed June 2019.
4. *Poems of John Clare's Madness* (London: Routledge and Kegan Paul, 1949), 31.
5. See *John Clare in Context*, 259–78, and the somewhat overlapping account in Porter's own *A Social History of Madness: Stories of the Insane* (London: Weidenfeld & Nicolson, 1987), 76–81.
6. This habit seems to have begun with Janet Todd's *In Adam's Garden* in 1973; others who write of Clare's 'pre-asylum' poetry include Mark Storey, in *Critical Heritage*, and Tim Chilcott (both of whom do also give the earlier asylum years their due), Johanne Clare, and more recently Paul Chirico, *John Clare and the Imagination of the Reader* (Basingstoke: Palgrave Macmillan, 2007), 5, and Adam White, *John Clare's Romanticism* (Basingstoke: Palgrave Macmillan, 2017), 108, 300.
7. John Goodridge, *John Clare and Community* (Cambridge: Cambridge University Press, 2013), 6, and passim; Kövesi (talking here, admittedly, about asylum writings, and establishing a critical frame for the later poetry), 204; Chirico, 1, 18.
8. *Romantic Poetry and Literary Coteries* (Basingstoke: Palgrave Macmillan, 2015), 165–88.
9. I am thinking here in particular of the work of Peter Barham and Robert Hayward: *From the Mental Patient to the Person* (London: Routledge, 1991), and the piece cited below.
10. *Poems of John Clare's Madness*, 3, 31.
11. *Poems of John Clare's Madness*, v, 6, 28, 23. Grigson's sense of Clare's *dementia praecox* is very much a mid-twentieth-century conception of schizophrenia, before work by psychiatrists such as Manfred Bleuler and

Luc Ciompi established, as Barham and Hayward quote Ciompi, that 'the developmental course of schizophrenia is not compatible with the conception of a progressive disease process but, rather, that such courses, upon closer inspection, show themselves as being almost as protean as life itself'('Schizophrenia as a Life Process', in *Reconstructing Schizophrenia*, ed. by Richard Bentall (London: Routledge, 1990), 62). The point is that even the most serious mental illnesses, like schizophrenia, or dementia, do not necessarily mean the end of life itself.

12. *Poems of John Clare's Madness*, 32, 2.
13. *St Andrew's Hospital Northampton: the first 150 Years (1838–1988)* (Cambridge: Granta, 1989), 3. Dr. Trick, at least, was a working psychiatrist.
14. These and the medical judgements of neurologists and psychologists such as Walter Russell Brain (who splendidly not only became The Lord Brain, 1st Baron Brain, but also edited the journal *Brain*), Seán Haldane, and Evan Blackmore, constitute the other standard references on Clare and madness.
15. *The Later Poems of John Clare* (Manchester: Manchester University Press, 1964), 3; Goffman, *Asylums: Essays on the Social Situation of Mental Patients and Other Inmates* (1961) (Harmondsworth: Penguin, 1976), 25–6.
16. See Bartlett's *The Poor Law of Lunacy: The Administration of Pauper Lunatics in mid-Nineteenth Century England* (London: Bloomsbury, 1999), now the standard reference point on this topic.
17. 'Parsimony, Power, and Prescriptive Legislation: The Politics of Pauper Lunacy in Northamptonshire, 1845–1876', *Bulletin of the History of Medicine* 81.2 (2007): 370.
18. 'Parsimony, Power, and Prescriptive Legislation', 373.
19. *New Essays on John Clare*, ed. by Simon Kövesi and Scott McEathron (Cambridge: Cambridge University Press, 2015), 3.
20. *Letters*, 669.
21. 'Kindness and Reciprocity: Liberated Prisoners and Christian Charity in Early Nineteenth-Century England', *Journal of Social History* 47.3 (2014): 721. For similar dynamics of gratitude in the asylum, see Len Smith, '"Your Very Thankful Inmate": Discovering the Patients of an Early County Lunatic Asylum', *Social History of Medicine* 21 (2008): 237–52.
22. The key sources used in most biographical accounts to date here are clearly MSS 410 and 412–14 in the Northampton catalogue, from the 1970 accession to the archive.
23. *Later Poems* (1964), 9.
24. Robinson and Summerfield's mistake is repeated elsewhere, for example, in the introduction to *John Clare in Context*, 9, where Knight is called

'Clare's doctor'. This error was pointed out in the useful cluster of essays on Clare at Northampton in *Northamptonshire Past and Present*, 3 (1971): 85–102, which also gives the information on salaries cited here, taken from the asylum records.

25. His retirement on a pension of £216 is reported in 1891 by the *Birmingham Daily Post*, September 29 and November 27. Knight had worked at the Birmingham Lunatic Asylum, later All Saint's Hospital, for 41 years. By then he was 77 years old, which tells another sort of story: this was a long shift at an institution 'enlarged repeatedly between opening and the late 1870s in order to contain ever increasing numbers of pauper inmates fuelled by the relentless expansion of Birmingham'. County Asylums website, https://www.countyasylums.co.uk/all-saints-winson-green-birmingham/. A much earlier article praises his 'faithful and efficient services', 'high character', 'kindness', and 'great humanity', reproducing a visitor's report to this effect, while also reporting on a Dickensian debate among local councillors as to 'whether they were always to be purchasing kindness and humanity with high wages?' (Knight's salary had just been raised modestly with the expansion.) 'Local Intelligence', *Aris's Birmingham Gazette*, October 17 (1853): 4.

26. Foss and Trick, *St Andrew's Hospital*, 58, 135–6.

27. *Northampton Mercury*, March 2 (1850): 3.

28. For anxieties relating to stewards and the possibility of embezzlement, see, for example, Jo Melling and Bill Forsythe, *The Politics of Madness: The State, Insanity and Society in England 1845–1914* (Abingdon: Routledge, 2006), 41–2, or Foss and Trick, *St Andrew's Hospital*, 88–9, for a later case of this at the Northampton Asylum; cf. Clare's line in 'Don Juan' about the steward 'open[ing] shop' and having a 'jolly flare up' with stolen tobacco: *Later Poems*, 1: 38.

29. Robinson and Summerfield, *Later Poems* (1964), 10.

30. '"No 'Sane' Person Would Have Any Idea": Patients' Involvement in Late Nineteenth-century British Asylum Psychiatry', *Medical History* 60.1 (2016): 37–8, 47.

31. Kövesi, *John Clare*, 199.

32. Rebecca Wynter, '"Good in all respects": appearance and dress at Staffordshire County Lunatic Asylum, 1818–54', *History of Psychiatry*, 22.1 (2010): 40, 41; Jane Hamlett and Lesley Hoskins, 'Comfort in Small Things? Clothing, Control and Agency in County Lunatic Asylums in Nineteenth and Early Twentieth-century England', *Journal of Victorian Culture* 18.1 (2013): 93–114; see also Hamlett, 'Public Asylums' in *At Home in the Institution* (Basingstoke: Palgrave Macmillan, 2015), 16–37. The sketch of Clare's coat and smalls is from Spencer Hall's account of his

1843 visit, later recounted in his *Biographical Sketches of Remarkable People* (London: Simpkin and Marshall, 1873), 166.

33. 'The Role of Landscape in Relation to the Treatment of Mental Illness in the Early Nineteenth-Century Asylum', *Garden History* 33.1 (2005): 49, 51–2 for the cottage.

34. 'Cheerfulness and tranquillity: gardens in the Victorian asylum', *Lancet Psychiatry* 1.7 (December, 2014): 506–7.

35. *Family Secrets: Shame and Privacy in Modern Britain* (Oxford: Oxford University Press, 2013). Foucault: *Madness and Civilization*, trans. Richard Howard (London: Routledge Classics, 2001), 195. My awareness of some of the social and medical historical work cited here was informed by two recent conferences; the asylum panels at the Society for the Social History of Medicine conference in 2018, and the 'Rethinking the Institution' conference at Liverpool John Moores University in 2017; thanks and acknowledgements to Kate Taylor for organising the latter.

36. 'Playing Cards, Cricket and Carpentry: Amusement, Recreation and Occupation in Caterham Imbecile Asylum', *Journal of Victorian Culture* 24.1 (January, 2019): 73, 80–2.

37. Foss and Trick, *St Andrew's Hospital*, 98–9.

38. Roger Sales offers some lively comment on 'asylum culture' in his *John Clare: a Literary Life* (Basingstoke: Palgrave, 2002; chapters 4 and 5), specifically addressing 'the everyday theatricality of asylum life' (120) in relation to Clare's boxer roles, although not really in this actual everyday sense, and not with much detail that is specific to Northampton Asylum; rather, as a form of symbolic contest with authority, his reading of Clare's time in the asylum being more marked by the anti-psychiatric critique (and some of the generalising) of earlier revisionary accounts, especially Porter's.

39. *Letters*, 660.

40. *Later Poems*, 1: xv; quoting, partly critically, Tibble and Thornton, *Midsummer Cushion*, xii.

41. Peterborough MS G5; quoted in Bate, *Biography*, 477. This was also used as the title of a play about Clare in the asylum, produced for BBC radio in 1978 by Roger Frith and later staged in 1989 and for the bicentenary in 1993.

42. Goodridge, *John Clare and Community*, 190.

43. *Later Poems*, 2: 666–7.

44. See Joanna Ball, '"The Tear Drops on the Book I Read": John Clare's Reading in the Northampton General Lunatic Asylum, 1841–1864', *Wordsworth Circle*, 34.3 (Summer, 2003): 155–8. There are 34 articles mentioning Lind in the *Northampton Mercury* up to February 1849 (Gale British Library Newspapers database).

45. See Chaney, "No Sane Person", 45, which reproduces and comments upon such an image.
46. See Benjamin Reiss, *Theaters of Madness: Insane Asylums and Nineteenth-Century American Culture* (Chicago, University of Chicago Press, 2008), 1, 15.
47. Judith Pascoe, '"The House Encore Me So": Emily Dickinson and Jenny Lind', *Emily Dickinson Journal* 1.1 (1992): 2.
48. 'Objects & Apparitions: For Joseph Cornell'; Elizabeth Bishop, *Complete Poems* (London: Chatto & Windus, 2004), 275.
49. Kövesi, 203; Anahid Nersessian, *Utopia, Limited: Romanticism and Adjustment* (Cambridge, MA: Harvard University Press, 2015), 25.
50. Mark Storey, 'The Poet Overheard: John Clare and his Audience', *JCSJ* 10.1 (1994): 9.
51. Northampton MS 52, quoted in *Later Poems*, 2: 666.
52. *OED*, online edition, senses 1–7.
53. *Giving up the Ghost* (London: Fourth Estate, 2003), 217.

BIBLIOGRAPHY

Adam, J. R. *The Gartnavel Minstrel*. Glasgow: the author. NHS Glasgow and Clyde Archives, HB13/2/229. Wellcome Library. 1845 https://wellcomelibrary.org/item/b21891412. Accessed April 11 2019.
Ball, Joanna. 'The Tear Drops on the Book I Read': John Clare's Reading in the Northampton General Lunatic Asylum, 1841–1864''. *Wordsworth Circle* 34 (2003): 155–8.
Barham, Peter, and Robert Hayward. 'Schizophrenia as a Life Process'. In *Reconstructing Schizophrenia*, edited by Richard Bentall, 61–85. London: Routledge, 1990.
———. *From the Mental Patient to the Person*. London: Routledge. 1991.
Bartlett, Peter. *The Poor Law of Lunacy: The Administration of Pauper Lunatics in mid-Nineteenth Century England*. London: Bloomsbury, 1999.
Bate, Jonathan. *John Clare: a Biography*. London: Picador, 2003.
Bishop, Elizabeth. *Complete Poems*. London: Chatto & Windus, 2004.
Blackmore, Evan. 'John Clare's Psychiatric Disorder and its Influence on his Poetry'. *Victorian Poetry* 24 (1986): 209–28.
Brain, Walter Russell. 'A Diagnosis of His Madness, in Four Views of John Clare'. *Northampton Chronicle and Echo*, May 20 (1964).
Chaney, Sarah. '"No 'Sane' Person Would Have Any Idea": Patients' Involvement in Late Nineteenth-century British Asylum Psychiatry'. *Medical History* 60 (2016): 27–53.
Chirico, Paul. *John Clare and the Imagination of the Reader*. Basingstoke: Palgrave Macmillan, 2007.

Clare, John. *Poems of John Clare's Madness*, edited by Geoffrey Grigson. London: Routledge and Kegan Paul, 1949.

———. 1964. *The Later Poems of John Clare*. Edited by Eric Robinson and Geoffrey Summerfield. Manchester: Manchester University Press, 1964.

Cohen, Deborah. *Family Secrets: Shame and Privacy in Modern Britain*. Oxford: Oxford University Press, 2013.

Cornell, Joseph. *Theater of the Mind: Selected Diaries, Letters, and Files*, ed. Mary Anne Caws. London: Thames and Hudson, 1993.

County Asylums website. https://www.countyasylums.co.uk/all-saints-winson-green-birmingham. Accessed April 11 2019.

Eastoe, Stef. "Relieving gloomy and objectless lives': The Landscape of Caterham Imbecile Asylum'. *Landscape Research* 41 (2016): 652–63.

———. 'Playing Cards, Cricket and Carpentry: Amusement, Recreation and Occupation in Caterham Imbecile Asylum'. *Journal of Victorian Culture* 24 (2019): 72–87.

Faubert, Michelle. 'Cure, Classification, and John Clare'. *Victorian Poetry* 33 (2005): 269–91.

Foucault, Michel. *Madness and Civilization*. Trans. Richard Howard. London: Routledge Classics, 2001.

Foss, Arthur, and Kerith Trick. *St Andrew's Hospital Northampton: The First 150 Years (1838–1988)*. Cambridge: Granta, 1989.

Fulford, Tim. *Romantic Poetry and Literary Coteries*. Basingstoke: Palgrave Macmillan., 2015.

Goffman, Erving. *Asylums: Essays on the Social Situation of Mental Patients and Other Inmates*. Harmondsworth: Penguin, 1976.

Goodridge, John. 'A First Line Index to the Poetry of John Clare: Introduction'. http://www.johnclare.info/firstlineintro.html. 1999. Accessed June 30 2019.

———. *John Clare and Community*. Cambridge: Cambridge University Press, 2013.

———. 2005. 'This Sad Non-Identity': Clare, Cowper, and 'Madness'. *Cowper and Newton Bulletin* (2005): 5–13.

Haldane, Seán. 'John Clare's Madness'. *PN Review* 30 (2004): 42–6.

Hall, Spencer. *Biographical Sketches of Remarkable People*. London: Simpkin and Marshall, 1873.

Hamlett, Jane, and Lesley Hoskins. 'Comfort in Small Things? Clothing, Control and Agency in County Lunatic Asylums in Nineteenth and Early Twentieth-Century England'. *Journal of Victorian Culture* 18 (2013): 93–114.

Hamlett, Jane. 'Public Asylums'. In *At Home in the Institution*, 16–37. Basingstoke: Palgrave Macmillan, 2015.

Hickman, Clare. 'The Role of Landscape in Relation to the Treatment of Mental Illness in the Early Nineteenth-Century Asylum'. *Garden History* 33 (2005): 47–60.

————. 'Cheerful Prospects and Tranquil Restoration: the Visual Experience of Landscape as part of the Therapeutic Regime of the British Asylum, 1800–1860'. *History of Psychiatry* 20 (2009): 425–41.

————. 'Cheerfulness and Tranquility: Gardens in the Victorian Asylum'. *Lancet Psychiatry* 1 (2014): 506–7.

Kövesi, Simon. *John Clare: Nature, Criticism and History*. Basingstoke: Palgrave Macmillan, 2017.

Kövesi, Simon, and Scott McEathron, eds. *New Essays on John Clare: Poetry, Culture and Community*. Cambridge: Cambridge University Press, 2015.

Lafford, Erin. Forms of Health in John Clare's Poetics. DPhil diss., University of Oxford, 2016.

Mantel, Hilary. *Giving Up the Ghost*. London: Fourth Estate, 2003.

Melling, Joseph, and Bill Forsythe. *The Politics of Madness: The State, Insanity and Society in England, 1845–1914*. Abingdon: Routledge, 2006.

Nersessian, Anahid. *Utopia, Limited: Romanticism and Adjustment*. Cambridge, MA: Harvard University Press, 2015.

Pascoe, Judith. "The House Encore Me So': Emily Dickinson and Jenny Lind'. *Emily Dickinson Journal* 1 (1992): 1–18.

Porter, Roy. *A Social History of Madness: Stories of the Insane*. London: Weidenfeld & Nicolson, 1987.

Powell, David. *Catalogue of the John Clare Collection in the Northampton Public Library*. Northampton: Northampton Public Library, 1964.

Reiss, Benjamin. *Theaters of Madness: Insane Asylums and Nineteenth-Century American Culture*. Chicago, University of Chicago Press, 2008.

Rogers, Helen. 'Kindness and Reciprocity: Liberated Prisoners and Christian Charity in Early Nineteenth-Century England'. *Journal of Social History* 47 (2014): 721–45.

Sales, Roger. *John Clare: a Literary Life*. Basingstoke: Palgrave, 2002.

Smith, Catherine. 'Parsimony, Power, and Prescriptive Legislation: the Politics of Pauper Lunacy in Northamptonshire, 1845–1876'. *Bulletin of the History of Medicine* 81 (2007): 359–85.

Smith, Leonard. '"Your Very Thankful Inmate": Discovering the Patients of an Early County Lunatic Asylum'. *Social History of Medicine* 21 (2008): 237–52.

Storey, Mark. 'The Poet Overheard: John Clare and his Audience'. *John Clare Society Journal* 10 (1991): 5–16.

Summerfield, Geoffrey. Manchester: Manchester University Press. *The Later Poems of John Clare, 1837–1864*. 2 vols. Edited by Eric Robinson and David Powell. Oxford: Clarendon Press, 1984.

White, Adam. *John Clare's Romanticism*. Basingstoke: Palgrave Macmillan, 2017.

Wynter, Rebecca. '"Good in all respects": Appearance and Dress at Staffordshire County Lunatic Asylum, 1818–54'. *History of Psychiatry* 22 (2010): 40–57.

INDEX

© The Author(s) 2020
S. Kövesi, E. Lafford (eds.), *Palgrave Advances in John Clare
Studies*, Palgrave Advances,
https://doi.org/10.1007/978-3-030-43374-1

Printed by Printforce, the Netherlands